T0215225

Learn Unity for Windows 10 Game Development

Sue Blackman

Adam Tuliper

Apress®

Learn Unity for Windows 10 Game Development

Sue Blackman
Temecula, California, USA

Adam Tuliper
Lake Forest, California, USA

ISBN-13 (pbk): 978-1-4302-6758-4
DOI 10.1007/978-1-4302-6757-7

ISBN-13 (electronic): 978-1-4302-6757-7

Library of Congress Control Number: 2016962195

Copyright © 2016 by Sue Blackman and Adam Tuliper

This work is subject to copyright. All rights are reserved by the Publisher, whether the whole or part of the material is concerned, specifically the rights of translation, reprinting, reuse of illustrations, recitation, broadcasting, reproduction on microfilms or in any other physical way, and transmission or information storage and retrieval, electronic adaptation, computer software, or by similar or dissimilar methodology now known or hereafter developed.

Trademarked names, logos, and images may appear in this book. Rather than use a trademark symbol with every occurrence of a trademarked name, logo, or image we use the names, logos, and images only in an editorial fashion and to the benefit of the trademark owner, with no intention of infringement of the trademark.

The use in this publication of trade names, trademarks, service marks, and similar terms, even if they are not identified as such, is not to be taken as an expression of opinion as to whether or not they are subject to proprietary rights.

While the advice and information in this book are believed to be true and accurate at the date of publication, neither the authors nor the editors nor the publisher can accept any legal responsibility for any errors or omissions that may be made. The publisher makes no warranty, express or implied, with respect to the material contained herein.

Managing Director: Welmoed Spahr
Lead Editor: Steve Anglin
Technical Reviewer: Marc Schärer
Editorial Board: Steve Anglin, Pramila Balan, Laura Berendson, Aaron Black, Louise Corrigan, Jonathan Gennick, Robert Hutchinson, Celestin Suresh John, Nikhil Karkal, James Markham, Susan McDermott, Matthew Moodie, Natalie Pao, Gwenan Spearing
Coordinating Editor: Mark Powers
Copy Editor: Sharon Wilkey
Compositor: SPi Global
Indexer: SPi Global
Artist: SPi Global

Distributed to the book trade worldwide by Springer Science+Business Media New York, 233 Spring Street, 6th Floor, New York, NY 10013. Phone 1-800-SPRINGER, fax (201) 348-4505, e-mail orders-ny@springer-sbm.com, or visit www.springeronline.com. Apress Media, LLC is a California LLC and the sole member (owner) is Springer Science + Business Media Finance Inc (SSBM Finance Inc). SSBM Finance Inc is a Delaware corporation.

For information on translations, please e-mail rights@apress.com, or visit www.apress.com.

Apress and friends of ED books may be purchased in bulk for academic, corporate, or promotional use. eBook versions and licenses are also available for most titles. For more information, reference our Special Bulk Sales–eBook Licensing web page at www.apress.com/bulk-sales.

Any source code or other supplementary materials referenced by the author in this text are available to readers at www.apress.com. For detailed information about how to locate your book's source code, go to www.apress.com/source-code/. Readers can also access source code at SpringerLink in the Supplementary Material section for each chapter.

Printed on acid-free paper

For Adam's wife, Artemis, and kids, Asa, Axl, and Zoe,
who so graciously let this project take up so much of his time

Contents at a Glance

Contents

About the Authors

Sue Blackman has been an instructor in the 3D field for nearly 20 years at art schools and community colleges. She has been involved with the commercial development of real-time 3D engines for more than 10 years. In the past, she has been a contributing author for New Riders Press (*3ds max 4 Magic*) and written for ACM SIGGRAPH on serious games. She has written product training materials and instruction manuals for developing content with real-time 3D applications, used by multimedia departments in Fortune 1000 companies including Boeing, Raytheon, and Lockheed Martin, among others. In addition to writing and teaching, Sue has been the lead 3D artist on several games for Activision Publishing and its subsidiaries. Sue can be contacted at Sue@3dadventurous.com or sueblackman3djunkie@gmail.com.

Adam Tuliper works as a senior software engineer for Microsoft, helping others achieve their technical vision across Windows, the Web, and the cloud. He works a lot with the gaming community in the western United States, co-runs the Orange County Unity Meetup, and is also an indie game developer working on new titles. He can be reached via his web site, www.adamtuliper.com, and Twitter (http://twitter.com/adamtuliper).

About the Technical Reviewer

 **Marc Schärer** is an interactive media software engineer and contributor to the Unity forums as a full-time professional Unity user since 2007. As a Swiss local, he attempts to support the local development communities in Switzerland to help them unleash their potential, applying his experience delivering interactive 3D learning, training, and entertainment experiences to mobile, desktop, and web platforms for customers around the world.

He has a strong background in the fields of 3D graphics, network technology, software engineering, and interactive media, which first interested him as a teenager. He studied computer science as well as computational science and engineering at the Swiss Federal Institute of Technology in Zürich.

He is currently the chief VR officer at vantage.tv, a company he co-founded in 2014, which seeks to revolutionize the way we see and experience events of any type and scale in the future by removing the barrier of distance.

Acknowledgments

I started writing this book well over two years ago, to help a friend break into both writing books and the Unity community. The friend, a big fan of mobile games, was going to handle the Windows Store section and assist throughout the rest of the book. Unfortunately, the friend had to pull out of the project, leaving me to pick up the pieces. Mobile development being well out of my comfort zone, I had to find a new co-author. The choice was easy. We had met Adam Tuliper during our research into Windows Store and he had graciously offered to help out in whatever way he could. Well, who better than Microsoft's liaison with Unity, and a senior programmer besides, whose duties include traveling the country and helping Unity users make the most out of their Windows games, apps, and Windows devices.

The problem (or benefit, as the case may be), was that as a Microsoft "insider," Adam was tuned in to what was in development. So we waited until the time was right to continue with the book, and as a result, were rewarded with Windows 10 and the fruition of the Unified Windows Platform (UWP) and all of the device families that encompassed. The little game that started out as a vehicle to use the accelerometer on Windows Phone and tablets blossomed into a great testing ground for handling input from touch, mouse, keyboard, and gamepad. The most exciting part, however, was the addition of Adam's work on publishing to Windows Store. Seeing the game on Windows Store, and getting the app and running it on another Windows 10 device was awesome! Adam burned the midnight oil to bring it all together by Chapter 12 and has my unending gratitude! Without Adam, this book would not have been possible. A *huge* thanks to you!

Introduction

The Unity community is very large and very helpful. Videos, code, and 3D assets are available on any number of topics, and the Unity help documents continue to evolve, keeping the community abreast of the latest functionality and features. One of the biggest challenges, however, is to learn how to bring it all together. In this book, you will begin with the aim to create a small Windows 10 game, taking full advantage of the Universal Windows Platform (UWP), and be able to publish it to Windows Store. Along the way, you will not only have a chance to learn the fundamentals of game development with the Unity engine, but also experience the concept of starting simple, testing early, and adding bonus functionality as time and budget permit. In the end, you will be taken through the process of publishing an app to Windows Store, a task filled with its own set of new terms, concepts, and procedures. As with creating games with Unity, the publishing process is well documented in the Microsoft Windows Dev Center, but in such detail as to be overwhelming. This final chapter of this book breaks down the essentials and leads you through the process of building and publishing to Windows Store one step at a time.

About the Unity Game Engine

The free version of Unity provides an excellent entry point into game development, offering features and functionality that remove barriers to creative game development. With its huge user community, Unity removes the elitist separation between programmers, artists, and game designers that is typical of high-priced game engines. It makes it possible for anyone to take the first step to bringing their ideas to life. In this book, you will get to wear many hats as you create your first Unity game, discovering where your interests lie as well as gaining an understanding of what is required to develop a casual game and bring it to market.

Will I Have to Learn to Script?

Most game play needs to be scripted in Unity, but hundreds of scripts are already available that can be readily reused. Unity ships with several of the most useful. More can be found by searching the Unity Forums, wiki, or Unity Answers. Many forum members will even write bits of script for less-adept users. In the Collaboration section of the forum, you can even find scripters looking to trade for art assets. By the end of this book, you should know enough to be able to take advantage of the wealth of material available from the Unity community. Although C# (pronounced *C sharp*), the coding language you will be using in this book, is not as user-friendly as Unity's version of JavaScript, it has become the language of choice for most users, in part because it is better suited to mobile platforms. Regardless of reasons, nowadays the majority of code samples are in C#, so it makes more sense to use it.

Assumptions and Prerequisites

This book assumes that you are new to scripting, 3D, and game design, and/or the Unity engine as well as publishing to Windows Store.

What This Book Doesn't Cover

This is not a book on how to become a programmer nor a high-level adept at asset creation. It uses programming best practices when possible, but the scripting in this book is designed to ease a nonprogrammer into the process by providing instant visual feedback as often as possible. While there are usually several ways to attain the same goal, the scripting choices made in this book are generally the easiest to read and understand from a newbie's point of view. You won't have to provide your own art assets or go foraging through the Unity Asset Store for suitable items for the book's project either. Art assets will be provided for you, giving you the opportunity to learn the basics of managing them in your game. Although the Asset Store is a great place to find all manner of assets for your games, the legalities of redistributing them in the Unity project for each of the book's chapters was prohibitive. Although it makes writing the book more difficult, the advantage of having the project in its current state at the end of the chapter is invaluable. Be sure to download the game project with the chapter assets from the book's page on the Unity web site, [url here, please].

Conventions Used in This Book

This book uses various conventions. Examples are shown here.

1.   Instructions look like this.

> **Tip**   Notes, tips, and cautions follow this format.

```
Code looks like this.
```

Platform

This book was written using Unity 5.4 in a Windows 10 environment.

Chapter 1

The Unity Editor

On the off chance that you are completely new to Unity, this first chapter reviews the basics of the Unity editing environment and a few key concepts. If you are already somewhat familiar with Unity, be aware that Unity is a fast-evolving application. This book was written while Unity 5.4 was in beta, so it is based on those features; future configurations could be slightly different. Be sure to check this book's thread in the Teaching & Certification ➤ Community Learning & Teaching section of the Unity Forums for updates, clarification, and changes introduced by subsequent releases.

Installing Unity

Your first task, if you have not already done so, is to download and install Unity. You should also set up a Unity account. Unity now has four license types: Personal, Plus, Pro, and Enterprise. Unity Personal is free, provided your company doesn't earn more than $100K a year. For the most part, the remaining offerings provide you with services that will help you refine your games for better monetization and player experience.

Creating a Unity User Account

If you don't already have one, you will be encouraged to create a Unity user account during the installation process. Your user account will provide access to the downloads, Unity Forums, Unity Answers, and the Unity Asset Store. The forums provide a place for discussion of all things Unity. Unity Answers is where you can go to get quick solutions to your queries, and the Unity Asset Store is where you can find assets of all kinds (3D models, animated characters, textures, scripts, complete game environments, and more) to help you with your project. After Unity is installed, you will find a direct link to each of these resources through the editor's Help menu.

© Sue Blackman and Adam Tuliper 2016
S. Blackman and A. Tuliper, *Learn Unity for Windows 10 Game Development*,
DOI 10.1007/978-1-4302-6757-7_1

To get started, go to https://store.unity.com or follow the Get Unity links from the Unity3D home page. Currently, you will be given the following license options (Figure 1-1) as well as a comparison of the differences. Select the Personal edition.

Figure 1-1. The current Unity license options

You will be taken to the next page, where the Personal edition's system and eligibility requirements are stated; click the Download Installer button to download the installer (Figure 1-2).

System Requirements for Unity version 5.4.0f3, released 28 July 2016.
OS: Windows 7 SP1+, 8, 10; Mac OS X 10.8+.
GPU: Graphics card with DX9 (shader model 3.0) or DX11 with feature level 9.3 capabilities.

Looking to download the installer for Mac OS X? Choose Mac OS X

If your company currently makes more than $100k in annual gross revenues or has raised funds in excess of $100k, you are not permitted to use Unity Personal as defined in our EULA Agreement. You may use Unity Pro with an unlimited revenue capacity.

Figure 1-2. The Unity system and eligibility requirements and Download Installer button

The site automatically offers the version that matches the platform you are currently on, but also provides a link to other operating system versions.

> **Tip** If you are installing Unity to a machine that does not have Internet access, you can usually find the separate component downloads by following the links for the Unity beta releases. Be aware that Visual Studio Tools for Unity requires Internet access to install and use.

Because the porting section of this book is written specifically for Windows Store and the Universal Windows Platform (UWP), you will eventually need access to Windows 10. For the time being, you will be able to create most of the book's project on the operating system you have at hand. Unity's *develop once, deploy everywhere* mantra, while not quite as simple as it sounds, does go a long way toward that goal. The majority of the book offers many tips, tricks, and best practices valuable for any target platform.

Performing the Installation

This book was written using Unity 5.4. Because Unity regularly makes changes that can affect your projects, you may wish to use the 5.4 version even if the current version is newer. If you prefer, you *can* install multiple versions of Unity on the same machine, provided you name the folders accordingly (for example, Unity 5.4, Unity 5.6). Since Unity 5, you have the option to run more than one instance of Unity at the same time. Because changes in the Project view directly affect the project on your hard drive, it is not advisable to open two instances of the *same* project. If you choose to have multiple versions of Unity, you will be required to start Unity from the desired version rather than from the desktop icon or the project itself, as the previously run version will open by default.

When you install Unity, you will be given a choice of components to install. Common choices are the Unity engine, Documentation (if you work offline on a regular basis), Standard Assets, Example Project, Microsoft Visual Studio Community 2015, Android Build Support, iOS Build Support, Windows Store .NET Scripting Backend, and Windows Store IL2CPP Scripting Backend (Figure 1-3). Links are provided in the Unity Build window if you decide to add more of the options at a later date.

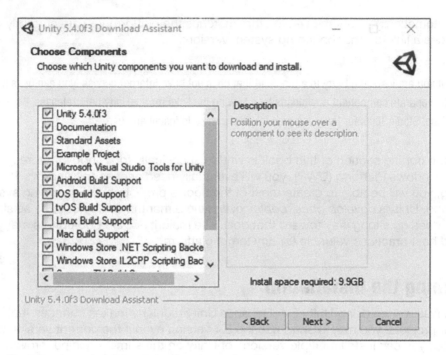

Figure 1-3. The Unity component options using the Download Assistant

For this book, you need Unity 5.4 (or the current build), Standard Assets, Microsoft Visual Studio Community 2015, and Windows Store .NET Scripting Backend. In Chapter 12, you will find in-depth explanations for several of the options, but for now, just install them.

1. Install Unity, following the prompts, including the previously suggested components.

On a Windows machine, Unity will be installed in the Program Files folder. The sample project (should you opt to install it) will be installed in Documents ➤ Public Documents ➤ Unity Projects. On a Mac, you will find Unity in Users ➤ Shared ➤ Unity. If you do not install the sample project and sample assets, they can be downloaded from the Unity Asset Store at a later date or through the installer.

At this point, you should see the Unity icon on your desktop (Figure 1-4).

Figure 1-4. The Unity application icon on the desktop

Click the icon to open Unity.

If you have not yet created an account, you will be given the opportunity to do so now, or you can choose to work offline. Next you will see the Unity start screen, where you can select a previously opened project, browse for a new project, or create and set up a new project (Figure 1-5).

Figure 1-5. The Unity start screen

This screen shows information including the location and version of previously opened projects. Unity makes very little attempt at backward compatibility as it strives to improve frame rate and feature sets, so don't be surprised if an older project does not work in a newer version. Also be aware that opening an older version will cause a project to be updated to run on the current version (as much as possible). When the update is completed, you will not be able to open it in earlier versions, so it is advisable to save a backup copy of the project folder prior to updating. Fortunately, you will be warned first and will have the opportunity to decline the update.

From the start screen, you can watch an overview video by clicking Getting Started. This overview is brief but will point you toward several of the Unity learning resources. Feel free to take a few minutes to watch the video. It is installed with Unity and does not require an Internet connection. If you do not have a Unity account, you will see a Sign In button instead of My Account in the top-right corner.

Let's begin by examining the editor with an almost empty new project loaded:

1. On the start screen, select the New button at the upper right to begin a new project (Figure 1-6).

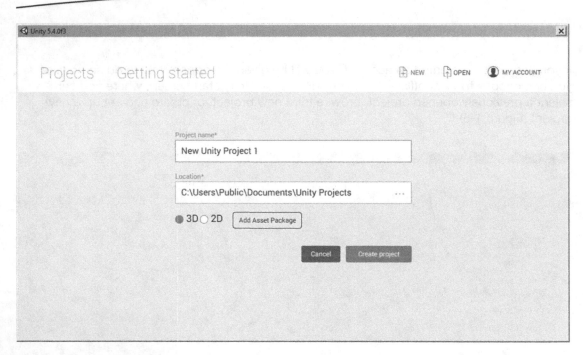

Figure 1-6. Creating a new project

Besides setting the name and location of the project, you are also given the option to preload assets relevant to 3D or 2D scenes. You won't be preloading any assets this time, but they can be imported into your scenes at any time through the editor. Best practice is to avoid loading unnecessary assets to keep your project clean and easy to manage.

2. Set the Project Name and Location manually using the Browse icon (…), or accept the default name and location.

Tip   When you create a new project, Unity creates a folder to house that project, using the project name you provide. The folder *is* the project.

3. With the project name and location specified, click the Create Project button.

    The new project and new *scene*, Untitled, opens in the Unity editor (Figure 1-7).

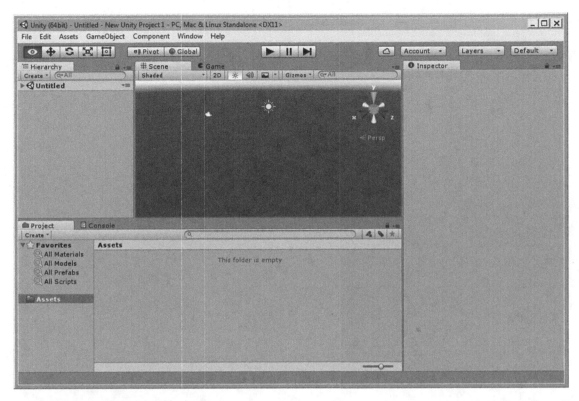

Figure 1-7. The new project in the Unity editor

Exploring the General Layout

With the project loaded, you should see Unity sporting its default layout. If you are using the Personal edition, the UI should appear in light gray, as in Figure 1-7. If you have purchased or are evaluating Unity Plus or Pro, the background will reflect the dark theme (Figure 1-8). For this book, the screenshots utilize the light theme for better contrast. If you have Plus or Pro and prefer the lighter version, you can change the Editor Skin in the General section of Unity Preferences (Figure 1-9).

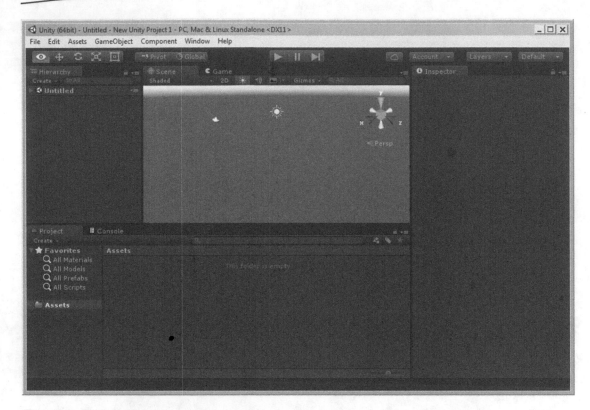

Figure 1-8. The Unity UI dark theme

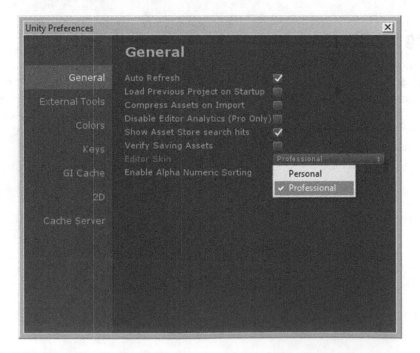

Figure 1-9. The Editor Skin options for Plus and higher

Unity's UI consists of four main *views* and several important features. The Scene view, Game view, Hierarchy view, and Inspector view (typically referred to as the *Inspector*) are generally accessible in any of the layout options, as are the playback controls, coordinate system options, and object/viewport navigation buttons (Figure 1-10). If the term *views* seems a bit odd, it helps to know that depending on which view is active, your input (or the events it triggers) will generate different results. The first click in a different view sets the focus to it.

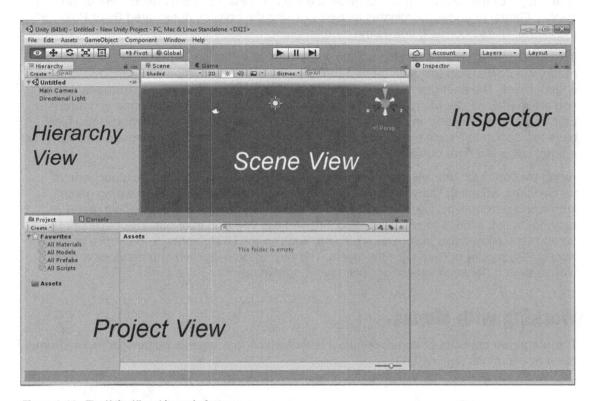

Figure 1-10. The Unity UI and its main features

With the default layout, the main feature is the Scene view. This is where you will be able to arrange your 3D assets for each scene, or level, in your project.

In the tab next to the Scene view, you will find the Game view. In the default layout, when you click the Play button, the Game tab is automatically opened. In the Game view, you will interact with your scene at runtime to test your game play.

To the left of the Scene/Game viewports, you will find the Hierarchy view. Here you will find the objects that are currently in the loaded scene, or level.

Below the Scene/Game view is the Project view. This contains the resources or assets available to the current project. This folder corresponds directly to the project's Assets folder on your operating system. Deleting files from the Project view will send them to the trash on your computer. If you author from an external hard drive, you should be able to locate the deleted files in the drive's own trash folder. The main point here is that there is no "undo" for these deleted files in the Unity editor.

To the far right, you will find the Inspector. This is where you can access the parameters, options, and other particulars of selected assets, from the Hierarchy or Project views, as well as general project-related settings.

At the top left, the navigation controls allow you to move and arrange objects in your scene and reorient the Scene view itself for easier access to the various objects.

To the right of the navigation tool controls are the coordinate system options. Here you can specify Global or Local coordinates as well as using the object's designated Pivot Point or the Center of its bounding box as the rotation point.

In the top center, you will find the playback buttons. The Play arrow puts you in Play mode, where you can test your game's functionality and presentation in a Windows or Mac environment. The background color of the UI will also change, alerting you to the fact that you are in Play mode. Many types of changes during runtime will be lost once you return to Edit mode. The Play button becomes a Stop button when you are in Play mode. You also have the option to Pause the game, using the middle button, or to step through one frame at a time, using the right button.

Along the top right, you will see a button and three drop-down menus. The cloud icon is for Services, enabling Unity to provide a "suite of integrated services for creating games, increasing productivity, and managing your audience." The Account drop-down menu provides quick access to your Unity account and lets you sign in or out. The Layers drop-down menu allows you to set various layers, such as the UI elements, to be active or inactive during Play mode, or to define new layers. The Layout drop-down menu provides a quick way to switch between several popular layout configurations.

Working with Menus

The menu bar consists of seven menus, a few of which may already be familiar to you from other applications (Figure 1-11).

Figure 1-11. The Unity menu bar

With the File menu (Figure 1-12), you can save and load both scenes and projects. This menu also enables you to build, or compile, your game before sharing it with others. In Unity, the *project* consists of all the assets or resources used to create each *scene*, or level. Scenes can be anything from complex 3D levels to simple 2D menus and anything partway between. As usual, keyboard shortcuts are shown where applicable.

Figure 1-12. The File menu

In the Edit menu (Figure 1-13), you will find the usual editing options: Undo, Redo, Cut, Copy, Paste, Duplicate, and Delete. The next couple of menu sections deal with functionality generally accessed through keyboard shortcuts or UI buttons, but that are useful for identifying the shortcuts.

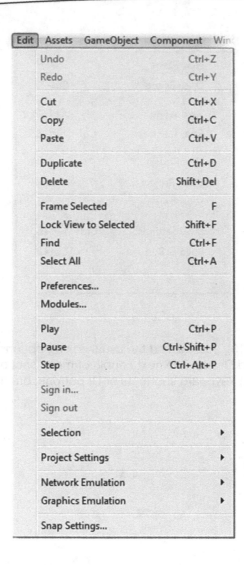

Figure 1-13. The Edit menu

You will investigate Frame Selected and Find later in the chapter. You use options from this section of the menu to locate and manipulate the viewport to the selected item. The Preferences option enables you to customize the Unity editor for matters other than layout.

With the exception of the Step option, the Play options are fairly self-explanatory. If the concept of stepping through a real-time game seems odd, think of physics. In that scenario, it could be useful to watch the progress of an object set into motion and affected by force, gravity, and other physics-based elements.

In the Selection section, you can create and load selection sets of objects for easier management of large scenes. While it may seem like more trouble than using parenting or groups to stay organized, it avoids the extra overhead of managing nested transforms. Children inherit the transforms of their parents, and position, location, and scale must have each offset calculated for each frame.

The Edit menu also provides access to project settings. These settings are not associated with any particular scene object. You will find yourself accessing the project settings regularly for everything from mapping user input to specifying the visual quality of your game.

At the very bottom of the Edit menu, you can gain access to the snap options to help with the arrangement of your 2D or 3D scene assets. Unity's snapping system is powerful and makes the layout of your environments fun and easy.

In the Assets menu (Figure 1-14), you will see the various options for creating, importing, and exporting assets. This extremely useful menu can also be accessed in a couple of places in the editor, as you will see throughout the book. Topping the list is the Create submenu. You use this option to create most of your Unity-specific assets, such as scripts, materials, and a variety of other useful things. Along with the menus for importing assets such as textures and 3D models, you will find a mainstay of Unity game development: the means of importing and exporting Unity packages. *Packages* are the vehicle for transferring all things Unity with their relationships and functionality intact.

Figure 1-14. The Assets menu

With the GameObject menu (Figure 1-15), you can create several types of preset objects, from the most basic of Unity objects, an Empty gameObject, to primitives (basic geometric shapes), lights, cameras, and a nice variety of 2D and 3D objects. Also of note in this menu are three of the last four commands. They are the means for positioning objects relative to one another, including cameras and their views.

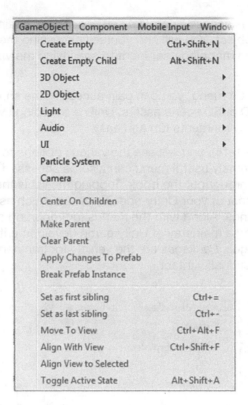

Figure 1-15. The GameObject menu

In Unity, anything that is put in your scene or level is called a *gameObject* (lowercase *g*). More than just Unity's name for an object, *gameObject* specifically refers to an object that inherits attributes and functionality from the GameObject class (uppercase *G*), the code that defines the top-level object and its basic behavior.

The Component menu (Figure 1-16) is where you can add components to define or refine your gameObject's functionality. Any of the premade objects from the GameObject menu *could* be built from scratch by adding the appropriate components to an empty gameObject.

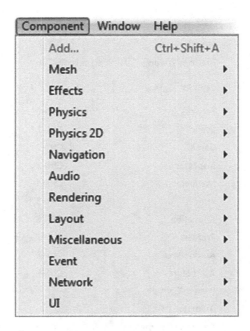

Figure 1-16. The Component menu

With Window menu (Figure 1-17), you can open or change focus to Unity's standard and specialty views or editors. The shortcut keys are listed if they exist. Unity's editor UI is completely customizable so it is possible to dock, float, or tab the component parts. This menu allows you to locate them again if you inadvertently lose them. Note the Asset Store item. This takes you directly to Unity's Asset Store, where you can import assets directly into your game. If you are not using Unity Pro, you will find that Pro-specific features are grayed out.

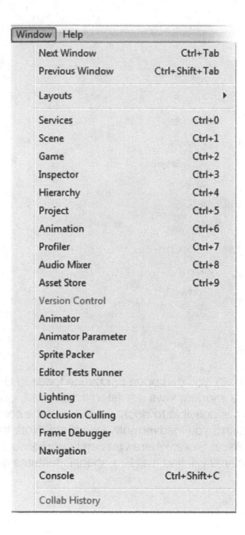

Figure 1-17. The Window menu

The Help menu (Figure 1-18), as expected, will provide you with the version number and license information of your Unity installation as well as manage the current location of your Unity license. This gives you an easy way to move your Plus or Pro license between different machines and platforms while authoring. This menu also provides access to the two main parts of Unity documentation: the Unity Manual, where you can find information on the workings and concepts behind much of the Unity workflow and features, and the Scripting Manual, where you can find Unity-specific API classes, examples, and scripting tips. Additionally, the menu supplies links to the Unity Forum, Unity Answers (when you just need a quick solution), a means of reporting a bug should the need arise, and other useful links to keep you connected with the Unity community.

Figure 1-18. The Help menu

Getting Started

As you may expect, you need something more than an empty project before exploring the Unity editor. The demo scene that Unity ships with changes occasionally, so yours may be different from the one shown in this chapter. Many useful Unity sample scenes can be found at the Unity Asset Store (under the Unity Essentials category, and the Complete Projects category under Unity Technologies). They are generally fairly complicated and are meant to show off what is possible to do with Unity, but a few have been designed for tutorials, so looking through and checking out the descriptions is worthwhile.

Loading Projects

If you did not install the Sample Project during the Unity Installation process, fetch it from the Asset Store now. The Asset Store generally should be opened through the Unity editor, as most available assets must be imported directly into your current project. Full projects, however, can be downloaded and stored in the location of your choosing. As the current sample scenes are packaged into a single project, you should see a Download button. Follow these steps:

1. From the Windows menu, select Asset Store.

2. Do a search of publishers for *Unity Technologies*.

3. Select the Standard Assets Example Project.

4. Click the Download button's drop-down arrow (on its right side).

5. Select Download Only and make note of the location.

6. Close the Asset Store window when the project has finished downloading.

From the current project, you can load the sample project:

1. From the File menu, select Open Project.

2. If you installed the sample project, you can select it directly from the Recent Projects list. If you downloaded it manually, select Open Other.

3. Navigate to the folder where the Standard Assets Example Project (the parent folder) was saved, select it, and click Select Folder.

When the Unity editor opens, the previously loaded scene will be loaded. If this is the first time you have opened a project, a new scene, Untitled, will be loaded (Figure 1-19). It consists of a camera and a Directional Light (which also provides a sky environment).

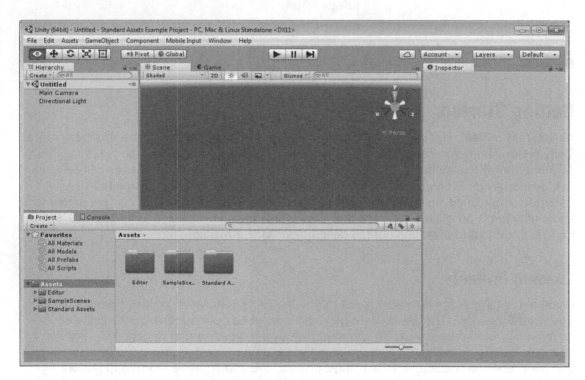

Figure 1-19. The Unity sample project opened with a new Untitled scene loaded

One of the first things you will learn to do in Unity is to keep your projects organized. While it's not mandatory to do so, most developers create a folder called *Scenes* to store the game's scenes or levels. You will find that the Scenes folder in the Standard Assets Example Project has been stashed inside the Sample Scenes folder. Unity provides icons to help you locate various types of resources. The icon used for scenes is, appropriately, the Unity product icon.

1. In the Project view, under Assets, click the arrow to expand the Sample Scenes folder.

2. Select the Scenes folder.

3. In the second column of the Project view, select and double-click the CharacterThirdPerson scene to load it (Figure 1-20).

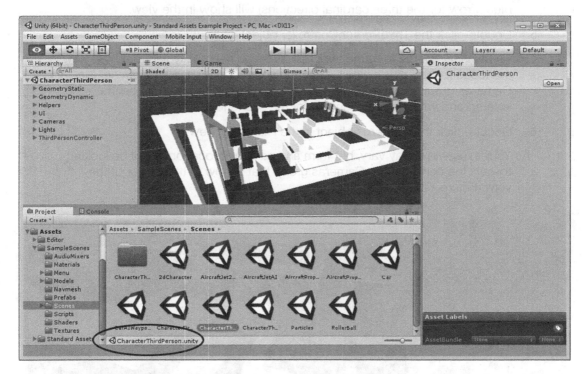

Figure 1-20. The CharacterThirdPerson scene loaded

The contents of the scene are shown in the Hierarchy view. The Scene view reflects the last observation point from the last scene seen in the Unity editor, regardless of what project it was in. You may have to adjust the view to see the contents better.

Navigating the Scene View

The first thing you will probably want to do is reposition and then explore the loaded scene in the Scene view. Because viewport navigation varies quite a bit in 3D applications, this is a good place to start your Unity experience. Let's begin by adjusting the view:

1. Move the cursor to the Scene view.

2. Hold the middle mouse button down and move the mouse to pan the view.

3. Using the middle mouse roller, zoom the view until you can see most of the contents of the scene.

    To orbit the view, it is best to have a center point set. The quickest way to set the focus of the Scene view is to choose an object and then force the view to frame or center it in the viewport.

4. In the Hierarchy view, single-click the object names to see where they are located in the scene.

    As you select them, their transform axis (a gizmo with a red, green, and blue arrow for the three cardinal directions) will show in the view.

5. Double-click the ThirdPersonController object.

    As the view zooms to frame the character, you can easily see that he is now the focus (center of the view). Although you probably can't see any of the Cameras group's contents, the center of the group looks to be centrally located and will be a good choice for the scene focus.

6. Double-click the Cameras object in the Hierarchy view.

    Your exact view may vary, but from any particular location, it will be looking toward the center of the Cameras group that is now in the center of the view (Figure 1-21).

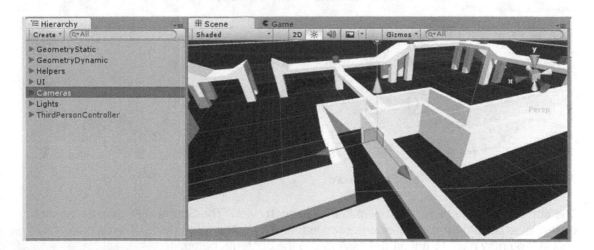

Figure 1-21. The Cameras group framed in the Scene view

7. To orbit around the Scene view's center point, hold the Alt key down on the keyboard, press the left mouse button, and move the mouse around. The Scene view is orbited around the current center.

8. To look around from the scene's viewpoint, hold the right mouse button down and move the mouse. Note that this changes the center of the view. With the Alt key plus the right mouse button held down, you can zoom the view.

9. You can also perform fly-through navigation through the scene. Hold the W key down on the keyboard and then press the right mouse button. Move the mouse to perform direction changes.

The speed increases the longer the mouse button is held down, so you may want to try a few starts and stops. Try experiments with the A, S, and D keys along with the right mouse button.

Understanding the Scene Gizmo

In the Scene view, you have several options for working in the viewport as you create and refine your scene. The two main options are to view the scene in perspective mode or in isometric mode.

1. Double-click the Cameras object once again in the Hierarchy view and then zoom back to get a good view of the scene contents.

2. Using the right mouse button (or any of the alternative methods), rotate the view and observe the Scene gizmo.

The Scene gizmo indicates the cardinal direction of the global or world directions (Figure 1-22). Currently, you are seeing the perspective view, Persp, but you can use the Scene gizmo to change to an isometric view, Iso. An isometric, view is often used in drafting to create a 3D view without the vanishing-point perspective of the human eye. Unlike in Persp, where objects farther back in the scene *appear* smaller, in Iso, their size relative to each other is always correct. When coupled with the cardinal directions (front, back, top, bottom, left, and right), Iso will show a flat orthographic view that can make positioning objects much more accurate. When rotated off of the side or top/bottom views, the view becomes isometric. You can toggle the label to return to a perspective view.

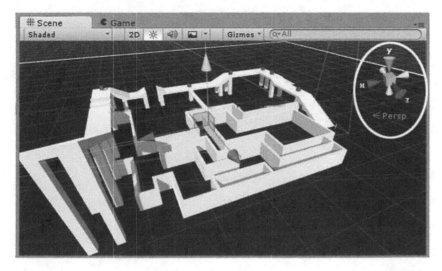

Figure 1-22. The Scene gizmo in the upper-right corner of the Scene view

3. You can also use the Scene gizmo to see the scene in traditional orthographic views after it is set to Iso. With the Scene gizmo set to Persp, select the y, or top, view arrow on the gizmo.

Tip   In Unity, y is in the world. The Unity Scene and Transform gizmo follow the x,y,z = R,G,B convention, where the x axis is red, y is green, and z is blue.

The scene is seen from the top (Figure 1-23), but it's still the perspective view, as indicated by the wedge-shaped icon next to the Top label, just below the gizmo.

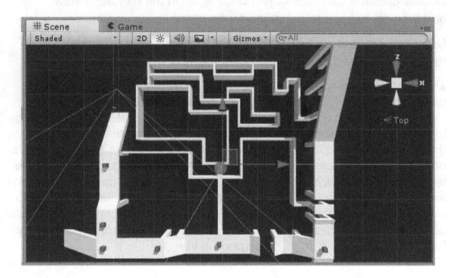

Figure 1-23. *The perspective Top view*

4. Click the Top label. Now the view is a flat orthographic view, as indicated by the three parallel bars next to the Top label (Figure 1-24).

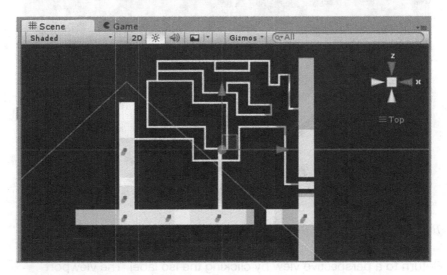

Figure 1-24. The orthographic Top view

5. Try clicking the other Scene Gizmo arrows to see the other views. These views will allow you to position objects with respect to each other with far more accuracy than a perspective view.

6. Use the right mouse button or its equivalent to rotate away from the current orthographic view.

The view once again becomes an isometric view (Figure 1-25). If you have an engineering background, you will recognize this as a typical means of depicting objects in 3D without having to calculate true (human-eye-type) perspective. It is also used in many world-building games, such as Blizzard's Warcraft 3 or StarCraft.

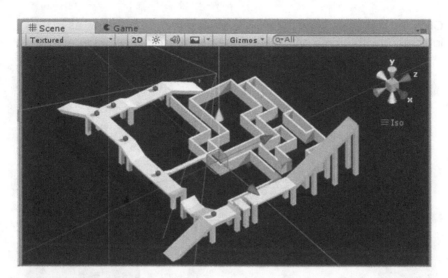

Figure 1-25. The Iso, or isometric, view

7.   Return to a perspective view by clicking the Iso label. The viewport
      and label are returned to a perspective view (Figure 1-26).

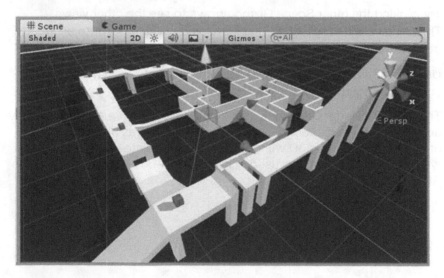

Figure 1-26. The Scene view once again showing a perspective view

Exploring the Views

Now that you are becoming more adept at manipulating the viewport, you can check out several of the tools and features available to you with each of the main views.

Hierarchy View

The Hierarchy view is essentially a list tree of the objects currently in the loaded or active scene. During runtime, objects can be *instantiated* (created on the fly) or destroyed (deleted from the scene). This is an important concept in Unity, and it is one of the reasons that most changes made during runtime are not permanent. On exiting Play mode, the Hierarchy view will be returned to its former state. This allows you to experiment with changes during runtime without worrying about the consequences.

Although this scene looks fairly simple in the Hierarchy view, you will discover that a parent object may contain any number of children, each able to have their own children.

1. Click one of the small, magenta boxes in the Scene view. This object's parent, GeometryDynamic, is expanded and highlighted in the Hierarchy view (Figure 1-27).

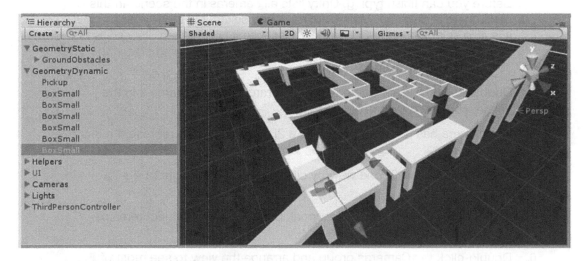

Figure 1-27. Picking an object in the Scene view to locate it in the Hierarchy view

Although this scene is simple, you can imagine how difficult it can be to locate particular objects in either the Scene or Hierarchy view in a more complex scene. Fortunately, Unity has a nice search function for that purpose. At the top of the Hierarchy view, to the right of the Create drop-down arrow, you will see a small magnifying glass icon and its drop-down arrow. This drop-down menu lets you filter for All, Name, or Type. Let's start with Type (Figure 1-28).

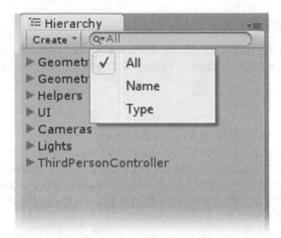

Figure 1-28. The Search feature's filters

2. Press the drop-down arrow next to the search icon and select Type.

3. In the text file to the right, type **camera**.

    Before you can finish typing, Unity lists all cameras in the scene. In this case, there is only one, Main Camera. If you select it in the Hierarchy view, it is also selected in the Scene view. Because it is a camera, its view is also shown in the Camera Preview window. Note how everything else in the scene has been grayed out.

4. Double-click the Main Camera in the Hierarchy view to frame it in the scene, and then zoom in closer to it.

    The camera has no mesh object, so a 2D icon is used to represent it in the Scene view.

5. Return to a normal Scene view by clicking the x to the right of the word you typed in.

    The Scene view is returned to normal, but the selected object remains highlighted in the Hierarchy view.

6. Double-click the Cameras group and arrange the view to see most of the boxes.

7. Deselect the Cameras group by clicking in a blank area of the Hierarchy view.

8. Change the filter back to All and type **box**.

    Because there are several objects in the scene with the word *box* in their name, the list of possible objects is quite long. In the Scene view, they are all "ungrayed," helping you to find the one you want fairly quickly (Figure 1-29).

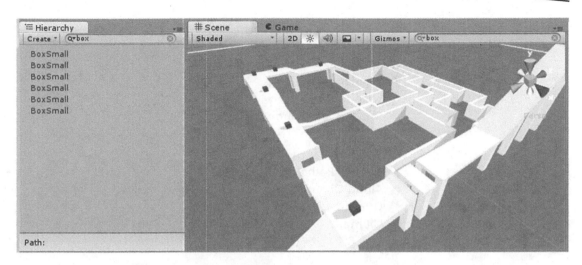

Figure 1-29. The options for a scene object with "box" in its name

9. Click the x to return the Scene view to normal.

Scene View

The Standard Assets Example Project doesn't really contain any complex scenes, but you should be able to see some of the more commonly used Scene view tools and features in action. The tools and options are found along the top of the Scene view (Figure 1-30).

Figure 1-30. The Scene view tools and options

1. Deselect any objects you've selected by clicking in a blank area of either the Hierarchy or Scene view.

2. Zoom back far enough to see most of the scene.

3. On the far left, just under the Scene tab, click Shaded to see the other viewport display options (Figure 1-31).

    Of the five, the first three are the most commonly used and should be easy to understand, especially if you have had any background in 3D modeling or have ever watched a "making of" video of any of the pioneers of the CG movie industry's 3D animated films.

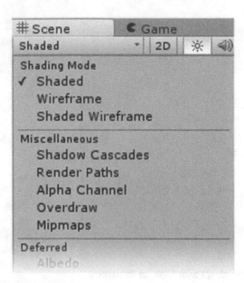

Figure 1-31. A few of the viewport display options

4. Try selecting Wireframe.

    You may have noticed that meshes automatically show as textured wire when selected. The difference here is that the wire is black, not light blue, allowing you to continue to locate the selected item in the Scene view. In Wireframe, you can see how 3D objects came to be called *meshes*, as they resemble wire meshes. Unfortunately, the Skybox environment is dark enough to make seeing the wireframe display difficult. You will learn where that can be turned off shortly.

5. Check out Shaded Wireframe next. Because of the light-colored materials in this simple scene, you can readily see the density of the various objects (Figure 1-32).

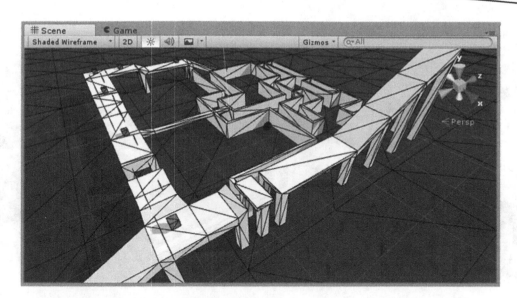

Figure 1-32. The scene viewed with Shaded Wireframe

The Deferred display options are grayed out because the render path is set to Forward in this scene. If you have Unity Pro, you have the option to use Deferred as the Rendering Path. It can be found in Edit ➤ Project Settings ➤ Player. It allows for more-sophisticated lighting and shaders. The display options will help you see the various components available to that render path.

If you are familiar with the alpha channel of a 32-bit texture or image, you may be thinking that Alpha is about transparency, with 0 as fully transparent and 255 as fully opaque. In Unity, however, the alpha channel can do duty as anything, from a glossiness channel to self-illumination to height maps. Some of Unity's shaders are designed to make use of the alpha channels' textures to maximize effect and minimize texture usage. With the Alpha option selected for the viewport texture display, you will be able to see the alpha channel but not what it has been used for (Figure 1-33).

Figure 1-33. Textures displaying alpha channels in a former sample scene, AngryBots

6. Select the Overdraw option and orbit the scene to observe the overdraw or overlap of the objects.

    Overdraw shows how many objects must be drawn on top of each other from the current vantage point. The denser or brighter the display (Figure 1-34), the more objects there are that must at least be sorted, if not actually drawn. On mobile devices, regardless of device and operating system, this type of sorting is costly and should be kept to a minimum.

Figure 1-34. Possible overdraw problem areas showing as bright areas in the Scene view

The next option shows the MIP map distance. *MIP mapping* is the process of creating multiple versions of the same texture image, with each being half the dimensions of its predecessor and consequently more blurry. No color indicates where the full original-sized texture is seen. As the tint goes from blue to clear to gold through to red, the smaller, blurrier maps are substituted, preventing the sparkly *artifacting* effect seen as the camera pulls back away from the object. Blue uses a blurred version of the map when the camera is close enough to see pixilation in the texture. Figure 1-35 shows the effect in the AngryBots scene, as there are very few textures used in the Standard Assets Example Project scenes.

Figure 1-35. Color tinting indicating which version of MIP map is shown according to the distance

To see the MIP maps generated from the imported textures, you can select a texture in the Project view and examine it in the Inspector:

1. In the Project view, select the Textures folder from the SampleScenes folder in the Assets folder.

2. Locate and select the ChevronAlbedo texture in the second column.

3. At the bottom of the Inspector, in the Preview window, move the slider from the far right, slowly over to the far left.

   The images are shown in increasingly blurry versions (Figure 1-36). They appear pixilated as Unity zooms in closer and closer and the versions are smaller and smaller. This image shows that the original was 512 × 512 pixels. The MIP mapped versions would be 256 × 256, 128 × 128, 64 × 64, 32 × 32, 16 × 16, 8 × 8, 4 × 4, 2 × 2, and 1 pixel. By MIP 7, it is all the same blurry color.

Figure 1-36.   A texture and two of its MIP mapped versions

4. Set the Scene display view back to its default Textured.

The next option for the Scene view is the 2D toggle (Figure 1-37). If you are creating the GUI for your 3D game or creating a fully 2D game, the 2D toggle is a must. A little experimentation shows that the 2D option is a preset to the Back view, with the iso option turned on. The view points in the positive z direction. The Scene gizmo is hidden to prevent accidental viewport manipulation. Only Pan and Zoom are available.

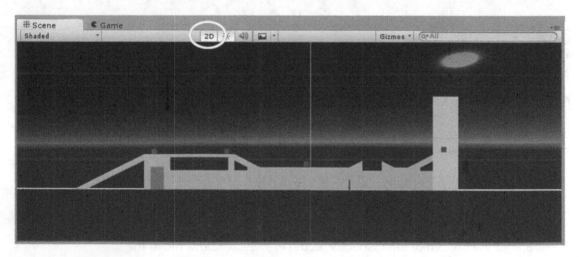

Figure 1-37.   The 2D toggle essentially a Back/iso view

The next toggle in the Scene view turns scene lighting off and on. When the scene lights are off, the scene is lit from the user's viewpoint, straight into the scene, ensuring that the visible objects will be well lit. In scenes where the lighting has already been "baked" into most of the textures, you will not see much difference.

5. Toggle the Scene Light button off and on to see the effect (Figure 1-38).

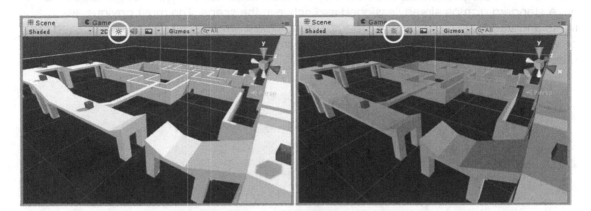

Figure 1-38. The Scene Lights toggle: lights on (left) and lights off (right)

Note the blue tint and shadows visible with the scene lighting, left. A search of the scene for light will show that there are two lights. When selected, you will see (in the Inspector) that the color of the main light is white and is set to use shadows. The color of the fill light is bluish, providing an economical way to fake bounced or ambient light.

The next button to the right is the Play Sound Effects toggle. It toggles audio on or off. To hear it in action, you would need an object with an Audio Source component with a sound assigned and set to Loop. You must also be close enough to hear it if it is set to be a 3D sound.

The Effects drop-down menu to its right allows you to select which scene effects will be shown in the Scene view (Figure 1-39). As you may remember, this scene uses a Skybox for the environment that interfered with the Wireframe display. You can toggle all of the effects off or on by clicking the Effects button, or you can selectively choose which you want to see from the drop-down menu. Feel free to deactivate the Skybox effect and try the Wireframe display again.

Figure 1-39. The Effects drop-down menu

The next option is the Gizmos drop-down menu (Figure 1-40). This controls which specialty icons show in the Scene view and how they are presented. Several types of gameObjects have standard gizmos already assigned and active in the scene. The most obvious are lights and audio, and—if you remember the new, almost empty scene when you opened the project—the camera. The gizmos help you to locate objects in the Scene view that have no mesh associated with them.

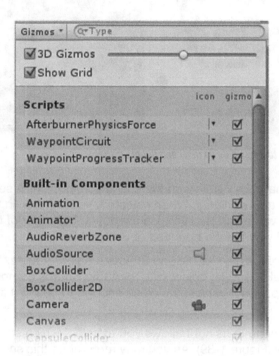

Figure 1-40. *Gizmos drop-down menu*

1. In the Project folder's Scenes folder, open the Car scene.

2. Double-click the Car and zoom in until you can see the camera, particle system, and audio icons (Figure 1-41).

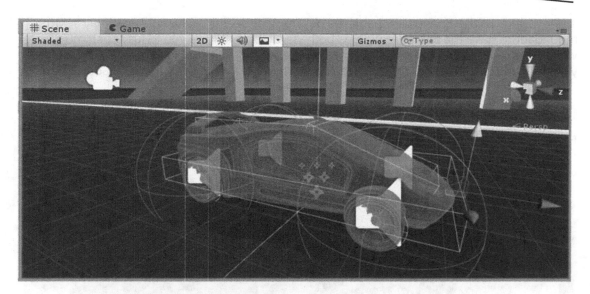

Figure 1-41. Camera and audio icon gizmos for the car

3. Zoom in closer.

    As the gizmos get larger, they start to fade out before they cover too much of the scene. As a default, they are set as 3D gizmos. They are obviously 2D icons, but they are adjusted in size depending on how close you are to them, giving you a better feel for where the actual gameObject is in 3D space. They are also occluded by mesh objects to prevent the scene from getting too cluttered. If you find the dynamic sizing distracting while working mostly in an overhead view, you may prefer to switch them to 2D by deactivating the 3D Gizmos check box.

4. Deactivate the 3D Gizmos check box and zoom out to see how the icons retain their size regardless of distance.

    All of the gizmos within view will be shown at a standard size. While this is obviously not practical for a first-person vantage point, it is useful for overhead editing.

5. Switch the view to a Top iso view so you are looking down on the car.

    The icons are easily visible in this simple scene. In a complex scene, icons may clutter the scene too much, whether you are using 2D or 3D gizmos. Fortunately, you can opt to turn icons off and on by type.

6. Open the Gizmos list again, and click the AudioSource icon from the icon column. All of the AudioSource icons are turned off in the Scene view.

In Unity, you have the option of assigning custom icons as well as generic icons to specialty scripts. In Chapter 6, you will have a chance to assign some custom icons to some of your scene objects.

The last item on the Scene view bar is the now familiar search feature. While it may seem redundant to have the search feature on both views, Unity allows you to fully customize which views are turned on and where they are placed, so you could find it very convenient if you are using two monitors and have the Hierarchy view far removed from the Scene view.

Game View

For the most part, the Game view is about the runtime functionality of your scene, and its tools and options reflect that as well (Figure 1-42). Having dealt with the most complicated view, you can now take a look at the Game view:

1.   Click the Game tab to the right of the Scene tab.

Figure 1-42. *The Game view options*

On the far left, the Free Aspect drop-down menu allows you to specify an aspect ratio so you can make sure you will be seeing what your player will see (Figure 1-43, left). You can also add custom, fixed sizes by clicking the Add button (the plus sign) at the bottom (Figure 1-43, right).

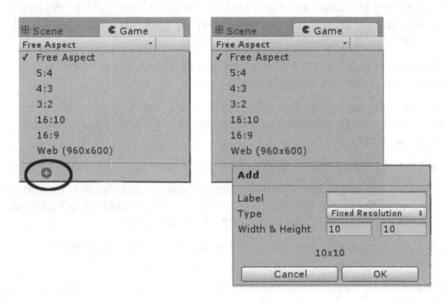

Figure 1-43. *The Free Aspect drop-down menu*

2. The next option is Maximize on Play (Figure 1-44). When toggled on, this hides all other views and maximizes the Game view during play. If you have stipulated a fixed window size, Unity will do its best to match it, scaling it smaller when necessary. Toggle the Maximize on Play option on.

Figure 1-44. Maximize on Play toggle

3. Click Play in the Player controls above the Game view. The Game window is maximized, and the other views are toggled off.

4. Stop Play mode by clicking the Play button again. The views return to their original layout.

   Next to the Maximize on Play option is the Mute Audio button. This lets you mute audio only during playback.

   Next to the Maximize on Play option is the Stats button. The Stats window will show you the statistics for your game during runtime. The most familiar will be the frame rate to the right of the Graphics label. The various items in the list may be a bit more cryptic, but all affect frame rate in one way or the other.

5. Toggle on the Stats window and click Play. Observe the frame rate and other items as you drive the car around the environment (Figure 1-45).

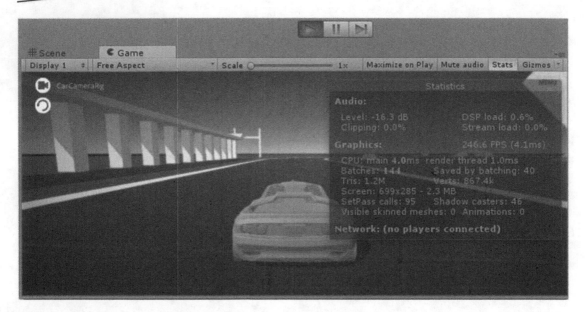

Figure 1-45. The Stats window during runtime

     6.   Stop Play mode, and turn off the Stats window.

The last item on the Game view bar is the Gizmos toggle. Like the Effects drop-down menu, this one works as a toggle when clicked or can be set to selectively see the gizmos you prefer.

Project View

Next up is the Project view. This is where all resources for your project are stored and managed. The Assets folder on your computer is the Assets folder you see in the Project view. The most important thing to remember is that you can add to the folder through the Explorer (in Windows) or the Finder (on Mac), but you should not rearrange resources except from within Unity unless you also include the asset's .meta file (it will have the same name). Deleting assets from the Project view will delete them from your computer. The Two Column Layout is shown as a default. It has some options that are useful when working with unfamiliar assets.

The big advantage of the Two Column Layout is the ability to easily scrub between text with a tiny icon when you know the name, but do not know what the image looks like, and a large thumbnail image when you are trying to locate a particular image or something that looks right for the purpose. Follow these steps to explore the Project view:

     1.   Under Assets, expand the folders to Standard Assets ➤ Environment ➤ TerrainAssets ➤ Surface Textures (Figure 1-46).

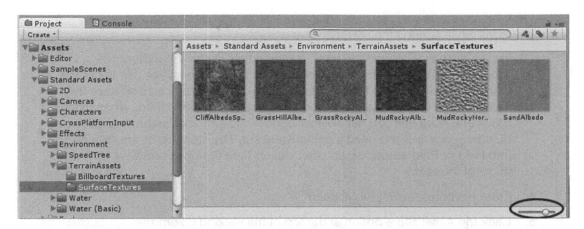

Figure 1-46. Adjusting the thumbnail display

2. Try adjusting the thumbnail slider at the lower right. The thumbnails scale nicely. Note that at the far left, you will get the 16-pixel version in list format. Also note that whatever the display scheme, as soon as you select an individual asset, it will be displayed in the bottom of the Preview section of the Inspector, where you will get an even better view of it.

3. Another of the main features of the two-column Project view is the Favorites options found above the Assets folder section (Figure 1-47). It allows you to see all assets of the listed types in the second column. Select each of the filters, and watch the results in the second column.

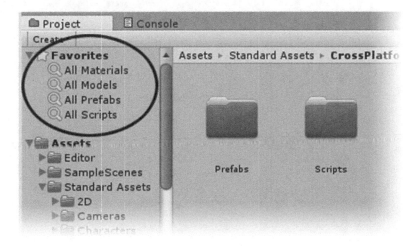

Figure 1-47. The Favorites options

With regular assets, you will be able to see thumbnails instead of generic icons while filtering the selections.

You've probably noticed the familiar search field at the top right of the Project view. With folders selected, you can type in a name or use the small icons at the right of the field to filter by type or label. You can also save the search if you find yourself repeatedly looking for the same item. When using the filters, however, you get another option. You can search the Asset Store directly if you find you need a particular asset. The store items are divided into Free or Paid assets, so you can search the thumbnail previews for items of interest.

4. From Favorites, select All Models.

5. Click the Asset Store option at the top of the second column.

6. Open the Free Assets section, and click a model that looks interesting.

The information about the model is shown in the Inspector, and you have the option of importing it directly to your scene or going out to the Asset Store for some serious shopping (Figure 1-48, left). For the Paid Assets, you will see the price instead of the import option (Figure 1-48, right).

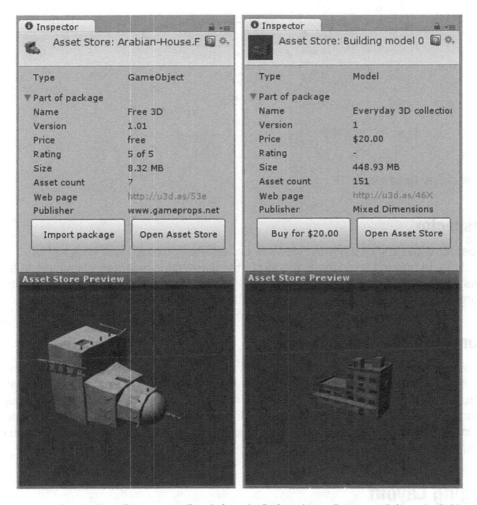

Figure 1-48. Accessing the Asset Store assets directly from the Project view: a Free asset (left), and a Paid asset (right)

7. For fun, type in an object of interest to you in the search field. The item or related items, if any can be found, appear in the project view.

When working with familiar assets, you may find it advantageous to use the original One Column Layout (Figure 1-49). The column options can be located by right-clicking over the Project tab. The One Column Layout is more compact and behaves more like the Explorer (Windows) or Finder (Mac). You will get a chance to give it a try later in the book.

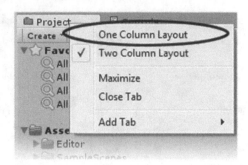

Figure 1-49. Column layout options

The Inspector

The Inspector is the last of the main views or panels. As you may have noticed, its functionality and options are directly related to the item that is selected elsewhere in the editor. As you become more familiar with Unity, you will spend a lot of time in the Inspector. It is where you will gain access to almost everything related to your game in Unity.

The Console

The console is where messages are printed out during runtime and whenever there are issues with your project. In the default Editor layout, you will find the console view's tab next to the Project view tab. In other layouts, it may not be active, but can be opened through the Window menu. As with all Unity views or windows, it can be left free-floating or can be docked in the location of choice. You will get more practice with the console in Chapter 3 when you investigate scripting.

Managing Layout

As you open various projects by different authors, you will see many layout preferences. The current default layout shows the loaded scene and Assets folder off to nice advantage, so is a good choice for a first look. As you start developing your own games, however, you may find it useful to try other preset layouts, or even customize your own:

1. Locate the Layout drop-down at the upper right of the editor. Open it and check out some of the preset layout options (Figure 1-50).

Figure 1-50. A few layout options

2. Select the 2 by 3 option. This layout is useful for changing and checking on objects during runtime as you get to see both Scene and Game views at the same time. Its tall vertical views or panels make it easier to access large numbers of assets in the Hierarchy view without resorting to the Search feature. Its main drawback is that the Project view's Two Column Layout does not lend itself to a tall, vertical column very well. This is when the Single Column Layout is useful.

3. Right-click over the Project tab and select the Single Column Layout.

   The Project view is now essentially the contents of the Assets folder, and the file structure has the standard operating system hierarchy (Figure 1-51).

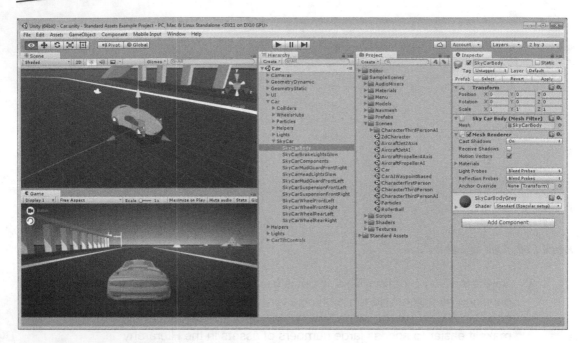

Figure 1-51. The 2 × 3 layout and Single Column project view

4. Besides the preset layouts, you can also float and rearrange the views manually. Click and drag the Hierarchy tab around the editor.

    The view snaps into various locations, ready to be dropped. If you have multiple monitors, you can even leave it floating outside the editor window. If you have trouble getting it to dock again, you can choose one of the preset layouts in the Layout drop-down menu.

Understanding the Project Structure

Before you jump in and start creating a game, you ought to have a basic understanding of how Unity projects are organized. Pretty much everything you create will reside in the Assets folder. It is up to you to keep things organized as you develop your game. Unity projects have a highly structured system of dependencies. To be on the safe side, avoid rearranging the contents of the project view outside the Unity editor to keep these intact.

File Structure

The file structure in Unity's Project view is drawn directly from Windows Explorer (or the Mac Finder). To see how Unity manages the folders that you create or import into your project, you can add a new folder to the current project:

1. Close the three main folders in the Project view. You should see the Editor, SampleScenes, and Standard Assets folders in the Project view.

2. With none of the existing folders selected, right-click in the Project view and select Create ➤ Folder (Figure 1-52).

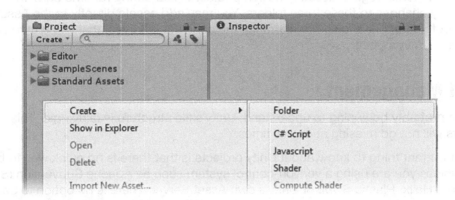

Figure 1-52. *Creating a new folder from the right-click menu*

3. Name it **Test Folder.**.

Before you can execute the next step, you have to know the location of the current project. A quick way to find that is to select New Project from the File menu and make note of the path shown for it.

4. In Explorer (or Finder on the Mac), navigate to where the Standard Assets Example Project resides and examine the contents of the Assets folder (Figure 1-53).

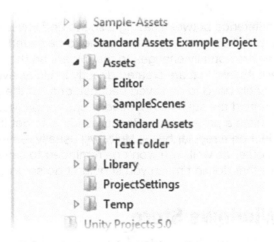

Figure 1-53. *The new folder, Test Folder, in the project's hierarchy in the OS's browser*

As you can also see, there are three extra folders that you cannot access through the Editor. The Library folder stores relationships between assets. Project Settings stores game-related data not contained in regular assets. The Temp folder exists during runtime only. You should not make any changes to these three folders. You may add assets directly to the Assets folder or subfolders, but should not rearrange the contents (and yes, that is the third time that has been mentioned!).

Project Management

As you are probably beginning to understand, Unity's file structure is fairly rigid. This ensures that assets will not go missing at crucial times.

Another important thing to know about Unity projects is that there is no quick way to back them up unless you are using a version-control system such as Apache Subversion (SVN), Git, Perforce Helix, Plastic SCM, or Unity's own Asset Server. There is no option to Save Project As. To be able to copy a project, you must first close it. You will find that as you refine scripts along the development process, earlier test scenes may no longer work. Unity project files can get quite large, so it is well worth the time and space to make occasional backup copies for emergencies, for referencing earlier functionality, or for experimenting with alternative ideas in a nondestructive way.

The finished projects for each chapter of the book are included in the book's asset file download from the Apress web site (www.apress.com/9781430267584). They will provide you with a means of comparing your results with a working copy at the end of each chapter. If you are already familiar with version control, you may want to do a search for *Unity metadata* and how the .meta files can be managed.

Load/Save

Also worth noting is the difference between saving a scene and saving a project. Changes made to the Hierarchy view will always require the scene to be saved. Changes in the Project view, because they are actually changes to the folders on the operating system, may not need to be saved. Assets that are created directly in Unity, even though residing in the Assets folder, will probably need to be saved because of all of the path and relationship metadata they generate behind the scenes. Anything scene- or project-related that does not directly involve assets requires a project save. Best practice is to get in the habit of saving both your scene and project on a regular basis. Unity will usually remind you to save one when it is required by the other as well. You won't be reminded to save scene and project very often in the book, but that doesn't mean you shouldn't do so on your own!

Preparing for Windows Store

If you are already on a machine running Windows 10, you can create a simple test scene to make sure you have most of the components required for the end goal of the book's project. This first go at the procedure is mainly to get all the required components installed and working. In Chapter 12, you will go through the procedure in depth with the project you will be creating in this section.

Building for Windows

Before you jump into building for Windows, you might want a bit of background on the process, specifically, what it means to build for Windows. This could include building for devices such as a phone, tablet, Xbox, PC, Microsoft HoloLens, Surface Hub, and more. There's been a long journey to support multiple versions of Windows, various stores that eventually merged into one store, and multiple platforms between ARM, 32-bit, and 64-bit systems.

Since this book is for building on Windows 10, that means one of two things: you can have a stand-alone build in Unity or a Windows Store build. *Stand-alone builds* are the traditional executable apps you download or install from media and run as a classic Windows application. These are the EXE files and their supporting files Unity generates.

However, we live in a world now that has a dizzying array of devices available, many of them mobile devices and tablets. These devices have different power requirements than a system that is plugged in all the time, and applications need to run differently on these devices. Traditional executables have many characteristics that make them less ideal for modern portable devices. The Windows Runtime, also called WinRT, is an application framework created by Microsoft to address many of the concerns of running modern applications on modern devices. Applications that run on WinRT are called *Universal Windows applications* and also commonly referred to a *Windows Store apps*. They can be downloaded and installed from the Windows Store or they can be side-loaded (this is what enabling Developer mode does for you), a process for installing Windows Store apps outside the store, a process that happens automatically we run our Windows Store apps from Visual Studio.

A Bit of History

Windows 8 had a store. Windows Phone 8 had a different store. If you bought something in one store, it wasn't reflected in the other store. Windows 8.1 brought changes so you could share an application ID across the stores and share app purchases and in-app purchases between the stores. Windows 8.1 finally brought a universal project to Visual Studio that had a separate Windows Phone project, a shared project, and a Windows Store project. It was a better way to share code between them. Unity still supports this. Windows 10, however, finally brought everything together in a much more cohesive environment.

The Universal Windows Platform

Windows 10 brought the *Universal Windows Platform* (*UWP*), which unifies all Windows 10 platforms in a common application programming model. UWP enables you to take an app and have it run across a multitude of devices without concern for the underlying device type—unless you want to customize an experience for a type of device (for example, an Xbox or HoloLens). While our end goal for this book is for you to be able to publish a little game to the Windows Store, you will be creating it with multiple devices in mind.

Applications that run on the UWP are called Store apps or UWP apps. Store apps have a particular life cycle to them that differ from traditional EXE programs (called *classic Windows applications* or *Win32 apps*, depending on who you talk to).

What platforms are those? We can look at this in two ways: the actual types of devices supported or the device family.

Thousands of devices can run Windows 10. For example, phones, tablets, IoT (Internet of Things) devices, desktops, laptops, and Xbox consoles all support Windows 10. Clearly, very different architectures are used on these devices to support processors such as x86 and ARM. As you'll see, when publishing a UWP app, it will (by default) compile all the different process architectures so you don't need to worry about it.

Device families represent a set of APIs given a name and a version number. Current device families include Mobile, Xbox, Desktop, IoT, and HoloLens. This is extremely powerful because our UWP applications can technically run on any device family—even IoT, though you wouldn't try to run a game on an IoT device for performance reasons. The Universal device family means any API defined there is available on any other Universal device (Figure 1-54).

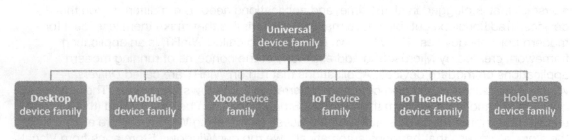

Figure 1-54. The Windows 10 device families

When you submit your applications to the Windows Store, you can specify which device families can run your application. If you want to write your own custom code to ask for Contacts on a device, you will see at https://msdn.microsoft.com/library/windows/apps/br224849 that the Contacts API runs on any Universal device family, which means it's available on any Windows 10 device (Figure 1-55).

Requirements (Windows 10 device family)

Device family	Universal, introduced version 10.0.10240.0
API contract	Windows.Foundation.UniversalApiContract, introduced version 1.0

Figure 1-55. Windows 10 device family requirements

Part of the power of a device family becomes apparent when you publish to the store. You may choose, for example, Mobile only or PC only. Because there is one Windows Store across all Windows 10 devices, this will determine how your application appears for each device family in the store. You can read more about device families at `https://msdn. microsoft.com/windows/uwp/get-started/universal-application-platform-guide`.

Application Life Cycle

It's important to understand how a UWP application runs on a Windows 10 system and what this means for your Unity game. When your application runs, it shows a splash screen and then loads. When you switch away from your app, it can be suspended by the operating system, in contrast to classic Windows applications that stay running. You can read more on the UWP application life cycle at `https://msdn.microsoft.com/en-us/windows/uwp/launch-resume/app-lifecycle`. The important takeaway is that your application will not continue running in the background. There are certain background programming tasks you can do in a UWP application, but they are outside the scope of this book and not applicable here (although a use case could be to define a background task to update your application's tile on a frequent basis to entice the user back—assuming they've pinned it to their start screen).

Installing UWP Applications

UWP applications aren't installed like traditional applications, where you manually run an installer and a bunch of DLLs and EXEs are copied to various locations. They are either downloaded from the Windows Store or side-loaded, which means installed from some other means like Visual Studio, an installer script, or managed by an enterprise such as a large company that runs its own software in-house. To test your game, you must install it (or deploy it) onto your machine. Luckily, Visual Studio does this seamlessly, which is one of the reasons you will be setting up Developer mode shortly. Before you do that, however, you will have Unity create your UWP application in the form of a *Visual Studio solution*.

Before proceeding, it is assumed that you have installed Unity and Microsoft Visual Studio Community 2015 and that you are connected to the Internet.

Enabling Developer Mode

You will also have to make sure Developer mode is enabled on your computer to be able to deploy (install) a Windows 10 application from Visual Studio to your computer. If Unity has installed Visual Studio for you, the first time you run it, you should be prompted to enable developer settings. If not, or if you already had Visual Studio installed, you can manually enable Developer mode:

1. Click the Start button in Windows on the taskbar and click the settings icon to load Windows settings.

2. Type in **developer** and select one of the resulting options.

3. Select the Developer Mode radio button, shown in Figure 1-56, and click Yes on the resulting prompt. You may then be shown a message to reboot; do so if prompted.

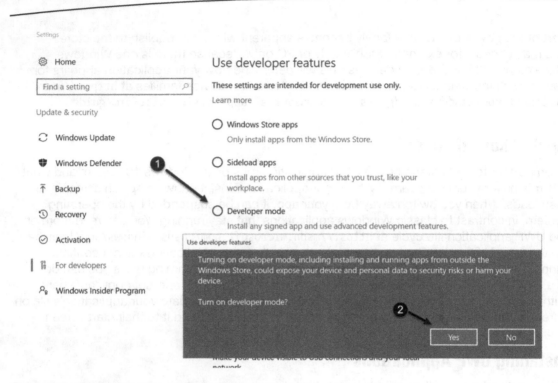

Figure 1-56. *Enabling Developer mode on a Windows 10 machine*

Creating a Test App

To help you complete the required installations, you will begin by creating a new Unity project. The installation procedure, especially for Microsoft Visual Studio Community 2015, can be time-consuming, and, depending on what else has been installed on your machine, may require perseverance. Fortunately, when things go wrong, you will usually be given links or instructions on how to find the missing components, as per Figure 1-57.

Figure 1-57. *A typical Missing Features dialog box*

1. Make sure you are connected to the Internet.

2. Double-click the Unity icon on your desktop.

3. When the Projects dialog box appears, click the New icon (option A in Figure 1-58).

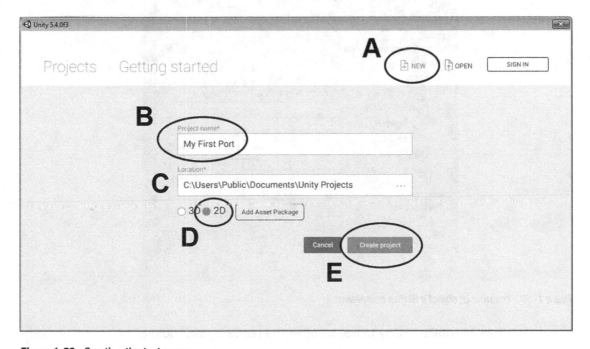

Figure 1-58. *Creating the test scene*

4.   Name the Project **My First Port** (Figure 1-58, B).

5.   Select the location for the project (Figure 1-58, C).

Unity creates a folder named My First Port. The folder *is* the Unity project.

6.   Change the project type to 2D and select Create Project (Figure 1-58, D and E).

The Unity editor opens.

A simple bit of interaction will be enough for your first test.

7.   From the GameObject menu, choose UI ➤ Button.

8.   On the left side, in the Hierarchy view, double-click the new Button object to center it in the Scene view window.

9.   On the right, in the Inspector, scroll down to locate the Button (Script) component.

10. Click the color bars for Normal Color, Highlighted Color, and Pressed Color and give each a different color (Figure 1-59).

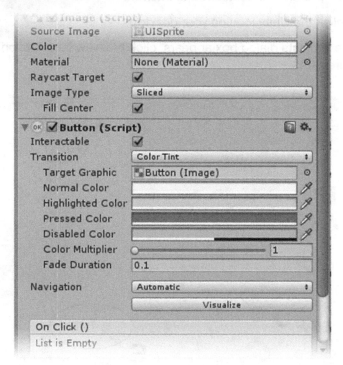

Figure 1-59. The new UI object's Button component

This will make it easy to see whether the game is responding.

11. Back in the Hierarchy view, select and then double-click the Canvas object to focus the view on it.

12. In the Hierarchy view, in the Canvas Scaler (Script) component, set the UI Scale Mode to Scale With Screen Size (Figure 1-60).

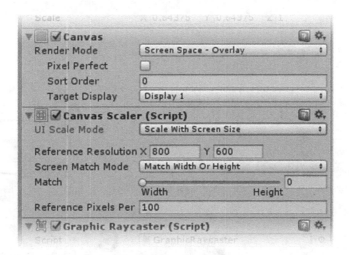

Figure 1-60. *The Canvas object's Canvas Scaler component*

13. Click the Button in the Scene view and click and drag it to the center of the canvas.

14. From the File menu, choose Save Scene As and type in **Button Test**.

   Next you will change some of the build settings.

15. From the File menu, open Build Settings.

16. Click the Add Open Scenes button (Figure 1-61, A).

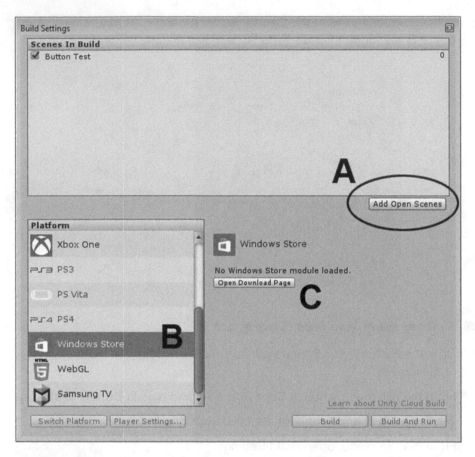

Figure 1-61. The Build Settings, adding a scene to the build (A), Selecting Windows Store as the platform (B), and the message if the Windows Store module is not yet installed (C)

17. Select Windows Store from the Platform list (Figure 1-61, B).

    If it shows that the Windows Store module is not loaded, do the following:

18. Click the Open Download Page button (Figure 1-61, C) and download the file UnitySetup-Metro-Support-for-Editor-5.4.0f3.exe (or whatever Unity version is currently available).

19. Save the project and close Unity.

20. Install the file, following the prompts on the installer.

21. Open the My First Port project (it will be in the Recent Projects list).

    You should be able to continue now.

22. Back in Build Settings, select Windows Store and click Switch Platform.

    The Unity icon will move to Windows Store and it will become the default platform.

Now you should see options for Windows Store.

23. Under SDK, select Universal 10 (Figure 1-62). Leave Build and
     Run On set to Local Machine. Leave UWP Build Type set to XAML.
     Deselect the Unity C# Projects check box.

Figure 1-62. *The build settings for your test build*

24. Click the Build button and create a new folder *outside* your Unity
     project (folder) named **Small Test**.

25. Inspect the contents of your new folder.

     If nothing is added to the folder, you are probably missing the Windows10
     SDK. Check the Unity console for a cryptic message about the missing SDK.

     If you have the SDK and your folder is not empty, you can obviously skip
     the section on locating and installing the SDK.

Installing the Windows 10 SDK

If you already have Visual Studio installed and don't have the Windows 10 SDK installed,
read this section. If you aren't sure, see the following "Verifying Installations" section. The
Windows 10 SDK can be downloaded and installed from https://developer.microsoft.
com/en-us/windows/downloads/windows-10-sdk. A quick way to check whether it is installed
is to open Visual Studio, choose File ➤ New Project, and navigate to the Universal section in
the new project dialog box. You can launch the installation from here as well, which simply
launches Visual Studio with the new option selected for the SDK, as shown in Figure 1-63.

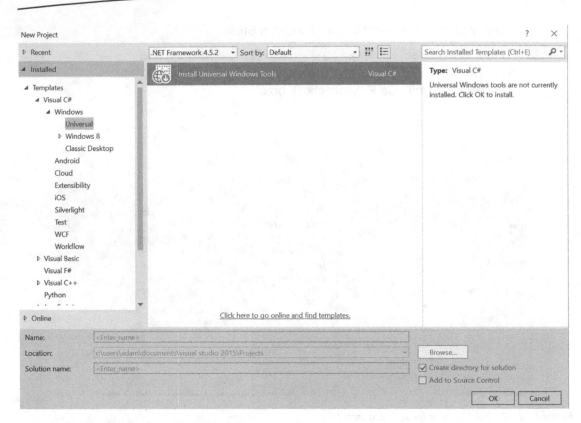

Figure 1-63. Installing the Windows 10 SDK from inside Visual Studio

This launches the Visual Studio installer, where you can accept the defaults and click Next to install the Windows 10 SDK (Figure 1-64).

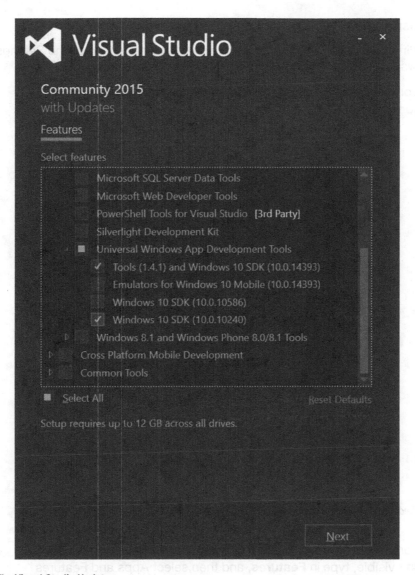

Figure 1-64. The Visual Studio Updater

Verifying Installations

For a more direct approach to verifying your installations, you can use the Settings panel on your Windows 10 PC as follows:

1. From the Windows Start menu, type **settings** or click the Settings icon (Figure 1-65).

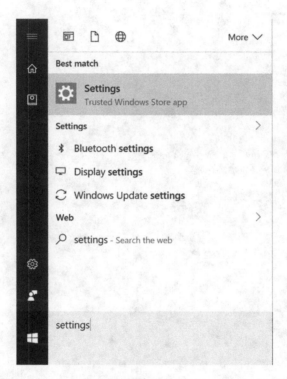

Figure 1-65. Checking on installed components through the Settings' Apps and Features

2. From Settings, select System ➤ Apps and Features. If this option isn't visible, type in **Features**, and then select Apps and Features (Figure 1-66). You will then see the list of installed applications.

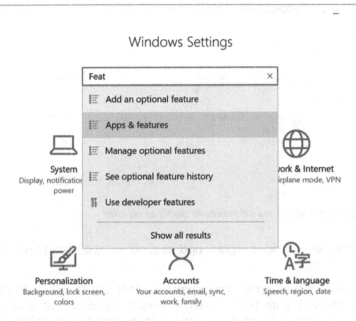

Figure 1-66. Locating Apps and Features in Windows Settings

3. Scroll down to Microsoft Visual Studio C++ Redistributable. You should see a version for 2015 (x64) and (x86) as well as the build numbers. Below those, you should see Microsoft Visual Studio Community 2015 with updates (Figure 1-67).

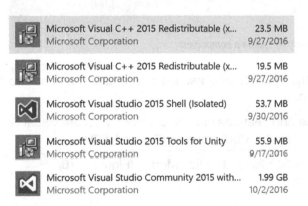

Figure 1-67. Checking on installed Microsoft components

4. Scrolling down farther, locate the Windows entries.

There you should have Windows SDK AddOn and Windows Software Development Kit (Figure 1-68).

Figure 1-68. Selecting a component to see the options to modify or uninstall

Obviously, this software undergoes regular updates, so you will want to use the most current versions.

If you do find that you are missing anything, you could modify the Visual Studio installation to select the new options (Figure 1-69). Again, ensure that you have at least Update 3 for Visual Studio. You can always check this via the Help ➤ About menu in Visual Studio.

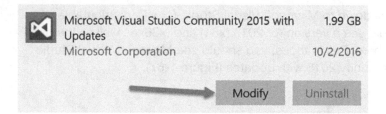

Figure 1-69. Selecting Modify to update a component

To manually update the Visual Studio installation and add the Windows 10 SDK, you can modify the installation:

1.   In the Apps and Features opened previously, locate Visual Studio again and click the Modify button (Figure 1-69).

2.   When Visual Studio loads, click Modify (Figure 1-70).

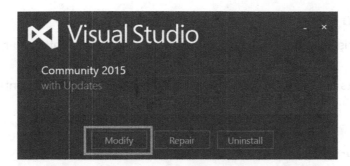

Figure 1-70. The Visual Studio modify options

3. Choose the latest SDK version available to you. If other items in the list are already selected, beyond what is shown in Figure 1-71, that is okay.

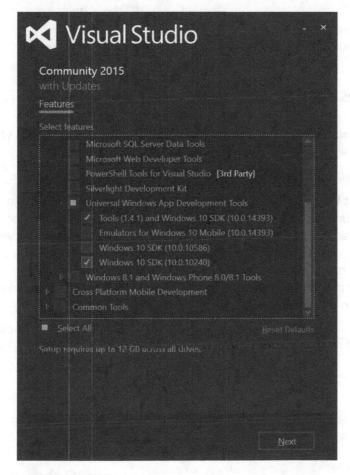

Figure 1-71. Updating the Windows 10 SDK

Continuing the Build

If you have just finished installing the SKD, return to Unity's Build settings and try the build again.

When the build has finished, the browser will open and you will see the contents of your new folder (Figure 1-72).

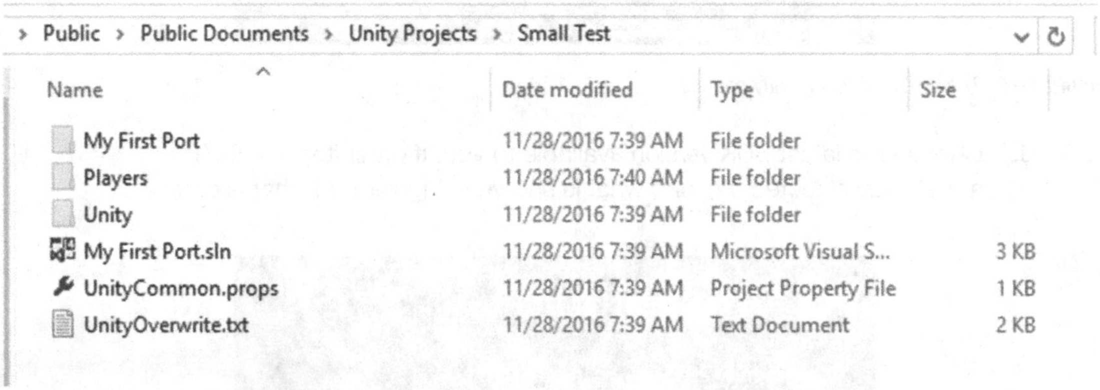

Name	Date modified	Type	Size
My First Port	11/28/2016 7:39 AM	File folder	
Players	11/28/2016 7:40 AM	File folder	
Unity	11/28/2016 7:39 AM	File folder	
My First Port.sln	11/28/2016 7:39 AM	Microsoft Visual S...	3 KB
UnityCommon.props	11/28/2016 7:39 AM	Project Property File	1 KB
UnityOverwrite.txt	11/28/2016 7:39 AM	Text Document	2 KB

Path: Public > Public Documents > Unity Projects > Small Test

Figure 1-72. The results of the successful build

Unity has generated a UWP Visual Studio *solution,* the .sln file, SmallTest.sln. Now you will open the solution with Visual Studio to complete the build process.

1. Double-click to open the My First Port.sln file in Visual Studio.

2. The first time you open Visual Studio, you will be asked to sign in with your Microsoft account. If you have previously purchased or downloaded just about any Microsoft product, you probably already have an account. If not, create one following the prompts. If you already have one and can't remember it, follow the prompts to recover it. Signing in is a one-time event on each machine, so you won't be bothered again.

   Having signed in, Visual Studio Community Edition will open, showing the new solution (Figure 1-73).

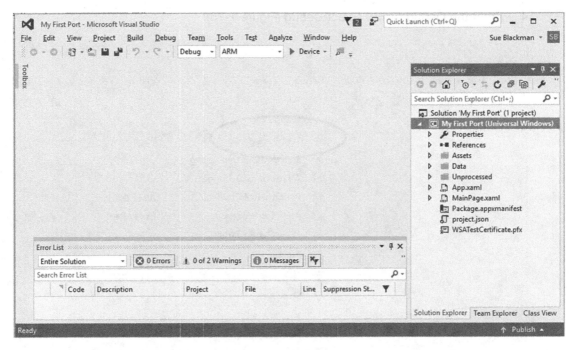

Figure 1-73. Visual Studio and your first build

3.   For Windows 10, select x86 (Figure 1-74).

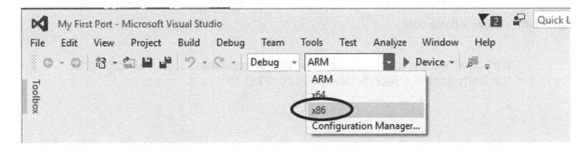

Figure 1-74. Selecting the processor type

4. From the Debug menu, select Debug (Figure 1-75).

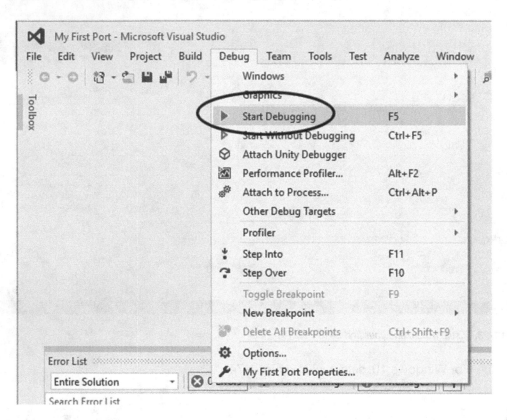

Figure 1-75. Creating a Debug build

If all goes well, you should see your project appear in its own window after the Unity splash screen finishes (Figure 1-76).

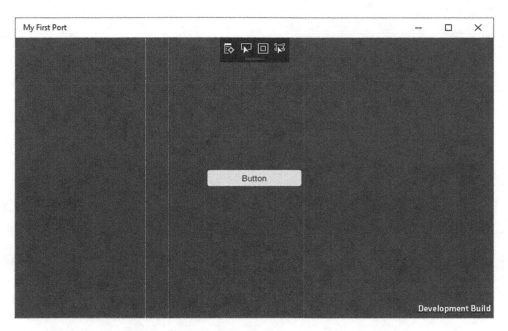

Figure 1-76. Your first build running on its own

5. Touch or click the button to see whether the functionality is working.

    It should change colors upon pressing, but will not show the hover color if you are using touch.

6. Close the game window and Visual Studio (the settings will be retained).

You've deployed and run your first test scene outside the Unity editor!

Summary

In this chapter, you took a first look at the Unity editor. Besides getting a brief overview of the major areas, you had a chance to investigate some of the functionality that will help you as the book's project progresses. The biggest takeaway was in scene management, where you learned that you could add to the Assets folder from your OS's Finder or Explorer, but that you should not rearrange assets outside the Unity editor after they have been added.

If you are feeling overwhelmed at the amount of new information to digest, don't worry. Anything that is critical to know and understand will be covered again later in the book. A few of the things mentioned in this chapter are more just to give you an idea of what can be done as your knowledge of Unity increases. Feel free to revisit this chapter at a later date.

In the last section, you created a tiny scene to get a head start on the process and installations required to build for the Windows Store.**Electronic supplementary material** The online version of this chapter (doi:10.1007/978-1-4302-6757-7_1) contains supplementary material, which is available to authorized users.

Chapter 2

Unity Basics

Although you can create assets directly inside Unity, the building blocks for your scene will usually be based on imported assets. The in-game functionality, location, and final appearance, however, will be managed and completed within the Unity editor. For that, you need a good understanding of Unity's key concepts and best practices. In this chapter, you will explore and experiment with a good portion of the Unity features that don't require scripting to be useful in your scenes.

Working with Unity GameObjects

In Unity, *assets* can be anything from textures and materials to meshes, scripts, and physics-related components. Whether they are imported or generated inside Unity, components are combined and manipulated to bring objects to life. Unity uses the term *gameObject* to represent objects because internally they belong to a scripting class named GameObject. When referring to a generic gameObject, this book uses the lowercase *g*. When scripting, the uppercase and lowercase g refer to either the particular gameObject, lowercase, or to the GameObject class, uppercase *G*, that holds the definitions and available functionality for all gameObjects.

The most basic of gameObjects (in the formal sense of the word) consists of little more than a transform. A *transform* indicates an object's scale, orientation, and location in space. The gameObject itself can be used as a parent to manage multiple gameObjects, or can be filled with components that define all manner of visual appearance and functionality. Unity provides many prebuilt gameObjects. Some are simple primitives, ideal for quickly prototyping your game. Others are full-fledged systems for complex and sophisticated objects and special effects.

If you have no prior experience with 3D assets, let alone game-type functionality, don't worry; you will begin with the basics and go on from there.

© Sue Blackman and Adam Tuliper 2016
S. Blackman and A. Tuliper, *Learn Unity for Windows 10 Game Development*,
DOI 10.1007/978-1-4302-6757-7_2

Creating Primitives

A *primitive* object is, by definition, an object that can be defined by a set of parameters. Although Unity offers several primitives of its own, those of you who have worked with traditional digital content creation (DCC) applications such as Autodesk 3ds Max, Autodesk Maya, or the open source Blender, will note that there is very little you can do to modify primitives other than change their scale. Be that as it may, primitives are extremely useful for prototyping your game's functionality and flow.

In Unity, the sphere, cube, capsule, and cylinder are a few of the available primitives. A sphere is defined by a radius and the number of longitudinal and latitudinal segments it has. A box, or cube, is defined by height, width, length, and its number of segments. When an object cannot be described by a set of parameters, it is called a *mesh*. A mesh is a collection of vertices, edges, and faces that are used to build the object in 3D space. The smallest renderable 3D element is a triangle, or tri. It consists of vertices, edges, and the face that they define (Figure 2-1). Unless specified by the shader in charge of drawing the face, the face is single-sided. The direction it is drawn on is called its *face normal*, where an imaginary line is perpendicular to the face.

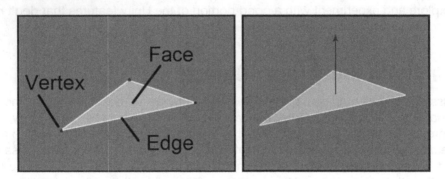

Figure 2-1. A face defined by its vertices and edges (left), and its face normal (right)

A primitive is a mesh, but a mesh (no parametric way to define or describe it) is not necessarily a primitive. In Unity, you do not have access to most of the primitive's parameters, but they can be used as is or as the base for more-complex gameObjects.

Let's begin by creating a new project:

1. If Unity is not already open, click the Unity icon on your desktop.

2. In the start window, select New Project.

3. In the location of your choice, name your project **Unity Basics**.

4. Underneath the Location, make sure 3D is selected and click Asset Packages.

5. Select Characters, Environment, and Prototyping asset packages.

6. Click Create Project.

Unity remembers the last layout you used. If you haven't opened anything else since the first chapter, it will be in the 2 × 3 configuration. Since you will be dealing with scene layout for a while, you can switch back to the Default layout if you wish.

7. Click the Layout button at the top right of the editor to open the list of presets.

8. Select Default.

The layout reverts to having the Hierarchy view on the left, the Inspector on the right, the Scene and Game views tabbed in the center, and the Project view underneath.

The project has a default, nameless scene, but it has not yet been saved. Unity will prompt you to save scenes when exiting, but it is a good idea to rename them before you begin working on them.

9. From the File menu, choose Save Scene As and save the scene as **Primitives**.

The new scene asset appears in the Project view, sporting the Unity application icon (Figure 2-2).

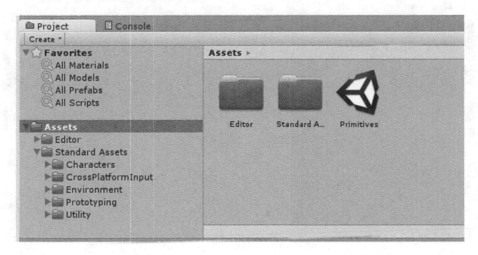

Figure 2-2. The new Unity scene asset in the Project view

10. From the GameObject menu, choose 3D Object ➤ Cube (Figure 2-3).

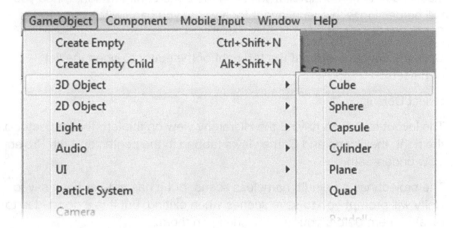

Figure 2-3. *Creating a Cube*

A Cube is created in the center of the Scene viewport (Figure 2-4).

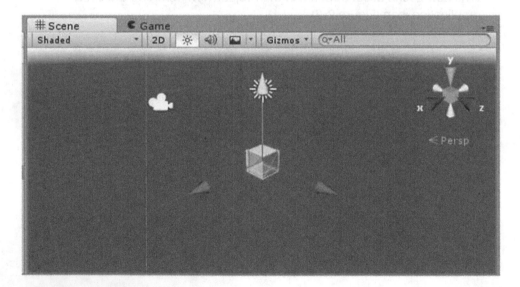

Figure 2-4. *The newly created Cube with its Transform gizmo*

Using Transforms

All gameObjects have a Transform component. Simply put, *transforms* represent move (translate), rotate, and scale actions. The Transform component keeps track of where the object is in space, what its orientation is, and whether it has been scaled. GameObjects can be moved, rotated, or scaled within the 3D world. You can transform them in Edit mode, and their transforms can be animated during runtime.

If you have not touched the Scene view since the project was created, the Cube should have been created at 0,0,0. In Unity, y is up in the world. If you use Autodesk products where z is up in the world for modeling your assets, don't worry. With a few exceptions, Unity corrects orientation on import. You should see your Cube with its Transform gizmo, specifically the Position gizmo, clearly visible. The arrows follow the convention of RGB = x,y,z, or, the red arrow is the x direction, the green arrow is the y direction, and the blue arrow is the z direction. z is the direction Unity considers as *forward*. Follow these steps to explore transforms:

1. With the Cube selected, look at the Transform component at the top of the Inspector (Figure 2-5).

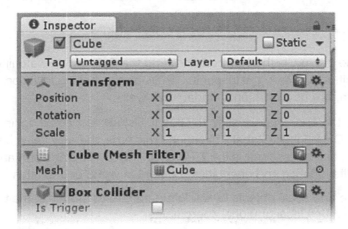

Figure 2-5. The Cube's Transform component

2. If the X, Y and Z Positions are not all 0, you can type it in to move the Cube to that location.

   In the Inspector, take a look at the Cube's Scale. It defaults to 1 × 1 × 1. Unity considers 1 unit equal to 1 meter. (That is approximately 3 feet if you are not used to thinking in metric units.)

   Besides being able to type values directly into the number fields, many of Unity's entry box labels act as sliders.

3. Position your cursor over the Rotation's Y label.

4. Click and drag it left and then right to rotate the Cube in the Scene view. Leave the Cube at about -120 degrees.

5. At the top of the editor, make sure the coordinate system is set to Local (it is a toggle), not Global, and the Transform is set to Move (Figure 2-6).

Figure 2-6. The coordinate system set to Local, and the Move transform active

6.   Click the z arrow in the viewport and drag the Cube while watching the Position values in the Inspector. The Cube is moving in its local z direction, but its x position is updated as well.

7.   Change the coordinate system to Global. Using the z arrow again, pull the Cube in the Global z direction. This time, the only value being updated in the Inspector is the Z Position. When you transform an object, its location and orientation are kept in world coordinates.

You can also rotate and scale objects by using the transform modes at the top left. Just like Position, Rotate can use local or global coordinates.

1.   Click to activate Rotate mode (Figure 2-7).

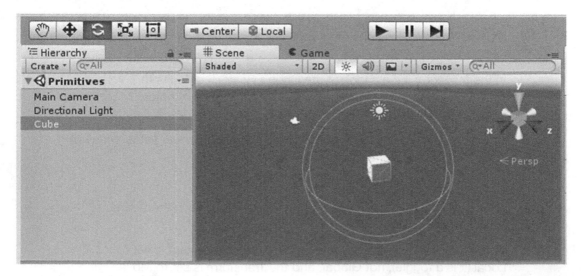

Figure 2-7. Rotate mode and the Rotate gizmo

2. Rotate the Cube by placing the cursor over the circular parts of the gizmo and dragging.

3. Change the mode to Scale (Figure 2-8).

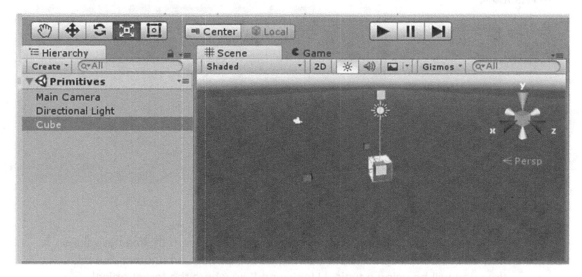

Figure 2-8. Scale mode and the Scale gizmo

Note that the coordinate system is grayed out. You can only scale an object on its local coordinate system. This prevents objects that have been rotated from getting skewed.

4. Scale the Cube on any of its axes.

5. In the Inspector, set all of its Scale values back to 1.

6. Set the coordinate system to Local.

With multiple objects, there are some tools that will help you with positioning. Let's add another primitive gameObject:

1. Hold down the middle mouse button and pan the Scene view so that the Cube is off to the left, but not out of the viewing *frustum* (the boundaries of the viewport window).

2. From the GameObject menu, choose 3D Objects ➤ Sphere. The Sphere is created in the center of the *viewport*, not at 0,0,0 (Figure 2-9).

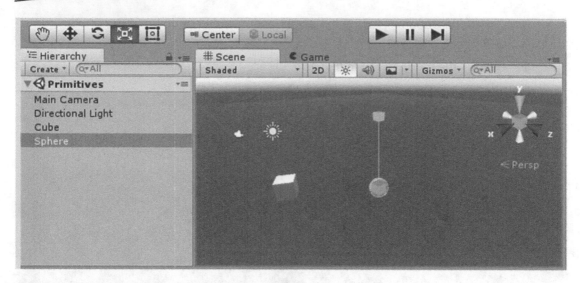

Figure 2-9. The new created Sphere—not located at 0,0,0

When you begin to work with components, you will learn that all the values from one can be copied to the same type component on another, but this time you will be using a typical Unity workflow where the target object is *focused*, or *framed*, in the viewport, and the object selected and then moved to that location. Unfortunately, this technique does not change the object's orientation to match. Realistically, most objects do not require exact orientation. Those that do are generally orthographically aligned, making their orientation easy to handle.

3. Select the Cube in the Hierarchy view.

4. Double-click the Cube in the Hierarchy view, or move the cursor to the Scene view and press the F key. The Scene view zooms in to the selected object. Unity calls this action *frame selected*.

5. Now select the Sphere by clicking it in either the Hierarchy view or the Scene view.

6. From the GameObject menu, select Move to View. The Sphere is moved to the new center of the viewport, as defined by framing the Cube (Figure 2-10).

Figure 2-10. *The scene focused to the Cube and the Sphere moved to the scene's focus*

7. Select the Cube and check the Inspector for its Rotation values. It should still have -120 (or whatever you left it at) as its Y Rotation value.

8. Select the Sphere and check its Rotation values. You can see that the Move To View option moved the Sphere to the location but did not change its orientation.

Duplicating GameObjects

In Unity, you will often find it necessary to duplicate objects. To do so, you can use Ctrl+D (⌘+D on Mac) or select Duplicate from the right-click menu. Some items—such as materials, textures, scripts, and many other assets—must have unique names. An objects automatically has its name incremented upon duplication. GameObjects can, however, share the same name.

In this section, you will name the duplicates for easier identification:

1. Select the Sphere in the Hierarchy view.

2. At the top of the Inspector, to the left of its name, turn off the check box to *deactivate* the Sphere in the Scene view. The Sphere disappears from the Scene view, but its Transform gizmo remains visible as long as it is selected.

3. Click in an empty spot in either the Scene or Hierarchy view to deselect the deactivated Sphere.

In the Hierarchy view, the deactivated Sphere's name is grayed out (Figure 2-11) indicating that it is not active in the scene. In case you are wondering, it is typical to activate a gameObject during runtime.

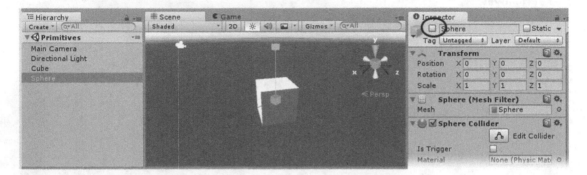

Figure 2-11. The deactivated Sphere in the Hierarchy view

4.   Select the Cube from either the Scene view or the Hierarchy view.

5.   From the right-click menu, select Duplicate. The clone is automatically renamed Cube (1).

6.   Switch to Move mode.

7.   Pull Cube (1) away from Cube so they are at least a meter (the original size of the cubes) apart.

8.   With either cube selected, press Ctrl+D (⌘+D on Mac) to clone another cube. The new clone is automatically renamed Cube (2).

9.   Move Cube (2) away from the other two.

Arranging GameObjects

Typically, you will make duplicates of imported 3D assets when setting up your 3D environment. Duplicates don't reduce the overhead during runtime, but they will reduce disk space, which equates to download time.

The end result is that duplicate assets must be arranged in the scene, either manually or through scripting. To help with that task, Unity has a very nice vertex snap feature:

1.   Arrange the view so that you can see all three cubes easily.

2.   Select Cube.

3.   Hold the V key down on your keyboard and move the cursor around the cube. The Transform gizmo jumps to the closest vertex.

4.   When the cursor snaps to the lower vertex closest to the next cube over, press and hold the left mouse button, and then drag it over to the next cube.

5. With the mouse button down, move the cursor around the target cube and watch the original vertex snap to its new target.

6. When you are happy with the alignment, let go of the mouse button to finalize the arrangement.

7. Repeat the process with the third cube in the row or stack you started with the first two (Figure 2-12).

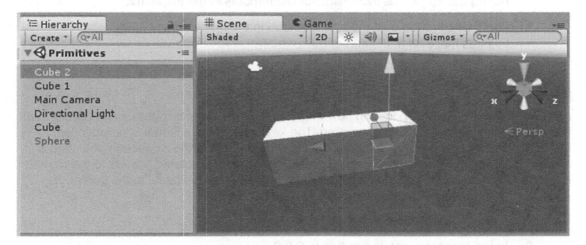

Figure 2-12. The cloned cubes aligned using Vertex Snap

You can also set objects to snap at intervals and use a rotation snap:

1. Select one of the cubes and set its rotation values back to 0.

2. From the Edit menu, at the very bottom, select Snap Settings.

    The grid snaps are set to 1 unit. This means that the object must be within 1 unit or meter of the grid intersection before they will snap. Because the cubes' pivot points are at their centers, the cubes were not sitting directly on top of the scene's construction grid. The first thing to do is move your selected cube up.

    Of interest is that the cube keeps the same offset as it snaps 1 unit each direction. If you want it to snap to corners, you can use the buttons at the bottom of the Snap Settings dialog box to center the cube on an intersection, add 0.5 to the X and Z in the Inspector, and then happily snap between corners.

3. Select the cube again and set its Y Position to **0.5** in the Inspector.

4. Try snapping the cube to the grid in the Global x or z direction.

    Angle or Rotational snaps are set to 15 degrees as a default. You will want to set them to a number that makes sense for your needs before you use the snap rotate functionality.

5. Change the mode to Rotate.

6. Hold the Ctrl (or Cmd) key down and rotate the cube on its y axis, noting the 15-degree increments or decrements in the Inspector.

7. Feel free to round up if the rotation value in the Inspector is infinitesimally off at the end of the rotation.

Parenting

At this point, you may be wondering how to group multiple objects together and parent them to a single gameObject for easier handling. The key concept here is that *children inherit the transforms of their parents*. If a parent is moved 2 meters in the z direction, the child is moved that same 2 meters. If the parent is rotated, the child is rotated *relative* to the parent. If the parent is scaled, the child receives the same scale, again, relative to the parent. It sounds straightforward, but it is a crucial rule to remember.

1. From the GameObject menu choose 3D Object ➤ Capsule.

2. In the Inspector, set its position to **0,0,0**.

3. Select Cube (2) and position it at least a couple of meters away from the Capsule.

4. Select the Capsule in the Hierarchy view and drag and drop it onto Cube (2) in the Hierarchy view.

5. Check the Capsule's transforms in the Inspector and make note of them.

    They now reflect its *offset* from its parent rather than its World space location in the scene.

6. Toggle the Transform gizmo from Center to Pivot.

    The gizmo moves from midway between Cube (2) and its child, Capsule, to the parent, Cube (2).

The newly created hierarchy is apparent in the Hierarchy view (Figure 2-13).

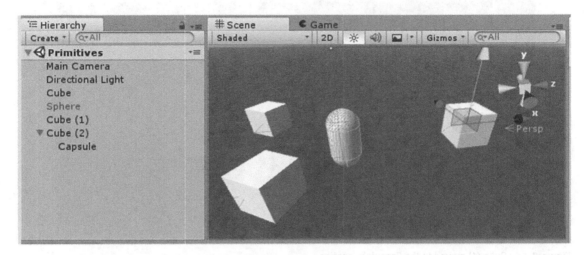

Figure 2-13. The parent, Cube (2), and its new child, Capsule

7. Now rotate Cube (2).

   The Capsule rotates around its parent as expected.

8. Inspect the Capsule's Position transforms.

   They remain the same as when it was first parented to Cube (2).

9. Double-click the Capsule in the Hierarchy view to frame it in the viewport.

10. Select Cube (1).

11. From the GameObject menu, use Move to View to position Cube (1) at the scene's focal point (Figure 2-14).

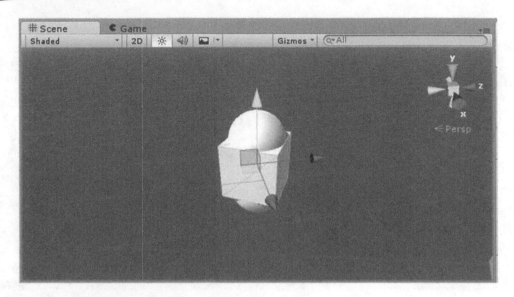

Figure 2-14. Cube (1) moved to the Capsule's location

12.   Now look at Cube (1)'s transform values.

As you may have expected, the two values do not match (Figure 2-15).

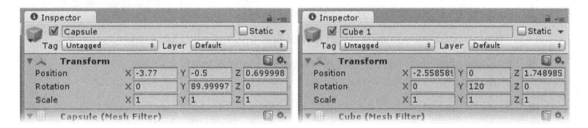

Figure 2-15. The Capsule's Position values (left), and Cube (1)'s Position values (right)

13.   Select the Capsule in the Hierarchy view and drag it out of Cube (1)'s group and drop it in a clear space below the other gameObjects.

Tip   You may have noticed that new objects added to the scene are added at the bottom of the hierarchy, making them easier to find as you fill out your scene. You can, however, move them around in the hierarchy without changing their location in the Scene view.

Now the Capsule's Position values match (Figure 2-16).

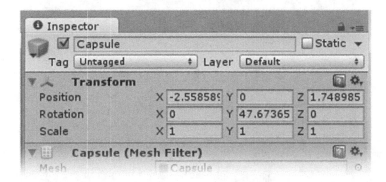

Figure 2-16. The Capsule's unparented Position values

Working with Components

In the previous section, you had an introduction to the Transform component. In Unity, all gameObjects are a collection of components that help define their appearance and functionality, and all gameObjects have a Transform component. You have already used several ready-made gameObjects. They already contain a standard set of components, generic or unique, that make them what they are. In addition to the mandatory Transform component, each of your primitive objects has a Mesh Renderer, a collider (of an appropriate shape for its primitive), and a Mesh Filter (for its particular primitive's geometry). With the exception of the Transform component always being at the top of the Inspector, component order can be rearranged. Order does not affect game play.

Mesh Renderer

The component with the most obvious effect on a 3D object is the Mesh Renderer component. This component is what causes the object's Mesh Filter component to be *rendered*, or drawn, into the Scene view. Its first two parameters dictate whether it can cast or receive shadows (provided there is a light in the scene set to cast shadows). It also holds an array for the material or materials assigned to the mesh. There are specialty renderers for things like skinned meshes (typically characters), but nondeforming objects generally use the regular Mesh Renderer.

1. Select one of the cubes in the scene.

2. In the Inspector, locate the Mesh Renderer component.

3. Click the arrow next to the Materials parameter to see what material or materials are used on the object (Figure 2-17).

Figure 2-17. *The Mesh Renderer component*

Each test object has only one material, so the Material array Size is 1, and that material resides in the Element 0 slot. Arrays always start counting at 0, not 1. The material, in this case, Default-Material, is shown at the bottom of the Inspector, along with a preview of the material. The material itself is not a component, but is a parameter in the Mesh Renderer component. This is an internally generated material that is applied to several of Unity's built-in meshes, and you will not be able to adjust it.

1. Select each of the cubes, and disable their Mesh Renderer components by deactivating the check box to the left of the component name.

Unlike *deactivating* a gameObject from the top of the Inspector (as you did with the Sphere), *disabling* the Mesh Renderer merely causes it not to be drawn in the scene. All of the rest of its functionality remains the same.

Mesh Filter

The Mesh Filter component is what holds the 3D mesh for gameObjects that are rendered into the scene. You will rarely need to do anything with it, but occasionally the actual mesh will go missing, so it is worth a quick look.

1. Select the Capsule object.

2. Click the little circular Browse icon to the far right of the Mesh parameter's loaded Capsule mesh (Figure 2-18).

Figure 2-18. The Browse icon for the Capsule's Mesh Filter

When the Browse window appears, you will see several imported meshes at the top and several internally generated primitives that Unity includes for its own use near the bottom. The Capsule is currently selected, and information about the mesh is shown at the bottom of the Browse window. The Browse window, just as with the second column of the Project view, has a scaling slider that allows you to adjust the thumbnail size or to drop down to text with a small icon. Because it is a floating window, you can also adjust its size and aspect ratio for easier browsing.

3. Adjust the thumbnail size with the slider at the top right of the Browse window.

4. Adjust the size and shape of the window as you would with any application (Figure 2-19).

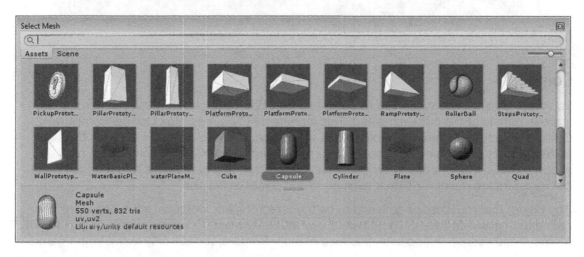

Figure 2-19. The Browse icon for the Capsule's Mesh Filter

5. For fun, double-click and select the EthanBody mesh instead of the Capsule.

6. Focus the Scene view on the Capsule to see the result.

The Capsule mesh is gone and the EthanBody mesh takes its place (Figure 2-19). The replacement mesh has inherited its material from the original Mesh Renderer component.

7. Click the Browse icon next to the Material parameter Element 0's currently loaded Default-Diffuse material, and check out various more-interesting materials.

    The material is immediately loaded as you click through the browser (Figure 2-20).

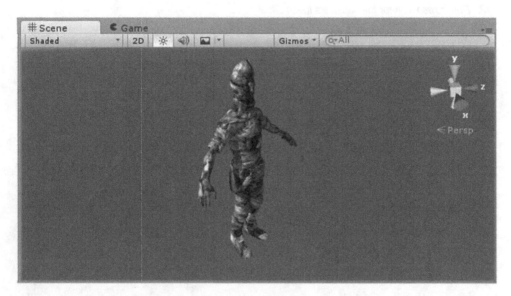

Figure 2-20. One of the Branches materials on the Capsule's EthanBody Mesh Filter

Colliders

You may have noticed when you selected and disabled each cube's Mesh Renderer, that a green outline of the cube remained. This represents the cubes' Box Collider component. Collider components have two main types of functionality. The default is to block physics-based objects from going through the volume defined by the Collider component. The second, the Is Trigger parameter, when activated allows objects to pass through the object but registers the event for further evaluation and possible action.

Any object that must cause an event to be triggered on pick, collision, intersection, or ray-cast *must have a collider* of some type. Even with their Mesh Renderer turned off (set to not render in the scene), the objects, because of their colliders, are still fully active in the game.

Colliders come in several primitive shapes, but can also be automatically generated from a mesh object. The latter is more costly, in terms of frame rate, and should be used only when absolutely necessary. There is a size limit (number of tris) and other limitations, so it is not unusual to import a custom mesh to stand in as a collider for a highly detailed mesh.

1. Select the Capsule, and check out its Capsule Collider component in the Inspector (Figure 2-21).

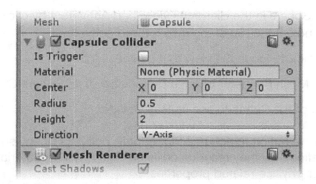

Figure 2-21. *The Capsule Collider component*

2. Disable the Capsule's Mesh Renderer to get a better look at its Capsule Collider in the Scene view (Figure 2-22).

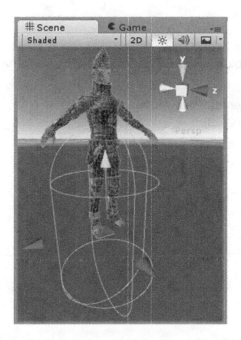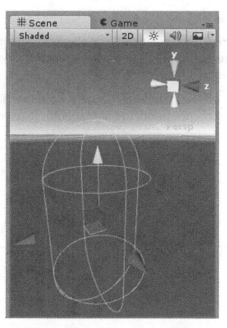

Figure 2-22. *The Capsule object (with the EthanBody mesh) and its Capsule Collider*

The Capsule collider was original fit correctly to the original Capsule Mesh, but colliders can be adjusted in both size and location through their parameters.

3. Select the Sphere in the Hierarchy view, and Activate it by clicking the check box at the top of the Inspector to activate it.

4. Double-click it to focus the view to it if necessary.

5. Disable its Mesh Renderer to get a better view of its Sphere Collider.

6. Select one of the Cubes to see its Box Collider.

In addition to having the option to act as a trigger only, colliders of any shape can use a Physic Material to define how they react on collision. The Physics Material lets you set bounciness and other physics-related properties.

Common to the collider shapes based on primitives is a set of adjustments for the shape itself, including the x, y, and z adjustments for its center offset. Mesh colliders can be used when the shape requires more-accurate collision testing, but it is far more efficient to use one *or more* of the other shapes and adjust each to fit. Colliders are a mainstay of interactivity and as such, you will get quite familiar with them.

Camera

As you may have guessed, not all gameObjects have mesh components or are drawn in the scene at runtime. The Main Camera is a typical nonrendering object. Let's see what components it has.

1. Select the Main Camera from the Hierarchy view, and look at its components in the Inspector (Figure 2-23).

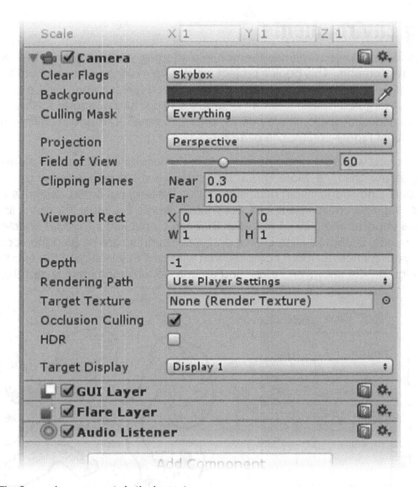

Figure 2-23. The Camera's components in the Inspector

Along with the mandatory Transform, it has a pretty robust Camera component and three components that have no exposed parameters at all. Because there is no mesh associated with a camera, it has no Mesh Filter, Mesh Renderer, or collider components. The GUI Layer component is what enables the camera to Unity's legacy GUI objects. The Flare Layer component allows the camera to "see" lens flare effects. Most of Unity's effects are now image based and do not require a Flare Layer.

The Audio Listener component is a specialty component. It enables sound in the entire scene or level. Unity automatically adds one to any camera objects that are created in your scene. A default camera is created with each new scene, which ensures that your scene will be sound ready. Unfortunately, every time you create a new camera, you will get another Audio Listener. Because there can be only one Audio Listener to a scene, you will see an error message requesting that you "ensure there is exactly one Audio Listener in the scene."

As you progress through the book, you will have a chance to investigate all sorts of components and find out what kind of functionality they add to each gameObject.

Creating Environments

If your goal is to create casual games for mobile platforms, you may or may not require outdoor 3D environments. This book's project will not be making use of an outdoor world, but it is worth delving into the Unity Terrain editor to get a feel for what can be done with it. When Unity first targeted mobile platforms, terrain was not fully supported. Now, with each release, speed and optimization have been improved so that 3D outdoor environments are feasible on at least higher-end mobile platforms.

More than ever, you will want to "compartmentalize" your world so that only a small amount of it is visible at any one time. More important, you will want to devise a way to control the nonvisible areas. Unity contains an occlusion culling system, but smart design is the first step to managing your environment well. For mobile, where the initial file size is limited, it is even more important to think in modules that can be packed into *asset bundles* to extend your games. Both occlusion culling and asset bundles are beyond the scope of this book, but as your games get more complex, you will want to investigate the two topics. Meanwhile, Figure 2-24 shows an indoor and an outdoor environmental layout that present opportunities for managing the visibility.

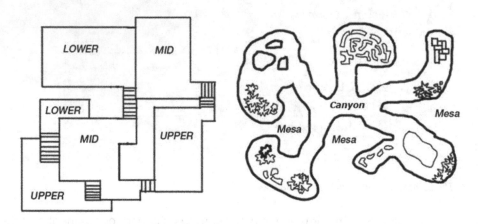

Figure 2-24. Efficient layout for indoor and outdoor scenes

Using the Terrain Editor

Unity's Terrain editor offers a lot of opportunity to create scene bloat, so you will be creating a small test scene to become familiar with the basic dos and don'ts. The Terrain component is well covered in the Unity documentation, at http://docs.unity3d.com/Documentation/Components/script-Terrain.html, should you wish to delve deeper into the Terrain editor.

Creating the Terrain GameObject

Let's begin with the base Terrain object:

1.   From the File menu, Save your current scene.

2.   From the File menu, choose New Scene.

3. From the File menu, choose Save Scene and name it **Terrain Test**.

    In the spirit of managing your project well, now is a good time to organize your scenes.

4. Right-click the Assets folder in the Project view, and choose Create ➤ Folder.

5. Name the new folder **Scenes**.

6. Drag the Terrain Test scene and the Primitives scenes into the new Scenes folder.

Now you are ready to create your new terrain:

1. From the GameObject menu, choose 3D Object ➤ Terrain (Figure 2-25).

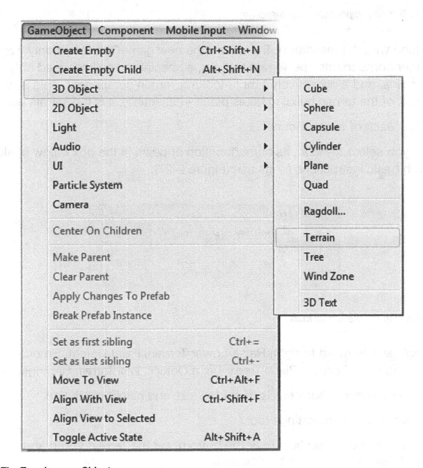

Figure 2-25. The Terrain gameObject

2. Double-click the Terrain object and inspect it and its unique
    components in the Inspector (Figure 2-26).

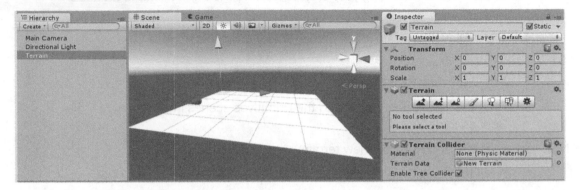

Figure 2-26. The Terrain components in the Inspector

Along with the mandatory Transform, the new gameObject has only two
other components: the Terrain Collider, a specialized collider used only for
terrains, and a deceptively simple-looking Terrain component. This is where
most of the terrain building takes place—essentially, it *is* the Terrain editor.

3. Click each of the tool icons.

As you select the icon, its name/function appears in the box below it, along
with basic instructions for its use (Figure 2-27).

Figure 2-27. Checking out the Terrain tools

Tools are, from left to right, Raise/Lower Terrain, Paint Height, Smooth
Height, Paint Texture, Place Trees, Paint Details, and Terrain Settings.

The first order of business is to set the size and height resolution.

4. Select the Terrain Settings tool.

5. In the Resolution section, near the bottom, set the Terrain Width and
    the Terrain Length to **100 × 100** meters.

6. Set the Height to **75** meters.

    The Height consists of the lowest point—a lake bottom, for example—to the highest peak. If you want mountains that are 130 meters high from a valley floor and a lake bottom that is 20 meters deep from that same floor, you would make the Height 150 meters.

7. Make note of the warning at the bottom of the Resolution sections.

    Modifying the Resolution settings may clear the heightmap, detail map, and splatmap. When you paint the various features and assets onto your terrain, a texture is created to store your brush strokes. The heightmap is a grayscale image that holds the topography. The detail map is an RGBA image that stores the location of details such as Terrain system–generated trees, bushes, and rocks. The splatmap is a color map that holds the terrain textures in its RGB and alpha channels. Each splatmap and detail maps can hold information for four textures or objects. When you exceed that number, a second map is created, using more memory for both the map and the assets it represents.

    The next step establishes "ground level," and as with the Resolution settings, must be done before sculpting, painting, or populating the terrain.

8. In the Inspector, in the Terrain's Paint Height tool, set the Height to **20** and click the Flatten button (Figure 2-28).

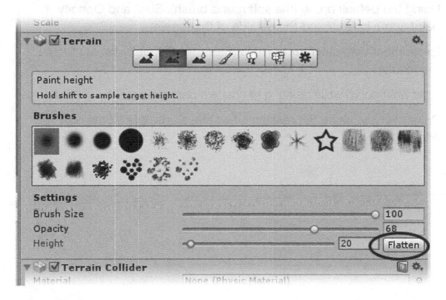

Figure 2-28. The Flatten height setting

Note that once you select a terrain tool, the basic instructions for its use appear in the box immediately below the Terrain toolbar.

The Terrain jumps up 20 units in the viewport, but the Y Position in the Inspector is not affected.

With your terrain defined, you are ready to sculpt the features and paint the textures and details. Painting and/or sculpting is achieved by pressing the left mouse button down while moving the mouse.

Raise/Lower Terrain

The first of the tools is Raise/Lower Terrain. With it, you can paint mountains and valleys by using a variety of brush shapes. The two parameters are Brush Size and Opacity (strength of the effect). In this module, painting is additive. As with all tools, the brush size shows as a light blue area on the terrain in the Scene view as you paint.

Tip   Terrain topography is generally easier to work with when scene lighting is toggled off.

---

1. At the top of the Scene view, toggle off Scene Lighting.

2. Select the Raise/Lower Terrain tool.

3. Rotate the view so that the terrain is closer to a top view.

4. Using the default brush (the soft round brush), Size, and Opacity, paint some hills around the outside of the terrain.

5. Experiment with different brushes, Sizes, and Opacity values to see the results.

6. Hold Shift down while painting to create a depression in the valley floor.

7. Paint over the same depression a few times until it bottoms out (Figure 2-29).

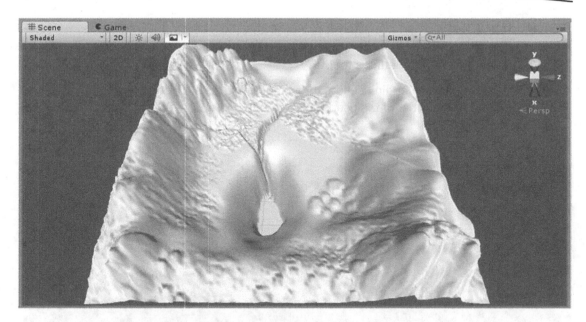

Figure 2-29. *The terrain as sculpted with the Raise/Lower Terrain tool*

Note how the detail softens as soon as you release the mouse button. This is Unity's Scene view Level of Detail (LOD), at work. If you zoom in, you will see the detail you originally saw as you painted.

You can also control the amount of mesh resolution for the terrain through the Settings tool:

1.   Change the Scene view display from Shaded to Wireframe (Figure 2-30).

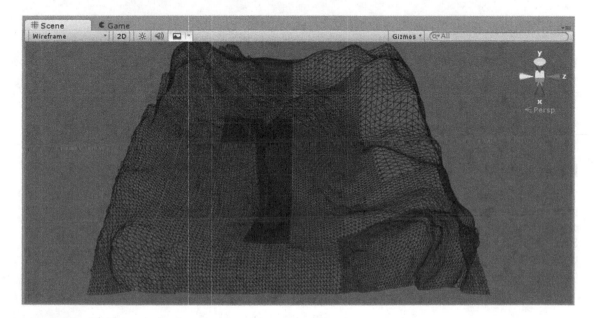

Figure 2-30. *The Wireframe display making the terrain topography more apparent*

2. Zoom in and out to see how the mesh resolution changes in response to viewing distance.

3. Select the Terrain Settings tool.

4. Under the Base Terrain section, try changing the Pixel Error setting to reduce the number of tris used for the terrain (Figure 2-31).

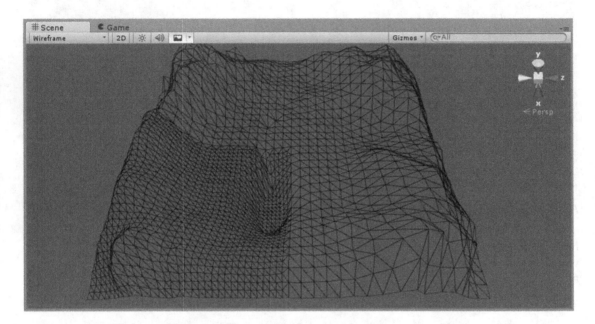

Figure 2-31. Using the Pixel Error setting to reduce the number of tris on the terrain mesh

The Pixel Error setting provides one means of adjusting a terrain mesh for lower-end devices while continuing to retain the higher-resolution image used to generate the terrain height. LOD functionality is retained.

5. Set the Pixel Error down to about **10** instead of the default 5 for a good compromise.

6. Set the Shading Mode back to Shaded.

Paint Height

The next tool is the Paint Height tool. Like the Raise/Lower Terrain tool, it is also additive, but you can set the cap height to have more control when painting building pads, mesas, or even sunken walkways. Because you are already defining a target height, this time the Shift key will sample the terrain's height at the cursor's location when you click. This is quite useful when you want to go back to a certain feature to increase its size but can no longer remember the height setting you used.

1. Select the Paint Height tool.

    Note that the previous settings for Brush Size and Opacity are retained. Let's create a plateau, slightly above the base level.

2. Hold the Shift key down, and click once to sample the valley floor near the depression.

    The Height parameter changes to match the sampled point.

3. Repeat the process until you find an area slightly higher than the base height of 20, or choose an area and set the Height manually to about 21 or 22.

4. Paint a nice plateau on the valley floor, encroaching into the depression a bit (Figure 2-32).

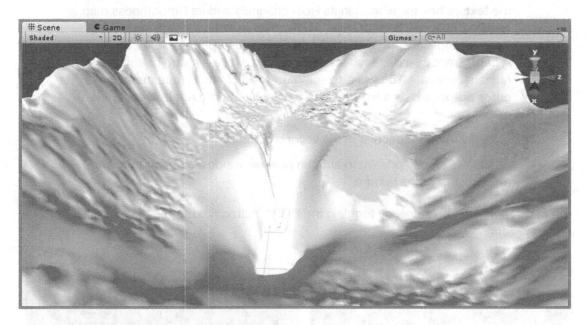

Figure 2-32. A low plateau to the right of the depression

Smooth Height

The next tool is the Smooth Height tool. Having undoubtedly ended up with a few spiky mountains somewhere on your terrain, you were probably wondering how you could tame them down a bit without having to undo your work. The Smooth Height tool will simulate some nice weathering to relax the rough areas.

Paint Texture

With the topography blocked in, it's time to add some textures. The Environment package you imported has some textures that are perfect for experimentation. The first texture you choose will always flood the entire terrain.

1. In the Project view ➤ Assets folder ➤ Environment ➤ TerrainAssets, select the SurfaceTextures folder.

2. Use the size slider to see the thumbnails at their maximum.

    The names of several textures are appended with *Albedo*. In earlier versions of Unity, and in Maya, the base texture is often called *Color*. In 3ds Max, it is called *Diffuse* in the basic materials. With the move to Physically Based Shading (PBS), the title *Albedo* is now used for the base texture. A few of the textures also have been appended with *Specular*. This indicates that the texture has the albedo in its RGB channels and its Smoothness map in its alpha channel. *Smoothness*, also known as *specularity* and *glossiness* in some applications, controls the surface's absorption or reflection of light. A hard, smooth surface reflects a lot of light, while a rough or soft surface reflects very little. You will also see MudRockyNormals, a texture whose entire purpose is as a Normal map to simulate bump not present in the mesh.

3. Click CliffAlbedoSpecular in the second column.

4. Adjust the Inspector's width and the preview window's height to get a good view of the texture.

You can see its alpha channel by toggling the RGBA button next to the Mipmap slider (Figure 2-33).

Figure 2-33. The texture's RGB channels showing the albedo (left), and the alpha channels showing the specular (right)

Textures, as with the rest of the trees, detail meshes, and grasses, must be loaded into the appropriate Terrain component tool before they can be used. Let's begin by flooding the terrain with the Grass(Hill) texture.

1. Select the Terrain object again to get back to the terrain tools.

2. Click the Paint Texture tool.

3. Under the Textures preview area, select Edit Textures.

4. From the list that appears, select Add Texture (Figure 2-34).

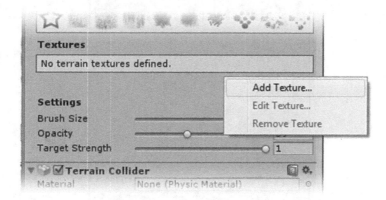

Figure 2-34. The Edit Textures list

The Add Terrain Texture dialog box appears (Figure 2-35).

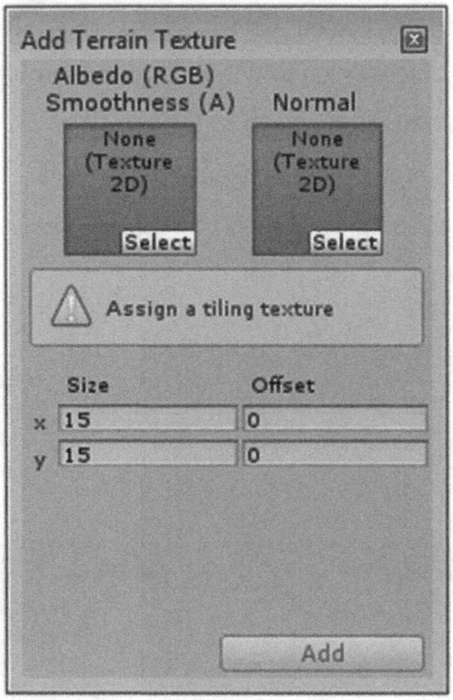

Figure 2-35. *The Add Terrain Texture dialog box*

5. Click the Texture's Select button to bring up the Select Texture2D dialog box.

6. Select GrassHillAlbedo.

7. Click Add.

The GrassHillAlbedo texture is now shown in the available Textures area beneath the brushes (Figure 2-36). In the Scene view, the terrain is filled with the GrassHillAlbedo texture, tiled at the default 15 × 15 size. Note that this is a tiling *size*, not amount. If you wanted the texture to appear smaller or more detailed on the terrain, you would decrease the Size parameters.

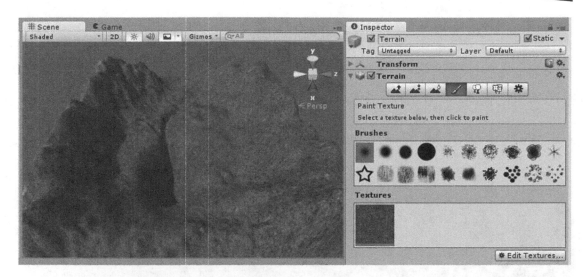

Figure 2-36. *The first texture flooding the Terrain*

To get some practice painting a terrain texture, you will need to add another texture:

1. Toggle on the scene lighting now that you have a texture on the terrain.

2. Click the Edit Textures button again, and select Add Texture again.

3. Select GrassRockyAlbedo and click Add.

   The new texture Is added to the available textures (Figure 2-37). Note that the GrassHillAlbedo texture has a light blue strip at its base. This tells you that it is the currently active texture for painting.

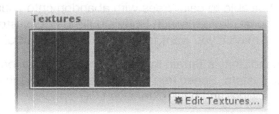

Figure 2-37. *The two available terrain textures*

4. This time, load MudRockyAlbedoSpecular into the Albedo and then load MudRockyNormals into the Normals slot.

5. Add the SandAlbedo texture and experiment with painting your terrain (Figure 2-38).

Figure 2-38. The freshly textured Terrain

The Normal map used in the MudRocky material is probably too costly for mobile devices and may not be supported on all devices, but it's fun to see the nice effect it has on the environment. The strength of the normal map is adjusted in the map itself. You will get to experiment with normal maps in Chapter 4.

Place Trees

With the texture in place, the next tool you will by trying is the Place Trees tool. As you may imagine, you will not be able to paint trees with abandon onto your terrain for mobile devices. Even on conventional platforms with Unity's built-in LOD system for trees, you have to design with occlusion in mind if you want to create a heavy stand of trees.

One of the nicer additions to Unity's Terrain system is the incorporation of Interactive Data Visualization's SpeedTree system. SpeedTree trees have more realistic interaction with wind, better rendering and shadowing, and have extensive LOD options.

Before populating your terrain with trees, let's take a few minutes to examine the trees on an individual basis:

1. From the Project view ➤ Standard Assets ➤ Environment ➤ SpeedTree ➤ Broadleaf folder, select Broadleaf_Desktop.

2. Drag it onto your Terrain object in the Scene view and adjust the view so you can see it nicely.

    The tree is rather large for the little 100 × 100 meter plot of land. Let's scale it down so you can plant more trees later.

3. Scale the tree down to about **0.375** for x, y, and z and readjust the view.

4. With the tree selected, click the tiny lock in the upper right of the Inspector to lock the Inspector to this object (Figure 2-39).

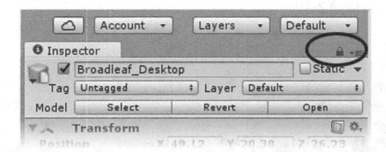

Figure 2-39. *Locking the Inspector to the Broadleaf_Desktop object*

5. Deselect the tree in the Hierarchy view.

    You now have a nice view unencumbered by mesh edges and colliders (Figure 2-40).

Figure 2-40. *The Broadleaf_Desktop tree in the Scene view*

6. From the Gizmos drop-down just above the view, activate 3D Icons so they won't block the view of the tree.

7. In the Scene view, zoom in and out from the tree and watch the Scene view display as it indicates the LOD version that you are seeing (Figure 2-41).

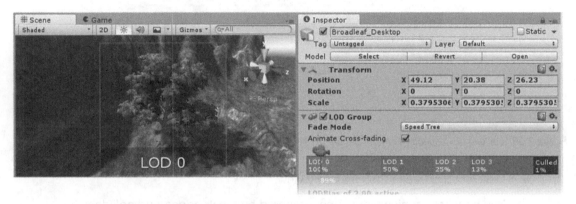

Figure 2-41. Inspecting the LOD versions in the Scene view

The bounding rectangle in the Scene view is color coded to match the LOD levels.

8. Unlock the Inspector.

9. From the Project view, drag the Broadleaf_Mobile tree into the scene next to the desktop version (Figure 2-42).

Figure 2-42. The Broadleaf_Mobile tree in the Scene view next to the Broadleaf_Desktop tree

The mobile version is nowhere near as robust as the desktop version, the leaves aren't anti-aliased against the background, and the color isn't as nice.

Let's get the camera set to the nice view of the two trees before going any further.

10. Select the Main Camera and from the GameObject menu, select Align with View.

When you go to Play mode after planting trees, you will have a better view of the trees.

11. Expand the Broadleaf_Desktop asset in the project view and locate the mesh assets (Figure 2-43).

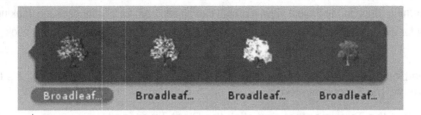

Figure 2-43. The four tree meshes used for the Broadleaf_Desktop tree's LOD versions

12. Select each LOD version of the mesh and check the Preview window to see the number of tris that each has.

13. LOD0 has 7188 tris, LOD1 has 4420 tris, LOD2 has 879 tris, and LOD3 (the billboard image) has 4 tris.

14. Expand the Broadleaf_Mobile asset and compare the triangle counts.

15. This time, LOD0 has 999 tris, LOD1 has 689 tris, LOD2 has 331 tris, and LOD3 (the billboard image) has 4 tris.

Additionally, the desktop tree has 13 colliders, and the mobile tree has 3. Collision calculations, as you may have guessed, cost time, which also equates to frame rate. The fancy rendering of the desktop tree also uses more frame rate.

Be sure to check online for lots of ways to economize your SpeedTrees.

Let's make some adjustments to the desktop version to make it a bit more economical.

1. Select the Broadleaf_Desktop tree in the Hierarchy view.

2. Turn off Animate Cross Fade so you can see the LODs pop in and out easier.

3. Drag the LOD dividers so the LOD changes happen sooner

4. Create a folder named Prefabs in the Project view.

5.   Rename your desktop tree to **Broadleaf_Comp** (for *compromise*).

6.   Drag it into the new Prefabs folder.

You have now created a customized version of the tree that can be used with the Terrain system. You don't have access to the SpeedTree prefabs except through the Terrain editor, but they already exist internally.

> **Note**   Dragging a scene object from the Hierarchy view into the Project view creates what Unity calls a *prefab*. Prefabs differ from imported assets in that they can contain Unity components— which means that you can have any useful object conveniently set up and ready to use. As an example, a common prefab for shooter-type games is a projectile. It might contain the projectile object and its components, a particle system or two, and the script that tells it what to do when it hits something. Once in the Project view, a prefab can be exported as a Unity package, making it available for use in multiple projects. You will be creating many prefabs throughout this book.

Armed with a better knowledge of where the resources can be spent on trees, it's time to plant a few using the Terrain system:

1.   Select the Terrain object and click the Plant Trees icon.

2.   In Edit Trees, select Add Tree, load your Broadleaf_Comp tree, and click Add.

3.   For fun, select the tree, click Mass Place Trees, and accept the default 10,000 trees.

   The Terrain object looks like an overgrown Chia Pet (Figure 2-44). If you try to rotate the view, however, you will probably see that it has brought your machine to a crawl.

Figure 2-44. Mass planting 10,000 trees

Note that with more than one tree available for planting, you will get an even percentage of each species or variety.

Let's get the terrain back under control.

4. Undo (Ctrl+Z or Cmd+Z from the Edit menu) until your terrain is clean again.

    There are basically two ways to plant your trees. You can click or you can click and drag. Single clicks drop a sparse number of trees, while dragging over the same spot fills in bare spots until the target density is achieved.

5. Set the Brush Size to **20** and the Density to **80**.

6. Click once on the terrain.

    A few trees are planted.

7. Click a few more times in different places.

8. Now click and drag in the same spot until it is quite dense.

9. Undo to remove the densely painted area.

10. This time, turn the density down to **10** and paint to fill in an area more completely.

    Now the density is capped at a more reasonable amount (Figure 2-45).

Figure 2-45. Careful planting resulting in a more reasonable density

11. Load the mobile version of the tree into the Terrain editor and add it to the terrain by using the same settings.

   Note that introducing a new tree doesn't alter the maximum density. If there is no room for it, the new tree will not be added.

12. Click Play and turn on Stats in the Game view (Figure 2-46).

Figure 2-46. Checking on frame rate

The density is reasonable, and the frame rate hasn't suffered too much.

13. Select the Terrain and in Settings, under Tree & Detail Settings, turn off Draw.

The trees and detail objects are no longer being drawn, but you may see several gray spheres hanging around in the Scene view. These are the light probes that can keep dynamic objects "in the shade" when using only baked light. You may disable them directly under the Draw parameter.

Let's try something else expensive but fun. One of the great features with SpeedTrees is how they react to wind. To see the wind, you will need a Wind Zone object.

1. From the GameObject menu, choose 3D Object ➤ Wind Zone.

   The Wind Zone comes in with the Mode set to Directional, so it doesn't matter where it is in the scene. The Spherical mode is useful when attached to low-flying helicopters. It has a Radius parameter.

2. Click Play and watch the frame rate to see how much the wind "costs" as the tree waving ramps up to full speed.

3. Experiment with the parameters.

Paint Details

Paint Details is for painting all other sorts of objects onto your terrain. There are two types of Detail object: Grass Textures and Detail Meshes. *Grass Textures* are images on planes that are *billboarded*, which means they always turn to face the camera. Using an alpha channel, they are meant for creating grass and other plants or objects that are layered against each other rather than volumetric in nature. *Detail Meshes* are for objects that require a 3D mesh, such as rocks, cactus, or succulents.

Detail Meshes do not have a built-in setting to keep them from getting too close to each other. Painting (mouse button held down) even with Density settings at their lowest will generally produce too many overlapping objects. The best practice is discriminating mouse button pressing rather than painting.

The main thing to remember with either Grass Textures or Detail Meshes is that the objects will fall under Unity Terrain's LOD system. Unlike the SpeedTrees that go between various versions of the tree down to a billboard image and finally are completely culled (turned off), Detail objects are either off or on. If, for example, you want to create large rock formations around the terrain, keep in mind that they will be distance culled.

Let's try a few detail objects:

1. Select the Terrain and then select the Paint Details tool.

2. Click Edit Details.

    You have the choice of Add Grass Texture, Add Detail Mesh, Edit, or Remove (Figure 2-47).

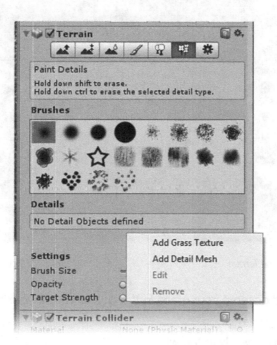

Figure 2-47. Detail object options

3. Select the Add Grass Texture option.

    The Add Grass Texture dialog box appears. If you click the Browse button, you will have to select from all of the scene textures. For the Grass Texture, you want a texture with an alpha channel. Two very nice grass textures came in with the Environment package.

4. From the Project view, Assets folder ➤ Environment ➤ TerrainAssets, open the BillboardTextures folder and choose GrassFrond01Albedo or GrassFrond02Albedo and click Add.

5. Set the Brush Size to **25**, the Opacity to **0.03**, and the Target Strength to **0.06**.

6. Zoom in close enough to the terrain so that the grass won't be distance culled.

7. For now, paint the grass heavily so you can see the pattern from the two tint colors.

8. Go back into Edit Details and edit the Grass Texture, changing the Healthy and/or Dry Colors.

    The color changes on the grass that was painted previously.

9. Hold the Shift key down and paint to thin out the grass (Figure 2-48).

Figure 2-48. Grass painted on the Terrain

10. Click Play and observe your grass in the Scene view if your camera is not set to it well.

    The grass waves gently in the wind.

11. In the Terrain Settings, under Wind Settings for Grass, adjust the Speed, Size, and Bending to better match your trees' movement.

Let's try a Detail Mesh next. There is nothing remotely useful for a Detail Mesh in your current project, so you will import a new Unity package.

1. From the Chapter 2 Assets folder, load the Rock.unity package.

   You will find the Rock in the Prefabs folder.

2. Load the Rock in as a Detail Mesh and set the Dry and Healthy Colors to white and gray.

3. Change the Render Mode to Vertex Lit.

4. Examine the Min and Max size settings and click Add but do not close the edit window.

5. Set the Brush Settings to Brush Size **100**, Opacity **0.1**, and Target Strength **0.625**.

6. Make sure the Rock is selected and click once on the Terrain to make some rocks (Figure 2-49, left).

7. In the Edit Details window, adjust the Min and Max sizes until you see good differentiation in the rocks, somewhere around 0.08 for the Min and 1.2 for the Max (Figure 2-49, center). You do not have to click Apply.

8. Click and drag on the Noise Spread label to see different fractal patterns (Figure 2-49, right).

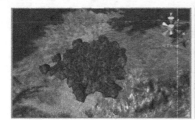

Figure 2-49. A single rock click: default settings (left), Min and Max size adjusted (center), and Noise Spread adjusted (right)

9. Click Apply and zoom out in the view to see when the rocks are distance culled.

10. When they disappear, go to the Settings section and under the Tree and Detail Objects, increase the Detail Distance until they reappear.

Unfortunately, the grass is also drawn again, so as you can see, using detail objects for something that should be seen at a great distance is probably not a good idea.

One last piece of information you should know about Detail Meshes is that Unity internally combines several Detail Mesh textures together for batching. If the rock's UV mapping spills out over the edge of the map (Figure 2-50, left), instead of staying within the mapping boundary (Figure 2-50, center), the object will pick up a neighboring texture (Figure 2-50, right).

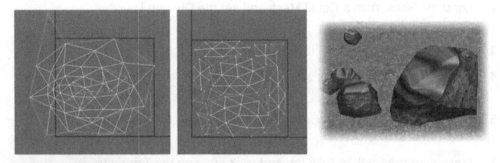

Figure 2-50. An overlapping UV unwrap (left), and the results (right). The correct unwrap is shown in the center.

Adding Water

With the newer shaders, you will be able to create some nice water to fill the hole in your terrain:

1. Temporarily deactivate the Draw check box in the Terrain Settings Tree and Detail Objects section.

2. Hover the cursor over the hole in the Terrain and press the F key on the keyboard to zoom in.

3. From Environment Water ➤ Water ➤ Prefabs, drag the WaterProDaytime prefab into the hole in the Scene view. In this prefab's Water component, set the Water Mode to Simple (Figure 2-51).

Figure 2-51. Caption

4. Adjust the scale and position to fit and then adjust the view.

5. Select the Main Camera. From the GameObject menu, choose Align with View.

6. Click Play to see the results.

    The water ripples gently as if with a light breeze, but the water color is uniform (Figure 2-52, left). The there is no reflection or transparency or indication of depth. Let's try the two other Water Mode options. Be sure to check up on the frame rate in Stats to see whether you can detect any large differences in the three options.

Figure 2-52. WaterProDaytime: Simple (left), Reflective (center), and Refractive (right)

7. While still in Play mode, set Water Mode to Reflective (Figure 2-52, center).

   The color remains constant, but the reflection makes this variation much more believable.

8. Now set the Water Mode to Refractive (Figure 2-52, right).

The Refractive version is very transparent with a bit of reflection, making it more suitable for shallow bodies of water.

The next water prefab you will try is a lot more complex than WaterProDaytime. It was designed more for oceans, and as such comes with multiple pieces to help fill out the scene.

1. Disable WaterProDaytime.

2. From Environment ➤ Water ➤ Water4 ➤ Prefabs, drag the Water4Advanced prefab into the hole in the Scene view.

3. Disable all but one of the child Tile objects, position it, and then click Play.

   This one has nice reflection (provided by its own camera), refraction, and transparency that is reduced near the center, providing a nice sense of depth. The only problem is that it was obviously meant to be an ocean. Fortunately, you can tame the wave displacement.

4. Select the parent, Water4Advanced, and disable the Gerstner Displace component.

5. Select the active Tile object and experiment with the Water4Advanced shader's parameters.

> **Tip** Changing the shader's parameters even during runtime will be permanent. You may want to take a screenshot of the original settings.

You can ignore the lower parameters with *Wave* in their name, as you have already turned off the Gerstner Displace component. Note that many of the X, Y, Z, and W values are for unrelated parameters (shown in parentheses). You may notice the sun's reflection on the water, depending on your lake's orientation and your camera position. The "sun" is not being calculated from the Directional Light; it is handled in another child of the Water4Advanced object, the Specular object. Its only component, the Transform, dictates where the highlight will fall on the water. Be sure to experiment with it as well.

Figure 2-53 shows the settings used to achieve the lake in the accompanying image.

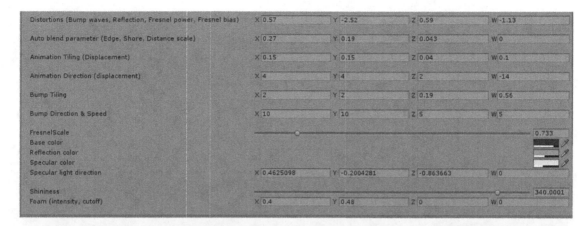

Distortions (Bump waves, Reflection, Fresnel power, Fresnel bias)	X 0.57	Y -2.52	Z 0.59	W -1.13
Auto blend parameter (Edge, Shore, Distance scale)	X 0.27	Y 0.19	Z 0.043	W 0
Animation Tiling (Displacement)	X 0.15	Y 0.15	Z 0.04	W 0.1
Animation Direction (displacement)	X 4	Y 4	Z 2	W -14
Bump Tiling	X 2	Y 2	Z 0.19	W 0.56
Bump Direction & Speed	X 10	Y 10	Z 5	W 5
FresnelScale				0.733
Base color				
Reflection color				
Specular color				
Specular light direction	X 0.4625098	Y -0.2004281	Z -0.863663	W 0
Shininess				340.0001
Foam (intensity, cutoff)	X 0.4	Y 0.48	Z 0	W 0

Figure 2-53. Settings (top) for the example Water4Advanced after a bit of tweaking (bottom)

Creating the Sky

In Unity, the sky is created through the use of a *skybox*. Clouds can be included in the images that make up the skybox. Moving clouds would have to be handled separately. Fog is handled through Image Effects.

Using Skyboxes

Just as the name implies, six images are used to create the visual bounds of your scene. Rather than create an actual cube that could interfere with other 3D objects, Unity's skybox is generated by a shader.

There are three shaders to choose from. The first builds a cubemap internally from a procedurally generated "sky." The second uses the standard DDS cubemap format, and the third creates a cubemap using six individual images.

Let's begin with the procedurally generated sky. Every scene you create is automatically set to use the existing Default Skybox material that was built with the Procedural Skybox shader.

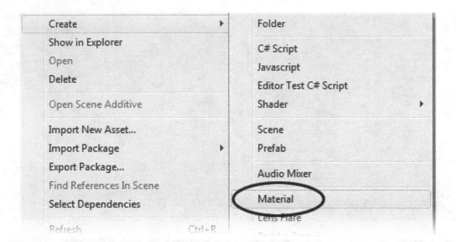

Figure 2-54. *Create ➤ Material from the Assets menu or the right-click menu in the Project view*

1. In the Project view, select the Materials folder.

2. Right-click over the folder or in the second column where its contents are shown and choose Create ➤ Material (Figure 2-54).

3. Name the Material **Procedural Sky**.

4. In the Inspector, click the Shader drop-down and choose Skybox ➤ Procedural (Figure 2-55, left).

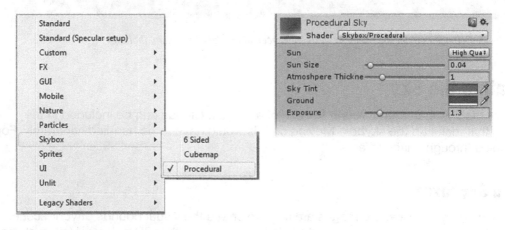

Figure 2-55. *The Procedural Skybox shader option (left), and selected (right)*

The shader has only five parameters, and the resulting sky is shown at the bottom in the Preview window (Figure 2-55, right).

5. Tweak the parameters until you get something interesting. Be sure to include a visible sun (you may have to drag in the preview window to see the sun).

Once the material is ready to go, you will load it into the scene.

6. From the Window menu, select the Lighting window.

7. In the Scene section, load your new Procedural Sky material into the Skybox field (Figure 2-56).

Figure 2-56. The Lighting window with the new Procedural Sky loaded

Note that the Ambient Source is currently set to use the skybox and that its intensity can by adjusted to suit.

The great thing with the Procedural skybox is that the shader uses the Directional Light in your scene to place the sun on the skybox.

8. Pan and orbit the Scene view so you can see the sun.

9. Select the Directional Light and rotate it about the x and y axes to see how the sun is positioned to match.

Note how the sky color and light change as it goes down toward, and then below, the "horizon."

If you want your skybox to have clouds, you have two shader choices. The Cubemap shader uses a ready-made cubemap, and the 6 Sided shader uses six individual images to generate one for you.

The sky you will be using next was generated using a free sky generator (www.nutty.ca/?p=381). It has the option for adding simple clouds, adjusting the position of the sun, and allows you to modify the colors of just about everything. The image was rendered out in a horizontal cross configuration and then processed in Photoshop and exported as a DDS formatted cubemap. For more information on cubemaps, a nice reference page is at www.cgtextures.com/content.php?action=tutorial&name=cubemaps.

1. From the Chapter 2 Assets folder, drag the Skies folder into the Project view.

2. In the Project view, select the Materials folder and from the right-click menu, create a new material.

3. Name the material **Cubemap Sky**.

4. In the Inspector, click the Shader drop-down and choose Skybox ➤ Cubemap.

5. Drag the Highnoon.dds (cubemap) image into the shader's Cubemap (HDR) field.

HDR stands for *High Dynamic Range*, where a more accurate intensity value is stored for the light areas than is possible with standard RGB. Your cubemap is not HDR and will not be as accurate when used for the Ambient Source. Nevertheless, it will contribute to the ambient lighting as is and has the advantage of using less resources than a true HDR cubemap would.

6. Drag the new Cubemap Sky material into the Lighting window's Skybox field.

7. Orbit and pan the view to see the results (Figure 2-57).

Figure 2-57. The Highnoon cubemap in the Cubemap Sky

8. In the Cubemap Sky material's Cubemap shader, try adjusting the Exposure and the Rotation.

The Highnoon cubemap's sun is somewhere near the top of the cube, so rotating it is more about getting a nice view of the clouds from the important locations in your scene than about deciding from which direction the sun will be shining. While less crucial in this case, you will be synchronizing the Directional Light in your scene with the cubemap's sun by using a few little tricks.

1. Rotate the cubemap to the desired orientation by using the shader's Rotation parameter.

2. Using Alt + left mouse button, orbit the view until the cubemap's sun is roughly centered in the Scene view.

3. Select the Directional Light and use Move to View.

    The light is in the true center of the view, so now you can adjust the sun to match.

4. Orbit the view to finish aligning the sun to the Directional Light.

5. Select the Directional Light. From the GameObject menu, choose Align with View.

6. Use the middle mouse roller the minimum amount to zoom the light back into view.

    The light's angle matches the sun in the cubemap, but it is facing the wrong direction.

7. Add or subtract 180 degrees to the Directional Light's X Rotation to get it pointing in the correct direction.

8. Double-click the Broadleaf_Mobile tree in the Hierarchy view and orbit the view to see how the shadows and lighting look.

The final shader uses six images and generates the cubemap for you; otherwise, it works essentially like the Cubemap shader. Let's try that one next:

1. Create a new Material and name it **SixImage Sky**.

2. In the Inspector, click the Shader drop-down and choose Skybox ➤ 6 Sided.

    The only tricky part about using individual images is knowing where each belongs. If they are already generated, the naming will generally follow one of two naming conventions. They will either be left, right, front, back, top, and bottom or they will be -X, +X, -Z, +Z, -Y, and +Y. You may also see them use positive and negative rather than + and -. Figure 2-60 will help you to decide which image is which, especially if the image is in the horizontal cross configuration and you will be manually separating it into the six individual images.

3. Drag the appropriate Morning_ images from the Skies folder into the 6 Sided shader.

   Something hasn't gone well (Figure 2-58). The easiest fix when breaking in a new cubemap source is to label each of the images with their side names and then swap either the left and right or the front and back. In this case, it looks like Unity currently has Left and Right opposite from the standard horizontal cross and Nvidia strip configuration names.

Figure 2-58. The Morning images showing incorrect ordering

4. Load the Left image in the Right slot, and the Right image in the Left.

   Everything is looking good again (depending on your version of Unity, of course).

5. Assign it to the Skybox parameter in the Lighting window and experiment with the Rotation to get the sun in the right location for your scene.

6. Use the technique outlined in the previous section to synchronize the Directional Light with the new cubemap's sun (Figure 2-59).

Figure 2-59. The early morning sun position—with most of the terrain in shadow

With the early morning light, you may decide that the Directional Light could be a bit stronger and maybe a bit bluer. Feel free to adjust its Intensity to **1.25** and give it a slightly bluish Color.

Introducing Fog

If you happen to live somewhere near a decent-sized body of water, you are probably missing a bit of morning fog, or at least some morning mist. Let's make that the final experiment for your little environment.

Unity now handles all but the most minimal fog through effects. Turning the trees on will give you good visual feedback for your fog.

1. Select the Terrain object and activate the Draw check box in the Settings, Tree and Detail Objects section.

2. In the Lighting window, scroll down until you find the Fog check box and activate it.

3. Zoom slowly back from your little environment.

The default fog is a nice generic gray color, but you have no means of adjusting its density, and it doesn't affect the skybox.

4. Select the camera and set it to Align to View.

5. Press Play and observe the frame rate (FPS) with and without the fog turned on.

    The frame rate jumps around a lot, but doesn't particularly seem to affect the frame rate.

To use the Effects fog, you will have to import the Standard Assets Effects package. Also be aware that this fog requires graphics cards that support Depth Textures. See Unity's

Graphics Hardware Capabilities and Emulation page for further details and a list of compliant hardware.

1. Import the Effects package from the Assets menu's Import Package option.

2. Select the Main Camera. From the bottom of the Component menu, choose Image Effects ➤ Rendering ➤ Global Fog.

3. Switch to the Game view and disable the Fog in the Lighting window.

4. Disable the Exclude Far Pixels check box.

    The skybox is now affected by the fog. You would probably want to turn the Camera's Clear Flags parameter to Solid Color and match the Color to your fog if this was your intended mood or style.

5. Disable the Distance Fog.

    Note the hard horizon line. You could lower the Height Density, but then the trees would no longer be hidden after you raise the fog height.

6. Raise the Height value until only the tops of the trees are showing.

7. Enable the Exclude Far Pixels check box and set the Height Density to about **0.5**.

    Now you get the best of both—except that the Water4Advanced is not affected by the fog. You will need to go back to using the simpler WaterProDaytime.

8. Deactivate Water4Advanced and activate WaterProDaytime.

9. Click Play and check the Stats for frame rate again.

If you are feeling adventurous, you might want to do a search of Unity Answers for *GlobalFogExtended by rea*. It has a lot more settings that you can tweak for some very nice effects (Figure 2-60). In the two Global Fog Extended images, the Raleigh setting (controls the color of the fog) was around 98. Luminance, Bias, and Contrast were tweaked to get a brighter look to the fog. The zipped file contains a shader and a script. Place the two files in the same folders as the Unity versions. Add the script to the camera and load the shader into it as well as setting the Directional Light as the Sun parameter.

Figure 2-60.   Global Fog, Distance (left); Global Fog Extended, Height Fog (center); Global Fog Extended, Distance and Height Fog (right)

As with just about anything you consider using for mobile platforms, you should always check frame rate and eventually test on the lowest targeted platform you plan on supporting.

Summary

In this chapter, you were introduced to the Unity gameObject and some of the components that help define its visual aspect and behavior. You discovered that Unity has several primitive 3D objects that are handy for experimenting.

You learned that all gameObjects have a Transform component that keeps their position, orientation, and scale. In the Scene view, you can use either the Local or the Global coordinate system with the Transform gizmo to arrange your objects. Double-clicking an object in the Hierarchy brings the object to the center of the Scene view, where you can then use the GameObject options, Move to View and Align to View, to great advantage.

Another means of alignment in Unity, you found, is the ability to snap objects to each other by using their vertices as snap points with the help of the V key. Cloning objects by using Ctrl+D (Cmd+D), you were able to quickly create and align your test cubes. You also got some practice activating and deactivating gameObjects from the top of the Inspector.

With multiple objects in your scene, the next experiment was to parent objects by dragging and dropping them onto other objects in the Hierarchy view. The key concept learned was that children inherit the transforms of their parents and that their transforms reflect their *offset* from the parent rather than their actual location in world space.

Getting back to components, you discovered how they became the building blocks of Unity gameObjects. With 3D objects, you saw that the Mesh Renderer component is responsible for drawing the object into the scene. Some components are somewhat generic, and others, such as the Light and Camera components, are quite specialized.

Plunging into Unity's Terrain system, you became aware of many factors that can impact frame rate. Painting the terrain with textures, and populating it with trees and detail objects (meshes or billboard planes), showed you how quickly you can bring the frame rate to a crawl.

A quick look at water, skyboxes, and fog rounded out the environment experiments and reinforced the importance of being aware of the graphic capabilities of your target platforms.

In the next chapter, you will delve into scripting, where you will begin your journey into making interactive and engaging games and applications.

Chapter 3

Scripting with C#

In Unity, very little happens without at least a small amount of scripting. Even if you consider yourself more of an artist or game designer, you should learn enough of the basics of scripting to be able to prototype game ideas, track down code for desired functionality, and become familiar with concepts and techniques commonly used with Unity game development. If your palms are getting sweaty and your pulse rate is increasing at this point, don't panic! The syntax involved is no more difficult to pick up than learning to text; it is generally fairly descriptive. The major concepts are fairly straightforward. More important, just as you don't need to understand the workings of an internal combustion engine in order to drive a car, in scripting you don't necessarily have to understand how a bit of code works in order to make good use of it.

Creating a New Test Project

If you are *already* familiar with programming, you will discover that only a small part of scripting in a game engine has to do with what you may have learned in a conventional programming class. The fun part is that scripting in a game engine gives you a lot more visual feedback for your efforts.

Let's begin by creating a new Unity project:

1. Create a new Unity project and name it **ScriptingTests**.

    You won't require any packages for this little test project.

2. Use the 2 × 3 layout and the One Column Layout for the Project view.

3. From the GameObject ➤ 3D Object submenu, create a Cube and a Sphere.

4. Move the Sphere a couple of meters away from the Cube on the x axis.

5. Orbit the Scene view until the Cube is on the left and the Sphere is on the right (Figure 3-1).

© Sue Blackman and Adam Tuliper 2016
S. Blackman and A. Tuliper, *Learn Unity for Windows 10 Game Development*,
DOI 10.1007/978-1-4302-6757-7_3

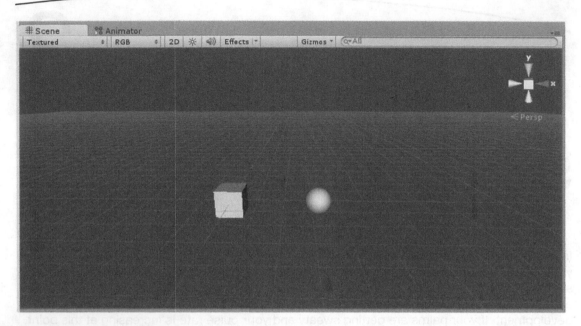

Figure 3-1. Scene view with the Cube and the Sphere

6. Select the Main Camera in the Hierarchy view. From the GameObject menu, choose Align with View.

7. Add a Directional Light and adjust its direction so that the two objects are well lit in the Game view.

8. Save the scene as **Scripting Sandbox**.

The scene is very simple but it will give you a lot of interesting possibilities for scripting tests beyond the classic Hello World message used in traditional programming courses.

Why C#?

In the earlier days of the Unity game engine, targeted users were typically familiar with Adobe Flash. As a result, most of the learning material and documentation was done with UnityScript, a JavaScript derivative similar to Flash's ActionScript. Besides having the great advantage of being the main scripting language in most examples, UnityScript tends to be a lot more user friendly than C# for beginners.

Unity supports multiple languages. JavaScript, C#, and Boo (although Boo is being phased out), and uses the Mono framework that allows you to author for multiple operating systems at the same time. With the push toward mobile, however, C# is becoming the language of choice for the Unity community. It is considered to be more powerful and more flexible, is getting to be better documented, and it is easier to find sample code for most Unity uses.

In this book, the scripting is kept fairly basic, but you are encouraged to investigate C# in a more traditional manner if you find the topic intriguing.

Working with Script Editors

Because the syntax for most programming languages is highly structured, people typically use a *script editor*. Unlike a simple text editor, it is full of features that monitor your syntax, offer suggestions, and highlight problem areas. Unity currently ships with MonoDevelop. It consists of several areas for more serious programming, but you will generally use just the editing area. With more recent releases, the option to install Visual Studio Tools for Unity has been added. Whatever your preference, you will need a test project for your experimentation.

Exploring the Editing Environment

Let's create a new C# script and check out the editing environment:

1. Right-click in the Project view and from the Create menu, choose C# Script.

2. The new script goes immediately into rename mode.

    Name it **MyFirstScript**.

    In the Inspector, you will see the new script with its bare-bones content. Of note is the name that you supplied in the *class declaration* (Figure 3-2).

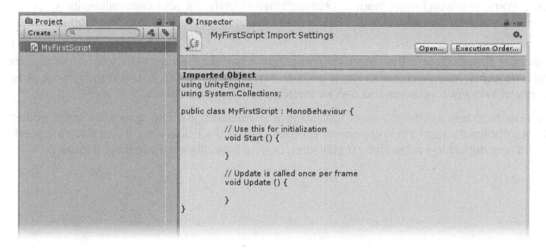

Figure 3-2. The newly generated script with its name showing in the class declaration

---

Tip   If you decide to change the script's name *after* it has been generated, you must also change it in the script's class declaration.

---

3. Because the script cannot be edited in the Inspector, it must be opened in the script editor. Click the Open button at the top of the Inspector, or double-click the script in the Project view to open the script.

One of your options when installing Unity was to install Microsoft's *Visual Studio Tools for Unity* (*VSTU*), a free version of the industry standard, Visual Studio, as your script editor. This feature-filled toolset allows you to develop and debug your Unity games by using Visual Studio.

Although installation may be problematic on older versions of Windows, you will need VSTU to port to the Universal Windows Platform (UWP). It can also be useful when developing for Android. If you did not choose to install it when you installed Unity, you can run Unity's installer again to have it installed, or you can do a search for *Visual Studio Tools for Unity* and install it directly from the Microsoft site. Either way, you will need Internet access, as some of its components are loaded from other locations. Additionally, you will have to log in with your Microsoft account to run VSTU for the first time.

Currently, the default installation for Unity loads Visual Studio Community edition. This version integrates with VSTU. If you are already familiar with coding and Visual Studio, you know that VSTU provides capabilities not only for rich refactoring, debugging, source code analysis, formatting, and custom debugging visualizers, but also for generating code methods in your code. If you are unfamiliar with all of the features just mentioned, don't worry, you won't need them to create games in Unity. As your capabilities increase, however, you may want to look at VSTU's many features for ways to improve workflow and productivity.

The other script editor is the *MonoDevelop* editor. It has shipped with Unity for several years, and although it may not have as many bells and whistles as VSTU, it runs happily on a wide variety of Windows versions and can be installed on offline machines.

If you want to use a different editor than what was installed, you can select the script editor of your choice through the Preferences submenu under the Edit menu. If you have installed the editors during the initial Unity installation, both will be offered as options (Figure 3-3).

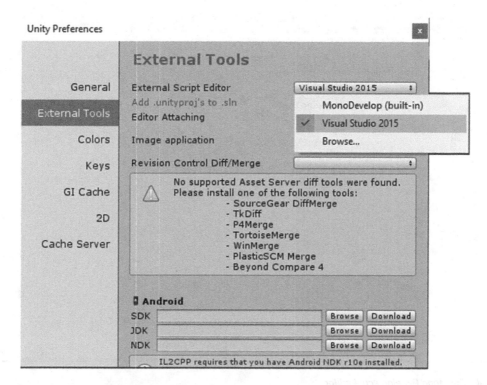

Figure 3-3. Selecting your script editor in Unity Preferences

The MonoDevelop script editor opens in its own window (Figure 3-4).

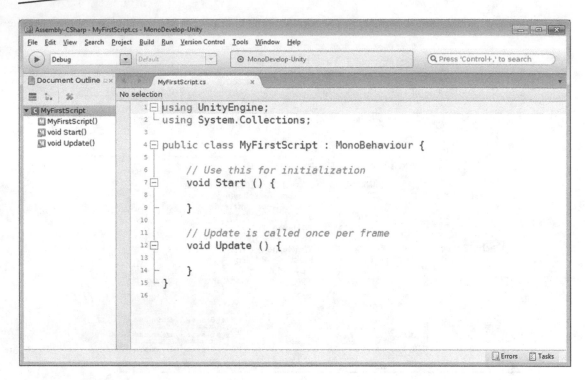

Figure 3-4. The Mono Develop script editor

In the left pane you will find the Document Outline. Try clicking each of its content elements. The element selected is located in the editing pane to the right. As your scripts become longer, this can provide a quick way to navigate to the desired location in your script.

If you have chosen Visual Studio as your script editor, it will also open in its own window (Figure 3-5).

Figure 3-5. The Visual Studio script editor

One thing you will notice about both editors is the traditional color coding of the contents of your scripts. As you become familiar with scripting, this feature will help you as you write your code. Another major reason to use a script editor rather than a simple text editor is that they will also identify errors and help you fix the problems. Let's try a little test:

1. Below the void Start () { line, type this:

    something wrong

    In Visual Studio, the error is reported immediately (Figure 3-6).

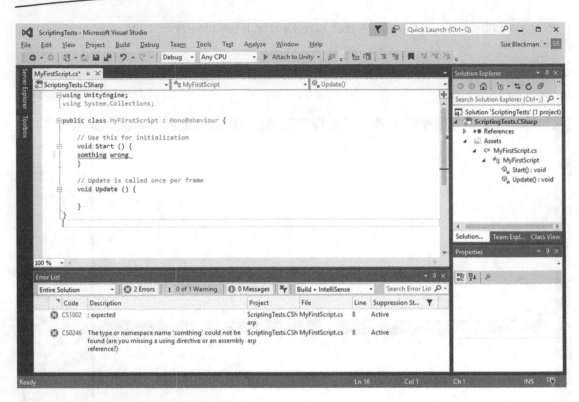

Figure 3-6. An error in the Visual Studio script editor

2. The asterisk next to the script's name at the top of the editor window indicates that the script has not yet been saved. To save a file in Visual Studio, use the Save icon on the toolbar (Figure 3-7).

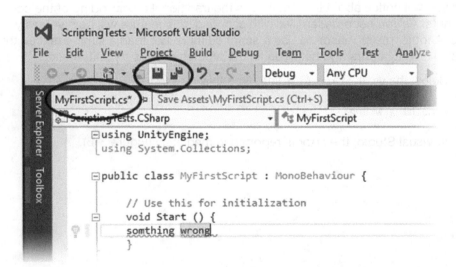

Figure 3-7. Use the Save button to save the script. The asterisk in the script name indicates it hasn't yet been saved.

3. In MonoDevelop, the error is not found until the file has been saved, and even then it will show in Unity's console (as soon as you switch focus to the Unity editor) first (Figure 3-8). To save the script in MonoDevelop, choose File ➤ Save or press Ctrl+S (Cmd+S).

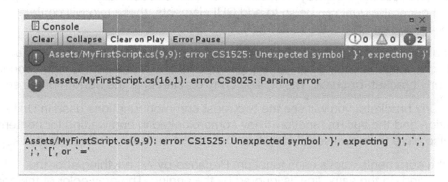

Figure 3-8. The error reported in Unity's console

4. For the error to show inside MonoDevelop, choose Build ➤ Build All (Figure 3-9).

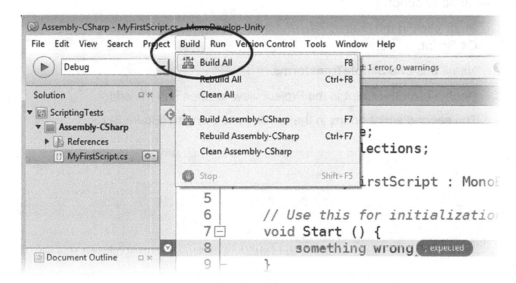

Figure 3-9. Using Build All to pinpoint the error in MonoDevelop

5. Remove the text you added to the editor and save the script.

Examining the Contents

In either editor, you will see the code for your script in the main window.

At the very top of the script, you will find the libraries used to interpret the code. `UnityEngine` and `System.Collections` are always added as a default. Occasionally, you may require other libraries, but generally, until you begin to add GUI elements, these two will contain most of what you will be using.

The next feature is the class declaration, `public class MyFirstScript MonoBehaviour {`. In Unity, a script is generally a single class. Its contents are contained within an opening and a closing curly bracket, or brace. The closing curly bracket is at the bottom of the script.

Inside the curly brackets, you will see the two most common functions used in Unity: the `Start` function and the `Update` function. They come blocked in and waiting for content. Note that they also have their own set of curly brackets to define where their content is kept.

Also note the comments above each function. Prefaced by `//`, anything after the backslashes, and on the same line, is ignored by the engine. The gray color of the comment text (green in Visual Studio) is a visual reminder that it is not to be read. Comments are often put above code, as in this case, as a description of what the code is doing as well as shorter notes at the end of lines. You can also use the `//` to temporarily disable lines of active code to help in the debugging process and as a way to locate code tagged for future attention.

Let's make another script:

1. Right-click in the Project view and from the Create menu, select C# Script.

2. Name this one **SimpleTransforms**.

3. Double click the script in the Project view to open it in the editor.

   The second script opens in the editor, in its own tab (Figure 3-10).

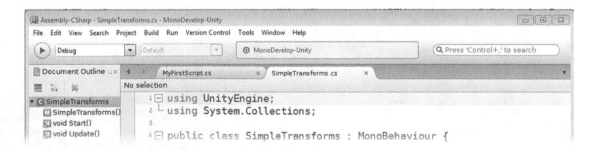

Figure 3-10. The second script open in the MonoDevelop editor

On its own, a script will do nothing unless it is in a scene. To add it to the scene, it must be added to a gameObject, where it becomes a component of the object.

4. Click and drag the SimpleTransforms script from the Project view onto the Cube in the Hierarchy view.

The SimpleTransforms script becomes a component of the Cube object, as you can see in the Inspector when the Cube is selected (Figure 3-11).

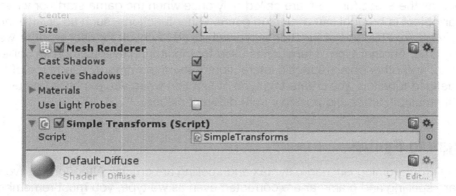

Figure 3-11. The SimpleTransforms script as a component of the Cube object

The script is added as an instance. That means the same script can be added to as many objects as you wish. If the script is changed, the changes will affect all of the objects that contain that script.

Building a Script

There are a few ways to make an object do something without scripting. Both traditional key-frame animation and the use of a physics in your scene can cause objects to move, rotate, or scale. But the essence of a game is to control what happens to your objects as the player interacts with the game. Doing that requires scripting. To script, you have to become familiar with functions, syntax, and variables at the very least.

To create a game, you create a lot of individual scripts that define the functionality of your game. Most scripts reside on and control specific gameObjects. Some scripts control a single action or event, while others eventually handle many game-play scenarios. More important, scripts quite often have to communicate with each other.

Whatever the complexity or purpose, scripts in most modern programming languages generally have the same basic components. *Functions* contain the instructions that make things happen. *Variables* store information such as an object, a state, or a value that can represent just about anything. *Comments* are the part of the code that is not interpreted by the engine and can be used to make notes in the code as well as temporarily disable code.

Later in the book, you will use specific comments to store tasks through // Todo and // Fixme, which then will appear in the task view of MonoDevelop, Xamarin Studio, and Visual Studio. Let's begin with functions

Introducing Functions

Functions are where the game functionality is handled. There are several types of functions. Some, such as the Start function, are called only once when the game starts or when a particular object is brought into a running game. Other functions, such as Update, are called every frame. This type of function is typically used to check for user input or watch for passing time. Another type of function is used for monitoring events such as collisions, mouse picks, and other object-specific interaction. A fourth commonly used type of function is a user-defined function. You create this type of function when you expect to be using its functionality multiple times and possibly from different places.

Investigating Syntax

As with any programming language, syntax and spelling are crucial. Although we live in a world where spelling and grammar are corrected even as we type, you must remember that letting devices do that kind of task costs time and resources. In games, that equates to frame rate, which can often make or break a game's chance of success.

Let's begin by examining one of the existing functions:

```
void Start () {

}
```

The first word, void, in this case, is the *return* type. With void, no information is returned.

The next word, Start, is the *name* of the function. The name may not contain spaces or certain special characters and cannot start with a number. In Unity, the convention is to use a capital letter for the first character of the name.

The parentheses are used to contain optional arguments. An *argument* is a piece of information that can be passed into a function for its use only.

Inside the curly brackets is where you put the body, or content, of the function. The curly brackets can be arranged in a couple of ways. Some people prefer them to always be on their own line, as follows:

```
void Start ()
{

}
```

The coding style for the curly brackets is taken very seriously by many companies. Always respect the preferences of people or companies you work with.

Inside the curly brackets, code is generally indented to show that it is inside the function. The MonoDevelop script editor automatically indents the code for you. Although indenting is not necessary, it makes the code more readable.

Let's add some content to the Update function of the SimpleTransforms script.Add the following line inside the Update function:

```
transform.Rotate(0,1f,0);
```

The Update function should now look as follows:

```
// Update is called once per frame
void Update () {
    transform.Rotate(0,1f,0);
}
```

Take a moment to look at the syntax of the line you just added. It uses *dot notation* to specify where to look for the various parts of the instructions.

As you may remember from the previous chapter, a transform is a move, rotation, or scale. In the preceding code, transform, with its lowercase *t*, refers to the Transform component on the object that the script is on, in this case, the Cube object. Rotate is a function (also referred to as a *method*) from the Transform class. The three numbers are the arguments passed into the Rotate method. In this case, they are the x, y, and z values that will be used to rotate the Cube. At the end of the line is a semicolon. This tells the engine that this is the end of the command.

Checking the Functionality

After adding the new code, you have to save the script before you can see any results. Saving the script compiles it into instructions that can be used more quickly during runtime. Follow these steps to save the script:

1. Look at the SimpleTransforms script's tab in the editor. Instead of the gray x next to the name, you will see a gray circle (Figure 3-12). This indicates that there have been changes to the script that have not yet been saved.

Figure 3-12. The SimpleTransforms script indicating unsaved edits

2. From the File menu, choose Save. Alternatively, you can press Ctrl+S (Cmd+S) to save the script.

3. With the script updated to include the new content in the Update function, you can now check out the results. Click Play and observe the Cube in the Scene and Game views.

The Cube rotates on its y axis. Depending on what else is running on your machine, you may notice that the rate of rotation is not constant. This might be a good time to see what the Rotate method is supposed to do by checking the scripting documentation.

4. From the Help menu, choose Scripting Reference. Set the scripting language to C# at the upper right.

5. Type **Rotate** in the search field and then click the magnifying glass to perform the search (Figure 3-13).

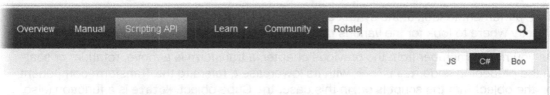

Welcome to the Unity Scripting Reference!

Figure 3-13. Searching the Scripting Reference for "Rotate"

6. Select the second offering in the search results, Transform.Rotate.

    The Description reports:

    Applies a rotation of /eulerAngles.z/ degrees around the z axis, /eulerAngles.x/ degrees around the x axis, and /eulerAngles.y/ degrees around the y axis (in that order).

    If relativeTo is left out or set to Space.Self, the rotation is applied around the transform's local axes. (The x, y, and z axes shown when selecting the object inside the Scene view.) If relativeTo is Space.World, the rotation is applied around the world x, y, and z axes.

    The relativeTo argument is optional, so the rotation, in degrees, is applied to the local axis. Because you have added the code to the Update function, the Cube should be rotated 1 degree each time the Update function is evaluated, or at least every frame. The problem, of course, is that frame rate varies depending on what else is being calculated at runtime, not to mention between devices.

    The solution to the problem is to use an important bit of code from the Time class. A search of the Scripting Reference will tell you that Time.deltaTime returns the "time in seconds it took to complete the last frame." If that sounds a bit confusing, read on. The bottom line is that multiplying a value by Time.deltaTime essentially changes the instructions from *per frame* to *per second*. It not only forces the rotation, in this case, to be consistent, but also ensures that the rotation will be the same on all capable platforms.

7. Change the 1f to `Time.deltaTime` * 1f so the line looks as follows:

    ```
    transform.Rotate(0,Time.deltaTime * 1f,0);
    ```

    The lowercase f next to nonzero numbers tells C# that the number is a *float*, or floating-point number. If the f was left off, it would be read as an *int*, or integer. The result of the multiplication would automatically be a float because time uses floating-point numbers. If it was written as 1.0, it would be considered a double without the clarifying f. Doubles require a larger memory allocation, though both can be fractional values.

8. Save the script.

9. Click Play. The Cube, now rotating at 1 degree per *second* instead of per frame, rotates at an extremely slow, but constant speed.

10. Change the 1f to 50f and save the script again.

11. Click Play and check out the updated speed.

Understanding Error Messages and the Console

If you are new to programming, you may easily get baffled by syntax errors as you add code to your scripts. Before moving on to other basic scripting topics, generating a few errors to see the results will be worthwhile. These examples use Unity's console in case you are using MonoDevelop, but feel free to compare the messages reported in Visual Studio if that is your script editor of choice.

Let's begin with a typical typo, an incorrect case. In C#, functions are usually capitalized and variables are usually lowercase.

1. In the SimpleTransforms script, change the t in `transform` to an uppercase T:

    ```
    Transform.Rotate(0,Time.deltaTime * 50f,0);
    ```

2. Save the script and then click on the Unity editor to switch the focus to it. An error message appears in the status line at the bottom of the editor (Figure 3-14).

Assets/SimpleTransforms.cs(13,27): error CS0120: An object reference is required to access non-static member "UnityEngine.Transform.Rotate(UnityEngine.Vector3)"

Figure 3-14. Error message on the status line

    The message indicates that Unity is missing a reference to an object on which it can perform the `Rotate`. The capital T refers to the `Transform` *class*, not the transform *component* on the Cube with the script.

3. Double-click the status line to open the full console. The console often gives you more information than is available to the status line (Figure 3-15).

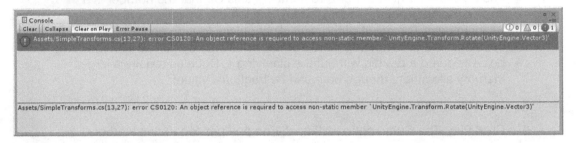

Figure 3-15. The error message in the console

Right now, your script is small enough to locate the problem without help, but when the script is large, you can use the console to find the issue. The script is identified at the beginning of the line. The two numbers inside the parentheses tell you the line number and character position. You can also have the console take you to the line in the script.

4. Double-click the error message in the console.

5. Switch focus to the script editor and note that the line with the error is now highlighted (Figure 3-16).

```
11        // Update is called once per frame
12        void Update () {
13            Transform.Rotate(0,Time.deltaTime * 50f,0);
14        }
15    }
```

Figure 3-16. The line located in the script

6. Put the lowercase t back into the line.

7. Delete the semicolon from the end of the line.

8. Save the script and check the console for the next error message (Figure 3-17).

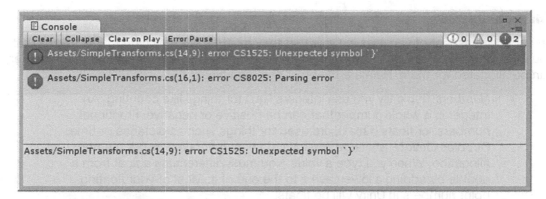

Figure 3-17. Two error messages

With the semicolon to signify the end of the line missing, the engine sees the } as the next character on the line and gets confused. That, in turn, causes a parsing error because the curly brackets no longer match.

9. Replace the semicolon and save the script.

10. Switch focus to the console. It updates and the errors are cleared.

Working with Variables

The next major feature of most programming languages is the *variable*. Variables are used to store *values*. They keep track of just about everything that your game will have to know to make things happen, and are accessed and can be updated as required.

Just as with function names, variables have their own naming conventions. In Unity, variable names generally start with lowercase letters. Like function names, they may not use certain special characters or spaces, and also may not use any reserved words. *Reserved words* are names already used by C# and Unity. If the variable name turns blue after you type it, that indicates that it is a reserved word so you must alter it for your own use.

The trick to naming variables is to keep the name descriptive without making it so long that it makes the code difficult to read. When naming in Unity, it is always preferable to use *camel case* (mixed uppercase and lowercase) rather than underscores to separate words. For instance, some_variable_name using underscores becomes someVariableName in camel case. As you will shortly see, the latter will become Some Variable Name when it is exposed to the Inspector.

Variable Types

An important aspect of variables in C# is that they must be strongly *typed*. This means that you must declare what type of information they will be used to store so that enough memory can be allocated for them. Here are the most common *types*:

- *Numbers*: Typically you use integers (`int`) for things like counting. An integer is a whole number that can be positive or negative. Fractional numbers, or floats (`float`), are used for things such as distance or time. Doubles (`double`) are large versions of floats that take a larger memory allocation. When you type a value, you must differentiate a float from a double by adding a lowercase f to the end of it. Most of your floating-point numbers in Unity will be floats.

- *Strings*: These are so named because they are strings of characters (`string`). They are always shown between quotation marks. The integer value 5 is not the same as the string "5", for example. The first has a numeric value, whereas the second does not. Also be aware that spaces and punctuation are characters, so "canary" is not the same as " canary ". And, as you may have guessed, capitalization also counts. "Canary" is not the same string as "canary".

- *Booleans*: Booleans (`bool`) pronounced *boo-lee-uhn* , for Charles Boole, a 17th century mathematician, are the most memory-efficient variable types. In C#, you use the values `true` or `false`.

- *Unity-specific variable types*: Pretty much anything can be a variable type in Unity, as long as it derives from a class. You can store all the information contained in an instance of a script (for example, when you've added a script to a specific object), all in a single variable. This concept is key to various scripts being able to communicate with each other.

Along with declaring the type of variable, you will also specify whether it can be accessed by other scripts and even whether it can be exposed to the Inspector. Variables exposed to the Inspector can be easier to set up for nonprogrammers as well as allow you to change their values during runtime for instant feedback. As a default, C# variables are always *private*; they cannot be accessed outside the scripts they are in. To make a variable accessible to other scripts and have it exposed to the Inspector, you must mark it as `public`. Occasionally, you may want to keep a variable public but not have it cluttering the Inspector. You can use `internal` for that scenario, though if you are already familiar with programming and understand the use of namespaces, you are better off using [`HideInInspector`] where the variable listed beside or below the line will be affected.

With a bit of background covered, you are probably anxious to create a few variables. Let's use MyFirstScript to experiment with a few variables:

1. Open MyFirstScript, or activate its tab in the script editor if it is already open.

2. *Under* the class declaration and *above* the Start function, add the following:

```
public int health;
public float reloadRate = 1.5f;
public string favoriteColor;
public bool isReady = false;
public Camera the_Camera;
public GameObject theSphere;
```

Variables that are available to the entire script or class must be listed inside the class's opening and closing curly brackets and are generally listed just below the class declaration and above the functions for readability. The order of the variables is not important, but it is good practice to keep them organized as your scripts get more complicated. In this book, unless told to put them in a specific location, you will usually add them below the existing variables so it is easier to compare your scripts with the finished scripts for each chapter.

3. Save the script.

To see the results of your additions, the script must be added to an object in the scene. This script doesn't do anything yet, but you will be contacting it from the other script, so let's go ahead and put it on the Sphere.

4. Drag the MyFirstScript from the Project view onto the Sphere in the Hierarchy view and select the Sphere.

The Sphere now has a My First Script component, complete with all the new variables showing as its *parameters* (Figure 3-18).

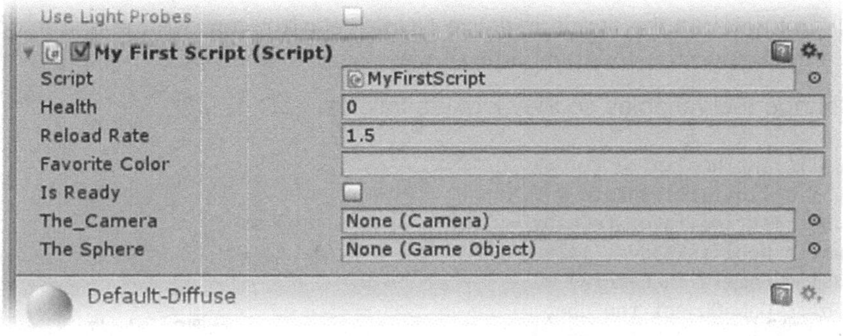

Figure 3-18. The Sphere's new My First Script component with the variables showing as its parameters

Note the way that the variable names using camel case in the Inspector. The first letter has been capitalized and a space has been added before new capitalized characters. The the_ Camera variable's underscore is less readable as a parameter in the component.

Let's take a moment to inspect the new additions.

The `health` variable was not initialized with a value, so it defaults to 0. The `reloadRate` variable requires an f to identify the value assigned to it as a float type in the script, but not in the Inspector. A value for the `favoriteColor` variable was not assigned, which is the equivalent of "", or no characters within the required quotation marks. Quotation marks are not used in the Inspector. The Boolean variable `isReady` was initialized to `false`, so the check box it displays for its parameters field is deactivated.

The last two variables are Unity-specific types, so you can see that in your script these types are both capitalized and the blue color of a reserved word. This is because they refer to predefined classes that already exist in the Unity engine. Note also that the type shows in the value field in parentheses after the *None*.

Let's load a camera, or rather a gameObject with a Camera component into the The_Camera parameter and then make some changes to the script to see how it affects the inspector:

1. With the Sphere selected, try to click and drag the Directional Light onto its The_Camera field. Because the Directional Light has no Camera component, it cannot be loaded there.

2. Now click and drag the Main Camera object onto the Sphere's The_Camera field. This time the object drops into the field nicely. The gameObject's name, Main Camera, shows in the field, but it is actually just its Camera component that is being referenced, so that remains showing in the parentheses.

3. Drag the Cube gameObject onto the The Sphere field. The Cube is a GameObject, the type specified, so there is no type shown for it in parentheses.

Let's see about those changes to the script next.

Order of Evaluation

Now you will go back into the script, initialize `favoriteColor`, remove the underscore from the_Camera, and change the variable name of theSphere to theCube to make it more logical:

1. Change the variables so they look as follows:

```
public int health;
public float reloadRate = 1.5f;
public string favoriteColor = "red";
public bool isReady = false;
public Camera theCamera;
public GameObject theCube;
```

2. Save the script again.

3. With the Sphere selected, check the results in the Inspector (Figure 3-19).

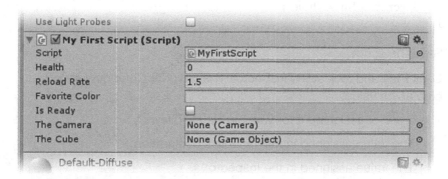

Figure 3-19. The updated My First Script component

Two things have happened, or rather one thing has happened and another hasn't. The two variables with name changes have been cleared of the values you assigned to them. As the names were changed, that is an expected result. Conspicuously missing, however, is the new Favorite Color value.

It turns out that as soon as a variable is exposed to the Inspector, that value will overwrite whatever was assigned to it in the variable's declaration and initialization. This allows the author to customize each instance of the script to tailor it to each of the scene objects that it has been assigned to. Unfortunately, it can wreak havoc with your efforts to track down problems in your script.

> **Tip** If your game is not behaving as expected, remember to check the Inspector to see what value is being used for the parameter in question.

4. In this case, because you haven't assigned any new values yet, you can reset the component to show the values assigned to it in the script. Right-click over the My First Script label in the Inspector and select Reset.

The new value, red, now shows in the Inspector. Note that the quotation marks are not used in the Inspector.

Let's try another experiment with the variable values. Let's change the favoriteColor value inside the Start function:

1. Add a line to reassign the `favoriteColor` value inside the `Start` function so that it looks as follows:

    ```
    // Use this for initialization
    void Start () {
        favoriteColor = "blue";
    }
    ```

2. Save the script.

3. Click Play and look at the Inspector. The Favorite Color now shows blue as its value.

    The order of assignment for variables is as follows:

    > The value assigned in the variable's declaration.

    > The value assigned in the Inspector.

    > The value assigned to the variable in the `Start` function.

    Another critical thing to know about variables that have been exposed to the Inspector is that changes made during runtime are only temporary.

4. While in Play mode, change the Favorite Color value to **green**.

5. Exit Play mode. The value returns to the original red.

> **Tip** Whenever you make changes to the values in the Inspector that you wish to be permanent, be sure to do so while not in Play mode. You should also remember to save the scene, as changes are local to the current scene.

You've seen how variables are used to store values, so now let's see one being used. In the SimpleTransforms script, you hard-coded a speed value for the rotation. More typically, you would create a variable named `speed` and use it in the command that rotates the Cube. That way, it could be used to control several things throughout the script. If it had to be changed, you would have to change only the value of the variable. A difficulty setting, for example, might be used to adjust several aspects of your game play.

Let's see how using a variable for speed affects your script:

1. Open the SimpleTransforms script.

2. Just below the class declaration, add the following variable:

    ```
    public float speed = 50f;
    ```

3. In the `Update` function, replace the original value with the variable speed:

    ```
    transform.Rotate(0,Time.deltaTime * speed,0);
    ```

4. Save the script.

5.   Click Play and select the Cube in the Hierarchy view.

6.   Change its Speed parameter and watch as the Cube's rotation changes in the Scene and Game views.

> **Tip**   You can change many numeric values in the Inspector by clicking and dragging on the parameter's label. The functionality is set up to behave like a slider.

7.   Stop Play mode.

Scope Within the Script

The next important thing to know about variables is their *scope*, or who they may be used by and how long they will persist in memory.

When variables are declared inside the class, but not inside a function, they are accessible throughout that particular instance of the script. That means they can be used or altered by the contents of any function.

If a variable exists *only* inside a function, it is said to be *local* to that function. It must be declared inside the function and is automatically destroyed (the memory allocated to store it is cleared) at the end of the function. Functions or methods *inside* other functions can have variables that are local to themselves. If a variable is declared within a particular set of curly brackets, it is local to that set.

Because of scope, you could easily use the same variable name in several places. Generally, however, best practice is to give even local variables different names just to avoid confusion.

When a variable is public, it may also be accessed by other scripts. Variables that have no reason to be used outside their class or show in the Inspector should be marked as *private*. In C#, `private` is the default.

> **Tip**   Because you may eventually find yourself converting Unity's JavaScript to C#, it is worth noting that in JavaScript, variables are public by default and must be specifically marked as private when you don't want them accessible outside their script.

1.   Open the MyFirstScript script.

2.   In the variables section, remove `public` from the `public int health` line:

```
int health;
```

3.   Save the script.

4.   Select the Sphere in the Hierarchy view and inspect the My First Script component in the Inspector. The Health parameter is no longer exposed to the Inspector (Figure 3-20).

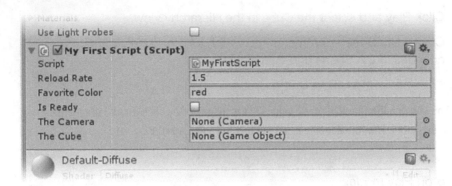

Figure 3-20. The Health parameter is no longer exposed in the My First Script component

At times you might not want to expose a variable to the Inspector, but require it to be accessible from other scripts. As mentioned earlier, this quick solution should not be used if you are an advanced user using namespaces. The `isReady` variable might be something that doesn't have to be exposed to the Inspector. Let's change it to `internal`.

1. Change the `public bool isReady = false` line to the following:

   `internal bool isReady = false;`

2. Save the script and check the Inspector.

   The Is Ready parameter is now hidden from the Inspector (Figure 3-21).

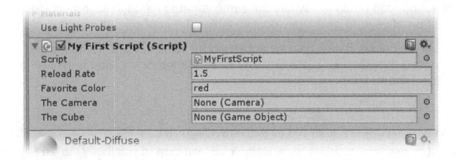

Figure 3-21. The Is Ready parameter is hidden from the Inspector

At this point, you may be wondering how you can check up on the values of variables hidden from the Inspector. As it turns out, you can set the Inspector to *Debug* mode instead of the default *Normal* mode to see private variables.

3. Right-click the Inspector label and select Debug from the list
    (Figure 3-22).

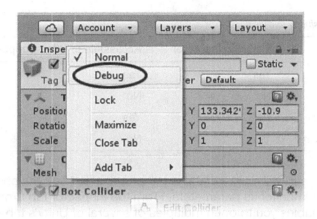

Figure 3-22. *Setting the Inspector to Debug mode*

The label name changes to Debug, and now you can see the private variables in the My First Script component (Figure 3-23).

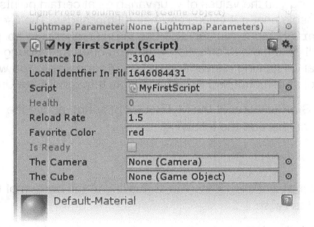

Figure 3-23. *The private variables visible, though grayed out, in the Inspector*

To further complicate the way variables can be accessed, you can use [SerializeField] in front of a private variable. This keeps the variable from being changed by other scripts, and it will allow you to easily set up or change the values through the Inspector instead of hard-coding them in the scripts.

For a side-by-side comparison of your choices, a table makes a good visual aid; take a look at Table 3-1.

Table 3-1. Variable Accessibility and Visibility

	Visible in Inspector	Accessible to Other Scripts
public	Yes	Yes
private	No	No
internal	No	Yes
[SerializeField] private	Yes	No

As your scene grows, you will realize that it is not practical to keep the one object selected all the time in order to monitor its parameters. From the Inspector tab drop-down list, the Add Tab submenu enables you to open multiples of several of Unity's tab views. This lets you keep focus on one object without the need to keep it selected. Feel free to set the Inspector back to Normal mode if it gets too cluttered.

Although Unity's tabs can be pulled off to float free, you will often want to know what multiple variable values are doing, and especially *the order in which they change*. The console, besides giving you nasty red error messages when your code has issues, can be quite helpful in telling you the values of your variables at certain points in your game. You can have the console print out values and helpful messages. The C# version is Debug.Log(<something to print>), but you can also use print(<something to print>). The Debug.Log version will yield more information when you open the debugger log, and the code adheres to the normal C# naming convention so *Log* is capitalized. You will find the print (note the lowercase *p*) statement used interchangeably throughout the Unity community.

1.   Inside the Start function of the MyFirstScript script, above the favoriteColor line, add the following:

     Debug.Log(isReady);

2.   Save the script and click Play. The status line at the bottom of the editor reports False.

3.   Double-click the status line to bring up the console and see the full report (Figure 3-24).

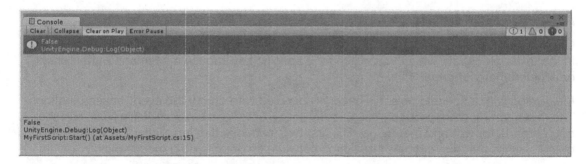

Figure 3-24. The console printing the value of isReady at startup

With the line selected, you can see more information at the bottom of the console. Regardless of the extra info, the message remains somewhat cryptic. Fortunately, you can also add your own message to clear things up.

4. Change the line to the following:

```
Debug.Log("The value of the isReady variable is: " + isReady);
```

5. Save the script.

6. Stop Play mode and then click Play again. This time, the message is a lot more helpful (Figure 3-25).

> ⓘ The value of the isReady variable is: False

Figure 3-25. The less cryptic message

You must stop Play mode and then restart it because the code for printing to the console is in the Start function and is evaluated only once, on startup. Following this line of thought, if your print statement was in the Update function, as soon as you changed the output instructions and saved (compiled) the script, the new values would show as soon as you switched focus back to Unity.

7. Stop Play mode.

The most helpful use of printing to the console is to flag some sort of an event. You can check where you are in a script when something happens as well as check on the value of relevant variables. For this, you will be testing some basic interaction in your scene.

Introducing Interaction

The most distinctive feature of games is that the user can interact with the game to generate events, move the story line forward, or work toward a specific goal. In Unity, with the exception of the UI system objects, interaction requires a collider. Whether you want to pick a 3D object in your scene, fire a projectile at it, or drop a boulder on it, you will be interacting with either the scene or a specific object.

Adding User Input

Generic input, such as keyboard, mouse, and device-specific input are generally monitored in the Update function, where you watch for a specific key, mouse movement, button press, or accelerometer change.

Interaction with a specific object is generally handled with one of the event-based functions. The most common are probably OnCollisionEnter, OnTriggerEnter, OnMouseDown, and their counterparts for exit and mouse-up. The first two functions flag interaction between scene objects, while the third catches interaction between an object and a mouse pick.

Let's see what other event-based functions are available:

1. Search the Scripting Reference for **MonoBehaviour** (note the British spelling here).

   Remember, when you create a new C# script, its default name is NewMonoBehavior. So your script, deriving from the MonoBehaviour class, has access to all variables, functions, and messages it contains.

2. Check the Messages category.

   These functions, also called *callbacks*, are called or evaluated when their specific event is detected and the message sent to the script. The easiest to test will be the OnMouseDown function. Let'' add it to the SimpleTransforms script. That script resides on the Cube object, so you will be adding pick functionality to your Cube.

3. Open the SimpleTransforms script.

4. Below the closing curly bracket of the Update function, but above the script's final closing curly bracket, block in the new function:

   ```
   void OnMouseDown () {

   }
   ```

Note   In this book, unless otherwise instructed, when you are asked to create a new function, add it *below* the existing functions, but *above* the script's final closing curly bracket. The convention is to have functions that are evaluated at startup first (such as Start and Awake), functions that are called every frame or at a fixed length of time next (Update and Fixed Update), and all others after those. After the script has been compiled, the order is irrelevant.

Caution   Be careful not to put a function *inside* another function.

5. *Inside* the new OnMouseDown function (between its curly brackets), add the following line:

```
Debug.Log("I've been hit!");
```

The MonoDevelop editor will automatically tab over to inset the line.

6. Save the script.

7. Click Play and pick the spinning cube with a left mouse click.

Your *I've been hit!* message appears in the console (Figure 3-26).

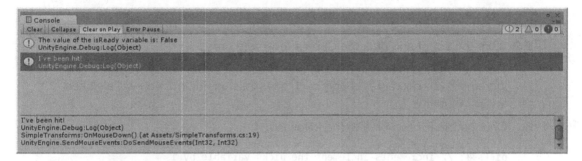

Figure 3-26. The less cryptic message

8. Click the Cube a few more times. As expected, each time the Cube is picked, the OnMouseDown function is called and evaluated.

Next let's try a bit of math and have the function print out the number of times the Cube has been picked after each new pick. For that, you need a variable to keep track of the picks. This is also a good time to include a comment to remind yourself what the variable is used for.

1. Stop Play mode.

2. Add the following variable declaration beneath the public float speed line:

```
int picks = 0; // number of times the object has been picked
```

Just as with functions, unless you're told to do otherwise, add new variables beneath the existing ones. If the new variable's purpose is not related to that of the previous variables, you may want to add a carriage return to make the new variable.

3. Add the following line above the Debug.Log line in the OnMouseDown function:

```
picks = picks + 1; // increment the picks variable
```

4. Change the Debug.Log line as follows:

```
Debug.Log("I've been hit " + picks + " times");
```

5. Save the script.

6. Click Play and pick the Cube several times to see the results.

The message updates nicely to show the number of times the Cube has been picked. There are a couple of other ways to increment an integer value. Because you will see them regularly in code, they are worth a quick look:

1. Change the picks = line to the following:

```
picks += 1; // increments increment the picks variable
```

2. Save the script and pick the Cube a few more times.

    The picks value is updated as before. The most abbreviated version increments or decrements only by 1, so is less useful, but you will also see it used regularly.

3. Change the picks = line to the following:

```
picks++; // increments increment the picks variable by 1
```

4. Save the script and pick the Cube a few more times.

    The picks value is updated as before. Note that this time, because the script changes were not in the Start function, you were able to check the results without having to restart Play mode.

5. Stop Play mode.

The interaction works well, as does the updating of the picks variable. What may have bothered you, though, is the message when the value is 1. Grammatically speaking, it should say *time* instead of *times*. The condition that should change the output exists only when the value of picks is 1. For that, you will be looking at the *conditional.*

Using the Conditional

If user interaction defines games in general, then the *conditional* is what directs the actual game play. It is where you specify what should happen in response to various events, depending on any number of variables or object states. A character, for example may die or continue fighting when attacked, depending on his health variable's current value. If a light is on, it may be turned off when a switch object is picked; otherwise, if the light is already off, it would be turned on.

The concept is straightforward: if <some expression evaluates as true>, then <do something>, else <do something else. The *else* is optional. The syntax is as follows:

```
if (<some expression>) <do this>;
else <do that>; // this line is optional
```

The only problem here is that there is only one command if the expression evaluates to true and only one if the expression evaluates to false. Because most conditions have multiple things to do for the two possibilities, you usually require a set of curly brackets. Think of them as shopping bags. You can hold only one object in your hand at a time, but a shopping bag lets you easily carry lots of things at the same time. This looks like the following:

```
if (<some expression>) {
    <do this>;
    <and this>;
}
else { // this part is optional
    <do that>;
    <and that>
}
```

In the expression to be evaluated, you can use various operators. Typically, you use the equivalency operator (==) or its counterpart, not equivalent (!=), where ! is the *not*.

When comparing number values, you can also use less than (<), greater than (>), less than or equal to (<=), and greater than or equal to (>=). If multiple conditions must be met, you can use the *and* operator (&&). If one of multiple conditions can be met, you can use the *or* operator (||) With multiple conditions, the first condition (leftmost) is evaluated first. With the *and* operator, if the first condition evaluates as false, the full condition can never be met, so the remaining condition or conditions are not evaluated. With the *or* operator, if the first condition evaluates as true, the remaining conditions are never evaluated because the condition has already been met. The bottom line is that you should always order your conditional by placing the one most likely to produce the required result first, and placing the least likely last. Math is evaluated in the traditional way: multiplication and division are evaluated before addition and subtraction. As with traditional math, you can use parentheses to force a different order of evaluation.

If you are checking the value of a Boolean variable, the variable is the only thing to go within the parentheses because it already evaluates to true or false.

Let's get some practice with conditionals by letting the user start and stop the Cube from rotating. To do that, you need a variable to manage the state of the rotation. It is either off (false) or on (true), so you will use a Boolean type variable:

1. Create a new variable in the SimpleTransforms script:

    ```
    public bool rotating = false; // Initialize as false
    ```

2. In the Update function, change the transform.Rotate line by putting the condition that must be met at the front of the line:

    ```
    if (rotating) transform.Rotate(0,Time.deltaTime * speed,0);
    ```

3. In the `OnMouseDown` line, add the following to change the `rotating` flag whenever the user clicks the Cube:

```
if (rotating == true) {
        rotating = false;
}
else { // it must be false
        rotating = true;
}
```

In the conditional, `if (rotating == true)` was used to make the code more readable. If you prefer the shorthand version, feel free to change it to `if (rotating)`.

4. Save the script.

5. Click Play and test the script by picking the Cube several times.

The Cube starts and stops with the user pick. Note that unlike the `if (rotating)` conditional in the `Update` function, you've set this one up with curly brackets. This allows for easy additions as the code develops. Let's go ahead and add one now. Using the `picks` variable, you can increase the speed each time the user pick causes the Cube to rotate.

6. Stop Play mode.

7. Add the following lines beneath the `rotating = true` line in the `else` section of the conditional:

```
// increase the speed by the current number of picks
speed = speed + picks;
```

8. Save the script.

9. Click Play and test by picking the Cube several times. The Cube rotates increasingly faster each time it is picked.

10. Exit Play mode.

Adding More Functionality

Lots of additional functionality is available that will be useful in many games and applications. In this section, you will look at two of the most commonly used techniques before moving on to the next chapter. Looping is a way to manage multiple objects or variables. User-defined functions are a mainstay of controlling game play, moving data around, and just about every other facet of game development.

Looping

Another commonly used bit of functionality is to iterate, or step through, a list, or array, of objects or variables. There are several ways to do this, depending on what you are iterating through. Because the for loop can be used on its own, you will take a short look at it now. Typically, you will iterate through a number of objects or perform an operation a set number of times in the Start function. Let's just do some simple addition to get a feel for how the for loop works:

1. Open the MyFirstScript script.

2. In the Start function, add the following:

    ```
    for (int x = 0; x < 10; x++) {
        print ("My favorite number is " + x);
    }
    ```

    The for loop requires four things. The first is an int type variable. It is *local* to the for loop and will act as a counter. This is one of the times you don't bother with a meaningful variable name.

    The variable is initialized with a value. Quite often you will be iterating through arrays with a first element number of 0. The second section tells the for loop when to stop: in this case, when the value of x reaches 10. The last section inside the arguments area tells the for loop how much to increment the variable after performing whatever tasks are set inside the body of the for loop (inside the curly brackets). In this case, you are telling it to increment by 1 by using the ++ shorthand. You could also use x += 1 or x = x + 1.

    Inside the body of the for loop, you put the instructions. With a for loop, they generally involve the use of the counter.

3. Save the script and click Play.

    The console reports your favorite number, or rather all 10 of them. At this point, you probably no longer want to clutter the console with the isReady printout. Rather than delete it, let's just comment it out for now.

4. Add // to the front of the Debug.Log line in the Start function:

    ```
    //Debug.Log("The value of the isReady variable is: " + isReady);
    ```

    The line goes gray, indicating that it will be ignored.

5. Save the script and click Play again. This time the console prints only the favorite number line.

Creating User-Defined Functions

As your last task in this chapter, you will create your first custom function. This task gives you a chance to try out an *argument* as well. You will have the Start function's for loop send the value of x off to be processed in your new function. Typically, you would create a user-defined function when you knew you would have to call its functionality from several functions or even from different scripts.

1. Continuing with the MyFirstScript, add the following function below the Update function, but above the script's closing curly bracket:

```
void MyCustomFunction (int newX) {
    Debug.Log("Wait, I prefer " + (2 * newX));
}
```

   This function doesn't return any values, so it begins with the usual void. The name follows the usual function-naming conventions by using camel case and starts with a capital letter. The argument takes an integer type variable that will be local to the function. Inside Debug.Log, a string is coupled with the variable that has been passed to the function where it is multiplied by 2. Using the parentheses around 2 * newX ensures that the value is computed before printing to the console. Now you can call your new function.

2. Inside the for loop, below the print ("My favorite number line, add the following:

```
MyCustomFunction(x); // send x off for more work
```

   With this line, you are calling the function and *passing* the current value of x to it. This is a means of passing local variables from one function to another, rather than allocating memory for a variable that is always reinitialized each time it is used.

3. Save the script.

4. Click Play and watch the results as they are printed in the console. Each iteration of the for loop prints the original message, jumps down to the new function, prints its message, and then goes back to the for loop for the next increment of x.

   The final piece of the puzzle is contacting another object's components. You may require a particular variable's value, want to change that value, or possibly make use of one of the other script's functions as you will in this little experiment. If this last section is over your head at the moment, don't worry; it will be just a quick look at one way to communicate between objects. You will have plenty of opportunities to learn more about interscript and object communication with the book's project.

   To call a function from another object, you must first make the function public.

5. Change the void `MyCustomFunction` line to the following:

    ```
    public void MyCustomFunction (int newX) {
    ```

6. Save the script.

7. Open the SimpleTransforms script.

    The first thing to do is to "introduce" the MyFirstScript to the SimpleTransforms script so it will know how to find and make contact with it.

8. Add the following variable:

    ```
    public MyFirstScript myScript; // the object/script with the function to contact
    ```

    The type is the script/class itself. The SimpleTransforms script will know which object that script is on when you load it onto the Simple Transforms component. Let's call the function from the `OnMouseDown` function and pass the `picks` variable to it.

9. In the `OnMouseDown` function, inside the `if (rotating == true)` block, under the `rotating = false` line, add the following:

    ```
    myScript.MyCustomFunction(picks); // send picks off to be processed
    ```

10. Save the script.

11. Select the Cube and drag the Sphere object onto the new My Script parameter.

12. Click Play and click the Cube several times.

    Now each time the Cube is clicked to a stop, the number of picks is sent off to the `MyCustomFunction`, where it is doubled and printed out with the message.

13. Save the Scene and save the project.

If you are new to scripting and find it intriguing, feel free to delve deeper into it with conventional courses or learning material. In the remainder of the book, you will be concentrating on using C# with Unity to achieve your game's functionality, but will not go deeply into traditional programming concepts and functionality except where required.

Working with Script Editors

By now, you may have noticed that, as you type, the script editor anticipates what you are typing and offers autocomplete choices for you (Figure 3-27 and Figure 3-28). Although you can use any text editor to write your scripts, dedicated editors such as MonoDevelop and Visual Studio are packed full of tools and functionality that seriously improve workflow. The simple color coding of reserved words is just the beginning.

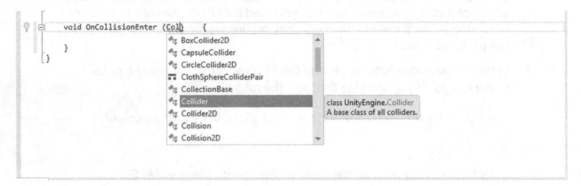

Figure 3-27. Autocomplete suggestions in MonoDevelop

Figure 3-28. Autocomplete suggestions in Visual Studio Community

But while MonoDevelop has been tied into the Unity API for years (recognizing Unity keywords, methods, and so forth), Visual Studio, unarguably the most popular and widely used editor in the programming world, is a relative newcomer to Unity. Because it is capable handling many programming languages that are not natively included in the Community edition, you must make sure that the tools developed to work with Unity have been installed.

If you opted to install Visual Studio Community edition when you installed Unity, it will also have installed Visual Studio Tools for Unity. If, however, you have uninstalled and reinstalled Visual Studio, you may be missing those essential tools. A quick check of Visual Studio will tell whether they have been loaded:

1. Double-click MyFirstScript in the Project view. The script will open in Visual Studio if Visual Studio is set as your script editor.

2. Right-click anywhere inside your code to bring up the right-click menu.

    You should see the Unity-specific options at the bottom of the menu (Figure 3-29).

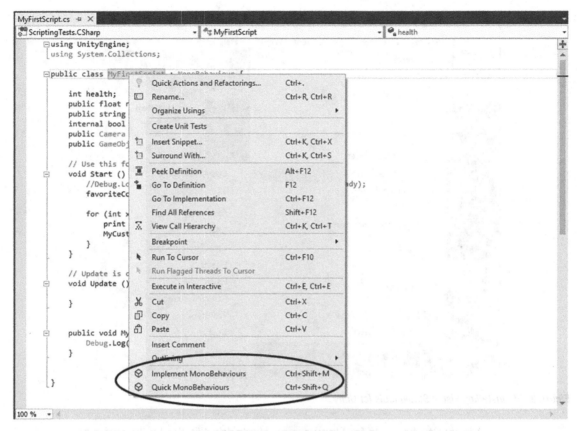

Figure 3-29. *The right-click menu confirming that Visual Studio Tools for Unity has been installed*

If you do not see the two Unity options at the bottom of the menu, Visual Studio Tools for Unity has not been installed. Fortunately, there is an easy way to get the tools installed.

3. In Unity, from the Assets menu, choose Import Package ➤ Visual Studio 2015 Tools (Figure 3-30).

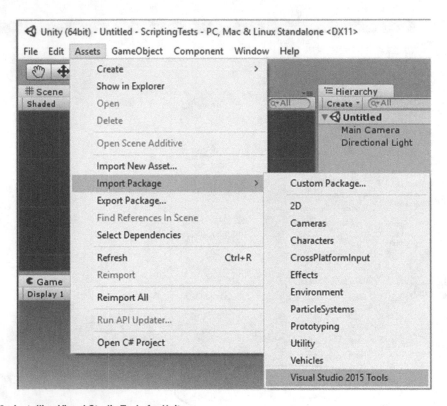

Figure 3-30. Installing Visual Studio Tools for Unity

The Visual Studio Tools for Unity are quickly added to the Unity editor (you may have to restart Visual Studio to see them).

If you do not see the option to import the Visual Studio 2015 Tools in the Import Packages submenu, it means you have not installed Visual Studio Community yet.

Once it's properly installed, you will want to get a first look at the two options at the bottom of Visual Studio's right-click window. While it may be a bit early in your scripting career to introduce you to them, eventually you will find them incredibly useful, so tuck them away in your memory or your notes on Visual Studio.

1. Back in Visual Studio, right-click anywhere inside the window where your MyFirstScript opened.

2. From the bottom of the right-click menu, select Implement MonoBehaviours.

    In this tool, you can create shortcut abbreviations for your most commonly used functions or methods (Figure 3-31).

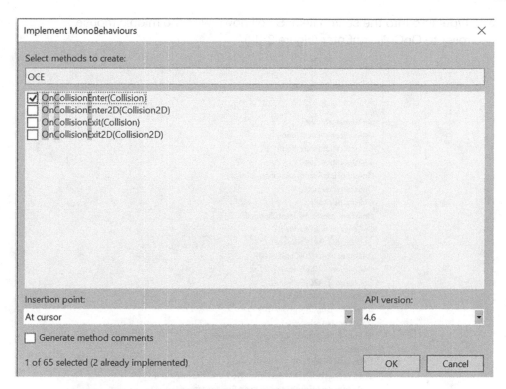

Figure 3-31. Creating typing shortcuts for Unity functions or methods

Let's look at the other Unity-specific option.

3. Close the Implement MonoBehaviours dialog box.

4. From the right-click menu, this time select Quick Mono Behaviours. The Quick Mono Behaviours tool opens up.

5. Type an **o** into the search field. Scroll down with the middle mouse roller to OnCollisionEnter (Figure 3-32).

Figure 3-32. Searching entries beginning with the letter o

Note the argument type the method expects, Collision.

6.   Scroll down farther and locate OnTriggerEnter (Figure 3-33).

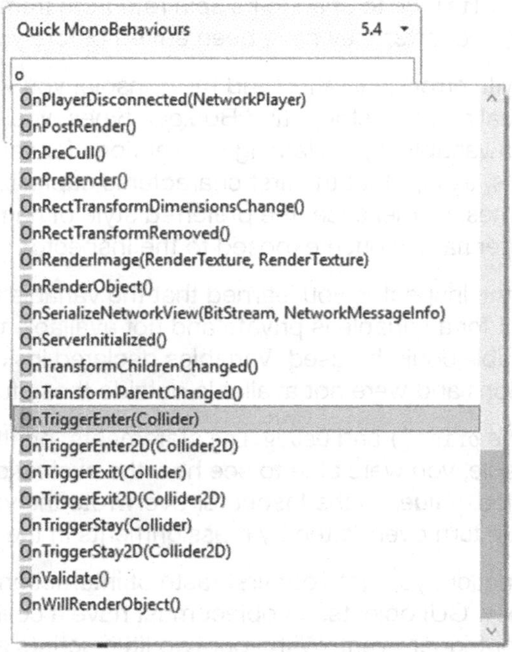

Figure 3-33. Locating the OnTriggerEnter method

This method expects a Collider type argument.

You will eventually be using these two functions quite often, as they are mainstays of interactivity in Unity. They both require a collider, but the first, OnCollisionEnter, is used when something bumps into the collider, and the second, OnTriggerEnter, is used when the object is allowed to pass through the collider so you can trigger an event. The two arguments are optional, and you may not use them for a while, but eventually you will want to retrieve information about the colliding or triggering object. This means you will have to remember which argument belongs with which function. Rather than opening Unity's Scripting Reference and searching for the method you are using, you can quickly find the method you want directly in Visual Studio.

Summary

In this chapter, you got your first introduction to scripting with C# in Unity with the help of a couple of Unity primitives. A script, you discovered, generally consists of functions, variables, and comments in most scripting languages. To author your scripts, you used the MonoDevelop script editor that ships with Unity but is a separate application.

With your first C# script, you learned that the name you give it on creation turns up in the class declaration. The libraries, UnityEngine and System.Collections, as well as the blocked-in Start and Update functions, are automatically added to your new scripts. Syntax is important for the naming and layout of functions, though the location of the curly brackets that encompass the body of the function can vary.

Adding a test script to each of your scene's two objects, you discovered that the scripts became components on the objects. With the first bit of functionality, you got your Cube to spin and then used Time.deltaTime to change its spin rate from frames to seconds. Scripts have to be saved, or *compiled*, after they have been edited before you can see the results.

After a few experiments with error generation and the console, you were introduced to variables. Besides the usual number, string, and Boolean types, you found that almost any script (or class) could be a variable type. Naming conventions for variables were similar to those used for functions, except that the first character is capitalized for functions and lowercase for variable names. Camel case, the preferred style of naming in Unity, translated to more-readable parameter names once exposed to the Inspector.

For a variable to show in the Inspector, you learned that the variable must be marked as public because the default for a variable is private and not available to other scripts. *Scope* in C# limited where a variable could be used. Variables declared inside functions turned out to be *local* to those functions and were not available outside those functions.

With the introduction to the print() and Debug.Log statements, printing variables and messages out to the console, you were able to see how the evaluation and reassignment of variable values was handled. Values in the Inspector overwrote the variable assignments in the declaration, but were in turn overwritten by reassignments in the Start function.

Using the OnMouseDown function, you got your first taste of interaction and learned that, with the exception of Unity's new GUI objects, an object must have a collider component to register a pick, collision, or trigger event. With your two little scripts and two simple scene objects, you got a first look at using conditionals to drive the results of the interaction. Finally, you had a quick peek at looping code and then made your first user-defined function and called its functionality from a different object.

In the last section, you took a first look at some extremely useful tools implemented in Visual Studio with the installation of Visual Tools for Unity.

Chapter 4

Importing Assets

Although Unity has several primitive objects, and others can be generated at runtime, unless your game tends toward the minimalistic, you will have to deal with imported assets. *Art assets* can be anything from textures and sound clips to fully rigged and animated characters or mechanical devices. The settings you choose for importing those assets will be determined by their use in the game. For mobile devices, where efficiency is extremely important, you need to be especially careful when selecting your import options.

Unity's import functionality varies according to the type of assets you are bringing into your project. Audio files are fairly straightforward, with a minimal number of choices. Textures can be used on meshes, sprites, and GUI objects and have a large number of parameters and setup options depending on intended use. 3D mesh objects are by far the most complicated, as they can come with animations and may require colliders. Even more challenging are animated characters with skinned meshes. Let's begin with the 3D assets.

Importing 3D Objects

3D mesh assets are generally the building blocks of a 3D game environment. While the terrain is usually built using Unity's terrain creation system, the remainder of the 3D assets will have to be imported. *Static* meshes can be objects such as buildings and other "permanent" objects. Objects that may animate or be moved around in the scene are often referred to as *props*, a term from film and theater for anything movable or portable. Obviously, just because an object is small doesn't mean that it will ever do anything or go anywhere, so props can also be static. The other major asset type in many games, 2D or 3D, is a *character*. Characters can range from humanoid to amorphous blobs. Assets *not* imported from digital content creation (DCC) programs tend to be particle systems for special effects, simple cloth objects, and terrains. The two latter types may be imported if they have complexity beyond the game engine's creation editors.

© Sue Blackman and Adam Tuliper 2016
S. Blackman and A. Tuliper, *Learn Unity for Windows 10 Game Development*,
DOI 10.1007/978-1-4302-6757-7_4

Supported 3D Mesh Formats

Unity supports several formats from most of the popular modeling applications. You can use two main types of files. The first are open source or at least open format types such as .fbx, .obj, .dxf, and .dae (COLLADA). These are file types that you would use to export assets from your modeling application. Unity can also read in proprietary file types such as 3ds Max, Maya, Blender, Modo, CINEMA 4D, LightWave 3D, and Cheetah3D. Whatever file types you use to import your 3D assets into Unity, they are internally converted to the .fbx format for use in the game. There are pros and cons associated with both file types. The generic types tend to be much smaller, as they save only essential information. Proprietary files, besides being larger, often require the authoring application to be installed and licensed on the machine where you are using Unity.

If you are a 3D artist and plan to sell your work on Unity's Asset Store, or are distributing files for learning material, you will want to export your files as .fbx so they can be used by everyone. If you are in a studio situation, and are using versioning software such SVN or Git, you may want to save the files directly into your project. Once they have been loaded into your project, they are converted internally for use, but remain editable directly from your DCC application. Without versioning software, you would have to overwrite your files, thereby abandoning earlier versions that you may want to return to.

Importing the 3D Assets

There are a few ways to bring art assets into your Unity Project for the first time. The most important concept to understand is that after these assets have been added to the project, they should not be moved around the Project view outside Unity, unless the meta files generated by Unity to keep track of the assets are moved at the same time. Let's do a few tests:

1. Create a new Unity project and name it **Import Test**.

2. Switch to the Default layout.

3. Locate the project/folder in the Explorer (Windows) or the Finder (Mac). See Figure 4-1.

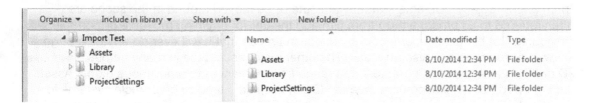

Figure 4-1. The project/folder in Windows Explorer

4. Open the Import Test folder until you can see the Assets folder.

5. From the Chapter 4 Assets folder, copy the Misc Textures folder and paste it into the Assets folder in the Explorer or Finder.

6. Switch the focus to Unity and inspect the Project view.

7. Select the Misc Textures folder.

    The new folder appears in the Project view (Figure 4-2).

Figure 4-2. The Misc Textures folder brought into the project

Dragging folders into the Assets folder through your OS's file hierarchy is the quickest way to bring multiple files, preorganized or not, into Unity. It also gives you the option to replaces files.

8. From the Chapter 4 Assets ➤ Misc Textures folder, drag the BambooFence.tiff image file into the new Misc Textures folder *inside* the Unity editor.

    When you drag the file in, it is automatically renamed BambooFence 1.

9. Delete the duplicate.

    This time, you will drag the image file into the same folder through the Explorer or Finder.

10. From the Chapter 4 Assets ➤ Misc Textures folder, copy the BambooFence image file and paste it into the project's Misc Assets ➤ Misc Textures folder.

    This time, the operating system asks if you wish to Copy and Replace, Don't Copy, or rename the copy (Figure 4-3).

Figure 4-3. *The options available when copying an existing asset into the project via Windows Explorer*

11. Select Copy and Replace.

For singular files, you can also use Import Asset:

1. In Unity, select the Assets folder.

2. Right-click and from the Create submenu, select Folder. Name it **3D Assets**.

3. From the right-click menu, select Import New Asset. From the Chapter 4 Assets ➤ Extra Assets folder, choose the Sugar Sack.fbx file.

    The file is imported into the project, into the selected folder (Figure 4-4).

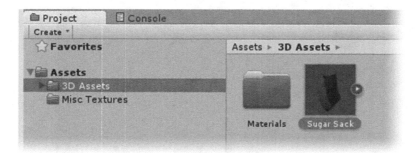

Figure 4-4. Importing the SugarSack.fbx file into the project by using Import New Asset

Another consideration when importing assets is to make sure the textures are imported before the 3D meshes. Theoretically, bringing them in at the same time should be sufficient, but to make *sure* the textures are found and materials generated for them, it is safer to bring the textures in first. If the texture is not found, you can add the proper texture manually, but each time you reimport the mesh object to update it, you will have to reassign the texture.

4. With the 3D Assets folder selected, use Import New Asset to import the DuckInflatable.fbx file from the Chapter 4 Assets ➤ Extra Assets folder.

5. Select the file and inspect its material at the bottom of the Inspector.

    The material has no texture (Figure 4-5).

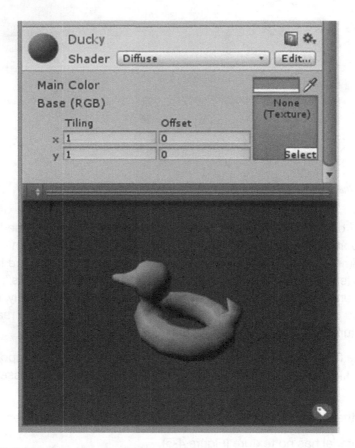

Figure 4-5. The DuckInflatable model imported before its texture

6. Import its texture, Ducky.tiff, into the project's Misc Textures folder.

7. Select the Ducky material from the Materials folder that was automatically generated when you imported the DuckInflatable.fbx file.

8. Click the Misc Textures folder, and then drag the Ducky texture onto the Ducky material's texture swatch.

    When an object is imported, its diffuse color is imported into the Main Color field and blended with the texture. This file was created in 3ds Max, where a texture fully overrides the diffuse color, so you will want to set it to white.

9. Set the material's Basic Color to white.

    The material is updated to include its texture (Figure 4-6).

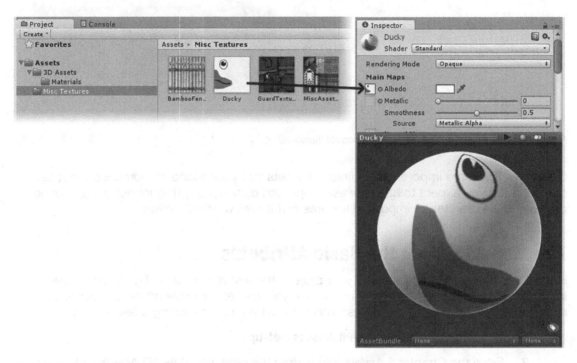

Figure 4-6. Dragging the Ducky texture into the Ducky material's texture slot

10. Reimport the DuckInflatable model via the OS and tell it to overwrite.

11. Check the asset in the Project view.

    With the correct texture loaded into the material, the reimported object shows correctly, but its thumbnail generated on the first import is not updated to include the texture.

12. This time, drag the DuckInflatable asset directly into the Project view.

    The name is appended, and the thumbnail reflects the corrected material (Figure 4-7).

Figure 4-7. The second import generating a correct thumbnail

Obviously, if you are importing fully finished assets into your scene, the process is not as crucial, but if you expect to have the asset updated occasionally throughout the authoring process, the extra step of importing textures first is well worth the effort.

The Model: Setting the Basic Attributes

Having imported the 3D assets into your project, the first place you will go to complete the import process is the Model tab. This is where you will set the scale, material guidelines, mapping options, and a few other essentials. Let's begin by importing a few more assets:

1. Save the scene and name it **Assets Set-up**.

2. From the Chapter 4 Assets folder, drag the *contents* of its 3D Assets folder directly into the existing 3D Assets folder in the Project view.

    Depending on the author of the assets and the application used to create them, the scale of the assets may require adjustment. A *unit* in Unity is considered to be 1 meter. That doesn't mean you *must* use that scale, but a few features, such as physics, are based on the default unit, so it is worth keeping in mind.

    If you are using assets that come from different sources, especially if they were not created specifically for Unity, you may have to adjust the Scale Factor. Often objects may be built to scale, but you have no clue what that scale is until you bring them into the scene. Scale is also relevant to the individual game. Objects are often made larger to draw attention or improve ease of interaction. One means of checking scale is to create an object of known scale to use as a *story pole*.

3. Create a Cube and position it at 0,0,0. A Cube comes in as 1 × 1 × 1 meter.

4. From the 3D Assets folder in the Project view, select the Wooden Barrel asset and drag it into the Scene view, next to the meter-sized Cube, and move both up to ground 0 (Figure 4-8).

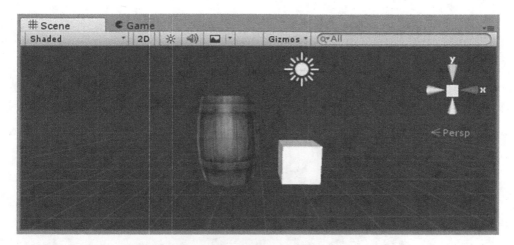

Figure 4-8. The Wooden Barrel in comparison with the meter-sized Cube

The Wooden Barrel appears to be overly large compared to the meter-sized Cube. You could use the object's transforms to scale it down to fit properly, but transforms cost resources, as they have to be calculated every frame. The best practice for both mobile platforms and desktops is to use the Scale Factor option in the Model tab to affect the imported asset rather than changing an instance of it in the scene. A word of caution: always scale characters before setting up their rigging, or you will have to go through the setup process for them again.

5. Select the Wooden Barrel asset in the Project view and, in the Model section, set its Scale Factor to **0.005** (Figure 4-9).

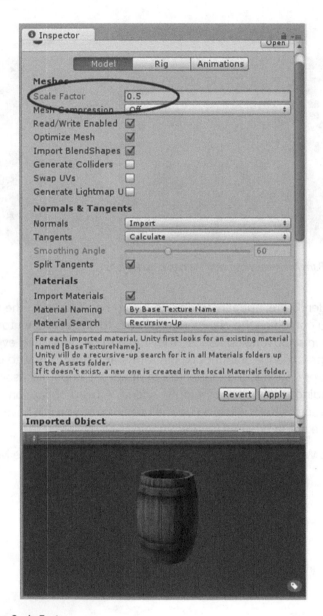

Figure 4-9. *Changing the Scale Factor*

6. Click Apply at the bottom of the import options area. The object's
    scale is updated in the Scene view (Figure 4-10).

Figure 4-10. The barrel asset's Scale Factor is reduced to make the barrel a bit over 1 meter tall

The other important setting in the Model section is Generate Colliders.
You've already experienced the role that colliders play in a 3D scene. They
can be used to block other objects from going through their associated
mesh as well as to trigger an event when intersected. Monitoring colliders
for whatever use can use up a lot of resources. In most cases, you should
manually add Unity's standard colliders, as they are the most efficient. For
more-complicated models, you may even add more than one collider to
approximate the object's shape.

Occasionally, especially when an uneven ground object is involved, you
will have to use a Mesh Collider. Mesh Colliders are the collider type used
when you select Generate Colliders in the Import Settings. Because they
are computationally expensive, you are always better off using multiple
primitive colliders to approximate the object's shape whenever possible.
Additionally, you should never use Mesh Colliders on anything but static
or nonmoving objects, as that would cause a recalculation of the internal
collision tree. Another issue to be aware of is that meshes with too many
triangles may not be able to generate a working Mesh Collider. With that
scenario, you could create a lower-poly version of the object, turn off its
Mesh Renderer, and add the Mesh Collider to it.

7. With the Wooden Barrel asset selected, activate the Generate
    Colliders check box and click Apply.

8. Select the Wooden Barrel in the Hierarchy view.

   The Mesh Collider is generated directly from the barrel's geometry, so you will not see the familiar green collider gizmo (Figure 4-11).

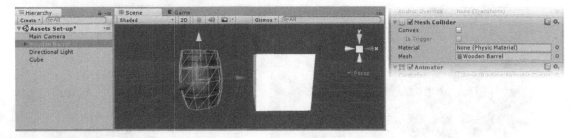

Figure 4-11. The Mesh Collider generated using the object's geometry

If your game involves projectiles that should hit the barrel and ricochet in various directions, then using the Mesh Collider will be a necessity. If the main function is to block player access, a Box Collider will probably be sufficient. If the barrel can be hit and moved by a projectile, a Capsule Collider may be the best choice. In this book's little game, you will use a Box Collider.

9. Select the Wooden Barrel asset in the Project view and deactivate the Generate Colliders check box.

10. Click Apply.

11. From the Component menu, choose Physics, and then add a Box Collider to the Wooden Barrel.

Let's try a more complicated model. If the goal with the little Guard House model was to prevent an object from reaching a corner, one large Box Collider would be perfect. But if the goal was to let an object through its doorway, but not its walls, you would want to use multiple colliders. To add other than Mesh Colliders to an imported asset, you must first add the object to a scene, add the collider or colliders, and then save it as a prefab if you want to reuse it in other scenes. Follow these steps:

1. Select the Guard House asset from the 3D Assets folder.

2. Drag it into the Scene view and then add a Box Collider.

   The object was designed to fit into a 90-degree corner, but rotated into that orientation rather than built into it. It may be easier to set up in an orthographic projection.

3. Set the Guard House's Y Rotation to **-90**.

4. Toggle on the Edit Collider button in the Box Collider component (Figure 4-12).

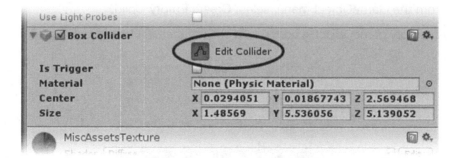

Figure 4-12. Accessing the Edit Collider mode

5. Drag the grips on the collider to size it to fit over the top section of the doorway (Figure 4-13).

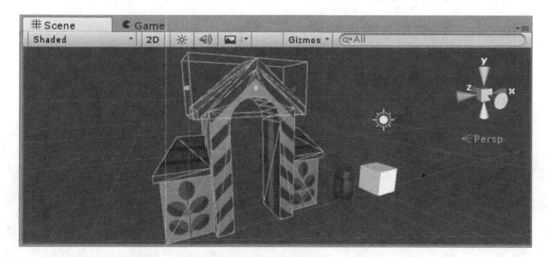

Figure 4-13. Fitting the Box Collider by using the grips

To add more Box Colliders, you have a couple of choices. You can add a child gameObject to the Guard House, or, unlike in earlier versions of Unity, you can now add multiple colliders of the same type to the same objoot. Thc first scenario tends to make setup easier, while the second should be slightly more efficient because there would be less overhead to keep track of.

6. From the GameObject menu, select Create Empty Child.

    An empty gameObject is added as a child of the Guard House (Figure 4-14).

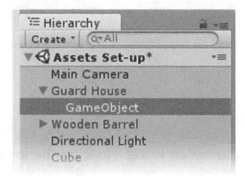

Figure 4-14. The newly created empty child object

7. Name it **Wall Collider** and add a Box Collider to it.

8. Move it roughly into place for the left wall.

9. Toggle the Edit Collider button and drag the grips on the collider to size it to fit the left-side wall (Figure 4-15).

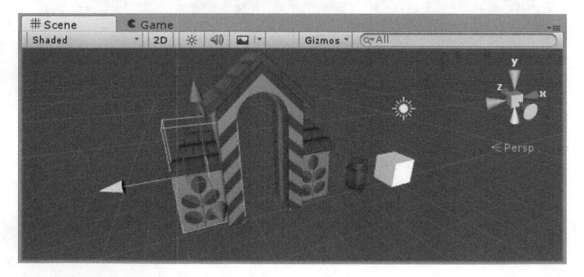

Figure 4-15. The Wall Collider's Box Collider adjusted

10. Duplicate the Wall Collider object and move it over to the right-side wall.

11.   Select the parent, Guard House, to see all the colliders at the same time (Figure 4-16).

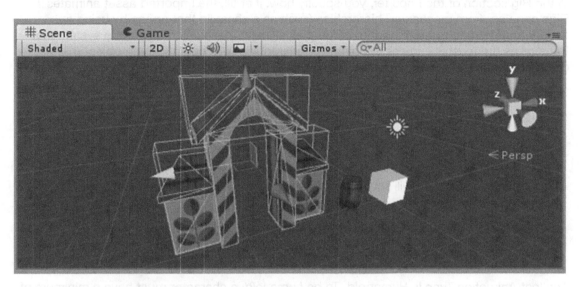

Figure 4-16. The Guard House's colliders

12.   Create a folder in the Project view and name it **Prefabs**.

13.   Drag the Guard House into it to create a prefab of the object with its new features and settings (Figure 4-17).

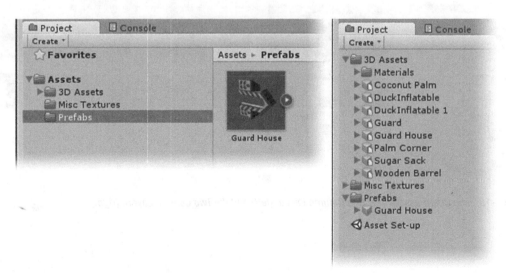

Figure 4-17. The new prefab in the Two Column Layout (left) and the One Column Layout (right)

Note the blue cube icons representing the prefabs in the One Column Layout. This gives you a quick means of differentiating between assets and prefabs.

The Rig Tab: Setting the Animation Type

In the Rig section of the Importer, you specify how, if at all, the imported asset animates. Rigs can vary from mechanical hierarchies (such as a chest lid that opens by using a simple transform to rotate the lid) to a complex skinned mesh (such as a bone system that transforms the mesh's vertices to animate a character). Let's begin with an object that doesn't animate, the Guard House:

1. Select the Guard House asset in the Project view.

2. In the Rig section, set Animation Type to None and click Apply.

3. Repeat for the Coconut Palm and Sugar Sack.

   The Wooden Barrel has a small animation. Because it is not even remotely humanoid, you will set its Animation Type to Generic. The Legacy type is kept only for backward compatibility.

4. Select the Wooden Barrel asset and check its Animation Type. It is set to Generic, as there are only two objects in its hierarchy, so it is good as is.

The last Animation Type is Humanoid. To be *humanoid*, a character must have a minimum of 11 bones that are roughly human-like in configuration. Let's set up the Guard character next:

1. From the 3D Assets folder, select the Guard asset.

2. Check out the contents of the Guard asset (Figure 4-18).

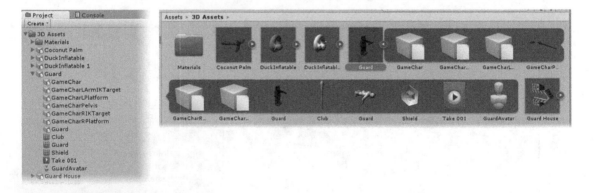

Figure 4-18. The Guard asset in the One Column Layout (left) and the Two Column Layout (right)

3. Drag him into the Scene view and assess his scale by using a Front iso view (Figure 4-19).

Figure 4-19. The Guard in the Scene view

You can set up an imported character without first checking on it in the scene. However, if the Scale Factor must be adjusted, you may have to redo some of the setup, so it is important to always check the scale first. For the book's game project, this character should be about 1.5 meters tall.

4. In the Model section, set the Guard asset's Scale Factor to **0.0075** and click Apply.

The Guard is scaled in the Scene view (Figure 4-20).

Figure 4-20. The Guard scaled in the Scene view

The preview in the Inspector, however, updates only the bones' scale, not their positions, so the character appears to have lost quite a bit of weight (Figure 4-21, right). The preview will have updated fully the next time you select the asset.

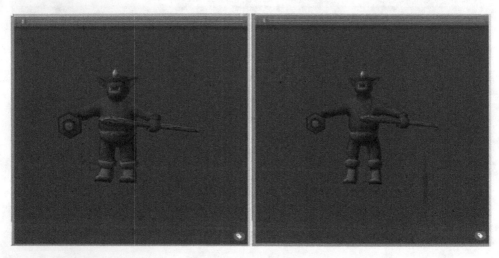

Figure 4-21. The Guard as imported (left) and not fully updated after the scale to a smaller size (right)

5. In the Rig section, select Humanoid and click Apply.

6. Under Avatar Definition, use Create From This Model. The other option is for multiple characters that are similar enough to share the same rig.

Having selected Humanoid, you must now configure the character—that is, make sure his bone system is set up so that you can use preset animations and behaviors that can map to the correct bones. This is one of the two major components of Unity's Mecanim animation system. Created originally for bipedal humanoid characters, Mecanim gives you settings and controls to mix and match characters and animations from different sources. You can, for instance, use the walk and run behaviors from a tall, skinny humanoid to animate a short, stocky character. The transforms that go with the gait can be baked into the animation or can be generated through scripting. More simply put, the character may have been animated moving along with the gait, or may have been animated in place, as if walking on a treadmill. The caveat to the interchangeable animation functionality is that all of the animations must come from the same build of character—because the scene character is adjusted globally to match the animations, not on a per animation basis. Basically, this means that you will not be able to use the walk sequence from a tall, skinny character and the run sequence from a short, stocky character.

The Guard character has his own animations, so his rig will be quick to set up.

7.   In the Rig section, click the Configure button (Figure 4-22).

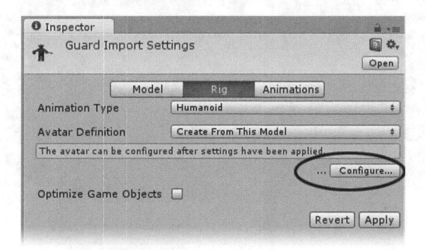

Figure 4-22. The Configure button in the Rig section

8.   Save the scene at the dialog box if you haven't done so recently.

Mecanim commandeers the Scene view as part of its setup procedure.

The Mapping panel shows a humanoid template, and the character and the bones are shown in the Scene view (Figure 4-23). Bones are automatically assigned, using both the bone names from the imported asset and their position in the hierarchy. Green indicates a successful assignment, and red indicates places where Mecanim was unable to find the bone in question. You can select and drag the correct bone from either the Scene or Hierarchy views and drop it onto either the correct location on the template humanoid or directly into the list.

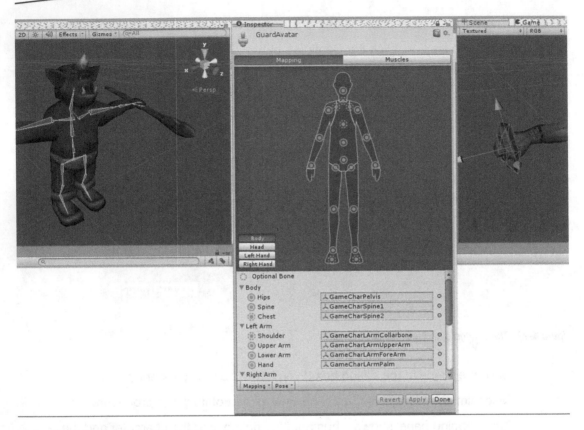

Figure 4-23. Configuring the character

With this character, the ribcage was used for a lot of the animation, but Mecanim doesn't recognize that bone and uses the top spine object for its Chest assignment. Although it may seem logical to reassign the ribcage as the chest, it's usually safer to go with Mecanim's choice. The ribcage bones show as gray, or unassigned, in the Scene view.

A warning appears, informing you of the differences (Figure 4-24). You can ignore the warning for this character.

△ MuscleClip 'Guard' conversion warning: 'GameCharPelvis/GameCharSpine1/GameCharSpine2/GameCharRibcage'
is between humanoid transforms and has rotation animation. This might lower retargeting quality.

Figure 4-24. The conversion warning

At the bottom of the panel, you will see drop-down menus for Mapping and Pose. The options contained within each may help you when a character doesn't import correctly. Note that the character is shown in classic T-pose in the Scene view. The T-pose is used to generate the mapping of bones to your character.

When the mapping is done, you can select the Muscles tab. Here you can test the rigging to see how well it holds up under extreme poses (the top section) or fine-tune it to fit the generic animations to your character's body type. With a fat character, for example, you would restrict the arm's range to prevent it from going through the character's body. Mecanim, when using various animations on the character, would restrict the rotation accordingly.

9. At the top of the Muscles section, move the sliders to see how well the Guard holds up to the various pose extremes (Figure 4-25).

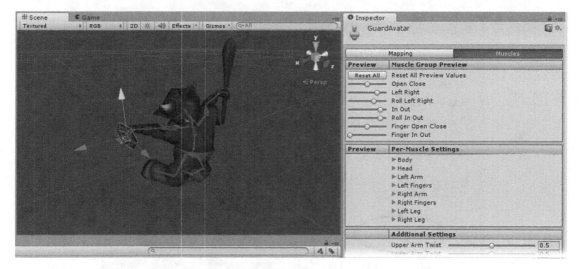

Figure 4-25. Testing the muscle assignments: contortion tests

10. This character doesn't have any special requirements, so you can return to the regular Importer. Click Done.

    The regular Scene view returns.

The Animations Tab: Setting Up the Animation Clips

The third section of the Importer is the Animations section. This is where you set up the animations that came in with your assets, if any. Follow these steps:

1.   Select the Guard House asset and click the Animations button.

     The Inspector shows that no animations are associated with this asset. If there were and you were not planning on using them, you would want to activate the Don't Import Animations check box.

2.   Select the Wooden Barrel asset.

     Under Clips, the imported Take 001 is highlighted.

3.   Below the Clip box, next to the animation clip icon, rename the clip to **Lid Open** (Figure 4-26).

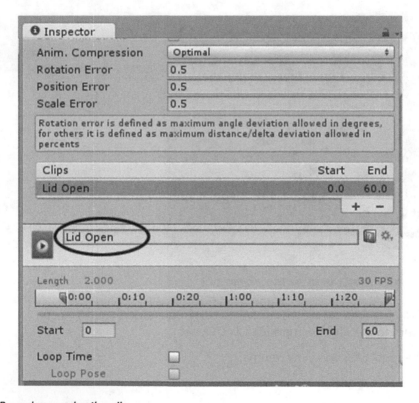

Figure 4-26. Renaming an animation clip

4.   Click the Play button in the Preview window to watch the animation. The animation shows the lid opening and closing.

     To reverse the animation clip, you can set its speed to a negative number, so there is no need to make a close animation unless you want it to behave differently than the reversed version of the open animation.

Depending on the authoring application, the assets will probably show a single animation with the default name Take 001. Best practice is to give your animation clips a meaningful name. Characters especially tend to have idle, walk, and run animations, so you will want to be able to differentiate between them.

The timeline is where you can break your clips into separate behaviors. The lid goes up over 30 frames and goes down over the last 30 frames. Note that the importer knows how many frames per second were used to generate the clip, so you needn't worry about its application of origin.

5. Set the Lid Open's End to **30** below the timeline.

6. Click the Play button in the Preview window at the bottom of the Inspector to see the animation. The preview loops through the frames for the specified clip.

7. Click the plus icon at the bottom of the Clips box to create a new clip.

8. Name it **Lid Close** and set its Start to **31** and its End to **60**.

9. Click Apply.

10. In the Project view, open the Wooden Barrel asset and check out the new clips (Figure 4-27).

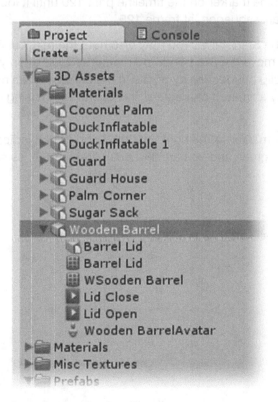

Figure 4-27. The Wooden Barrel asset's new animation clips

You may also notice the little torso icon. When an asset has animations, an Avatar is created. It represents the Mecanim animation system.

Let's set up the character next. When using the Humanoid Animation Type, you have more options in setting up the clips. The steps are as follows:

1. Select the Guard asset.

2. In the Animation section, rename Take 001 to **Guard Idle**.

3. Set its End to **120**.

   Many of the animations or behaviors that belong to characters should be looped.

4. Just below the Start field, activate the Loop Time check box.

5. Click Play in the Preview window to see the idle animation.

   If the animation doesn't quite loop cleanly, you can activate the Loop Pose check box and let Mecanim blend the bone locations to make them meet up. As long as the animation was meant to loop, it does a nice job; if not, it will probably cause more harm than good.

6. Click the plus sign to create a new clip and name it **Guard Walk**.

7. Drag the left-side marker on the timeline past 120 until it looks like he is fully in a walk sequence, at frame **125**.

   This will set the Start value. You may also note the mini curve that shows up when you move the Start and End markers. Quite often you will be able to judge the clip boundaries by peaks in the curves. While not crucial in conventionally animated characters, it is useful when using motion-capture (mo-cap) files.

8. Drag the right marker to the right until the Loop Match indicator goes from yellow to green and you are at a peak (frame **160**), as shown in Figure 4-28.

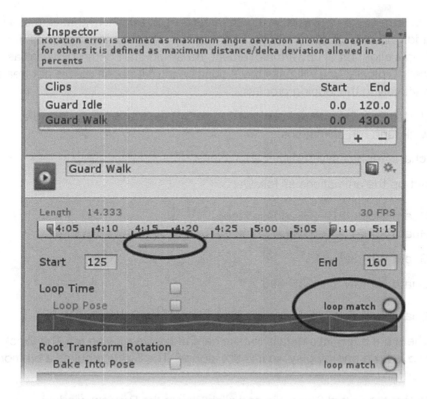

Figure 4-28. Finding the loop points for the walk sequence on the timeline

Walk sequences may be as short as a stride for each leg or may have three or more loops to introduce a bit of variation. This character uses a single repeat for his walk. The next behavior, the run sequence, has two. To conserve resources during runtime, let's use only one. Typically, you will want to find the best one.

9. Create a new clip for the run sequence and name it **Guard Run**.

10. Set its Start to **165** and its End to **205**.

11. Adjust the zoom bar to fit the range.

12. Drag the End time indicator back to frame **185** (the location of the last peak). The Loop Match indicator turns green.

13. Activate the Loop Time check box.

    The last option you will want to utilize is the Bake Into Pose option for the Root Transform Position (Y). Not only has this character been animated for a walk pose, but his root transform has also been animated so that he moves forward as he walks. If he had been animated walking in place, you would have to move him though scripting. When a character has been animated going forward, there is a possibility that a small amount of upward movement exists. Because the animations loop relatively (that is, they are additive), the character continues to move forward as the clip loops. If there was a slight bit of upward movement, he would start drifting upward as well. Typically, you will bake the Y position into the pose so it is not treated relatively in the looping process.

14. Under Root Transform Position (Y), select Bake Into Pose for the idle, walk, and run animations.

The Guard character has several other animations.

1. Set up the animations as follows:

     Guard Block, 210–268, doesn't loop
     Guard Strafe, 272–312

     Guard WIP, 325–345

     Guard Narrow Idle, 355–395

     Guard Jump, 400–425, doesn't loop, do not use Bake Into Pose

     There are a few little details to take care of before moving on. The Block clip is for a one-off play, so it is not looped. The Strafe requires a bit more work.

2. Select the Guard Strafe clip and click Play in the Preview window. The character carefully side-steps, but his right wrist snaps at the loop point.

3. Select the Loop Pose option to blend the positions better.

     To get the strafe right, you can use a negative speed. For animations that require a *mirrored* movement, there is a Mirror option, just above the velocity values.

     The walk-in-place (WIP) is typically used when turning a character whose regular walk includes the forward movement.

     The Narrow Idle can be used to fit the guard inside the Guard House, as he is awaiting some action.

     The Jump can help you understand what the Bake Into Pose option does.

4. Select the Guard Jump clip.

5. In the Preview window, toggle on the Pivot/Mass gizmo.

6. Click Play in the Preview window and watch as the gizmo moves up and down as the character jumps.

7. Turn on Bake Into Pose for Root Transform (Y).

    This time, the gizmo stays on the ground as the character jumps up and down. The important thing to note is that if the character is given a collider, it would stay with the ground instead of going up with the character (Figure 4-29). In normal situations, you want the collider to move with the character, so you usually do not use Bake Into Pose for jump clips.

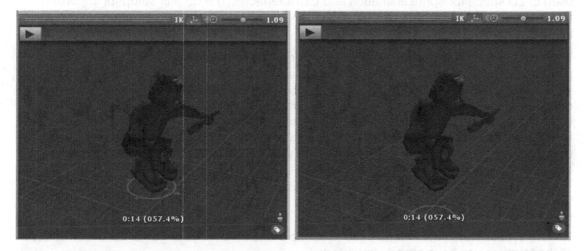

Figure 4-29. Without Bake Into Pose (left) and with Bake Into Pose (right)

8. Turn off Bake Into Pose for Root Transform (Y).

    As a final bit of information on animation clips and Mecanim, you may have noticed that there are a few spare keys between each behavior, where the character returns to its starting location and neutral pose. It is especially important to return the character to its former pose after the animation transforms his position.

9. Add one last clip and leave it at the full frame number.

    At frame 430, the character is in his full start configuration and location. This is the pose he will have in the scene before Play mode and the one where you will be adding his collider(s). If his last animation was a run, his mesh would be off in the distance, and you would be left to guess where the collider would have to be positioned and sized.

10. Click Apply to accept all of the Guard's clip animations.

You will have a chance to experiment with controlling the character in Chapter 11.

Importing Image Assets

Textures are an important part of enriching the player's enjoyment of your game. Through style and color palettes, textures can provide continuity and mood. They can also be your game's downfall, especially for mobile platforms, if not managed well. There are a lot of considerations to keep in mind when using textures.

There are two basic types of textures: those that are used on 3D models and those that are used in 2D space for sprite animation and GUI interfaces. The default setup for imported textures depends on whether you specified a 3D or 2D game when you created your project. So far, your textures are all for 3D objects.

The textures themselves normally have three or four channels. Red, green, and blue (RGB) are the standard channels for an 8-bit texture, and each channel has a range of 0 to 255 (256 shades). At a value of 128, the color is fully saturated. A value of 0 is black, and a value of 255 is white. The fourth channel, the alpha channel, is also 8 bits, but goes from black to white only. Traditionally, the alpha channel is used to determine transparency, where 0 (black) is fully transparent and 255 (white) is fully opaque. In Unity, the alpha channel is quite often used for purposes other than transparency, as you will see in the "Working with Materials and Shaders" section later in this chapter.

Setting the Texture Type

Texture Type dictates the default used to set up the texture for your game. Let's look at a few of the textures you have already imported:

1. From the Misc Textures folder, select the BambooFence texture.

2. Click the Texture Type drop-down list to see the choices (Figure 4-30).

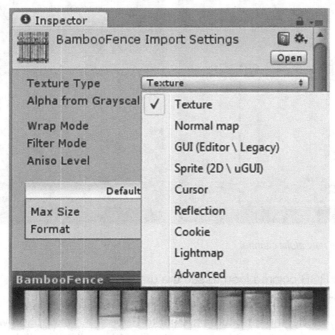

Figure 4-30. The Texture Type options for imported textures

The textures earmarked for 3D games come in as Texture. The BambooFence texture does not have an alpha channel, but you could have one automatically generated for it.

> **Note** In Unity 5.5, "Texture" has been renamed to "Default".

3. Activate the Alpha from Grayscale check box and then click Apply. A new icon appears in the Preview window's title bar (Figure 4-31, left).

> **Note** In Unity 5.5, Alpha from Grayscale can be found in the Alpha Source drop-down.

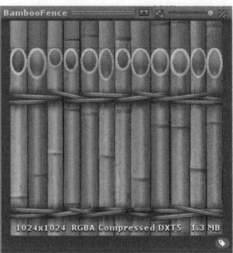

Figure 4-31. Viewing the new alpha channel

4. Click the RGB colored icon to see the grayscale alpha channel
    (Figure 4-31, right).

    For Wrap Mode, most textures are set to Repeat. An exception would be
    for textures used for cookies, or masks for objects like spotlights, where
    you want to project a single image.

    Filter Mode determines how the texture looks when seen from a distance
    or at sharp angles. Bilinear is usually a good default. Aniso, short for
    Anisotropic, is a filter that helps remove the artifacting (the sparkling effect)
    often seen on ground textures when viewed at oblique angles. Aniso
    filtering is quite costly, in terms of frame rate, so use it sparingly.

    Closely tied to filters is *MIP mapping*. In this process, smaller, blurrier
    textures are substituted as the texture recedes farther back in the
    3D world's environment. The concept is simple if you think about a
    checkerboard texture. As you view the texture from the front in the
    viewport, it covers a fixed number of pixels. As it recedes, you will hit the
    "sweet spot," where the numbers of pixels the texture covers comes out
    evenly for the two colors, but eventually, the game engine will have to make
    arbitrary choices about which color to draw. As the texture recedes, the
    color choice has no way to remain consistent, and the texture appears to
    sparkle. To avoid this artifacting, textures are MIP mapped. A series of base
    2–sized textures is made for the image (Figure 4-32).

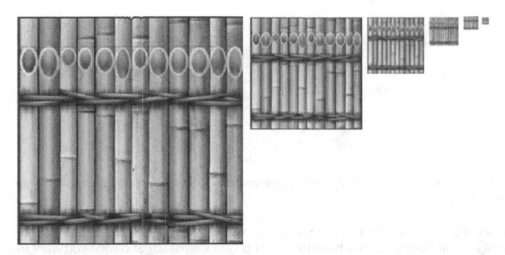

Figure 4-32. A few of the 512 sized image's MIP maps, from left to right, 256, 128, 64, 32, 16, and 8

The next option is for size. In the Preview window, you can see that the current size of the texture is 1024 × 1024 pixels. The size (in memory) is 1.3 MB. Both numbers are overkill for mobile devices, unless the texture will be covering a large part of the screen.

5. Set the Max Size drop-down to 512.

    Now the size is reported as 341.4 KB, approximately a quarter of the original. Just for fun, you may want to see how much lower it will be without the added alpha channel.

6. Deactivate the Alpha from Grayscale check box and click Apply. The size drops to 170.7 KB.

    The savings from 1.3 MB to 170.7 KB is substantial when you are dealing with limited memory. The original format of the texture asset makes no difference. On import, textures are converted to .dds format, using the most logical compression type in this case, DXT1. This means you can use image formats such as .psd with their layers intact and update or tweak them at will.

Depending on the platform you are authoring on, you also have the option to override the Max Size and Format options, based on the *target device* for the individual texture (Figure 4-33).

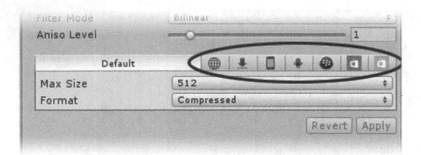

Figure 4-33.   Override choices: for Web, stand-alone (desktop), iPhone, Android, BlackBerry, Windows Store apps, and Windows Phone 8

Be aware that only tabs for installed platform modules will appear as options. For both devices and platforms, you will have to decide on the lowest target device you want to support and then research its capabilities. A good place to start is the Unity docs, where you will find guidelines for each platform.

Exploring Texture Dimensions

You may have noticed that the texture sizes offered are limited. Even if you are completely new to real-time engines, you've probably heard by now that textures should be in base-2 size. And if math isn't too far in your past, you may even remember that *base 2* means the numbers are derived by multiplying the previous number by 2. The "magic" numbers are 2, 4, 8, 16, 32, 64, 128, 256, 1024, 2048, and so forth. The reason is that in computers (or other electronic devices), memory blocks come in base 2–sized blocks. If a texture takes up just an extra pixel in the two directions, it jumps memory usage up by a magnitude of 4 (Figure 4-34).

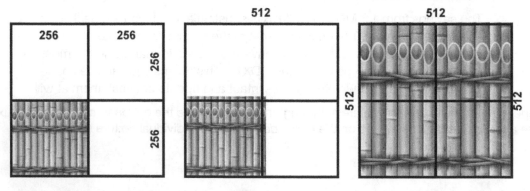

Figure 4-34.   Memory usage for 256 × 256 pixels (left), for 270 × 270 pixels (center), and for 512 × 512 (right)

Having spilled over into the adjacent memory blocks, the middle texture, 270 × 270, takes the same amount of memory as the 512 × 512 image. The other problem is that as a default, the Texture Type, Texture, will scale the image out to fit the full memory size, possibly causing poor image quality. For non-power-of-2 images, you should use the Advanced setting rather than the presets. From there, you can disable the forced power-of-2 setting. While the power-of-2 "rule" is less crucial with modern devices, it is always good practice to keep to it for performance reasons.

Understanding Mapping and Vertex Count

Another topic for economical 3D assets is that of mapping and vertex count. The same object's vertex count can vary substantially, depending on its edge treatments and how an image is mapped to it. This variation is caused by the information stored on each triangle's vertices. Lighting, colors, transparency, and other data can be stored there. If the information can be shared, the vertex can be shared. Part of the resource usage is in transforming and lighting objects—so the fewer vertices to process, the faster your frame rate.

The smallest renderable 3D element is a face, or triangle. It consists of three vertices, the three edges that connect them, and the face that they define (Figure 4-35, left). When vertices are shared between faces, the lighting is averaged between the direction of each face, or the face normal (Figure 4-35, center). When the edge between faces is "hard," the vertex cannot be shared, because each face will have lighting derived from its vertex (Figure 4-35, right). Lighting is calculated by using the angle of incidence between the light source and the vertex normal (Figure 4-36). The smaller the angle of incidence, the more light the vertex receives.

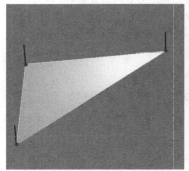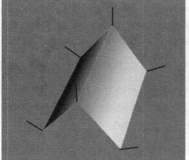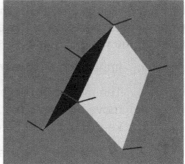

Figure 4-35. Vertex normals on a single face, or triangle (left), being shared or averaged between two quads (center), and not shared (right)

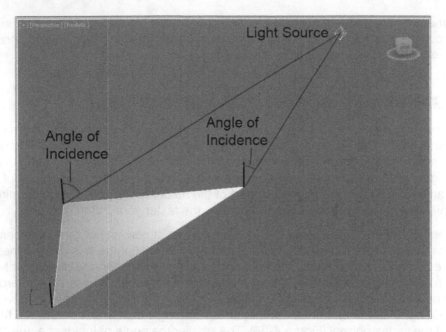

Figure 4-36. The angle of incidence determining the amount of light that a vertex normal receives

Let's use a fairly simple mushroom model as a test case. It was created using a lathe and then bent slightly afterward. The model is reported to have 74 vertices in the application where it was created. For this experiment, it was given several treatments. In Unity, you will see that the vertex count varies for the different configurations.

1. Import the Mushroom.unity package into the project.

    The mushroom assets come into the project at the root level. Feel free to move them into the 3D Assets folder with the rest of the imported assets to keep the project better organized.

2. In the Project view, select each mushroom mesh and note its triangles (tris) count.

In Figure 4-37, you see the mushroom model showing its geometry and two textures mapped onto three of the examples.

Figure 4-37. The base mushroom geometry and two of the textures used

Figure 4-38 describes the treatments and shows the vertex count for each after being imported into Unity.

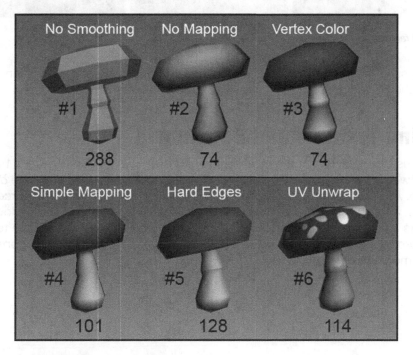

Figure 4-38. Several configurations of the mushroom model

For #1, there are no shared vertices; each triangle has its own set of vertices. With #2, all vertices are able to be shared, so the count is the lowest possible for the model. #3 has color added to the vertices, so the vertex count remains the same. To see this mushroom's vertex color, you would have to add it as a terrain Detail Mesh or find a shader that uses vertex color. The lower row of mushrooms in Figure 4-38 all use textures and have mapping coordinates. They are mapped as shown in Figure 4-39. Mushroom #4 uses 3d Max's default mapping for lathes, in which the top and bottom vertices are separated to prevent texture stretching (Figure 4-39, A). Because the texture is a simple gradient, it *could* have used mapping as in Figure 4-39, B, and would have dropped 14 vertices (two rows of 8 are collapsed to 1 vertex each). In # 5, mapping B was used, but adding hard edges forced extra vertices to allow for the lighting. Mushroom #6 uses a traditional *unwrap*: different parts of the mesh are laid out for minimal distortion and optimum layout. It comes in at 114. The downside of numbers 4–6, of course, is that their textures will take up memory.

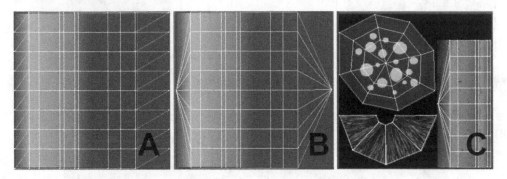

Figure 4-39. Three mapping layouts

As you have seen, economy and visual appeal usually have trade-offs, but as long as you understand the deciding factors, you should be able to make informed choices.

Managing Textures and Batching

In the previous example, two of the mushrooms had their own unique texture. If both mushrooms were in the scene and visible, Unity would have to make a separate *draw call* for each one. As you have probably guessed, draw calls cost resources. Resources equate to frame rate, and in mobile applications, battery usage. To economize, Unity allows you to *batch* objects by using the same material for multiple objects. To do so, first the textures are usually *atlased* together onto one texture sheet. Several of the objects you imported earlier share the same texture (Figure 4-40).

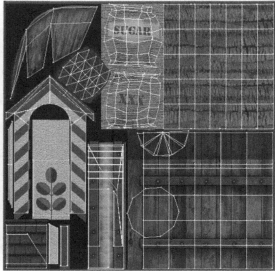

Figure 4-40. *The MiscAssets texture sheet*

This image contains the unwrapped textures for the palm tree, barrel, guard house, and sugar sack. The mapping can be seen to the right.

Batching has a few limitations. Besides using the same material, the objects must have fewer than 300 vertices each. Also, stored vertex information is limited to three types. Typically, this is the x, y, and z location; normal (the direction it faces); and UV (its mapping coordinate). This means that each mesh is limited to *900* vertex attributes. If the requirements are met, instead of making separate draw calls for each object at render time, batching can combine them into a single draw call.

Static batching, now available in Unity's Personal edition, is significantly more efficient, because it can batch objects of any size as long as they are marked as static and share the same material. Typically, objects that do not animate or move are marked as Static and can be batched. With the Asset Set-up scene loaded, drag the Coconut Palm and Sugar Sack into the scene and arrange them so that each can be seen (Figure 4-41).

Figure 4-41. The miscellaneous assets visible in the scene

When checking on draw calls, you must have the objects in question within the viewing frustum (the bounds of the screen) and at least partially visible:

1. Select the camera from the GameObject menu and then choose Align with View.

2. Add a Directional Light to the scene.

3. Click Play and then toggle on Stats from the Game view's toolbar (Figure 4-42).

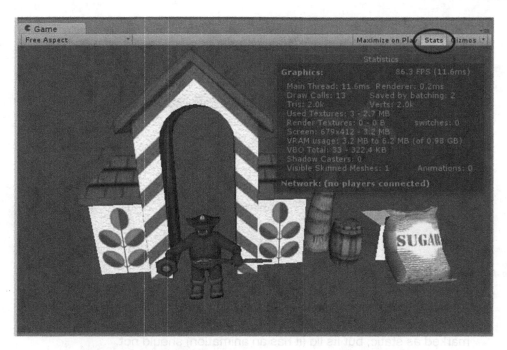

Figure 4-42. Stats toggled on in the Game view

On the second line, you will see Draw Calls and Saved by Batching. Currently, the stats show 13 draw calls and 2 saved by batching. A count of the renderable objects turns up 14 (3 for the guard, 2 for the barrel, and 6 for the palm). The 15th is, presumably, for the camera drawing the background. By deactivating the objects one by one, you will find that the two saved draw calls are from the guard's club and one of the tree's fronds.

The Coconut Palm, Guard House, and Sugar Sack all use the same material and do not animate in this test scene, so they are good candidates for batching.

4.   Select the Coconut Palm, Guard House, and Sugar Sack.

5.   At the top right of the Inspector, select the Static check box (Figure 4-43).

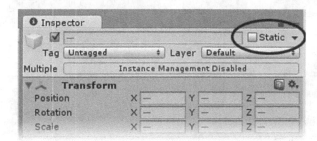

Figure 4-43. The Static check box in the Inspector

6. Click Yes, Change Children in the dialog box.

7. The Static flag has several individual options. Click the down arrow to see all the features that were marked as static (Figure 4-44).

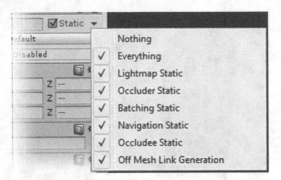

Figure 4-44. The various Static options

A few of the settings that use the Static flag are lightmapping, occlusion culling, batching, and path finding. The Wooden Barrel should also be marked as static, but its lid (it has an animation) should not.

8. Select the Wooden Barrel and mark it as static, but not its children (as the lid has an animation).

9. Click Play, and examine the changes in the Stats dialog box (Figure 4-45).

Figure 4-45. The Stats dialog box after setting several objects to Static

This time, the draw calls drop to 6, and 9 are reported saved by batching. The Cube doesn't share a material with any other objects, but it should be marked as static for several other reasons covered by the flag.

10. Stop Play mode.

11. Set the Cube to Static and click Play. As expected, the Draw Calls number does not change.

12. Stop Play mode.

As a quick recap, there are a few guidelines for successful batching. It is worth keeping them in mind when preparing objects for your scene:

- Objects must share the same material.

- Objects must be marked as Static.

- Vertex attributes must not exceed 900—that is, three attributes per vertex.

- Objects cannot use separate lightmaps. (The extra UV map makes a total of four attributes per vertex, unless you can do away with one of the standard ones.)

- Objects cannot be scaled in the scene. (Nonuniform scale is apparently allowed.)

- Instantiated objects must not use an instanced material (which they do by default).

- Materials used for batched objects must not be altered during runtime, as that will cause another instance of the material to be created and break batching.

Working with Materials and Shaders

In Unity, all materials use *shaders*—the calculations are performed on the GPU (graphics chip) rather than the CPU. As you might expect, the fancier the shader, the more resource-intensive it is. When 3D assets are imported into Unity, a material is generated by using the default Standard shader. The Standard shader has several optional parameters and was meant to be used in high-end games and applications where resources are more plentiful and a realistic style is the goal. The shader was designed especially for physically based materials so that the material will look correct in any given lighting and environmental setting. Although it is optimized for runtime, it is an expensive choice for low-end mobile devices on which the mood is more often playful than awe inspiring.

The material generated on import derives its name from the texture unless you change the import settings in the Model section. On import, only a diffuse texture and a lightmap texture (using map channel 2) will automatically be added to the material. The lightmap texture is for the legacy method, but of note is that Unity supports only two map channels.

Investigating the Standard Shader

Let's begin by taking a look at a few of the imported assets' materials:

1. Select the Sugar Sack in the Hierarchy view.

2. Open its Material array to see what material or materials it is using (Figure 4-46).

Figure 4-46. Identifying a material on an asset through its Mesh Renderer component

There are a couple of good reasons that you don't just open the material where it is clearly visible at the bottom of the object's components. The first is that the object must remain selected while you are working on the material. And the second is that opening just the material in the Inspector will give you a preview of it in the Preview window at the bottom of the Inspector.

3. Click the material's name in the Element 1 slot to highlight it in the Project view.

4. Now open the material from the Project view and inspect it.

It uses the MiscAssetsTexture material and is currently set to use the default Standard shader (Figure 4-47). With physically based materials, there are generally two ways to set up your material for realism. The first is by adjusting its *metallic* properties, and the second is by adjusting its *specular* properties. In each method, the other property is automatically set by the other. Preference is generally dictated by the application used to create these physically correct shaders, so Unity also offers a Standard (Specular Setup) shader for those who prefer that method.

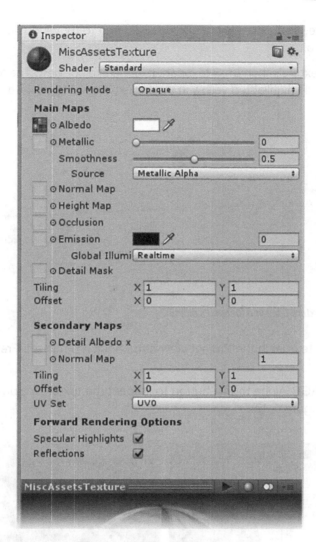

Figure 4-47. The MiscAssetsTexture material using the Standard shader

The material has options for quite a few parameters that can make your materials look extremely attractive. Even with the material optimized for runtime, a lot of the options will be too costly for mobile devices. Let's take a quick look at them anyway. Just as with anything else, economizing in other areas could justify splurging for that one special asset that could make your game a hit.

The first map and color is for Albedo. This is the main color or texture of the material. In other shaders, you will see it called Main Color, Main, or Diffuse. In Unity, material colors, especially for the main color, are additive. That is, the color will be blended (in Photoshop terminology) into the texture, if any, in an additive fashion. White adds nothing, gray darkens a texture, and black overwrites whatever it is added to. In this case, with the Albedo color being white, the texture is not altered. Feel free to try various color tints and observe the result.

5.   Click the texture's thumbnail to locate it in the Project view. The texture is temporarily highlighted yellow in the Project view (Figure 4-48).

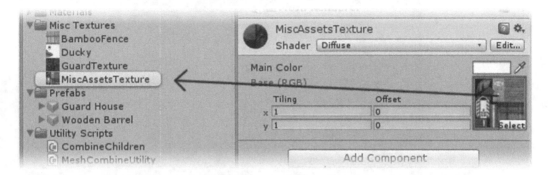

Figure 4-48. *Locating a texture used in a material's shader*

6.   Select the texture in the Project view and check it out in the Preview window.

7.   Click the RGB/Alpha toggle button to inspect the texture's alpha channel (Figure 4-49).

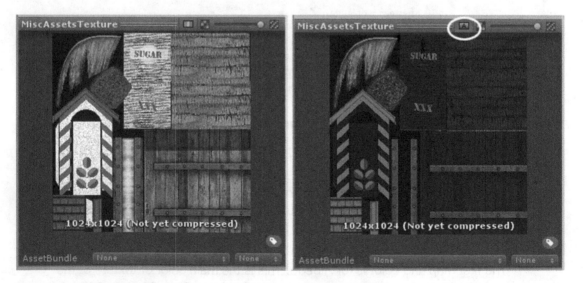

Figure 4-49. *Viewing a texture's alpha channel by toggling the RGB/Alpha button*

You will be using the alpha channel as a glossiness/specular/metalness map. In other words, it will affect the shininess and reflectiveness of the material. In places where the image is white, it will be very shiny; and where it is black, it will have no shininess at all.

8. Select the MiscAssetsTexture material again.

9. Drag the MiscAssetsTexture texture into the Metallic slot (Figure 4-50).

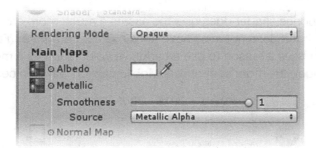

Figure 4-50. The Metalic slot using the alpha channel of the MiscAssetsTexture

As you may have noticed, the Smoothness has been set to 1, very smooth/reflective. The palm fronds and roof tiles are the most obviously affected, with the overhead lighting (Figure 4-51).

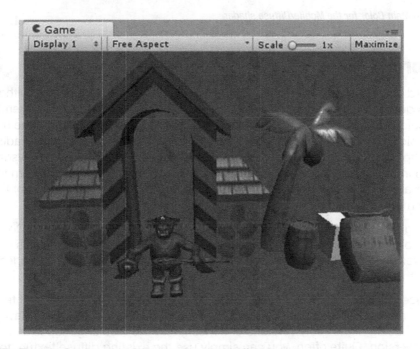

Figure 4-51. The The palm fronds and roof tiles sporting new highlights

Feel free to rotate the Directional Light in the scene on its x axis to see how the red stripes and painted leaves on the Guard Shack react to the light.

Although the Standard shader is tempting, you should become familiar with the shaders designed expressly for mobile devices. They use less resources and so less battery power.

10.   Click the Shader drop-down again, and from the Mobile submenu, select Diffuse.

This bare-bones shader does give the assets a much more casual look and feel. Note that it does not even have a main Color parameter (Figure 4-52). Unless you have a reason to use an additive color (such as a mouse-over color change), the more economical Mobile version will do nicely.

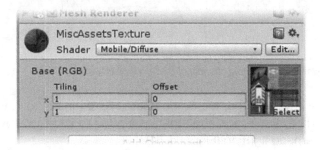

Figure 4-52. No Main Color for the Mobile/Diffuse shader

Using Normal Maps

For the Guard character, you will add a bump. A *bump* adds detail to a mesh without changing its geometry. If you think back on the way an object is lit, you will remember that the light is calculated at each vertex. A *bump map*, or its modern equivalent, the *normal map*, uses color to simulate geometry that doesn't exist. The bump map was traditionally a grayscale map in which white was bumped out and black bumped in. As a grayscale, it was often loaded in the diffuse texture's alpha channel. The *normal map* (*normal* from the vertex normals that are used to calculate lighting) uses color to indicate the direction of the fake normal for a much more accurate result.

You can recognize normal maps by their distinctive cyan and magenta colors. Do be aware that a large normal map adds a lot of extra lighting calculations, as each pixel is treated as if it were a vertex. The savings are in fewer actual vertices on a mesh to be managed. The cost is the space the texture takes up in memory.

Because it uses all three color channels, RGB, the normal map requires its own texture. Normal maps are typically generated in DCC applications (such as 3ds Max, Maya, ZBrush, or Blender) by using higher-poly versions of a mesh, and the resulting map is then applied to a lower-poly version. Quite often, you can simply use the existing diffuse texture to generate a useful normal map. The normal map is derived from its grayscale, where white is bumped out and black is ignored.

While experimenting with the normal map, you will not want the character's mesh edges showing (a third reason to open a material by itself):

1. Select the Guard group, and then select its Guard child object.

2. In its Skinned Mesh Renderer component, open the Materials array and click its Element 0, the repository for the first material used on the object. The material is located and briefly highlighted yellow in the Project view.

3. Select the GuardTexture material.

4. Change its shader to Mobile ➤ Bumped Specular.

5. Click the GuardTexture thumbnail and select it in the Project view.

6. Press Ctrl+D (Cmd+D) to duplicate the texture. Rename it **GuardTextureBmp**.

7. Change its Texture Type to Normal Map and then click Apply.

   With the default settings, the texture map is too detailed to make a nice normal map (Figure 4-53, left). Rather than changing the Filtering from Sharp to Smooth, you can reduce the size of the bitmap, improving the smoothness of the normal map, *and* reducing the number of calculations it requires in the scene as well as the amount of memory and disk space it requires.

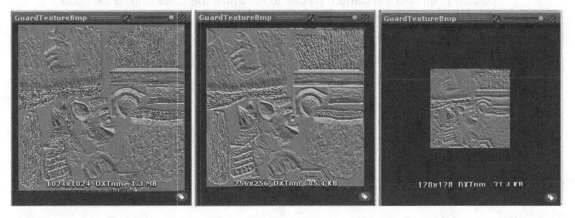

Figure 4-53. The GuardTextureBmp at the original 1024 (left), 256 (center), and 128 (right), where the repurposed map is even smoother

8. For the Default, select 256 as the Max Size and then click Apply.

9. Select the GuardTexture material again.

10. Adjust the Shininess slider until it is near the left side, producing a soft highlight (Figure 4-54, center).

Figure 4-54. *The default Diffuse shader (left), the Specular Bump shader before adding the normal map (center), and after adding the normal map (right)*

11. Drag the new normal map into the NormalMap slot.

    With the addition of the normal map (Figure 4-54, right), you may have noticed seams from the unwrap (Figure 4-55, left). If you plan on generating the normal map directly from the texture map, be sure to add extra "padding" around the pattern pieces to minimize the color difference used to generate the normal map (Figure 4-55, right).

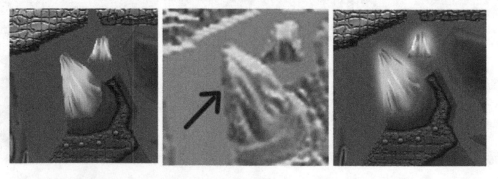

Figure 4-55. *The horn in the original texture (left), the normal map it generates (center), and a method of reducing seams created when the surrounding color contrasts too much (right)*

12. Drag the Guard parent object into the Prefabs folder in the Project view.

Just as with any shader that has multiple features, effects such as specular highlights and bumps can mean extra passes when an object is drawn in the scene. Always weigh the visual impact with the cost in frame rate. Don't be afraid, however, to leave a costly shader in the game. If the game requires "pruning" to improve frame rate further down the production pipeline, you can always revisit your assets and decide what visual candy can be sacrificed.

For now, let's go ahead and prepare a few of the assets you've experimented with for use in the game you'll be making:

1. Focus the Scene view to the Coconut Palm and create a new Empty gameObject.

2. Name it **Tropical Corner**.

3. Drag the Coconut Palm, Sugar Sack, and Wooden Barrel objects into it.

4. Drag the Tropical Corner object into the Prefabs folder.

5. In the Prefabs folder, select the Tropical Corner, the Guard, and the Guard House prefabs.

6. From the right-click menu, select Export Package. The assets and their dependencies are gathered up for inclusion in the package (Figure 4-56).

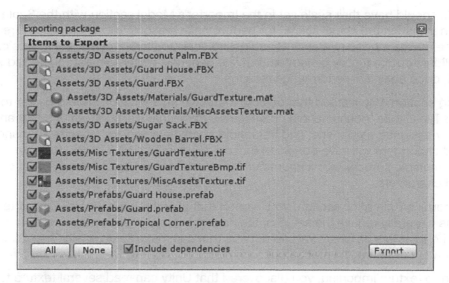

Figure 4-56. The prefabs gathered for export as a Unity package

7. Click Export and save the assets as **CornerObjects.unitypackage** in your Chapter 4 Assets folder.

8. Save the scene and save the project.

You've just created your first Unity package. Be aware that as of this writing, Unity does not yet support prefabs of prefabs, so plan accordingly when creating prefabs for reuse (they will not retain their reference relationship to each other).

Summary

In this chapter, you discovered that assets can be textures, sound clips, 2D textures, or 3D meshes. 2D images can be used as textures for 3D meshes, to create your game's GUI and use as animated sprites. 3D objects may be static or animated and may be as complex as fully rigged and animated characters. You also found that their intended use dictates the import settings for all assets types.

Next you discovered that Unity supports several 3D file types in their native format, but internally, it converts all to .fbx. To ensure that Unity can generate the proper material for your imported 3D asset, you learned that a safe practice is to import the textures into the project before the meshes. All types of assets can be imported by dragging directly into the Project view, copying into the Assets folder via the operating system, or by using the Import Assets option in the right-click menu. The important thing to remember is not to move assets around in the OS unless you are including the metadata files. Importing an updated asset into the project is best done through the OS, where you have the option to overwrite the original.

3D models should have their scale set in the Importer's Model section with the Scale Factor option rather than in the actual scene, for performance reasons. Next, you discovered that a meter cube makes a good reference for adjusting scale to fit your game. 3D assets can have Mesh Colliders automatically generated, but it is generally better to create the colliders from primitives, once again for performance reasons.

For the Rig section, you learned that objects that have no animation should be set to Animation Type None, nonhumanoid characters and mechanical contraptions that animate should stay assigned as Generic, and humanoid characters should be set to Humanoid. Humanoid characters will have bone and muscle assignments so that you can use animation clips from multiple sources. A minimum number of 11 bones is also a requirement for humanoid characters.

In the Importer's Animation section, you learned that objects that have been imported with animations generally require the setup of their animation clips. Clips may or may not loop. Humanoid characters have several clip options that can make setup easier, especially if the animation was created using motion capture.

Moving on to texture importing, you discovered that Unity can read several texture formats, but converts them to .dds format for optimal compression. Textures can be 24 bit or 32 bit, where the extra 8 bits hold an alpha channel. The textures can be given a size cap on a global or a platform-specific basis. To save disk space and memory, you learned that all textures should be sized in multiples of two. Textures used in the scene on 3D assets also have a series of MIP maps automatically generated.

Upon experimenting with materials and shaders, you found that rather than using an 8-bit bump from an alpha channel, Unity uses normal maps. A quick way to create a normal map is to duplicate a regular texture and set its Type to Normal. Because shaders can use the alpha channel for purposes other than transparency, you discovered that Unity can generate an alpha channel from a texture's grayscale version. This alpha version can be used to determine areas of glossiness, where white is fully glossy, and black is ignored, as well as many other useful shader parameters.

By experimenting with 3D assets imported and brought into a test scene, you discovered that objects meeting several requirements (including poly count and a shared material) could be automatically batched to combine several objects into a single draw call, seriously improving the efficiency of your scene.

With all of the various adjustments made to your imported assets, you learned that it was usually a good idea to make prefabs of the assets that had been set up in the Scene view. This enables you to reuse the asset, or group of assets, in multiple scenes. Finally, you created your first Unity package so it could also be used in other packages.

Chapter 5

Prototyping the Navigation

As with any game, it is always a good idea to lock down the basic functionality by using simple proxy objects wherever possible. This helps keep your development time agile, allowing you to adjust your game plan when an idea doesn't pan out. Even with a team of programmers, you can easily hit technical restrictions that will force you to make changes. Game play itself may require extra thought; what looks good on paper doesn't necessarily equate to fun game play. Creating mock-ups with simply geometry allows you to test your ideas without the overhead or commitment of expensive (in time and/or money) art assets.

Understanding the Basics

For this book's project, you will be making a little tip-puzzle game. The concept is simple, but the functionality can be challenging, especially using game physics. The player will rotate or tip a board to move a sphere, or marble, into key positions. This type of input will give you an excellent opportunity to experiment with input from various platforms and devices. To tip the board, you will click and drag the mouse on desktop applications, finger-drag on touch screens (tablet), and even use accelerometers on mobile devices if supported.

Taking the First Steps

To create your mock-up, you will use a few Unity primitives and begin to work out the functionality with your scripts. You will add objects and scripting a little at a time so you are not overwhelmed by the task ahead of you and can spot errors a lot easier. Start with these steps:

1. Create a new project with the defaults set up for 3D and name it **Tiltboard**.

2. Save the default scene as **Board Test**.

3. Create a Cube and name it **Board**.

4. Set its X and Z Scale to **26** and its Y Scale to **0.2**.

© Sue Blackman and Adam Tuliper 2016
S. Blackman and A. Tuliper, *Learn Unity for Windows 10 Game Development*,
DOI 10.1007/978-1-4302-6757-7_5

5.   Add a Directional Light and adjust its rotation until it shines down on the Board at a slight angle.

6.   Switch to 2 × 3 layout and set the Project tab to One Column Layout, if you are not already in it.

7.   Adjust the camera to get a good view of the Board in the Game view (Figure 5-1).

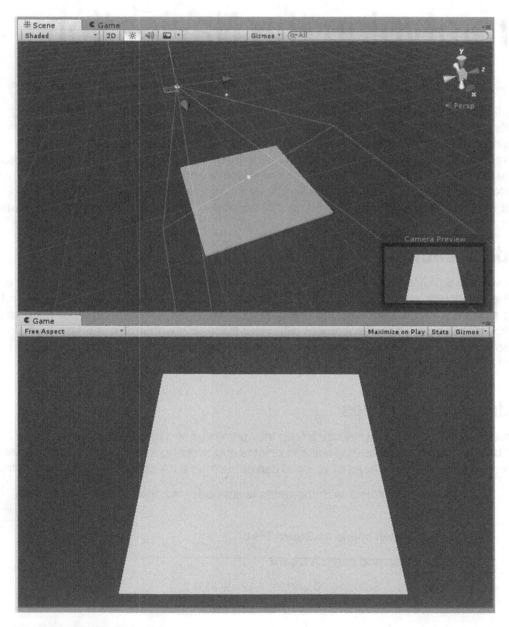

Figure 5-1. The Board in the Game view

Scripting User Interaction

Just as with the old-time handheld games, your player will have to tip the board to get the marble, or ball, to roll in the correct direction. There are several ways to script this behavior.

The logical place to start is with the desktop functionality. A search of the Unity Forums and Unity Answers found several possible solutions, but the following JavaScript code for using a mouse drag to control an object's rotation was one of the simplest. Here is the URL for the code:

http://answers.unity3d.com/questions/386625/rotate-object-following-mouse-movement-object-jump.html?sort=oldest

The code is as follows:

```
private var factor : float = 0.6;
private var v3StartPos : Vector3;
private var v3StartRot : Vector3;

function OnMouseDown(){
    v3StartPos = Input.mousePosition;
    v3StartRot = transform.eulerAngles;
}

function OnMouseDrag(){
    var v3T : Vector3 = Input.mousePosition;
    transform.eulerAngles = v3StartRot + Vector3.up * (v3StartPos - v3T).x * factor;
}
```

Most syntax changes are fairly simple to convert JavaScript to C#. C# is automatically private; the type is first, then the variable name, and then the optional assignment. Floats must have a lowercase f to distinguish them from doubles. The word var is not used. For functions, void (the type returned by the function) is put in front of the name. The word function is not used.

1. From the right-click menu in the Project view, create a new folder and name it **Game Scripts**.

2. Create a new C# script in the Game Scripts folder, and name it **TiltBoard**.

3. Open the script in the script editor and add the following under the class declaration:

```
public float factor = 0.6f; // adjustment
Vector3 v3StartPos; // mouse location
Vector3 v3StartRot; // board orientation
```

4. Add the following below the Update function:

```
void OnMouseDown(){
    v3StartPos = Input.mousePosition; // starting location of the cursor
    v3StartRot = transform.eulerAngles; // current orientation of board
}
```

```
void OnMouseDrag(){
    Vector3 v3T = Input.mousePosition; // get the current cursor position
    transform.eulerAngles = v3StartRot + Vector3.up * (v3StartPos - v3T).x * factor;
}
```

5. Save the script.

6. Drag and drop the script onto the Board object.

7. Click Play, and test by clicking the board and dragging the mouse left
   and then right.

The board rotates on its y axis, Vector3.up. It is using the change (delta) in the cursor's
horizontal, or x, direction as long as the left mouse button is held down.

For the game, the board's orientation will control the marble's movement as it tilts along its
x and y axes. Let's begin by changing the rotation axis in the code. While Vector3.up is easy
to decipher, it gives no clues as to how the other directions can be accessed. For that, you
will take a quick look at the scripting docs:

1. From the Help menu, select Scripting Reference and search for
   Vector3 but do not select it from the list that is generated.

   In the list, you will see that Vector3.up is shorthand for Vector3(0,1,0).
   Vector3.down is shorthand for Vector3(0,-1,0), Vector3.forward is
   Vector3(0,0,1), Vector3.backward is Vector3(0,0,-1), Vector3.left is
   Vector3(1,0,0), and Vector3.right is Vector3(0,0,-1). By now you've
   probably guessed that Vector3.up = Vector3.down. This allows you to use
   the delta of the x, y, and z values whether they are positive or negative.
   Armed with this information, you will change the code to tilt the Board on
   its x axis using Vector3.left.

2. Exit Play mode.

3. In the OnMouseDrag function, change the Vector3.up to Vector3.left
   as follows:

```
transform.eulerAngles = v3StartRot + Vector3.left * (v3StartPos - v3T).x * factor;
```

4. Save the script, click Play, and test, remembering to move the mouse
   left and right.

   The board rotates along the x axis, which makes it tip in the z direction. It
   might be more intuitive if the mouse vertical movement (y) tips the board on
   its x axis.

5. Exit Play mode.

6. Change the rotation line as follows:

```
transform.eulerAngles = v3StartRot + Vector3.left * (v3StartPos - v3T).y * factor;
```

7. Save the script and test the adjustments.

   This time, the cursor and the board seem more in sync. The problem now is that you also require the board to move in the other direction as well. The code is adding the adjustment for the one axis to the current orientation, so you ought to be able to add the other at the same time. It will require the same adjustments. To make sure the evaluation is done in the correct order, you will add a few parentheses.

8. Exit Play mode.

9. Change the rotation line to the following:

```
transform.eulerAngles = v3StartRot + (Vector3.left * (v3StartPos - v3T).y * factor) +
(Vector3.forward * (v3StartPos - v3T).x * factor);
```

10. Save the script and test again. This time, the Board tilts along both axes as you move the mouse around.

11. Exit Play mode.

With the basics working, you are probably anxious to drop a marble onto the board. It sounds easy, but keeping in mind that game physics are only approximations of the real thing, you will soon discover otherwise:

1. Create a Sphere in the middle of the board and lift it up so it is slightly higher than the Board's top surface.

2. Name it **Marble**.

   For objects to make use of physics, you must add a Rigidbody component.

3. Add a Rigidbody component to the Marble object.

4. Click Play and tilt the board.

   The Marble drops to the Board, but does not react when the board is tilted. To achieve interaction when the Board object is in motion, the board must also have a Rigidbody component. And because the board is controlled with user input rather than physics, it must be marked as Is Kinematic. This is also the case if it has key-frame animation or any other means of animation other than physics.

5. Add a Rigidbody component to the Board object.

6. Set it to Is Kinematic and deactivate the Use Gravity check box.

7. Click Play and test.

   The marble now rolls around as you tilt the board, but occasionally, it will fall through. A partial solution here is to make the board thicker so that the marble can't get through it between frames as easily. Physics behavior is not necessarily calculated every frame, so it is possible that an object can miss a collider altogether if it is moving too fast.

The farther the marble gets from the center of the board (the object's pivot point), the faster the board will change position in relation to the marble, and the higher the chance that the marble will get through it between the time the collision checks are made. Obviously, this will cause problems with game play, but rule number 1 is "don't waste good game ideas on learning material," so you will get creative during the course of this project and turn it to an advantage, or at least a plausible part of the game mechanics. To improve performance, you can also adjust the way the Marble is handled by physics.

8. Select the marble and in its Rigidbody component, set Collision Detection to Continuous Dynamic.

You can also help collision detection by making barriers thicker so that the objects aren't as likely to pass through between physics frame checks. The checks themselves can be altered, but it is not advisable to do so unless you really know what you are doing.

9. Select the Board and set its Y Scale to **2.0**.

10. Adjust its Y Position to **-1** so that its top surface is at 0.

11. Click Play and test.

This time, the marble is better behaved, but it is still too easy to lose it over the edge.

Before you add some walls, you will probably want to make the contents of the Scene view easier to see. A simple green material for the Board will be a big improvement.

12. From the right-click menu, choose Create ➤ Material.

13. Name it **Green**.

14. In the Inspector, Click the Main Color sample swatch and change it to an easy-to-see green (or any other color you wish).

15. Drag it onto the Board object in either the Scene view or the Hierarchy view.

Let's add some walls next. Visually, the walls shouldn't be too thick, but to keep the physics working, you will increase the collider size:

1. Create a Cube, **28** × **3** × **1**.

2. Name it **Wall**.

3. Increase the Collider's Z Size to **3**.

4. Set its Z Center to **-1** so that the collider hangs over the outside of the Board.

5. Set the Collider's Y Size to **2** and set its Y Center to **0.5** (Figure 5-2).

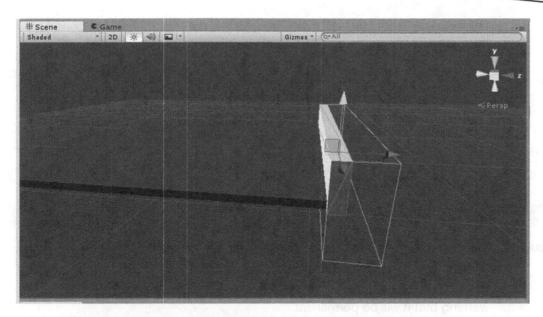

Figure 5-2. The Wall's collider scaled out beyond the cube

The next thing you will want to do is to add a Rigidbody component to the Wall. It already has a collider to stop other rigidbodies, but if it will be moving, it will use far less resources if it also has a rigidbody set to Is Kinematic.

6. From the Components menu, choose Physics and then add a Rigidbody component.

7. Activate the Is Kinematic check box and deactivate the Use Gravity check box.

Creating Prefabs

Now that the wall has been beefed up to help prevent physics mishaps, you can save setup time by turning it into a prefab. *Prefabs* are Unity's mechanism for storing reusable objects. In traditional desktop applications, when you instantiate an object such as a projectile, the object, its components, and its children are put into the scene on demand, ready for action. When the object is no longer required, it is destroyed. In mobile applications, the two functions are too costly to use with abandon, but the prefab itself also serves a twofold purpose. It can help save disk space and/or download time and it makes scene setup using identical objects, or instances, much quicker. Follow these steps to create a prefab:

1. Create a new folder in the project view and name it **Prefabs**.

2. Drag the Wall object into the new folder.

    The Wall prefab sports a blue cube icon in the Single Column Layout (Figure 5-3, left) and a thumbnail of the object in Two Column Layout (Figure 5-3, right). Its name in the Hierarchy view is blue instead of black, indicating that it is a prefab of an asset that exists in the project. If a prefab is deleted from the project, its instance in the Hierarchy view turns red, but the object remains.

Figure 5-3. The prefab and its icon in Single Column Layout (left) and Two Column Layout (right)

3. Delete the Wall prefab from the Project view and acknowledge the warning that it will be permanent.

    The name in the Hierarchy view turns reddish.

    You can repair the "broken" prefab through the GameObject menu.

4. Select the Wall in the Hierarchy view and from the GameObject menu, select Break Prefab Instance.

    The Wall's name turns black.

5. Drag the Wall object back into the Prefabs folder to create a new prefab.

    When the prefab was created, all of its components and their parameter values were stored as is. To reuse them, you can bring them into the scene during Edit mode in three ways.

    To bring a new prefab into the scene in the same location and orientation as the original, you can simply duplicate the original in the scene.

6. Select the original Wall in the Scene and duplicate it by pressing Ctrl+D (Cmd+D on the Mac).

    The duplicate occupies the same location and orientation as the original.

7. Set its Y Rotation to **180** and move it to the other side of the Board.

    Let's try another method.

8. Drag the Wall prefab from the Project view into the Hierarchy view.

    This duplicate also occupies the same location and orientation as the original did when the prefab was created.

9. Set its Y Rotation to **90** and move it to the appropriate side of the Board.

10. Finally, drag the Wall prefab directly into the Scene view, and move it around the Board, observing the changes in the Y Position as you do so.

    The bottom of the Wall object is automatically adjusted according to which object it intersects.

11. Set its Y Rotation to **-90** and set its Y Position to match the other three walls.

12. Move it to the remaining side of the Board object and drag the Wall object in the Hierarchy to the bottom of the list so it is with the other walls.

    Depending on how you arranged your walls in relation to the outside edges of the Board object, you may have noticed that you have some overhang. The beauty of using a prefab is that changes will affect the copies.

13. Select the Wall prefab in the Project view and set its X Scale to **27**.

    The walls in the Scene view scale to match.

14. Rename the four walls to **Wall Top**, **Wall Bottom**, **Wall Left**, and **Wall Right**, according to their location in the Game view (Figure 5-4).

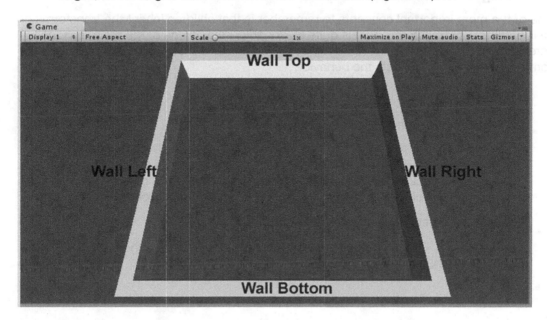

Figure 5-4. The four walls in the Game view

Tip Activate and Deactivate the walls to identify them in the Game view or turn on Gizmos in the Game view to see which is which.

Just as with transforms, the instances of the prefab may have unique names without breaking the prefab.

Before testing the new additions, you can use the same collider scaling method to help keep the Marble from falling through the floor while improving the visuals:

1. Select the Board and reduce its Y Scale to **0.5** and its Y Position to **-0.25**.

2. Set its collider's X and Z Size to **1.2** and its Y Size to **10**.

3. Adjust the collider's Y Center to **-4.5**.

   To have the walls *move* with the Board, you will have to parent them to it.

4. Drag the four wall objects onto the Board object in the Hierarchy view.

5. Click Play and test.

The functionality is there, but in the next section, you will quickly see a drawback to parenting everything to the board.

Working with Inheritance

One of the more important concepts to remember is that children inherit the transforms of their parents. For transforms, that is quite reasonable—that is one of the main reasons to parent objects. Problems arise, however, when rotation and scale come into play. Let's try some experiments to illustrate the behavior:

1. Stop Play mode.

2. Select one of the walls.

   Its Scale now reads $1 \times 1.5 \times 0.04545455$. In other words, the scale reflects the influence of the parent. Multiply the current values by the Board's values and you get $22 \times 3 \times 0.5$. Unfortunately, mixing scale and rotation is going to cause problems. Let's create a ramp for the Marble to roll up.

3. Create a new Cube and name it **Ramp**.

4. Make it **3** × **3** × **6** and rotate it so that one end is flush with the board (Figure 5-5).

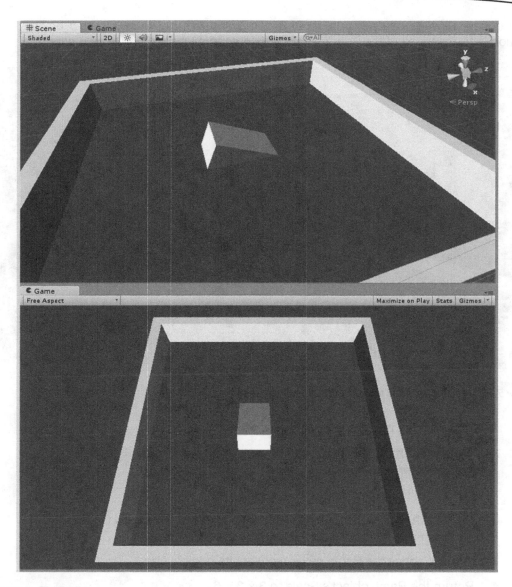

Figure 5-5. The Ramp

5. Move the marble above it so it will drop onto the high end of the
    Ramp object.

6. Click Play and watch the marble drop and roll.

7. Stop Play mode and drag the Ramp object onto the Board object.

The ramp is skewed because of the rotation combining with the scale (Figure 5-6). The solution is to parent all of the Board object's children to a unitized (value of 1) parent.

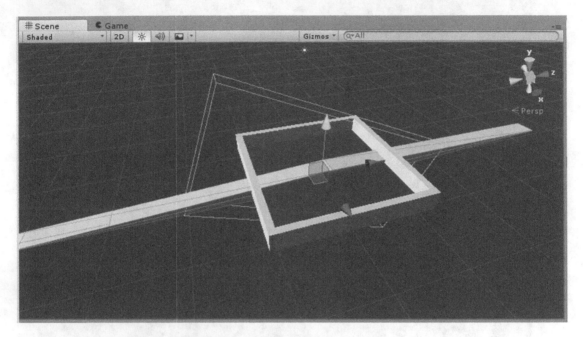

Figure 5-6. The Ramp parented to the Board and badly skewed

1. Double-click the Board object to focus the viewport to it.

2. Create an Empty gameObject and name it **Board Group**. It should be in the center of the Board.

    Note that its Scale is 1 × 1 × 1.

3. Drag each of the Board Object's child objects into the Board Group and then add the Board object to it as well.

    You will notice the Ramp never recovers its original size.

4. Return the Ramp object's Scale to **3 × 3 × 6**.

    Now the problem is that the code to rotate the board is on the Board object, not on the Board Group. You can easily add the script to the Board Group, but the function is using `OnMouseDown` and `OnMouseDrag`, so you will have to add a collider so that the player can interact with it.

> **Tip**   With Unity, any object that involves interaction must have a collider component.

5. Select the Board object, right-click the Tilt Board component, and select Remove Component.

6. Select the Board Group object and add a Sphere Collider component.

7. Turn on Gizmos in the Game view and increase the Radius of the Sphere Collider until it is large enough to let the player click and drag from anywhere onscreen: approximately **25**.

8. Set Is Trigger to on (true) so the collider does not create a physical barrier.

9. Add the TiltBoard script to the Board Group object.

10. Set its Factor to **0.1** so the player can't tip the board too quickly and cause the physics to fail.

11. Click Play and test the new assembly.

Rolling the ball around and trying to get it up onto the ramp is pretty challenging, but not terribly exciting. There are a few things you can do to improve things. The first is to reset the Marble object when the player allows it to escape the board environment. Typically, this is done with what is usually referred to as a *death zone object*.

Creating a Death Zone

Traditionally, you would Destroy the object and Instantiate a new one back at the start location. With mobile devices, however, instantiation is costly (uses a lot of battery power), so you will simply move it back to the start.

With the Board Group object, you created an Empty gameObject and added a collider. For more-complex colliders, such as the Box Collider, it is often easier to create a Cube and adjust its dimensions, and then delete or disable its Mesh Renderer:

1. Focus the Scene view on the Board Group and create a new Cube.

2. Name it **Death Zone**.

3. Move it down below the Board Group so that the tilting Board Group will not hit it (about -30 Y Position) and scale it to about **100 × 10 × 100**.

4. Disable its Mesh Renderer component, so that only the collider shows.

5. Set its Box Collider's Is Trigger parameter to on.

Is Trigger will allow the object to go through the collider, but will flag the intersection in an OnTriggerEnter function.

Next, you will create the script that controls the Death Zone's functionality. Before worrying about the reset functionality, it's always a good idea to make sure the detection is working:

1. Create a new C# script in the Game Scripts folder and name it **DeathZoneReset**.

2. Below the default Start and Update functions, add the following:

```
void OnTriggerEnter () {
    print ("got one!");
}
```

3. Save the script and drag it onto the Death Zone object.

4. Click Play and tip the Board Group until the marble goes over or through the board and into the Death Zone.

The console prints *got one!* when the Marble intersects the Death Zone.

To reset the sphere to its original location, the script must first be able to identify the sphere and to also know where the reset location is. You could query the Marble's starting location through an Awake function before the game gets underway and the Marble drops, or you can use a placeholder object. The latter affords you a nice amount of flexibility that can be useful as you add more sophistication to your game. If you had different levels, for example, the starting location could vary from level to level.

Additionally, the sphere may be subject to repositioning throughout the game due to various other events, say, a portal effect, so it is worth considering having the relocation code in a centralized place. Logically, a script on the Marble object makes the most sense as it is the marble that must be relocated. Let's also plan ahead and allow for multiple starting points by making the location variable an array:

1. Stop Play mode.

2. Create a new C# script and name it **MarbleManager**.

3. Add the following variable under the class declaration:

```
public Transform[] location; // drop point locations
```

> To define an array (multiple values for the variable), you add the brackets at the end of the variable's type. In C# (and Unity's version of JavaScript for mobile platforms), the elements in the array must all be of the same type. By declaring this one as public, you can assign the values directly in the Inspector. You will be assigning gameObjects, but only the object's *transforms* are being stored in the location array.

4. Create a variable to store the current starting location:

```
Transform currentStartLocation; // this could vary depending on level
```

5. In the Start function, assign one of the array elements as the current starting location:

```
currentStartLocation = location[0]; // assign the current start location
```

The 0 inside the brackets refers to element 0, the first element in the array. Arrays always start counting their elements at 0, not 1. For now, you will assume that the starting location will be stored in element 0.

6. Create a new function to move the marble to the specified location:

```
public void SetToStart () {
    // set the new position
    Vector3 tempPos = new Vector3(transform.position.x,transform.position.y,
transform.position.z);
    tempPos = currentStartLocation.position;
    transform.position = tempPos;
}
```

Note that this function is marked as public. This will allow you to access it from other scripts and even other objects. In C#, you cannot directly set a new transform. You must first create a temporary variable that holds the current transform, assign the new value to that variable, and then you can assign that variable's value to finally change the object's transform. To store just the position part of the transform, you are using a Vector3 type to hold x, y, z. Variables capable of storing multiple values are called *structs*. To access the individual parts of the variable's value, you use *dot notation*.

7. Save the script.

8. Drag it onto the Marble object.

Next you will create the placeholder location for the starting position of the marble:

1. Select the Marble in the Hierarchy view and focus the view to it.

2. Create a new Empty gameObject and name it **Start Location A**.

3. Select the Marble.

4. In the MarbleManager component, click the arrow next to the Location parameter to see the contents of the array.

At this point, the array is empty; it has a Size of 0. Rather than setting the Size to 1, and then dragging the Start Location A object into the Element 1 slot, you can shortcut the procedure and save a step.

5. Drag the Start Location A object from the Hierarchy view onto the Marble's MarbleManager component's Location line.

The array is automatically set to a Size of 1 and the object put in the new Element 0. The object shows as the value, but in parentheses, you can see that it is just the object's transform that has been stored (Figure 5-7).

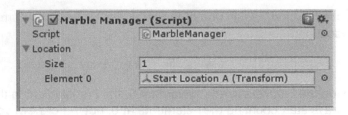

Figure 5-7. The Start Location A object assigned as Element 0, storing its transform

Now you can test the script by having it position the marble in the starting location when the game begins.

6. In the Start function, below the line that assigns the current location, add the call to the function that relocates the object:

```
SetToStart (); // move the object to the current start location
```

7. Save the script.

8. Move the Marble object off to the side in the Scene view.

9. Click Play.

The marble appears at the start location and drops onto the board.

With the repositioning code working well, you can return to the DeathZoneReset script and add its next bit of code. To call a function on another object's script, you must identify both the object and the script. Additionally, the function itself must be marked as public. A quick check of the SetToStart function will tell you that it is indeed set to public, so you are good to go ahead and reset the marble from the DeathZoneReset script.

1. Open the DeathZoneReset script.

2. Under the class declaration, create a new variable to store the reference to the Marble object:

```
public GameObject marble;  // the marble object
```

3. In the OnTriggerEnter function, comment out the print line and below it add the following:

```
//print ("got one!");
marble.GetComponent<MarbleManager>().SetToStart(); // put the marble back to the start
```

To call a function or access a variable on another object's script, you identify the object, and then you must identify the script (or other component), and finally, using dot notation, call the function (as in this case) or specify the variable.

4. Save the script.

5. Select the Death Zone object and drag the Marble object from the Hierarchy view to the DeathZoneReset component's Marble parameter.

6. Click Play, and test by sending the marble over a wall or through the floor.

The marble is dropped from the start location shortly after it goes over a wall.

Tweaking Physics

At this point, you are probably thinking that even with a bunch of obstacles, the marble control may be too slow to qualify as *fun*. Fortunately, there's no rule that says you have to stick to reality. You can change not only the object's "physical" properties through its colliders, but also the physics reactions on a global scale. Tweaking the physics will improve the player experience greatly. Let's begin by changing the gravity itself.

1. From the Edit menu, choose Project Settings ➤ Physics. The Physics Manager opens (Figure 5-8).

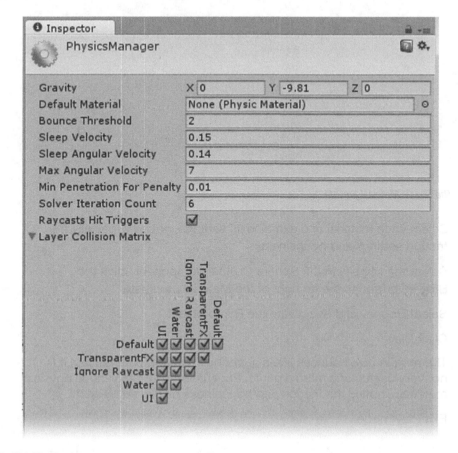

Figure 5-8. The Physics Manager

2.   In the Physics Manager, set the gravity to **-200**, or, if you prefer to be able to remember the default settings, add 20 to the default to make it **-209.81**.

3.   Click Play and test the new gravity setting. The marble is much more responsive.

     You can also experiment with the physic materials for the marble and board.

4.   Exit Play mode.

5.   From the right-click menu in the Project view, choose Import Package ➤ Physic Materials.

6.   Click Import.

     In the Standard Assets folder, you will find the Physic Materials folder with five handy presets (Figure 5-9). If you wish to experiment with them, feel free to duplicate an existing material for tweaking, or, if you are a physics whiz, create your own from scratch from the right-click menu, by choosing Create ➤ Physic Material.

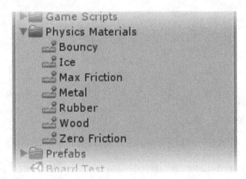

Figure 5-9. *The Physic Material presets*

7.   Select each material and examine its settings, noting especially the friction settings and bounciness.

8.   Select the Marble. In the Sphere Collider component, click the Browse button to the far right of the Material parameter.

9.   Select Bouncy and deactivate the Ramp object.

10. Click Play.

     The marble now bounces like a super ball. Though entertaining, it is not very useful for a marble game. Experiment with the various physics materials, noting the friction and bounciness displayed by each.

11. Exit Play mode.

12. Activate the Ramp and select Metal for the Marble's Physic Material.

13. Add the Wood Physic Material to the board for a bit more friction.

14. Click Play and test. The marble now has a nice amount of responsiveness.

You can also adjust the mass of the marble to further refine its behavior;

1. Select the Marble.

2. In its Rigidbody component, set its Mass to **500**.

3. Click Play and test. The responsiveness remains intact, but the marble has less of a tendency to bounce.

Improving the Basics

The little bit of game play you have blocked in is pretty basic. With each addition, you have undoubtedly had ideas about how to improve things. Let's move ahead and implement a few more goodies. There are any number of things you can do to affect the player experience, but a good place to start is by improving the marble reset functionality.

At the end of the preceding section, you probably noticed that a short pause before the marble reset would be a nice touch. It would allow you time to reset the board, update scores or health, or even fire off some special effects. While it is too early in the development to start adding the eye candy, now is a good time to set up some of the functionality that can be handled when the marble is reset or even ported to a different position as part of the game.

Using Co-routines

Setting a delay or pause before triggering an event is not as easy as it sounds in C#. In Unity's JavaScript, you could use a simple `yield new WaitforSeconds([pause time])`. In C#, however, adding a pause is a bit trickier. The problem is that code is evaluated linearly during each frame. To create a pause in C#, you have to start a *co-routine*—a type of function that can run at the same time as the rest of the code. When the pause times are up, the code will be evaluated regardless of what everything else is doing. Let's create a co-routine to delay the repositioning of the marble.

The first consideration is how to handle the pause when it can come from two different places. There are times, such as scene startup, when there should be no delay. This makes a good argument for keeping the transform code separate from the delay code. You might wonder why you can't use the same code and pass in a value of 0 for the delay. You could do that easily enough, but with mobile applications in mind, you are probably better off avoiding the extra overhead for an `IEnumerator` (the place where the delay code will live).

It also turns out that you can't call an IEnumerator from another script, so you will end up adding extra code regardless. Let's begin by reorganizing the MarbleManager script:

1. Open the MarbleManager script.

2. Create a new function for the outside objects to call:

```
public void StartDelay (float pause) {
    StartCoroutine(DelayReset(pause));
}
```

> The StartDelay function takes an argument, pause, which is a float value. It passes it on to the co-routine, DelayReset. Co-routines are always initiated with StartCoroutine.

3. Create the co-routine below the StartDelay function:

```
IEnumerator DelayReset (float pause) {
    // pause before reset
    yield return new WaitForSeconds(pause); // this starts the delay
    // add some FX here
    // reset
    SetToStart (); // call the original relocation function
}
```

4. Save the script.

   Now you can redirect the DeathZoneReset's OnTriggerEnter function.

5. Open the DeathZoneReset script.

6. Change the contents of the OnTriggerEnter function:

```
marble.GetComponent<MarbleManager>().StartDelay (3f); // set the delay going using 3 seconds
```

7. Save the script.

8. Click Play and send the marble over the edge.

After the marble intersects the Death Zone and the specified delay has passed, the marble is reset to the specified location.

A couple of issues may have become apparent at this point. Depending on the angle of the Board Group, the marble could get to the Death Zone quickly or after a longer fall. It may also be visible to the player while it falls into the void. The solution to the first problem is rather simple: invert the functionality of the Death Zone. Instead of triggering the reset when the marble enters the zone, trigger it when it *exits* the zone. This means that you will have to resize and reposition the Death Zone. The code change is even easier:

1. Stop Play mode.

2. Open the DeathZoneReset script.

3. Change the OnTriggerEnter function to OnTriggerExit.

4.   Save the script.

5.   Rename the Death Zone object to **Live Zone**.

6.   Change its scale to **30** × **10** × **30**.

7.   Move it up so that it covers the Board Group (Figure 5-10) and then add it to the Board Group in the Hierarchy view.

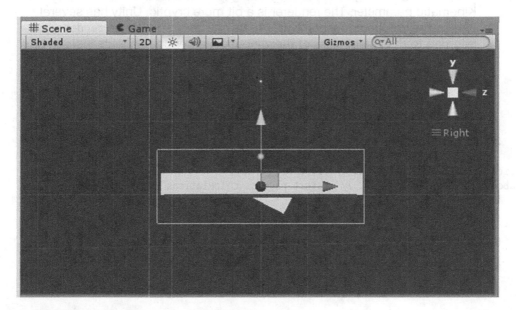

Figure 5-10. The Live Zone positioned over the Board Group

8.   Make sure the Start Location A object is *inside* the Live Zone.

Tip   To see where the Start Location A object is in relation to the Live Zone, set the Coordinate System Pivot to Pivot. Select the Start Location A object first, and then holding down the Ctrl key, add the Board Group to the selection.

9.   Click Play and test by once again sending the marble over the walls. This time, the delay time is more consistent and predictable.

Visibility control will also be a quick feature to add. Rather than Deactivate (easy) and Activate (not so easy) the Marble, you will simply tell it not to be rendered or drawn in the scene. In the interest of saving resources (for mobile devices), you can also suspend the physics calculations that are dropping the marble. You can't disable the Rigidbody component, but you can temporarily set it to Is Kinematic.

1. Open the MarbleManager script.

2. At the top of the StartDelay function, add the following:

```
renderer.enabled = false; // turn off rendering
rigidbody.isKinematic = true; // suspend physics calculations
```

> The code for the Rigidbody is fairly straightforward. You are turning on its Is Kinematic parameter. The renderer is a bit more cryptic. Unity has several types of render components similar to its colliders, so you use renderer, referring to the parent class of the various renderer components instead of the specific one used by the object. In both cases, not specifying the object directly infers that the components in question are on the same object that the script component resides on.

> The values will be returned to normal right after the delay time is up.

3. In the IEnumerator, just above the SetToStart() line, add this:

```
renderer.enabled = true; // turn on rendering
rigidbody.isKinematic = false; // restart physics calculations
```

4. Save the script.

5. Select the Marble in the Hierarchy view.

6. Click Play and test.

7. Watch the two components to see the values change.

Suppressing Player Input

With the marble's basic functionality well underway, you have probably noticed that the player may have left the board in an awkward position to restart the play. It would make sense to reset the board's transforms in preparation for the marble re-drop. The problem is that resetting the board won't guarantee that the player won't keep moving it during the delay time. So the goal here is to also suppress user input during the reset delay.

Player input is monitored every frame, so the place to suppress it is in an Update function. The code you will be using can actually go in any script's Update function with the same results. For now, to keep things simple, you will add it to the MarbleManager script. To turn the functionality off and on, you will create a flag, a simple two-state Boolean variable, to handle the functionality:

1. Open the MarbleManager script.

2. Below the existing variables, add the following variable:

```
internal bool repressInput = false; // allow player input at start-up
```

> The internal keyword means that the variable will not be exposed to the Inspector, but that it *will* be accessible to other scripts.

3. In the `Update` function, add the following:

```
if(repressInput) Input.ResetInputAxes(); // blocks user input
```

> `Input` is capitalized, referring to the actual `Input` class rather than an individual use of it on an object. This is why the code is object-independent. The `ResetInputAxes()` function, or method, sets all input values back to 0, effectively blocking user input for each frame.
>
> As you may have guessed, you will set the flag off and on in the same places you took care of the marble's activity.

4. In the `StartDelay` function, above the `StartCoroutine` line, add the following:

```
repressInput = true;
```

5. In the `IEnumerator`, above the `SetToStart` line, add this:

```
repressInput = false;
```

6. Save the script.

7. Press Play and test the new code by trying to tip the Board during the reset delay. The board remains unresponsive while the marble is being reset.

Resetting the Board

With player input safely suppressed, you can see about returning the Board Group to its original orientation. You could do that instantaneously, as you did with the marble's relocation, but because the board is fully visible and a main feature onscreen, it would be nicer to see it glide smoothly back to its original orientation. Smoothly changing an object's position is relatively easy using a `Lerp` (linear interpolation) function. Rotation, on the other hand, can be massively more complicated. Internally, Unity handles rotation by using Quaternion math. Basically, this means it deals with the direction the object's up vector is pointing. As humans, we generally prefer to use rotation in Euler (pronounced *oiler*, or if you are familiar with umlauts, euler). Euler angles allow us to think of rotation in degrees, but more important, to rotate the x, y, and z axes independently.

Fortunately, there is a Quaternion static variable that represents no rotation, `Quaternion. identity`, and a function, `Slerp` (for *smooth linear interpolation*), to take the board from its current orientation back to no rotation. The trickiest part of `Slerp` (and regular `Lerp` as well) is understanding the time argument, `t`. It is not time so much as a *location* on a timeline that is normalized to 1, or 100 percent of the time. You will derive it from `Time.time`, the amount of time that has passed since the game was started.

The first step is to create a script that will live on the Board Group and handle the functionality:

1. Create a new C# script in the Game Scripts folder and name it **BoardManager**.

2. Just below the class declaration, add the following variables:

```
internal bool resetBoard = false; // flag to run the reset
Quaternion from; // the object's current rotation when the reset is called
// time slicers
internal float endTime = 0.0f ;
internal float matchTime = 0.0f ; // seconds duration of the pause
```

3. In the Update function, add the following:

```
if (resetBoard) {
    float t = ( Time.time - endTime + matchTime) / matchTime ; // Goes from 0 to 1
    print (t); // so you can see that the numbers do what they are supposed to do
    transform.rotation = Quaternion.Slerp(from, Quaternion.identity, t);
    if (Time.time > endTime) resetBoard = false;// reset the flag

}
```

If the math calculating t makes your head hurt, don't worry; you can watch the numbers reported from the print statement.

The endTime and matchTime values are set in the function that starts the rotation reset. It in turn is triggered from the marble's MarbleManager script when the delay has been started.

4. Create the function that starts the board reset:

```
public void StartBoardReset (float pauseTime) {
    matchTime = pauseTime;
    endTime = Time.time + matchTime;
    from = transform.rotation;
    resetBoard = true;
}
```

This function is public as it will be called from the Marble's MarbleManager script. The argument pauseTime will be passed in from that script as well. It is assigned to the matchTime variable that is available to any other functions in the BoardManager's script. The endTime is calculated by adding the matchTime to Time.time, the amount of time that has passed since the game began. The from variable stores the Board Group's current orientation in Quaternion form, and the resetBoard flag is set to true to get things moving (or rotating, as the case may be).

5. Save the script.

6. Add the new script to the Board Group.

Before you can test, you will have to make a few additions to MarbleManager:

1. Open the MarbleManager script.

2. Add the following variable to be able to access the BoardManager:

```
public BoardManager boardManage-r; // the Board Group's BoardManager script
```

>   With this declaration, you are specifying the type as the script component, BoardManager. You will drag in the Board Group as the value, so the MarbleManager will know that it is communicating with that script on that object. Typically, you use the same name as the script for the variable name but with the first character lowercase. Let's continue writing the Board Group's reset functionality.

3. In the StartDelay function, above the StartCoroutine line, add the following:

```
boardManager.StartBoardReset(pause); // start the board reset, send the pause time
```

4. In the IEnumerator, above the SetToStart line, add this:

```
boardManager.resetBoard = false; // toggle off the board's reset flag
```

5. Save the script.

6. Select the Marble in the Hierarchy view.

7. Drag the Board Group object onto the new Board Manager parameter.

8. Click Play and try tipping the marble out of the board. The Board Group smoothly resets itself just in time for the marble to drop and allow the player another chance.

9. Stop Play mode.

10. In the BoardManager script, comment out the print(t) line and save the script.

11. Save the scene and save the project.

Summary

In this chapter, you made a good start with testing the basics of your little game by creating a simple mock-up without the need for fancy art assets. Along the way, you had your first taste of adapting someone else's script to your needs through trial and error. Using OnMouseDown and OnMouseDrag, you learned how to affect an object's rotation.

With a bit of script, a cube, and a sphere, you got your first look at using physics to control game play. After discovering that game physics are by no means a silver bullet, you learned some tricks to improve the odds of the functionality working as you had imagined by padding the collider scales. While creating your proxy geometry, you also got a look at a Unity mainstay—the prefab. Although you discovered that instantiating and destroying prefabs at runtime was usually too expensive to use for mobile devices, you found they can be extremely useful for scene setup as well as for conserving disk space or minimizing download times.

Next, with a handful of proxy objects to manage, you learned an important piece of knowledge about parenting objects. Children, you found, inherit the transforms of their parents. If the parent had a scale of something other than 1 × 1 × 1, you discovered that mixing scales and rotations could result in horrible skewed geometry. Upon dragging objects in and out of a group, you also discovered that the transforms reported in the Inspector were only local offsets when they were parented to other objects.

In anticipation of players getting too rough with your game, you created a death zone that would restart the game play when the marble went over the edge. While scripting the functionality, you used examples of variables that could have several values held in an array, and variables whose values had multiple parts, structs. With these, you started to get a feel for using dot notation as a means of accessing just the parts of objects, components, or variables you wanted.

Jumping into a few more advanced topics in C# code, you learned how to set up delays in code evaluation with co-routines by using the IEnumerator. Scripting a pause before the reset of the marble gave you an opportunity to manage some component properties, suppress user input, and finally, to smoothly rotate a gameObject back to its starting orientation.

Chapter **6**

Experimenting with Functionality

As you saw in the previous chapter, just because something is challenging (for example, driving the marble around the board) doesn't automatically make it fun. Given that challenging tasks can be fun for one person and tedious for another, you are never going to be able to please everyone. You can, however, try your best to make the challenges entertaining. Just as with the preliminary stage, you can block in the functionality without spending too much time. With mobile devices in mind, you will not have free rein to overload the game with fabulous (but costly) special effects, so intriguing concepts and clever or unexpected consequences will have to do the job. A combination of obstacles and power-ups or other "helpers" will form the basis of the game play required to move the marble to an end location.

With basic navigation and environment sorted out, it's time to decide on the functionality that will challenge the player while moving the marble to reach its goal. The goal in most little tip games is to get the marble or other spherical object to a particular location, usually a depression in the board. While a depression to catch a sphere is not practical for game physics, your marble will eventually have a location for a goal. In this chapter, you will experiment with various means of helping and hindering the player maneuvering the marble around the board.

Creating Portals

Although portals could generally be considered a more advanced feature because of the scripting involved, you already have much of the code written. The biggest difference is that the reset location could be unique to each portal. Also, you probably don't want a board reset to pause game play. You will want some sort of special effect to mark the event, but

© Sue Blackman and Adam Tuliper 2016
S. Blackman and A. Tuliper, *Learn Unity for Windows 10 Game Development*,
DOI 10.1007/978-1-4302-6757-7_6

that can wait until later in the book, when you add the "eye" and "ear" candy. This time, you will be re-creating the DeathZoneReset script to make it useful for various scenarios:

1. Create a new C# script and name it **PortalHopper**.

2. At the top of the script, just under the class declaration, add the following variables:

```
public MarbleManager marbleManager; // the MarbleManager script
public Transform destination; // the target location
internal float delay = 0.0f; // the time it will take to move the marble
```

Note that this time you will directly specify the script to be contacted, the MarbleManager script, by dragging it into the Inspector. Using GameObject. Find and GetComponent uses a lot of resources and time, and should be avoided whenever possible, especially outside the Start or Awake functions.

3. Add the trigger function:

```
void OnTriggerEnter () {
    marbleManager.PortalJump (delay,destination);
}
```

The PortalJump function will take two arguments, the delay time that will be the same for all portals, and the destination object's transform.

4. Save the script.

5. In the MarbleManager script, add the PortalJump function:

```
public void PortalJump (float pause, Transform destination) {
    renderer.enabled = false;
    rigidbody.isKinematic = true;
    StartCoroutine(DelayPortalJump(pause, destination));
}
```

Just as with the StartDelay function, the PortalJump function acts as a staging area for the transportation of the marble by turning off the renderer and disabling the physics calculations. Note that it passes both the delay time and the destination on to a co-routine.

6. Add the IEnumerator:

```
IEnumerator DelayPortalJump (float pause, Transform destination) {
    // pause before reset
    yield return new WaitForSeconds(pause);
    // add some FX here
    // reset
    renderer.enabled = true; // turn on rendering
    rigidbody.isKinematic = false; // restart physics calculations
    MoveToLocation (destination);
}
```

As you can see, there is little difference between the two IEnumerators. The renderer and physics calculations are turned on after a short delay and then the relocating is initialized.

7. Create the MoveToLocation function:

```
public void MoveToLocation (Transform destination) {
   // set the new position
   Vector3 tempPos = new Vector3(transform.position.x,transform.position.y, transform.
position.z);
   tempPos = destination.position;
   transform.position = tempPos;
}
```

This is the usual C# method of setting a new location. A temporary variable is created to hold the current values, a value (or values) is changed, and the new struct is fed back to the object's position parameters. In case you are familiar with Unity's version of JavaScript and are thinking the C# procedure is long-winded, JavaScript performs the same procedure, but it is hidden from the user.

8. Save the script.

Next you will create a couple of proxy objects to test your repurposed code:

1. Select the Directional Light and for its Shadow Type, choose Soft Shadows (or Hard Shadows if your Unity license does not include Soft Shadows).

    Dynamic shadows use a lot of resources during runtime, but are quite useful during setup because they help to alleviate visual ambiguity. Simply put, they help you to view the screen's 2D space as 3D space.

2. Create a new Sphere in the Hierarchy view and name it **Portal A**.

    This sphere will act only as a location or zone and will not require a Rigidbody component.

3. Set its collider's Is Trigger parameter to true.

4. Scale it to **2 × 2 × 2**, and leave it to intersect the board slightly (Figure 6-1).

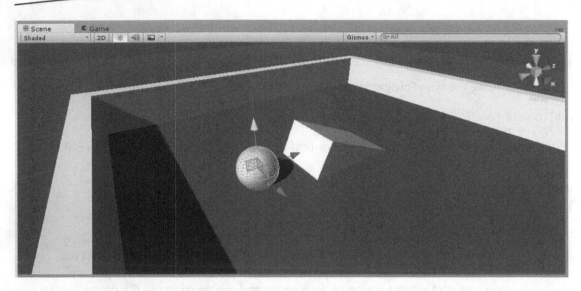

Figure 6-1. The Sphere intersecting the Board slightly

5.   Drag the PortalHopper script onto the new object.

6.   Drag the Marble object onto its MarbleManager parameter.

7.   To test, drag the Start Location A object onto its Destination parameter.

8.   Drag Portal A into the Board Group.

9.   Click Play and then test by rolling the marble into the Portal A sphere.

The marble is *ported* to the original drop spot regardless of board orientation. It will be crucial to have the portal destination spots part of the Board Group, as there is no pause or board resetting involved.

1.   Duplicate the Portal A object and name it **Portal A Destination**.

2.   Position the cursor over its PortalHopper component, right-click, and select Remove Component.

3.   Remove the Sphere Collider component as well.

4.   Move the Portal A Destination object to the other side of the Board (Figure 6-2).

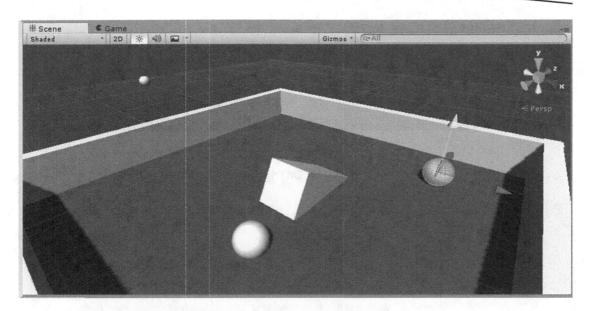

Figure 6-2. The Portal A Destination object relocated to the upper right of the board

5. In the Inspector, disable its Mesh Renderer.

6. Select the Portal A object and drag the Portal A Destination object in as its Destination.

7. Click Play.

    As soon as the game starts, instead of dropping from Start Location A, the marble is immediately moved to the Portal A Destination. The answer to the mystery lies in the fact that Portal A is already intersecting the Board's collider at startup, so the OnTriggerEnter code is triggered.

8. Stop Play mode and lift the Portal A object clear of the Board.

9. Click Play again.

    This time, the Marble drops into the game as expected.

10. Roll the Marble through the portal from several directions.

The marble continues rolling in the same direction it was going at its previous location.

Although lifting up the Portal A object so it no longer intersects with the Board solves the issue, there will be plenty of times when that option is not available. Fortunately, you have a few options for preventing the Board from triggering the code in the OnTriggerEnter function.

Let's begin by having the function report the name of the object that triggered it. Many functions can be *overloaded*. That means that they have optional arguments. You have used OnTriggerEnter with no arguments up to this point. So how do you know what the possible configurations are for a function? Simple: you check Unity's Scripting Reference.

1. From the Help menu, select Scripting Reference.

2. Select C# in the upper right and type **OnTriggerEnter** in the Search field (Figure 6-3).

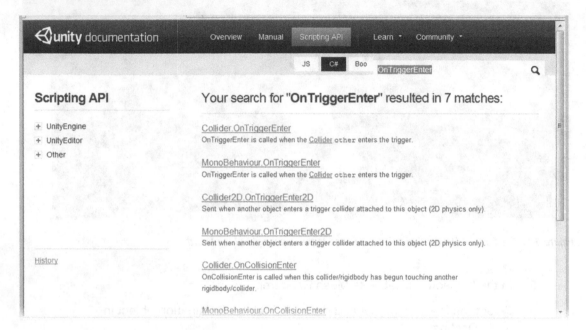

Figure 6-3. The results for a search of OnTriggerEnter

3. Select Collider.OnTriggerEnter.

   The argument wants a collider (Figure 6-4). This argument is different in that you don't pass it into the function manually; the object triggering the function passes its collider in automatically. Let's see how that works.

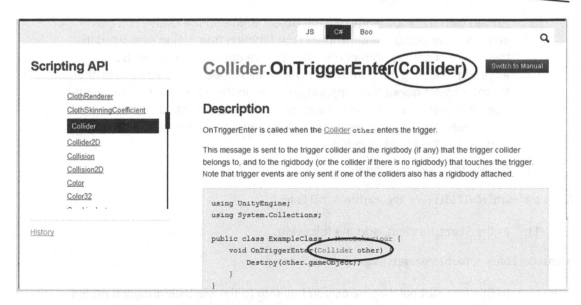

Figure 6-4. The optional Collider argument for OnTriggerEnter

4.   In the PortalHopper script, change the OnTriggerEnter function as follows:

```
void OnTriggerEnter (Collider theCollider) {
```

5.   At the top of the function, add the following:

```
print (theCollider.gameObject.name);
```

The collider component does not have a name field, so you must ask for its gameObject's name by using dot notation.

6.   Save the script.

7.   Select the Portal A object and move it back down so it intersects with the Board.

8.   Click Play and watch the console.

The console reports an intersection of Portal A and the Board. The Sphere is ported to the Portal A Destination object before it has a chance to drop from the start position.

9.   Roll the Sphere into the Portal A Object.

Now the console reports the Marble as the object with the collider that triggered the event.

Armed with the knowledge of what object triggered the event, you can see about stopping the code inside the function from being evaluated if the object is not the correct one. The return code exits the function so anything following the command is never evaluated. While you could check for the correct object by comparing names, in this scenario, you will want to use a quicker, more-efficient comparison. Because manually assigning yet one more object can get tedious, let's use an alternate way to quickly get and assign the Marble's collider.

10. Create the following variable:

```
Collider marbleCollider; // the marble's collider
```

11. In the Start function, add the following:

```
marbleCollider = marbleManager.gameObject.collider;
```

In this line, dot notation takes you back up to the MarbleManager's parent, the Marble, and then goes back down to the Marble's Sphere Collider component.

12. Add the following lines just above the print statement:

```
// if the collider didn't belong to the Marble object, leave the function
if(theCollider != marbleCollider) return;
```

13. Save the script.

14. Click Play.

This time, the Marble drops and rolls down the Ramp.

15. Roll the Sphere into the Portal A object.

It is ported to the drop site and its name reported as the evaluation of the function is continued.

16. Comment out the print line.

17. Save the script.

Depending on the level design, you could use portals to help or hinder the Marble's progress. With the single drop site, you could give the player shortcuts to reach the end position or goal. If, on the other hand, a site was randomly selected, the Marble could suffer a setback in its journey. The portals, in effect, become "chutes" and "ladders."

Before developing the multilocation code, let's take a little time to differentiate the "magic" portals from regular obstacles. A glow effect would be a nice touch, as well as letting the player know that the object is not "solid."

1. Select the Portal A object.

2. Disable the Mesh Renderer component.

3. From the Component menu, choose Rendering ➤ Light.

4. Set the Range to **4** and the Intensity to **1.5**.

5. Set the Color to a nice magenta H-**295**, S-**255**, V-**255**, and the Color's Alpha to about **175**.

6. Activate the Draw Halo check box.

    You should now see the halo in the Game and Scene views where the sphere used to be (Figure 6-5). A *halo* is an object drawn on a plane that is billboarded (or aligned) to always face the camera. It will generally require less resources than a post-processing effect such a glow but has the disadvantage of clipping other geometry.

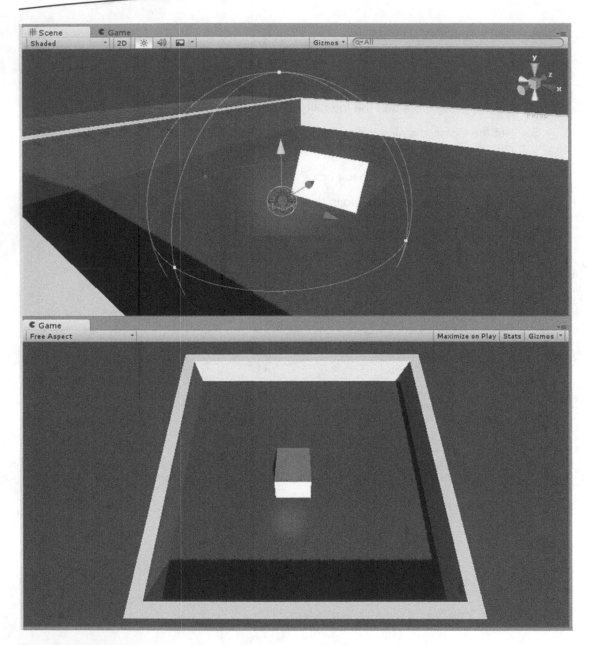

Figure 6-5. The halo option for the Light component now on the Portal A object

7. Reduce the Portal A object's Scale to **1** × **1** × **1** so the Marble will be lit briefly before the jump.

8. Click Play and make sure everything continues to work as before.

9. Stop Play mode and select Portal A.

10. Drag it into the Prefabs folder in the Project view.

11. Rename it **Portal Good**.

The portal object in the Hierarchy view is renamed to match.

12. Rename the original in the Hierarchy view to **Portal Good A**.

You will require multiple destination sites, so now is a good time to make a prefab for those as well. While you are at it, you can remove unused components:

1. Select the Portal A Destination object.

You could remove the Sphere (Mesh Filter) and Mesh Renderer components, but they will make the y positioning easier in the Scene view if you drag directly from the Project view, so it may be better to leave them disabled.

2. Repeat the prefab-creating procedure with Portal A Destination, naming the prefab **Portal Destination Good**.

Making Custom GameObject Icons

The main problem with making the drop sites nonrendering is that you won't be able to see them in the Scene view during setup unless they are selected. Fortunately, Unity gives you a way to make custom icons for your gameObjects and even for your scripts.

1. Select the Portal Destination Good object in the Prefabs folder.

2. In the Scene view, change the view to a Top iso view.

3. At the top of the Inspector, click the gameObject icon (the blue cube) and select the magenta label icon (Figure 6-6).

Figure 6-6. The icon options revealed at the top of the Inspector

In the viewport, the new icon appears along with the object's name (Figure 6-7). The name stretches the label out far beyond the object's location, and you really don't need to know its name. It would be more useful if it was a simple X-marks-the-spot sort of image.

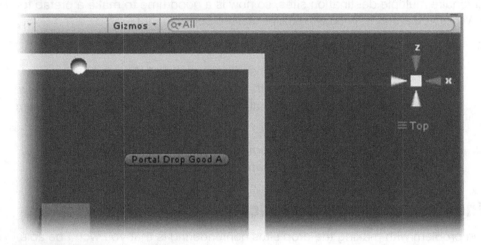

Figure 6-7. The icon in the Scene view with the object's name

4. Locate the Chapter 6 Assets folder in the assets you downloaded from the Apress web site.

5. Drag the Misc Textures folder into the Project view in the editor, or copy and paste it into the project's Assets folder in your OS's Explorer (Finder on the Mac).

6. Open the icon drop-down again and click the Other button.

7. In the browser, locate and select the magenta X image, GoodX.

    The X image is an improvement for marking a drop site, but the image is rather small if you are using 3D icons for the gizmos. You can scale the 3D icons (but that can clutter the view), or you can switch to 2D icons. The icons themselves are obviously all 2D images, but the 3D icons are scaled according to distance.

8. From the Gizmo icon on the Scene view toolbar, deactivate the 3D Gizmos check box.

    The icon is an appropriate size now (Figure 6-8).

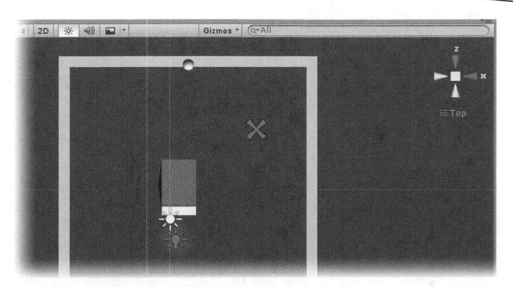

Figure 6-8. The custom image icon in the Scene view

Now you can easily create its counterpart, the "bad" drop site:

1. In the Prefabs folder, select the Portal Destination Good object and press Ctrl+D (Cmd+D) to duplicate it.

2. Name it **Portal Destination Bad**.

3. Select the BlackX image for its icon.

4. Drag the new prefab into the Scene view, across from the "good" site.

    The object's pivot point is at the Board's top surface, too low for dropping the Marble back into the scene.

5. Turn on the Mesh Renderer component and lift the sphere up until it just clears the Board.

6. Turn off the Mesh Renderer component and drag the object into the Board Group in the Hierarchy view.

7. Use Ctrl+D (Cmd+D) to make three duplicates.

8. Give them unique names by appending the default name with the numbers 1, 2, 3, and 4.

9. Move the objects to different spots around the board (Figure 6-9).

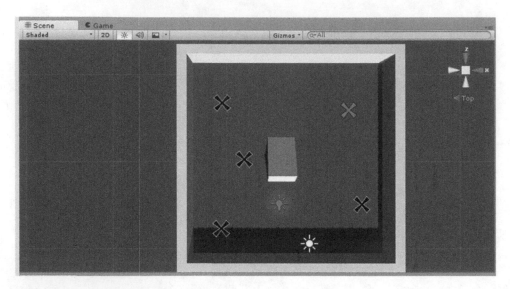

Figure 6-9. The new "bad" drop sites

You will also require a few "bad" portals.

10.   Select Good Portal A in the Hierarchy view and duplicate it.

11.   Move to an empty spot on the Board.

12.   Name the new object **Portal Bad**.

Because this object won't be associated with any particular landing spot, it can have a generic name. You will be making a few changes to this one, so the first thing to do is to break the association with the prefab.

13.   From the GameObject menu, select Break Prefab Instance.

14.   Change its Light color to reddish-orange for now.

You will be making a different special effect for it later in the book.

Adding Randomization

Now let's see about adapting the PortalHopper script to work with multiple landing sites. For this, you will be using a function that returns random numbers exclusive or inclusive of a given range, depending on number type:

1.   Open the PortalHopper script.

2.   Change the destination variable by making it an array:

```
public Transform[] destination; // the possible target location
```

3. In the `OnTriggerEnter` function, just below the `return` line, add the following:

```
int num = Random.Range (0,destination.Length);
Transform tempDestination = destination[num];
```

To access array elements, you require integers, so in this code you assign an integer randomly chosen from 0 to the length of the array. Note that Length is capitalized, but does not have the parentheses indicating a function call. With integers, the maximum number is excluded. If your array has five elements, the last element number is 4, so choosing a number between 0 and 5 (where 5 is excluded) gives you a quick way to randomly select array elements. Float values, on the other hand, are *inclusive* of the max value. Both variations include the min, or minimum, value.

In this bit of code, local variables `num` and `tempDestination` are created inside the function to keep the code more readable. The memory is allocated and then freed up as soon as the function is finished.

4. Change the `marbleManager` line to include the new randomly chosen destination:

```
marbleManager.PortalJump (delay,tempDestination);
```

Theoretically, because allocating and accessing sucks up resources, you would be better off just doing the calculations inside the `marbleManager` line. If you are comfortable with what is happening in the last three lines, comment out the first two and change the final line by adding [`num`] to the original `destination` variable, and then substituting the `Random.Range` line for `num`:

```
marbleManager.PortalJump (delay,destination[Random.Range (0,destination.Length)]);
```

5. Save the script.

6. Select the Portal Good A object and set the new Destination array Size to **1**.

7. Assign the Portal Destination Good object as its Destination Element 0.

8. Select Portal Bad and set its Destination array Size to **4**.

9. Drag the four "bad" drop sites into the array elements (Figure 6-10).

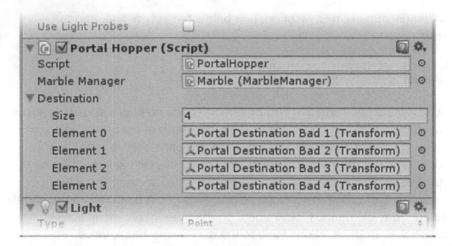

Figure 6-10. The "bad" drop sites loaded in as possible destinations

10. Click Play and roll the Marble through the "bad" portal several times.

     You will find that the random numbers are truly random; the random number generator will often select the same drop site twice in a row.

11. Stop Play mode.

More on Marble Physics

So far, the marble can be controlled only by tilting the board. With the new portal functionality, you might decide the player will want a way to avoid the bad portals, especially should they become mobile at some point. You might also decide that a rolling marble is too easy to predict. By using a bit of physics force, you can bring both scenarios into play.

Adding a Jump

A jump will be useful for evading marauding portals as well as helping the Marble reach its goal. You will begin by delving into Unity's Input class to fire it off. By using Unity's Input Manager to orchestrate the jump, you give the player the option to remap the keys, or you to remap the means of input as well.

1. From the Edit menu, choose Project Settings ➤ Input.

2. Open the Axes array by clicking the arrow next to the name (Figure 6-11).

Figure 6-11. The presets in the Input Manager

3. Open the two Jump elements.

    The first Jump is triggered from the spacebar, the second from joystick button 3. This means either input will fire off the event when scripted to use what is essentially a virtual button. When it comes time to trigger the event from the mobile platforms, you will be able to add another option by using the Jump "key." Let's find out how to script it.

    Input is another factor that can be called from any of the scripts. In this case, because it will be affecting the Marble, you will be creating another script for it.

4. Create a new C# script and name it **Booster**.

    Input is generally checked for every frame, so you will add the code to the Update function.

5. Add the following variable for the strength of the jump:

```
public float jumpStrength = 1000000f;
```

    If the amount of the jumpStrength sounds excessive, remember that you have increased the game gravity by quite a bit. By using a public variable, you will be able to test the jump during runtime to fine-tune the amount of force required.

6. Add the following code inside the Update function:

```
if (Input.GetButtonDown("Jump")){
    rigidbody.AddForce(Vector3.up * jumpStrength);
}
```

AddForce, as you probably guessed, is what pushes the object in the specified direction. In this case, it is Vector3.up, short for Vector3(0,1,0). This is a world coordinate, so even if the Board is tipped at an extreme angle, the Marble will go up relevant to the world rather than up relevant to the Board.

7. In the Scripting Reference, look up Input.GetButtonDown.

Its description reads as follows:

Returns true *during the frame the user pressed down the virtual button identified by* buttonName.

You need to call this function from the Update *function, since the state gets reset each frame. It will not return* true *until the user has released the key and pressed it again.*

Use this only when implementing action-like events, i.e., shooting a weapon. Use Input.GetAxis *for any kind of movement behavior.*

So the input triggers only once, when the virtual key is pressed.

8. Save the script and add it to the Marble.

9. Select the Live Zone and set its Y Scale to **15** to give yourself more jump room before triggering a reset.

10. Click Play and press the spacebar when the Marble rolls off of the Ramp.

11. Press the spacebar repeatedly in succession.

The Marble jumps higher with every successful press, but not all key presses register with this input type. Let's try an alternative Input option. The GetButton variation will return true while the virtual button is held down. This one is typically used for projectiles. The projectile rate is controlled with a timer.

1. Change the conditional:

```
if (Input.GetButton("Jump")){
```

2. Save the script.

3. Click Play and tap the spacebar *as briefly as possible*.

    This time the reaction is reliable, but the height of the jump is not. Let's test a timer to limit the jump time. You can find this code in the sample code for `Input.GetButton` in the Scripting Reference.

4. Add the variables for the timer:

```
float jumpRate = 0.5F;
float nextJump = 0.0F;
```

5. Add the timer check to the conditional:

```
if (Input.GetButton("Jump") && Time.time > nextJump){
```

    The *and* operator, &&, is used when you want to specify that more than one condition must evaluate as true.

6. Add the line that updates the timer at the top of the conditional:

```
nextJump = Time.time + jumpRate;
```

7. Save the script.

8. Click Play and test the jump several times to make sure it is responsive without excessive height. This time, the jump is well behaved and happens on cue.

This functionality should help your player move the marble up onto obstacles that are just out of its reach or to jump out of the way to avoid enemies. A remaining issue is to prevent the player from jumping the marble again before it has landed. Typically, you create an isGrounded flag and add that into the conditional:

1. Add the following variable to the Booster script:

```
 bool isGrounded = true;
```

2. Add the new flag to the conditional:

```
if (Input.GetButton("Jump") && Time.time > nextJump && isGrounded){
```

3. Just below that line, set the flag to `false` to prevent additive jumps:

```
isGrounded = false; // prevent jumping if in air
```

4. Save the script.

    To track when the Marble is grounded, you will watch for its collisions with other objects with an `OnCollisionEnter` event. Rather than checking for the ground by name, you will use another of Unity's mainstays, the *tag*.

5. Add the function to reset the flag:

```
void OnCollisionEnter (Collision collision) {
    if (collision.gameObject.tag == "Ground") {
        isGrounded = true;
    }
}
```

6. Save the script.

    Next you will define the new Ground tag and assign it to the Board object and the Ramp.

7. Select the Board object.

8. At the top of the Inspector, click the down arrow in the Tab drop-down and select Add Tag (Figure 6-12).

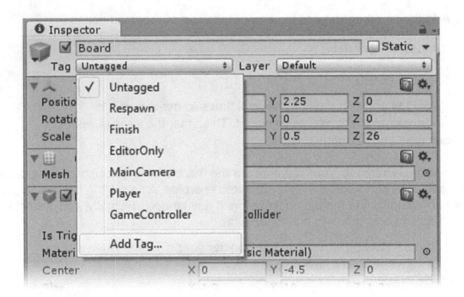

Figure 6-12. Adding a new tag

9. In the Tag array, type in **Ground** for Element 0.

    As soon as you start typing, an Element 1 is added for the next tag (Figure 6-13).

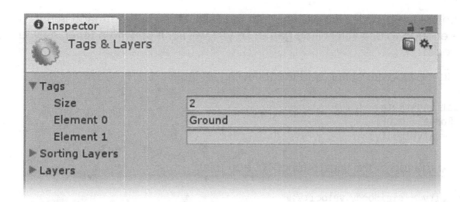

Figure 6-13. The new Ground tag

Creating a tag doesn't automatically add it.

10. Select the Board again and select the Ground tag from the drop-down.

The big advantage to using tags is that you can filter for multiple objects in a conditional without naming them individually. That means you can tag the Ramp as a Ground also.

11. Select the Ramp and set its Tag to **Ground**.

12. In the Booster script, initialize the isGrounded flag to false:

```
bool isGrounded = false;
```

13. Save the script.

14. Click Play and make sure the Marble remains jumpable.

Adding a Turbo Boost

Using the same AddForce code that you used for the jump, you should be able to give the Marble a speed boost. The tricky part here is to figure out which way the Marble is heading. Unlike a simple 2D environment, the tilting Board makes all three axes crucial to the calculation. So the first order of business is to get the current velocity (speed and direction) of the marble. Fortunately, velocity, or the *velocity vector*, is one of Rigidbody's variables. The most logical place to monitor that value is from the Update function.

Just as with the jump code, you will find that the GetButtonDown command is not consistent enough to use in this little game, so you will set it up with a timer, as you did with the jump code:

1. In the Booster script, add the following variables:

```
public float boostRate = 0.4F;
float nextBoost = 0.0F;
Vector3 currentVelocity;
```

2. At the top of the Update function, add this:

```
currentVelocity = rigidbody.velocity;
```

To test the functionality, you will want to be able to trigger the boost manually. But because you may also want to trigger it as a result of particular events, the code that does the work should be in its own function, a public function so it can be called from other objects. Let's begin by adding a variable for the boost strength.

3. Add the following variable:

```
float boostStrength = 5000f;
```

4. Add the following function:

```
public void Boost () {
    nextBoost = Time.time + boostRate; // set timer
    rigidbody.AddForce(currentVelocity * boostStrength, ForceMode.Impulse);
}
```

A couple of things happening are here. First, increasing the velocity is as easy as multiplying the current velocity. Second is the use of the optional ForceMode flag. If you look up ForceMode in the Scripting Reference, you will find the following description and list of variables:

Description: *Option for how to apply a force using Rigidbody.AddForce.*

Variables:

Force: Add a continuous force to the rigidbody, using its mass.

Acceleration: Add a continuous acceleration to the rigidbody, ignoring its mass.

Impulse: Add an instant force impulse to the rigidbody, using its mass.

VelocityChange: Add an instant velocity change to the rigidbody, ignoring its mass.

In this case, you are using `impulse` to give a quick boost to its current velocity.

To test the turbo boost before setting up trigger points, you will create your own custom virtual key. Once again, by creating a virtual input rather than hard-coding an event to a particular keyboard key, you keep your code more flexible for the player.

5. In the `Update` function, below the `currentVelocity` line, add the following:

```
if (Input.GetButton("Boost") && Time.time > nextBoost) {
    Boost ();
}
```

6. Save the script.

Before you can test the new functionality, you must create the virtual Boost button in the Input Manager:

1. From the Edit menu, choose Project Settings ➤ Input.

   The easiest way to create a new input axis is to copy the one that most closely resembles the one you want to make. In this case, Jump, a one-off type of functionality, is a good candidate.

2. Locate the first Jump, the one that is triggered with the spacebar.

3. Right-click its label and select Duplicate Array Element.

   The duplicate is created below the original, or perhaps the duplicate is created above the original and it is now the current one. Whatever the mechanism, they are identical, so it doesn't matter which one you modify.

4. Change its Name to **Boost**.

   The Name is the string you use to specify the input axis in scripting.

5. Set its Descriptive Name to **Boost Force**.

   This name/description shows in the Player Settings dialog box on startup on a desktop deployment.

6. Change the Positive button to **left shift**.

7. Unlock the Inspector by toggling the tiny lock icon to open.

   For a list of keys, buttons, and other input device names, search for *Conventional Game Input* in the Unity Manual and check out the Button Names section.

   With the code and input axis sorted out, you are ready to give the new turbo-boost a try.

8. Click Play and press the keyboard's left Shift key to see the boost in action.

The Marble shoots off faster when the key is pressed.

Let's see how game play is affected with a few "hot spots."

Just as with the portals, you will use spherical colliders as they are the most efficient (having to check only a single value, the radius). This time, however, you will want the spheres' pivot point on the Board's surface. Depending on the way the colliders are used, you may also want the player to see them.

9. From 3D Objects, create a Quad object on the Board.

10. Set its X Rotation to **90** and its Y Position to about **1.5**.

11. Drag the object into the Board Group.

Because the Quad is essentially just a flat square, you will want to be careful to keep it above the surface of the board slightly. If it was exactly on the surface of the Board, the renderer would not know which object to draw and could end up drawing pieces of both. As an object gets farther away from the camera, the problem intensifies. In some cases, you can use a custom shader that will help to solve the "Z-order fighting."

12. Name the Quad **Hot Spot**.

13. Set its Scale to **2.5, 2.5, 1**.

14. Remove its Mesh Collider.

15. Add a Sphere Collider and activate the Is Trigger check box.

16. Locate the BoostSpot texture in the Misc Textures folder and drop it on the Hot Spot in either the Scene view or the Hierarchy view.

Dropping a texture directly onto an object generates a basic material with a Diffuse shader. This texture has an alpha channel, so you will want to switch the shader to something more appropriate.

17. Locate the new Materials folder that was generated inside the Misc Textures folder.

18. Inside the folder, select the BoostSpot material.

19. Change its shader to a Transparent, Diffuse shader.

Now you need a way to call the boost functionality when the Marble intersects the Hot Spot's collider. Let's begin by creating a script for it:

1. Create a new script and name it **HotSpotBooster**.

2. Add the following variable:

```
public Booster booster; // the Booster script
```

3. Add an `OnTriggerEnter` function:

```
void OnTriggerEnter (Collider theCollider) {
    // if the collider didn't belong to the Marble object, leave the function
    if(theCollider.gameObject.name != "Marble") return;
    //trigger the boost
    booster.Boost (); // trigger the boost
}
```

As with its portal counterpart, you first check to make sure it was the Marble that tripped the trigger. If it was, you call the Boost function on the Booster script.

4. Save the script.

5. Add it to the Hot Spot object.

6. Drag the Marble object into its Booster parameter.

7. Drag the Hot Spot object into the Prefabs folder.

8. Duplicate the Hot Spot twice in the Hierarchy view and move the duplicates to new positions around the Board.

9. Click Play and roll the Marble over a Hot Spot.

The Marble shoots forward on its current trajectory.

Embracing UWP

In this last section, you will begin the process of making your little game playable on different devices. While desktop systems already allow you to use input from a gamepad as well as mouse and keyboard, consoles are less flexible. For the TipBoard game to be controllable on an Xbox One device, you will want to tilt the board with one of the analog thumb sticks on a gamepad.

Mapping the Gamepad

While Unity has a lot of functionality for joysticks already mapped into the Input Manager, the first challenge is to check the mapping on the current hardware. Button and axis assignments will also vary between operating systems such as iOS and Windows 10 so you will want to research your target devices and platforms early in development.

Another important bit of information is that there are two types of input on the Xbox controller. *Buttons* return `true` when pressed. *Axes* generally return a float value between -1 and 1 at all times. The left and right triggers are an exception in that they return 0 to 1 and 0 to -1, respectively. The current mapping for the Xbox One controller is shown in Figure 6-14.

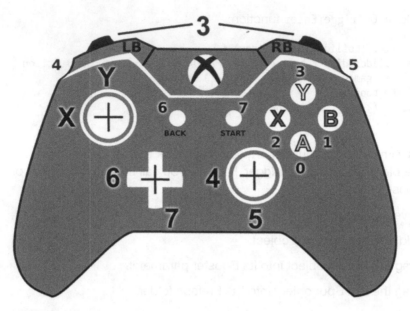

Figure 6-14. The Xbox One gamepad and its Unity mapping

For this last section, you will need an Xbox controller; either Xbox 360 or, preferably, Xbox One.

Testing Axes

Let's begin by testing the axis-type inputs. You had a quick peek at the Input Manager earlier in the chapter when you gave the marble some jumping functionality through the use of the virtual Jump button. If you were to increase the array of input elements, you would get a copy of the last element in the array, so rather than bloating the array, let's repurpose an existing element.

1. From the Edit menu, choose Project Settings ➤ Input.

2. Click the tiny lock icon at the upper right of the Inspector to keep the Input Manager open.

3. Create an Empty gameObject in the scene and name it **Test Input**.

4. In the Inspector, open the Axes array if it is not already open and open the Fire2 element.

5. Change its Name to **Test Axes**.

6. Clear all of the button names.

   The names are not used when you are using axis input, so it is a good idea to remove them to prevent confusion.

7. Set Sensitivity to **1** and select Joystick Axis as the Type.

8. If it is not already set to X Axis, open the Axis list and select X Axis from the top of the list.

9. Create a new script and name it **GamepadMapping**.

10. In the Update function, add the following:

```
if (Input.GetAxis("Test Axes") != 0) print(Input.GetAxis("Test Axes"));
```

11. Save the script and add it to the Test Input object.

The script deals with the Input class and as such could be on any object or script.

1. Click Play and open the console.

   A small number (not the expected 0) is constantly printed to the console, even though you haven't used any of the controller's buttons or sticks. It is called the *dead zone* and can cause the objects controlled by the axis to slowly wander without user input. The value varies according to each individual gamepad with older, worn thumbsticks generally registering higher values. For the tiltboard game, it will simulate players not being able to hold the board perfectly still, but for other uses, you might want to increase the size. Let's try that now.

2. In the Input Manager, with the game continuing to run, set the Dead value slightly larger than the value being printed.

   The values continue to be printed in the console, but the object will no longer be affected by them.

3. Now push the left stick all the way to the left and then to the right.

   The value tops out at 1 at the far right and -1 at the far left.

4. In the Input Manager, with the game continuing to run, change the Axis to the Y Axis.

5. Test the left stick's vertical axis.

   It tops out at 1 at the bottom and -1 at the top. If necessary, you could activate the Invert check box to invert the results.

6. Next, test the 3rd Axis (Joysticks and Scrollwheels) and press the two front triggers, one at a time.

   The left trigger goes almost to 1 and the right trigger almost to -1.

7. Change the Axis to the 4th Axis and make note of which stick, trigger, or dpad (the rocker control to the left of the right stick) is mapped to it.

8. Repeat for any other axes you are curious about.

Tilting the Board

Now that you have checked the input mechanism, you can see about using it to tilt the board. If you search the Internet for using a gamepad to rotate objects, you will find several solutions. Let's try one of the simpler solutions to get a feel for what you will require:

1. Open the TiltBoard script.

2. Add a speed variable:

```
float speed = 100f;
```

3. In the Update function, add the following:

```
float vert = Input.GetAxis("Vertical") * speed * Time.deltaTime;
float hor = Input.GetAxis("Horizontal") * speed * Time.deltaTime;
transform.Rotate(vert, hor, 0);
```

4. Save the script and test it by using the left stick.

    The board tips nicely on the vertical axis, but spins on the horizontal. In case you are wondering why the axes work at all, a quick check of the Input Manager will reveal a second set of virtual Horizontal and Vertical inputs. Let's sort out the mapping on the rotations.

5. Change Rotate(vert, hor, 0) to Rotate(vert, 0, hor).

6. Save the script and test the functionality.

    The rotation begins well, but it soon becomes apparent that the rotation is local as the board is tipped repeatedly.

7. Change the Rotation to the following:

```
transform.Rotate(vert, 0, hor,Space.World); // rotate relative to world
```

    The rotation is better, but it allows the user to turn the board upside down. Let's try a different approach by *setting* the angle of rotation rather than *animating* the rotation.

8. Replace the contents of the Update function with this:

```
float xRotation = Input.GetAxis("Vertical")  * speed;
float zRotation = -Input.GetAxis("Horizontal")   * speed;

transform.eulerAngles = new Vector3(xRotation , 0, zRotation);
```

9. Save the script and test the new code.

The limits are good, but the sensitivity is too high. You can adjust both the speed and the input's sensitivity:

1. In the script, change the speed to **50** and save the script.

2. In the Input Manager, set the Sensitivity for the joystick versions of the Horizontal and Vertical to **0.5**.

   Experimentation will show you that the lower the Sensitivity value, the tighter the rotation limits. While you are there, you can reduce the Dead value to 0. You have probably discovered that it takes some skill to keep the sticks from snapping back to 0. Setting the Dead zone to 0 will give the player more control as the values approach 0.

3. Set the Dead value for both inputs to **0**.

4. Test the new settings.

   The sensitivity is better now, but you can make it smoother by using Time.deltaTime.

5. Add Time.deltaTime to both rotations:

```
float xRotation = Input.GetAxis("Vertical")  * speed * Time.deltaTime;
float zRotation = -Input.GetAxis("Horizontal")  * speed * Time.deltaTime;
```

   Slowing the input with Time.deltaTime will require a speed adjustment.

6. Set the speed to **1500**.

   Feel free to make the speed variable public so you can fine-tune the number.

7. Test the latest additions

   The board control using the gamepad is much better.

As with anytime you make major changes in the code, you should always check to see whether the rest of the functionality remains intact:

1. Click Play and try tipping the board with the mouse drag.

   Nothing happens because the rotation is being set in the Update function using the (almost) 0 values from the gamepad. The first thing you should probably do is check whether a gamepad or joystick is present. If there is, you will also want a flag to bypass the Update code. Let's begin by adding a couple of flags.

2. Add the following variables:

```
bool gamepad = false; // is there a gamepad active on the system
bool useGamepad; // flag to bypass update code
```

3. In the Start function, look for the presence of any gamepads or
    joysticks:

```
if (Input.GetJoystickNames().Length > 0) gamepad = true;
```

4. In the Update function, wrap the transform.eulerAngles line in a
    conditional:

```
if (gamepad && useGamepad) {
    transform.eulerAngles = new Vector3(xRotation , 0, zRotation);
}
```

Now let's set the temporary flag when the player is using mouse-drag to tip
the board.

5. At the top of the OnMouseDrag function, add the following:

```
useGamepad = false;
```

Next you need to decide when to turn the flag back on. If you turned it back
on in an OnMouseUp function, the board would snap back to the input axes'
(almost) 0 values. If the player isn't using the gamepad, you would rather
it skipped the snap-back code entirely. The problem will be to allow the
player to switch back to the gamepad at will. By checking for a reasonable
value from the input axes, you can tell when it is active again.

6. In the Update function, above the if (gamepad conditional, add the
    following:

```
if (xRotation > 0.5f || zRotation > 0.5f) useGamepad = true;
```

It's not a very high-tech solution, but it is quite effective.

7. Save the script and test the functionality from both types of input.

Now the player can switch between mouse and gamepad without disrupting game play.

Testing Buttons

For the gamepad buttons, you can work with the button by name rather than with virtual
input buttons. Although that makes testing easier, hard-coding it will prevent the player from
remapping the input to a different gamepad. For now, let's use the quick method:

1. Open the GamepadMapping script.

2. Add the following lines to the Update function:

```
if (Input.GetKeyDown(KeyCode.Joystick1Button0)) print("A");
if (Input.GetKeyDown(KeyCode.Joystick1Button1)) print("B");
if (Input.GetKeyDown(KeyCode.Joystick1Button2)) print("X");
```

```
if (Input.GetKeyDown(KeyCode.Joystick1Button3)) print("Y");
if (Input.GetKeyDown(KeyCode.Joystick1Button4)) print("LB");
if (Input.GetKeyDown(KeyCode.Joystick1Button5)) print("RB");
if (Input.GetKeyDown(KeyCode.Joystick1Button6)) print("Back");
if (Input.GetKeyDown(KeyCode.Joystick1Button7)) print("Start");
```

3. Save the script.

4. Click Play and test your gamepad's button mapping, making note of any deviation.

    In Chapter 11 you will be making use of more button and axis functionality. You may have noticed that the marble jumped when you pressed the Y button. This is because the jump action is already being triggered by a virtual button/keyboard key.

5. Exit Play mode.

6. Locate the second Jump virtual input in the Input Manager and investigate its settings.

    It is already mapped to joystick 3. Also note the sensitivity used for buttons, 1000.

7. Delete or deactivate the Test Input object in the Hierarchy.

8. Unlock the Inspector.

9. Save the scene and save the project.

With a handful of useful snippets of functionality tested, you are ready to create the environment for your little tilt board game.

Summary

In this chapter, you experimented with functionality that will serve to help or hinder the marble's progress toward its goal. Repurposing the reset functionality from the previous chapter, you developed a portal system, and delving into physics forces, you developed a couple of interesting ways to temporarily disrupt the marble's progress.

You quickly discovered that the collision detection required a means to filter for the correct collider before executing the appropriate instructions. To do so, you used the optional Collision argument with the OnTriggerEnter event. It returned information about the colliding object so that you were able to jump out of the function with a return in case it wasn't the correct object.

While experimenting with the portals, you got a first peek at how Unity combines components to make various types of objects. By adding a Light component to your portals and activating its Halo parameter, you were able to create a low-resource glow effect to mark the portal's location.

To make things more interesting, you created an array to hold multiple destinations for your portals. You discovered that Random.Range was exclusive of the minimum and maximum integer values, making it ideal for use with arrays so that the portal's destination could be randomly chosen.

While looking into physics forces to make your marble jump or shoot forward on cue, you had a second look into Unity's Input system and were able to create your first "virtual" button or key. This, you found, was an excellent way to allow flexibility not only for you, but also for the player, as it allows the player to remap keys.

To make the trigger for the jump functionality more robust, you borrowed a technique used often for shooting projectiles. With the use of Time.time, the amount of time that has passed since the start of the game, you created a simple timer to prevent rapid triggering of the jump feature. Adding a second condition, you specified that the jump could not be triggered unless the marble was grounded. To determine the state of the marble, you once again used the Collision argument. This time, however, by making your own custom tag, you could check for any number of objects that used that particular tag.

Taking the boost functionality one step further, you abstracted the actual code that produced the boost into its own function. This enabled you to quickly test the results with the virtual key and to actually call the same functionality when the marble intersected a hot spot object's collider on its own.

Finally, you embraced the UWP concept by adding code to allow the player to use a gamepad instead of a mouse to tilt the board. In doing so, you learned how to detect gamepads and then use their two input types, buttons and axes, in place of the mouse and keyboard.

Chapter 7

Creating the Environment

Now that you have a tentative idea for a tip-board chutes-and-ladders type of game, you need your game to have some sort of path to give the player a goal and purpose for the marble. Good portals will move you farther along the path, and bad portals will drop you back. For the path itself, because a typical casual game is meant to be played multiple times, the path should be either generated at runtime or at least chosen from a pool of possible paths. Because creating the logic and code for a fully automated path is beyond the scope of this book, you will compromise by creating an authoring system that will let you design paths quickly and store them in efficiently small sizes.

For the path itself, you will be using hexagonal tiles, or cells. The six sides allow for the path to go in six directions, including some nice diagonals, making it more interesting than a simple square grid. Trying to stay *exactly* on the path would be too challenging with the tip board, so you will also be devising a way to track the last activated tile, allowing the player to complete the path without being penalized for rolling off it. As the marble rolls over a path tile, in order, it will be shown as activated. The marble can activate a path tile only if the previous one is already activated.

Generating the Paths

The key to today's casual games is that they must be fun to play multiple times. This means that each time the player starts the little tip-board game, the game should be a bit different. The power-ups and enemies will add a lot of randomness, but the path configuration will also help. If you search the Web for maze and path generators, you will find lots of material. Several maze generators are for sale from the Asset Store that could be adapted for this game. Writing an automated path generator by hand is not too hard, but it is a little time-consuming.

The best way to begin is to make a visual mock-up of cases where the scenario leads to failure (will halt path generation). See Figure 7-1.

© Sue Blackman and Adam Tuliper 2016
S. Blackman and A. Tuliper, *Learn Unity for Windows 10 Game Development*,
DOI 10.1007/978-1-4302-6757-7_7

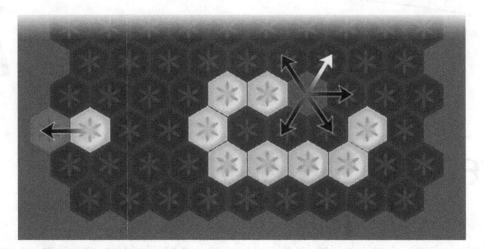

Figure 7-1. Path generation scenarios

The first test to halt path generation is when there is no cell, as in Figure 7-1's left-hand case. On the right, having found an existing cell for the location of the next path cell, it is tested for adjacent path cells. With no adjacent path cells (the parent direction is not checked), this location will be valid. From that cell, however, all but one of the directions will prevent the path from remaining linear. The top-left direction, in case you are wondering, would create an ambiguity, with two path cells leading off from the same cell. With the two most obvious fail cases identified, the rough procedure for the path cell generation would be as follows:

1. Create a grid of numbered cells for the board and put them into an array.

2. Find a random starting cell and choose a random direction to go.

3. Cast a ray in the direction to find out whether a cell is there.

4. If there is no cell in the location, rotate the ray 60 degrees and cast another ray until a valid location is found.

5. With a valid cell location found, check that cell's adjacent cells to make sure none of them are path cells.

6. If there are no adjacent path cells, accept this location as the next path cell.

   If there are adjacent path cells, rotate the ray 60 degrees and cast another ray until a valid location is found.

7. Go to step 5 and repeat until you have enough cells for the path. If you don't have enough cells for a long enough path, try a new path.

As you can see, the procedure does not lend itself well to a numbered list of steps. In this case, a visual representation in the form of a flow chart will be much more useful (Figure 7-2). It allows you to refine and work out the details of the procedure before you write your first line of code.

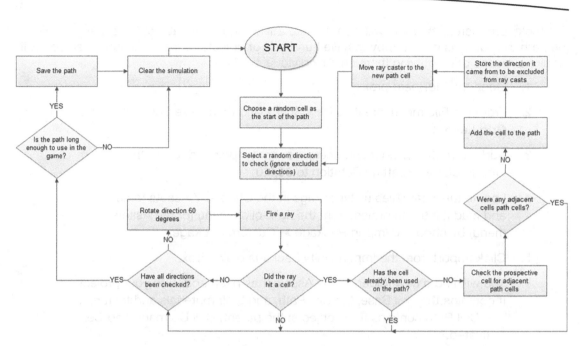

Figure 7-2. The path generation flow chart

Following this procedure, you will soon find that most of the valid paths are not terribly exciting, as they often "crawl" along the borders. You could set the cells along all three borders to not be usable, but that cuts out some nice solutions. Ideally, you should randomly decide whether a border cell could be included, but that will complicate the code. To keep things moving along in this project, you will store several solutions and choose from those at runtime. In case you are thinking that you will require too many solutions, you will be adding some functionality that will allow you to manually create and store paths easily. Storing the solutions will take up very little room, as you will be storing only a list of the path cells by grid location.

Introducing the Cells

Before settling down to create some paths, you should decide on the means of identifying an activated cell. The most obvious scenario is to change the material on the cell. Swapping materials during runtime, however, tends to be a bit costly, so it would be wise to come up with something more efficient for mobile platforms. If each cell contains three versions of the stepping stone or tile object, you will be able to turn the renderer for each off and on as required. The overhead required to keep track of the extra geometry will not be much of a burden, especially if you have two types of cells: path and nonpath. Eventually, all of the tiles will use the same material with an atlased texture, so the draw calls will be kept to a minimum.

Typically, when you are creating mazes, each square (or other shape) is called a *cell*. In this game, the hexagonal shape resembles a cell, but is almost flat like a tile. The term *tiles* also quite often refers to sections of terrains or other ground that can be tiled, so is doubly appropriate for the objects. Both terms will be used to refer to the objects.

The tricky part here is that you will want to take advantage of prefabs to build the grid for the path, but Unity is quite happy to have hundreds of objects of the same name, so you will require a means of identifying them on an individual basis.

1. Open the TipBoard project.

2. From the File menu, create a New Scene and then Save Scene As **Grid Layout**.

3. Add a Directional Light and orient it so that it points down at the ground plane by setting Rotation to **90,0,0**.

4. Locate the BoardTiles.unitypackage in the Chapter 7 Assets folder and load it into the project from the right-click menu (or the Assets menu) by choosing Import Package ➤ Custom Package.

5. Click Import from the Import Unity Package dialog box.

    You will find a new folder, Game Assets, has been added to your project. It contains the Cell Base, the Cell Path, and their materials and textures. The Cell Path contains three objects: the parent, Cell Dormant, and Cell Activated.

6. Drag the Cell Base and Cell Path assets into the Hierarchy view.

7. Press Ctrl+D (Cmd+D) to duplicate the Cell Path object and move it to the right.

8. On the first Cell Path object, deactivate the Cell Activated child object.

9. On the second Cell Path object, deactivate the Cell Dormant object.

The three cell objects, or tiles, should help the player identify the game's objective (Figure 7-3).

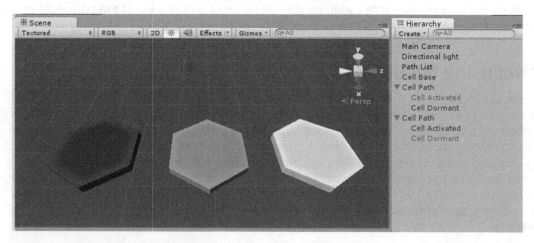

Figure 7-3. The three cell object configurations

Preparing the Assets

Anytime you plan on using an object more than once, you should immediately create a prefab for it. As your scene develops, you can add to the prefab and have the scene instances of it automatically update to receive the new changes. Follow these steps to create the prefab:

1. Delete the Cell Path object with the Cell Activated child object showing.

2. Select the other Cell Path object and activate its Cell Activated child.

    Deactivating an object during runtime is easy. Reactivating it is not, as it is inactive and cannot be contacted using GameObject.Find(). For your game, you will be enabling and disabling the Mesh Renderer to control visibility.

3. Disable the Cell Activated child's Mesh Renderer in the Inspector.

    To track the marble, the path tiles must have colliders. A Sphere Collider is the most economical and closely fits the hexagon shape of the cell.

4. From the Component menu, choose Physics and then add a Sphere Collider to the Cell Path object.

5. Set the collider's Radius to **0.85**.

    Keeping the collider smaller than the hexagon will prevent the player from slightly clipping a corner and activating the tile.

6. Set the collider to Is Trigger.

7. Right-click over the Sphere Collider's component label and select Copy Component.

8. Drag the Cell Path object into the Prefabs folder.

    A prefab for the Cell Path is created.

9. Select the Cell Base object in the Hierarchy view.

10. Position the cursor over any of the component labels, right-click, and select Paste Component As New.

11. Drag the Cell Base object into the Prefabs folder.

12. In the Prefabs folder, for both the Cell Base and the Cell Dormant objects, deactivate the Mesh Renderer's Cast Shadows parameter.

    Shadows are costly at any time and should be turned off whenever possible. The activated version of the cell uses an Unlit shader, so it will not receive shadows. Both of its shadow parameters can be turned off.

13. Turn off both shadow parameters in the Cell Activated's Mesh Renderer component.

With the Cell Path's prefab safely started, you can delete it from the scene. You will be doing a little bit of layout practice with the Cell Base object, so it can remain in the scene for now.

14. Check the objects in the scene to see that their shadow parameters have been updated to match the prefabs.

15. Select the Cell Path object in the Hierarchy view and delete it from the scene.

Let's see how easy it will be to create the grid with the Cell Base:

1. Select the Cell Base object in the Hierarchy view.

2. Using Ctrl+D (Cmd+D), duplicate the object about three or four times.

    As expected, in the Hierarchy view, the clones all have the same name.

3. Selecting the new cells from the bottom upward, move them apart in the x direction so that the first object in the list in the Hierarchy view is to the left in the Scene view and the last object is on the right (Figure 7-4).

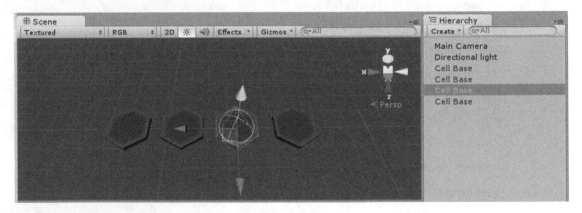

Figure 7-4. The grid of base tiles

Unlike older versions of Unity, the Hierarchy view is no longer shown alphabetically, but is shown in the order objects were added to the scene. This will be helpful for tasks such as grid layout, where you could have a lot of objects with the same name, yet need to process them in a particular order.

Aligning the objects is surprisingly easy when you take advantage of Unity's vertex-snapping functionality.

4. Select the second cell.

5. Hold the V key down on the keyboard and move the cursor to the lower-left corner of the hexagon (Figure 7-5).

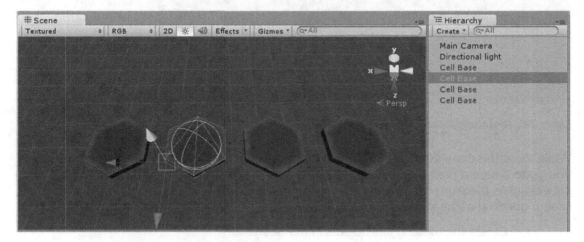

Figure 7-5. Using vertex snap

The gizmo snaps to the lower left.

6. Press the mouse button down and drag the cell to meet up with its neighbor on the left.

7. Continuing to hold the V key down, select the middle hexagon and move it to the left to snap to the second cell.

8. Repeat for the remaining cells, checking to make sure you are snapping the top vertices together.

So far, so good. You're probably thinking the grid layout will be a snap (pun intended). But the problem comes when you duplicate multiples. Their order in the Hierarchy list may be unexpected.

9. Select all of the cell objects and use Ctrl+D (Cmd+D) to duplicate them.

10. While they are still selected, drag them below the first row, and then use the vertex snap to put them into position.

11. Click the first cell on the left in the new row.

In the Hierarchy view, the cell is shown as the last in the list (Figure 7-6). As long as you remember how the order of creation is done, it probably won't cause problems, but if you wanted to parse the list in a more logical manner (at least for those of us who are used to reading from left to right), you would have a lot of rearranging to do.

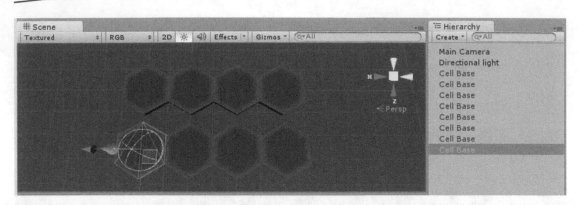

Figure 7-6. Unexpected list order for the duplicates

While the order doesn't matter for this experiment, it will for the final grid. What's more, when you go to create a prefab of the full grid, the order may change once again. Fortunately, especially as there are a lot of tiles in the final layout, in this next section you will be using a prefab grid that came in with the other objects in the Unity package you imported.

1. Delete the existing cell objects in the Scene view.

2. In the Prefabs folder, locate the Game Grid prefab.

3. Drag it into the Hierarchy view.

4. Set the Scene view to a Top iso view.

5. Select the Main Camera.

6. From the GameObject menu, choose Align with View.

7. Adjust the camera's position until you have a good view of the cell grid in the Game view (Figure 7-7).

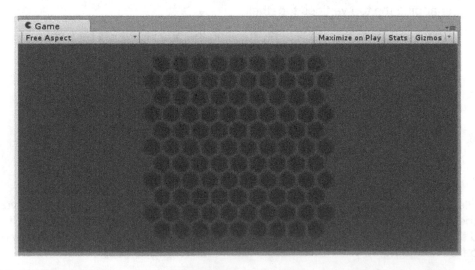

Figure 7-7. The grid of base tiles or cells in the Game view

8.   Select one of the cells.

Although a Cell Base prefab was used to create the Game Grid children, they did not update when you added the collider to the original Cell Base prefab. At the time of this writing, creating prefabs of prefabs is not yet supported. Fortunately, you can add components to multiple objects at the same time.

9.   Select the Cell Base prefab in the Project view, hover the cursor over the Sphere Collider component's label, and select Copy Component.

10. In the Prefabs folder, open the Game Grid and select *all* of its Cell Base children.

11. Position the cursor over one of the component labels in the Inspector, right-click, and select Paste Component as New.

12. In the Hierarchy view, select one of the Cell Base objects and make sure it received the collider component.

The collider appears on each of the Base Cell objects in the Hierarchy.

You could forge ahead and set up the grid for the actual game, but with a little more effort, you can add a bit more code and use it to generate some path data as well.

Making Paths

The first thing to consider is how many *path* cells or tiles you will want to use. As you've already heard a few times, using Instantiate and Destroy to add and remove prefabs from the scene tends to be too costly for mobile. For the path, you will use an array of existing objects that are activated and positioned on demand. This will also give you a means of adjusting the difficulty of the game.

To manually be able to design a path, the procedure will be as follows:

1.   Build an array of base cells and an array of path cells.

2.   Pick a base cell for the start of the path and record its element number.

3.   Take the next available path cell and move it to the base cell's location.

4.   Activate it.

5.   Add the base location to an array that will record the path.

6.   If the last added path cell is picked, reverse the process.

When dealing with objects that will be activated and deactivated during runtime, you will require a means of finding them when they are not active. To do so, you will create the array in the Awake function. The Awake function is evaluated *before* the Start function, where you will initialize the object's Active state. Let's create a script for each path cell parent. Because children inherit the transforms of their parents, you will want to make sure that the parents are both at 0,0,0.

1. Create a new empty gameObject and name it **Path Manager**.

2. Set its position to **0,0,0**.

3. Create a new C# script in the Game Scripts folder and name it **PathCells**.

4. Add the following variables:

```
public Renderer activatedCell;
public Renderer dormantCell;
```

> In this version of the game, you have only two children representing the states of the tile. In a more complicated version, you might want to keep track of several, so you will find the children with GetComponentsInChildren. As all of the path cells are alike, you know that element 0 will be the *activated* tile, and element 1 will be the *dormant* tile. The cell variables are set as public so you will be able change their parameters directly from other scripts.

5. Above the Start function, add an Awake function as follows:

```
void Awake () {
    // make temp array of children
    Renderer[] child = gameObject.GetComponentsInChildren<Renderer>();
    //identify and assign the children
    activatedCell = child[0];
    dormantCell = child[1];
}
```

6. Save the script.

7. Drag the script onto the Cell Path prefab in the Prefabs folder in the Project view.

8. Drag the Cell Path prefab into the Scene view, set its Y Position to 0, and drag it off to the right of the Game Grid.

> A quick check of the base cells will show you that they are a bit lower than 0, so the path tiles will visually be a bit higher.

9. Drop the Cell Path object onto the Path Manager object in the Hierarchy view.

10. With the Cell Path object selected, duplicate it until you have 35 objects.

The PathCells script doesn't do anything yet, but eventually it will store the cell's location in the array of path cells as well as an array containing the cell's children. The next script you make will help you to create paths on the board grid.

1. Create another new C# script and name it **PathCellManager**.

2. Add it to the Path Manager object.

3. Open the script and add the variable for the Path Cell array:

```
public PathCells[] allPathCells;
```

4. Create an Awake function and create the array:

```
void Awake () {
    // set the size of the array using the number of children
    allPathCells = new PathCells[transform.childCount];
    // find all the children containing the PathCells component & put them into the array
    allPathCells = gameObject.GetComponentsInChildren<PathCells>();
}
```

Awake functions are evaluated before the Start function. It is traditional to put the Awake function above the Start function, but the order doesn't affect anything.

Unity arrays are not resizable, so you either set the Size in the Inspector, as you have done previously, or, as in this case, you can set the size after the variable has been declared. The GetComponentsInChildren function will also search through children of children, so searching for a Transform component would have returned all of the Cell Path objects and each of their children. As you will be contacting the Cell Path objects through their PathCells script/component, you specify PathCells as the component type to search for. The childCount returns only the number of children an object has and does not include grandchildren, so it will not require any adjustment.

5. Save the script.

6. Click Play and check out the Path Manager object to see the list of Cell Path objects it generated for the All Path Cells array.

With the Cell Path Objects safely stored, you can take care of their active state in the Start function.

7. Stop Play mode.

8. In the Start function, add the following:

```
// deactivate the Cell Path objects
foreach (PathCells cells in allPathCells) {
    cells.gameObject.SetActive(false);
}
```

The foreach loop iterates through the array and, in this case, performs the change in active status. Because the objects have already added to an array that lives in memory, you will have access to turning them back on.

9. Save the script.

10. Click Play and check to see that the Cell Path objects are deactivated.

Let's also go ahead and block in the functions that will be handling the path picks.

11. Block in the two functions:

```
public void AddPathCell(int elementNum, Transform location) {

}

// FIXME used only for path design *********
public void RemovePathCell(int elementNum) {

}
```

As you create the various scripts throughout the chapter, some of the code will be used only during the game setup process. When it is time to publish, you will want to disable it for efficiency's sake and to prevent player-induced mishaps. By adding a comment beginning with FIXME, you will be able to quickly locate and make the changes before publishing.

12. Save the script.

Just as with the Cell Path objects, the Cell Base objects will be communicating with their parent, so they will require a script to manage data and other functionality:

1. Create a new C# script and name it **BaseCells**.

2. Select the first of the Cell Base objects on the Game Grid prefab in the Project view, and drag the new script onto it.

If you check the other Cell Base objects, you will see that it was not added to the rest of them. As you found when adding the Sphere Colliders, you will be able to select them all at once and add them quickly.

3. Select the *rest* of the Cell Base objects on the Game Grid prefab.

4. From the Component menu, choose Scripts, and select the BaseCells script.

Next you will create an array for the Cell Base objects. Once again, you will use GetComponentsInChildren to identify the objects. This time, you will search for the BaseCells component. The best place to manage the base cells, of course, is from their parent, Game Grid.

5. Create a new C# script and name it **GridManager**.

6. Drag it onto the Game Grid object in the Hierarchy view.

7. Open the script and add the variable for the Cell Base object's array:

```
public BaseCells [] allBaseCells;
```

8. Create an Awake function and create the array:

```
void Awake () {
    // set the size of the array using the number of children
    allBaseCells = new BaseCells [transform.childCount];
    // find all the children & put them into the array
    allBaseCells = gameObject.GetComponentsInChildren< BaseCells >();
}
```

> Now that you have generated the array, you can assign the element numbers to the Cell Base objects themselves by iterating through the new array and sending them off to the individual objects.

9. In the Awake function, after the array has been filled, add the following:

```
//inform the Cell Base objects of their element numbers
for (int x = 0; x < allBaseCells.Length; x++) {
    allBaseCells[x].elementNum = x;
}
```

10. Save the script.

Before you can test, the Cell Base objects will require a variable to store their element number. Later, when picked, they will have to contact the PathCellManager script to identify their element number. They already have a collider, so they are ready to receive a pick event. The colliders on the Cell Base objects are only for the path design process and will have to be removed before publishing.

Let's go back in and add some more code to the BaseCells script to get rid of the error reported by the console:

1. Open the BaseCells script.

2. Add the following variables:

```
public PathCellManager pathCellManager; // the component on the Path Manager object
public int elementNum; // the element number assigned to this cell object
```

> In a desktop application, where resource management is less of an issue, you would use GameObject.Find to locate the Path Manager object, and then use GetComponent to identify the PathCellManager component. The problem is that GameObject.Find must iterate through the entire scene to find the object. While a one-off use in a Start function shouldn't be

a problem, in this case you have over 100 objects that would all be looking for the same object and iterating through the scene to find it. By approaching the task from the opposite direction, you ought to be much more efficient.

3. Save the BaseCells script.

    The error about missing variables disappears.

4. Switching to the GridManager script for a minute, add the following variable:

```
public PathCellManager pathCellManager;
```

5. In the Awake function, below the allBaseCells[x].elementNum = x line, add this:

```
allBaseCells[x].pathCellManager = pathCellManager;
```

Now you can manually assign the Path Manager object just once and it will automatically be assigned to the 100+ Cell Path objects.

6. Save the script.

7. Select the Game Grid object in the Hierarchy view and drag the Path Manager object onto its Grid Manager component's Path Cell Manager parameter.

8. Click Play and then check a few of the Cell Base objects to see that the Path Manager object has been correctly assigned (Figure 7-8).

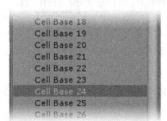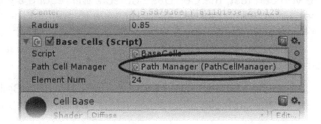

Figure 7-8. The Path Manager and its PathCellManager component found at runtime

With that little issue solved, let's head back to the BaseCells script.

The Cell Base object will have to send its element number back to the PathCellManager when picked, so you will require an OnMouseDown function. In case you are worried about multiple platforms, the functionality you are setting up now is only for game setup.

9. In the Base Cells script, create an OnMouseDown function to receive the pick:

```
//FIXME this is for path design only *************
void OnMouseDown () {
    pathCellManager.AddPathCell(elementNum, transform);
    gameObject.SetActive(false);
}
```

Besides the element number that the GridManager will have assigned it, to save time, the picked object will also send its location before it is deactivated.

10. Save the script.

11. Click Play and try picking the base cells in the Game view to create a path.

The cells disappear when picked (Figure 7-9).

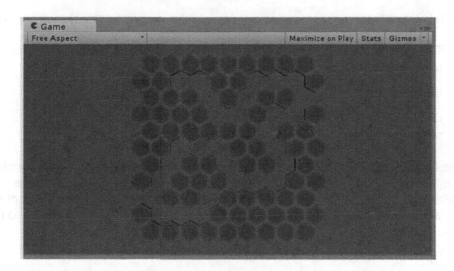

Figure 7-9. The path revealed as base tiles are picked and deactivated

Now you can see about filling the recently vacated spots with the Cell Path objects. You will bring a Cell Path object to the location and then activate it. The trick here is to be aware of which Cell Path objects have already been used. For that, you will keep track of the *next-in-line* element number. The Cell Path objects should also keep track of their own element numbers in their pool. Let's go back in and add some code to the PathCells script:

1. To the PathCells script, add the following variables:

```
PathCellManager pathCellManager;
public int pathElement; // the element number of this object in the path array
public int baseElement; // the element number of the cell it will replace
```

2. Save the script.

3. Open the PathCellManager script.

4. Add the following variable to keep track of the next-available Cell Path object:

```
public int nextInLine; // next available element number for the path objects pool
```

The Start function already has a foreach that iterates through the path cells and deactivates them. Rather than turning it into a for loop, you can add a local variable as a counter that will essentially be the element number.

5. In the Start function, above the foreach line, add the following local variable:

```
int x = 0; // the counter
```

6. Inside the foreach loop above the SetActive line, add this:

```
allPathCells[x].pathElement = x++; // assign its element number to it, then increment x
```

The x in this case, is not incremented until *after* the assignment, so is safe to use in this fashion.

7. Save the script.

8. Click Play and check the Cell Path objects in the Hierarchy view to see that they are storing their Path Element numbers.

With some of the "paperwork" out of the way, let's see about getting the Cell Path objects to activate and move to the vacated Cell Base locations. The pick takes you to the PathCellManager script, where the picked cell has just sent its location and element number to the AddPathCell function. The first task should be to make sure you haven't used up all of the Cell Path objects:

1. Open the PathCellManager script.

2. In the AddPathCell function, add the following:

```
if (nextInLine >= allPathCells.Length) return;
```

3. Now add the code that manages the path cell:

```
//activate the next path cell
PathCells cell = allPathCells[nextInLine]; // assign it to a temp variable for easier
handling
cell.gameObject.SetActive(true);
```

Here you are accessing the next Cell Path object in the array, assigning it to a temporary variable, and then activating it.

4. Add the following:

```
//transform it
cell.transform.position = location.position;
```

> Using the `location` of the Cell Base object that was passed into the function it is replacing, it is moved to the new position.

5. Now add this:

```
// store the base cell element's number in this path cell
cell.baseElement = elementNum;
```

> The Cell Base object's element number is stored so it can be identified and reactivated if the Cell Path object is removed from the path.

6. And finally, add the remainder of the code:

```
// increment the nextInLine
nextInLine++;

// deactivate the Cell Base
location.gameObject.SetActive(false);
```

> The last bit deactivates the Cell Base here, *after* a check for a valid Cell Path object to replace it so you can comment it out in the PathCells script (where no check was carried out).

7. Save the script.

8. In the BaseCells script, comment out the `gameObject.SetActive(false)` line, as it is now handled in the PathCellManager script.

9. Save the script.

10. Click Play and try creating a path.

Marking the Path Starting Tile

You are probably thinking that it would be nice to have a quick way to recognize the starting tile. Because the element 0 tile in the `allPathCells` array is always the first one used, you can simply assign a different material to it:

1. Locate the Cell Dormant material in the Game Assets ➤ Materials folder.

2. Duplicate it and replace the appended 1 with *Start*.

3. Tint its Main Color a light green to differentiate it.

Here's where you might think things should be easy. You might think you could change the first Cell Path's Cell Dormant material and all would be well, but the objects *may* not be loaded as per the order in the Hierarchy list. Assigning a different material to the first path cell *after* the path list has been generated will be a safe way to go:

1. In the PathCellManager script, add a variable to hold the start material:

```
public Material startMaterial;
```

2. At the bottom of the Start function, add this:

```
allPathCells[0].dormantCell.material = startMaterial;// assign the start tile material
```

3. Save the script.

4. Select the Path Manager object in the Hierarchy view and assign the new Cell Dormant Start material to its Start Material parameter.

5. Click Play and create a path.

    The starting tile is clearly marked (Figure 7-10).

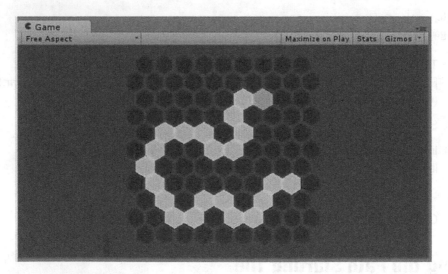

Figure 7-10. The starting tile clearly marked

Scripting the Undo

Now of course, you are probably thinking it would be handy to be able to undo a path cell when you change your mind. This functionality is less work, because you don't have to put the path cell back, just deactivate it. The next time the cell is used, it will be moved to the next location. Now you will script the undo functionality.

1. Back in the PathCells script, assign the `pathCellManager` component in the `Start` function:

```
pathCellManager = transform.parent.GetComponent<PathCellManager>();
```

By going up the component hierarchy with `transform.parent`, you can get the component's parent and from there go *back down* and get any of the sibling components.

2. Add the following function:

```
//FIXME this is for path design only *************
void OnMouseDown () {
    pathCellManager.RemovePathCell(baseElement);
}
```

Here, the element number of the Cell Base object that was turned off is sent back for processing.

3. Save the script.

4. Open the PathCellsManager script.

5. In the `RemovePathCell` function, add the following:

```
// deactivate the current path cell
PathCells cell = allPathCells[nextInLine - 1];
cell.gameObject.SetActive(false);

// reactivate the base cell at this location using the element number argument
gridManager.allBaseCells[elementNum].gameObject.SetActive(true);

// decrement the nextInLine
nextInLine--;
```

You will have to identify the Game Grid's GridManager component, before you can test the code as it holds the array of Cell Base objects.

6. Continuing with the PathCellsManager script, add the following variable:

```
public GridManager gridManager;
```

7. Save the script.

8. Select the Path Manager object in the Hierarchy view and drag the Game Grid object onto its Base Cell component's Grid Manager parameter.

9. Click Play and test the undo.

As long as you create and undo the path in the correct order, the functionality is sufficient.

> **Tip** To create valid paths, add and remove tiles in the correct order only.

There are obviously lots of ways you could make the little path designer more foolproof, such as an end-of-pool warning and a way to force you to create the path only in order. If you want to spend time making the code more robust, you can revisit it after you have been through the last section of the chapter that restricts the player from activating tiles out of order.

Saving Your Paths

As it is now, the functionality you have added will work for its intended purpose—a way for you to create paths that can generate a sequential list of Cell Base elements for a path. The big question is, how can you save them? The answer is: as a prefab. For that, you need to create an object whose sole purpose is to hold the array of Cell Path elements in their proper order:

1. Create a new Empty gameObject and name it **Path List**.

2. Create a new C# script and name it **PathLister**.

3. Add it to the Path List object.

   To store the numbers, this time you will try something a little different. You will use a *list* instead of an *array*. A list will grow and shrink on demand, allowing you to use as many or as few path cells as you wish. Easy levels could have fewer, less complicated paths, and harder levels could have more path tiles and complicated patterns.

   The first thing to know about lists is that they are not included with the regular includes at the top of the script.

4. At the top of the script, just under the regular includes, add the following as per Figure 7-11:

```
using System.Collections.Generic; // required for lists

// This script is used for path design only **************
```

```
  PathCellManager.cs  ×    BaseCells.cs        ×    GridManager.cs    ×    PathCells.cs      ×    PathLister.cs      ●
 PathLister ▸   Start ()
1⊟ using UnityEngine;
2 │ using System.Collections;
3    using System.Collections.Generic; // required for lists
4
5    // This script is used for path design only ***************
6
```

Figure 7-11. Including System.Collections.Generic for lists

5. Add the following variables under the class declaration:

```
public List<int> pathList;
public int lastIn = 0;
```

Note the syntax: the type follows List.

6. And add a variable to hold an optional texture:

```
// optional texture image for this path
public Texture thumbnail;
```

7. Add the two little functions that manage the list:

```
public void AddToList (int newNum) {
    pathList.Add(newNum);
    lastIn++;
}

public void RemoveFromList () {
    lastIn--;
    pathList.RemoveAt(lastIn);
}
```

With a list, elements are added at the end of the list with Add. By keeping track of the last element number, the lastIn variable, you can use RemoveAt to remove the element from the list. Note the use of ++ and -- to increment and decrement the value of lastIn.

8. Save the script.

The element numbers that feed the list will come from the PathCellManager script:

1. Open the PathCellManager script.

2. Add the variable that holds access to the list:

```
public PathLister pathLister;
```

3. At the bottom of the AddPathCell function, add the following:

```
//FIXME add to the path list, design only **************
pathLister.AddToList (elementNum);
```

4. At the bottom of the RemovePathCell function, add this:

```
//FIXME remove from path list, design only **************
pathLister.RemoveFromList ();
```

5. Save the script.

6. Select the Path Manager object in the Hierarchy view and drag the Path List object onto its new Path Lister parameter.

7. Click Play and select the Path List object before you start creating a path.

8. Open the Path List parameter to view the additions and removals.

The Cell Base elements are added and removed as you design your path.

Now it's time to create the prefab. Let's begin by making a folder to store your creations for use in the actual game:

1. In the Prefabs folder, create a new folder and name it **Paths**.

2. Click Play again and create a path worthy of saving.

3. *While still in Play mode*, drag the Path List object into the new Paths folder.

Tip You may want to make a screen grab of each path and reduce it to thumbnail size for reference so you don't repeat any of the paths. You can add it to the Path List objects in the Prefab's Path folder.

---

4. Stop Play mode.

5. Check out the list in the new prefab. The element numbers remain intact.

6. Repeat the process.

    The newly created prefabs' names are even incremented as you drop them into the folder.

7. Repeat until you have at least four path lists.

Figure 7-12 shows a few of the possible configurations.

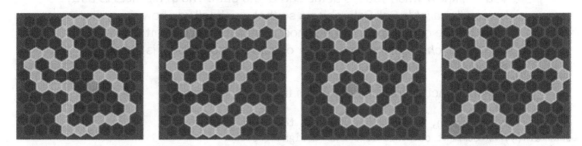

Figure 7-12. A few possible paths

Loading the Paths

Reusing the path templates should be fairly easy, as you already have most of the code. You will now add that functionality to the PathCellManager script:

1. In the PathCellManager script, add the following:

```
using System.Collections.Generic; // need for lists
```

2. Add the following variables:

```
public PathLister[] paths; // array of prefabs with path lists
int pathLength; // length of the chosen path
```

3. Save the script.

4. Select the Path Manager and set its Paths array Size to match the number of paths you created.

5. Drag the path prefabs into the waiting elements.

6. Back in the PathCellManager script, create the function that loads the paths:

```
void LoadPath () {
    // pick one of the paths
    int num = Random.Range(0, paths.Length);
    // iterate through the list and send each Cell Path object for processing
    foreach(int x in paths[num].pathList){
        AddPathCell(x,gridManager.allBaseCells[x].transform);
    }
    pathLength = paths[num].lastIn;
}
```

The last line stores the length of the chosen list, its `lastIn` parameter, so you will know when you are at the end of the path. The `allPathCells` array holds all *available* Cell Path objects so that won't tell you how many were used for the current path. The method `transform.childCount` returns the number of *children*, not the number of *active* children, so it is of no help either.

7.   Call the function from the bottom of the Start function:

```
// load a premade path, comment this line out to design more paths
LoadPath(); // comment out this line when designing paths
```

8.   Save the script.

9.   Click Play a few times to see the prefab paths loaded.

Because the random number chosen is truly random, you may get repeats. The game will eventually have enough going on that this shouldn't be a problem, but you may wish to investigate ways to have more control over randomly generated numbers.

Activating the Paths

With a means to quickly create and reuse paths, it is time to add the last bit of path functionality. The player must roll the marble along the path to reach the end tile. As the marble intersects a tile's collider, it should "light up," or otherwise indicate that it has hit that checkpoint. In order to keep the player on the path, the tiles will light up only if they are done in sequence. Additionally, portals can jump the marble backward or forward along the path. This will require full management involving the status of the path. You already have a nice list of the Cell Path objects to work with, so you will be making code to navigate the list.

Changing the Tiles

The first bit of game functionality to address will be the visual indication that the tile has been activated. For *activated*, you will turn on the Mesh Renderer on the Cell Activated child and turn it off on the Cell Dormant child. As the parent object already contains the code to manage itself, it will be worthwhile identifying the children's Mesh Renderer component for quicker access. You will be toggling the states from the PathCellManager script as it contains the array of Path Cell objects.

1.   Open the PathCellManager script.

2.   Add the following function:

```
public void ToggleTileState (PathCells cell) {
    // get the renderer component's current state
    if (cell.activatedCell.renderer.enabled) {
        cell.activatedCell.renderer.enabled = false;
        cell.dormantCell.renderer.enabled = true;
    }
```

```
else {
    cell.activatedCell.renderer.enabled = true;
    cell.dormantCell.renderer.enabled = false;
    }
}
```

In this function, you pass in the cell/tile you want to change, check the Mesh Renderer's state on the dormant child, and then toggle the two cells' Mesh Renderer's state accordingly.

Let's set up a simple way to test an intersection with the collider.

3. Save the script.

4. Back in the PathCells script, add the following:

```
void OnTriggerEnter (Collider collider) {
    if (collider.tag != "Player") return;
    pathCellManager.ToggleTileState(this);
}
```

In case you are wondering why you aren't toggling the tiles directly from the cell, remember that the path itself is managed on the PathCellManager script and it will ultimately be in control. So the argument, this, passes the cell (or, more accurately, its PathCells script) back to the PathCellManager script.

You also may have noticed that instead of checking for the hitting collider's object name, you are once again checking for its tag. As you found out earlier, Unity provides several ways to identify (or, in this case, filter) objects for special processing. Tags give you the freedom to check for several related objects.

5. Save the script.

Now you will want a quick way to test the new code. The easiest way to test is by dragging an object around in the scene view at runtime. That way, you don't have to add collision floors, worry about driving it around, or other little issues.

1. Double-click one of the base cells in the Hierarchy view to focus the view to it.

2. Create a new Sphere object and set its Tag to Player.

3. Add a Rigidbody component and deactivate the Use Gravity check box.

4. Check to make sure the Sphere intersects the game tiles, and then set the view to a Top iso and drag it off the grid.

5. Click Play and select the Sphere.

6. Drag the Sphere around the path and watch the tiles toggle between activated and dormant versions.

The next step is to find out which tile has just been toggled and report back to the PathCellManager. The cell already knows its order in the list of path tiles, or cells, and communication is already going back to the PathCellManager, so all you have to do is add an extra argument to the `ToggleTileState` function.

1. In the PathCellManager script, change the `ToggleTileState` function as follows:

```
public void ToggleTileState (PathCells cell, int pathPosition) {
```

2. Add a `print` statement at the top of the function to check the number:

```
print (pathPosition);
```

3. Save the script.

    Having changed the arguments in the function, you will have to change them each place the function is called.

4. In the PathCells script, change the `pathCellManager.ToggleTileState` line to the following:

```
pathCellManager.ToggleTileState(this,pathElement);
```

5. Save the script.

6. Click Play and use the Sphere to toggle the tiles in the path's order.

    The printout in the console should be sequential regardless of which end of the path you started from.

7. Comment out or delete the `print` statement.

8. Save the script.

Setting Sequential Progress

Now that you have a means of knowing where on the path you are, you can change the rules a bit. If you think about it, as long as you remember the number of the previously activated tile, if the next tile is +1, you can continue. The first task, then, will be to save the current path position. The PathCellManager script is in charge of path monitoring, so that is where you will begin.

1. Open the PathCellManager script.

2. Add the following variable:

```
int lastActivated = -1; // the last sequential tile visited
```

Note the initialization of -1. This is so that the first tile, element 0, will be valid.

3. At the top of the `ToggleTileState` function, add the following:

```
//check for a valid position before processing
if (pathPosition != (lastActivated + 1)) return;
```

4. At the bottom of the function, add this:

```
lastActivated++; // increment the position
```

5. Save the script.

6. Click Play and test using the Sphere.

This time, the cells will activate only when triggered from start to finish.

Working with External Influences

The last bit of path functionality will be to increment or decrement the last activated path position in response to some outside influences, say, the portals. The mechanism will be the same for both, but the position will go in either a positive or a negative direction, depending on the number fed to it. The mechanics of updating the path are similar to those in the `ToggleTileState` function. As you probably guessed, this functionality will also be handled in the PathCellsManager script:

1. Open the PathCellsManager script.

2. Add the following to the Update function for easy testing:

```
// this is just for testing **************
if(Input.GetKeyDown("up")) PathAdjuster(4);
if(Input.GetKeyDown("down")) PathAdjuster(-4);
```

3. Now start the `PathAdjuster` function:

```
public void PathAdjuster (int tiles) {
    if(lastActivated == -1) return;
```

No path adjustments are allowed until the player has rolled the marble onto the path. The `tiles` argument is the base amount of the adjustment.

4. Next, randomize the adjustment a little:

```
// randomize the base amount
int newAdj = Random.Range(tiles - 1, tiles + 1);
```

5. Start the for loop:

```
for (int x = 0; x < Mathf.Abs(newAdj); x++) {
```

This one is a bit tricky. You want to loop through the code newAdj number of times, but when newAdj is a negative number, the amount would already be less than the end condition. The solution here is to use the absolute value (remove any negative signs) of the number. The Mathf class will give you access to all sorts of mathematical functions not regularly available.

6. Search the Scripting Reference for Mathf to see what other interesting functions are available.

7. Add the code that does the work:

```
// forward, if it was a positive number
if(newAdj >= 0) {
    lastActivated++;
    // get the new tile to activate
    PathCells cell = allPathCells[lastActivated];
    cell.activatedCell.renderer.enabled = true;
    cell.dormantCell.renderer.enabled = false;
}
else { // backwards, if it was a negative number
    // get the last activated tile
    PathCells cell = allPathCells[lastActivated];
    cell.activatedCell.renderer.enabled = false;
    cell.dormantCell.renderer.enabled = true;
    lastActivated--;
}
```

8. End the for loop and close the function:

```
    }
}
```

9. Save the script.

10. Test by manually activating the path about halfway in the Scene view with the Sphere, clicking in the Game view to switch focus to it, and then pressing the up or down arrows to jump the activated tile position backward or forward.

The functionality is there, but you need a couple of checks to account for the start and end of the path. Let's say that the path cannot by reduced past the first tile, lastActivated = 0, and it can't be jumped all the way to the end tile, pathLength - 2.

1. At the top of the if(newAdj >= 0) conditional, add the following:

```
if(lastActivated > pathLength-3) return;
```

2. At the top of the else, add this:

```
if(lastActivated < 1) return;
```

3. Save the script.

4. Click Play and test.

    The new code safely prevents the path from out-of-range errors or allowing the player to finish without attempting the path.

5. Deactivate the test Sphere.

Adding New Game Pieces

The next chapter introduces the functionality designed in the previous chapter and ties it into new game pieces to enhance your new board environment. These game pieces will radically impact your marble's progress and so ought to be worthy of your new environment. Let's import the assets and do the initial setup:

1. Create a new scene and name it **Ani Test**.

2. From the Chapter 7 Assets folder, drag the three textures, BambooFence, CellTiles.tiff, and GamePieces.psd into the Game Assets ➤ Model Textures folder.

    The two *new* textures have been atlased to contain the textures for multiple objects (Figure 7-13).

Figure 7-13. The new atlased textures

3. Drag the four .fbx files—Bamboo Wall, Banana Peel, Gumdrop, and Peppermint—into the Game Assets folder.

    The three new game pieces all use the same material, GamePieces.

4. Select the GamePieces material in the Project view.

5. Set its Main Color to white.

> **Tip** Some DCC applications do not blend their diffuse color with their diffuse texture map as does Unity, so it is always a good idea to check the generated material's Main Color on import.

6. Check out the new game pieces in the Inspector (Figure 7-14).

Figure 7-14. The new Banana Peel, Gumdrop, and Peppermint game pieces

The Banana Peel, as you may have guessed, will serve as the boost trigger to speed up the marble. The gumdrops will become the Good portal objects, and the Peppermint will be the Bad portal objects. The Gumdrop and Peppermint objects both have simple transform animations. There is little setup to do for them, but the animation clips will require renaming.

7. Select the Gumdrop asset in the Project view. In the Animations section, rename its clip to **Squash.**

8. Under the clip name, click Clamp Range.

The file that the Gumdrop was created in was set to 60 frames of animation, but the Gumdrop was animated for only 30 frames—hence the prompt to Clamp Range.

9. Set the clip to Loop Time and click Apply.

10. Repeat for the Peppermint, naming its clip **Spin** and checking its Loop Time.

The Banana Peel object is more complicated. As with the character you set up in Chapter 4, it too has a bone system. This one is not humanoid, so you will leave its Animation Type set to Generic. Three of its four clips will be the random animation that occurs when the Marble rolls over the Banana Peel, and the fourth will be a standard idle animation. The Banana Peel is a bit large for the rest of the game pieces, so you will begin by setting its scale:

1. Select the Banana Peel asset, set its Scale Factor to **0.008** in the Model section, and click Apply.

2. In the Rig section, set its Root Node to Banana Peel.

3. In the Animation section, create four animation clips as per Figure 7-15.

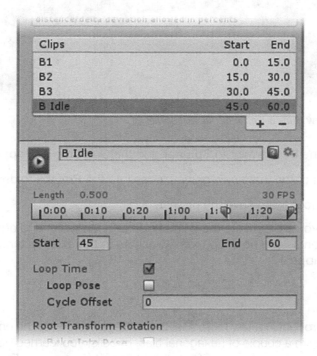

Figure 7-15. The Banana Peel animation clips

4. Set only the B Idle clip to Loop Time and then click Apply.

   To finish the animation setup, you will have to put the objects into a scene and hook up the Mecanim features.

5. Drag the three new game pieces into the Scene view (Figure 7-10).

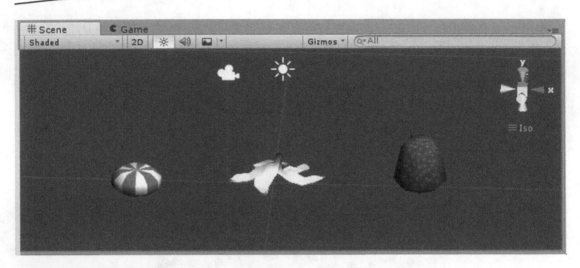

Figure 7-16. The three new game pieces in the Ani Test scene

6.   Rename the Peppermint to **Spinner** and the Gumdrop to **Popper**.

7.   Drag each of the three new game pieces into the Prefabs folder.

8.   Save the scene and save the project.

In the next chapter, you will activate the animations with Mecanim and add some unexpected animation as you hook up the new assets to the existing functionality and expand their visual appeal.

Summary

In this chapter, you brought in a few more assets and began to create the environment for your game. Starting with a couple of hexagonal tiles, or cells, you learned how using vertex snap could speed up the layout process for arranging assets in a scene. From there, you went through the process of creating the code that would manage the visibility of the path tiles through the use of their Mesh Renderers. Using a bit more economizing, you found that shadow casting was expensive and learned to assess an object's shadow-casting requirements.

Though you imported a finished grid of hexagons, you learned that presently, Unity does not support prefabs of prefabs, but that you could add components by selecting multiple objects. As you created code to manage the path tiles, you discovered that regular arrays in Unity are not dynamic in size. To make a list of path tiles that could grow and shrink during the path-authoring process, you discovered the list, but found that it was not included automatically and that you had to include system.Collections.generic to use it.

After adding code to manage the design and creation of your paths, you discovered they could easily be saved as prefabs during runtime, allowing you to read back in the data during the actual game. With randomly selected paths now available, you finished the path, managing code so that it would track the player's current position on the path, highlight the completed tiles, and allow for outside sources to move the player up and down the path.

Finally, you brought in a few new assets and set up their animation clips and saved them as prefabs in anticipation of incorporating them into your game.

Chapter 8

Combining Assets and Functionality

With your potential game functionality and the game board ready for further testing, your next challenge is to merge them and, along with some new game pieces, lock down the basic game play.

Merging Environment and Functionality

It's time to see how the functionality and board environment work together:

1. Open the Board Test scene.

2. Drag Start Location A, Marble, Directional Light, and Main Camera into the Board Group.

3. Delete the Ramp from the group.

4. Make a prefab of the Board Group by dragging it into the Prefabs folder.

5. Open the Grid Layout scene (don't save the Board Test scene).

6. Delete the main Camera, the Directional Light, and the Sphere.

7. Save the scene as Board Level.

8. Drag the Board Group prefab into the Hierarchy view.

9. Adjust its height until the tiles just peek through, about **-3.03** (Figure 8-1).

© Sue Blackman and Adam Tuliper 2016
S. Blackman and A. Tuliper, *Learn Unity for Windows 10 Game Development*,
DOI 10.1007/978-1-4302-6757-7_8

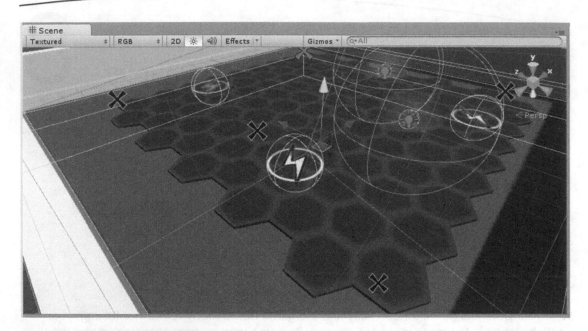

Figure 8-1. The grid and board objects merged

10. Take the Marble, Main Camera, Directional Light, and Start Location
    A out of the Board Group, agreeing to lose the prefab.

Shadows help define shape and keep us oriented in 3D space. Now, with the grid graphics
on the board and most of the action taking place close to the board's surface, it is not as
important for the light to cast shadows. As shadow calculations are quite costly, it is always
a good idea to turn them off if the game will work well without them.

1. Set the Directional Light's Shadow Type to No Shadows.

    As you saw in Chapter 5, anything that must move with the tilting board
    must be added to its group.

2. Drag the Game Grid and Path Manager objects onto the Board
   Group in the Hierarchy view.

    In the previous chapter, you used a marble stand-in to check the path
    collisions. The condition was that the colliding object was tagged as
    Player. Let's go ahead and set the same tag on the real Marble object.

3. Select the Marble.

4. Tag the Marble as Player.

    Testing the Marble on the path will be easier if the portals and hotspots are
    deactivated.

5. Select the portals and hotspots and deactivate them.

6. Click Play and then test by rolling the marble from the start of the path to the end (Figure 8-2).

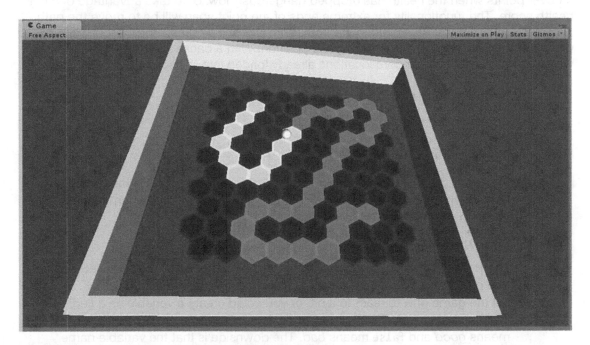

Figure 8-2. Rolling the Marble along the path by tipping the Board

The action is difficult and boring at this stage but will form the basis of the little game. In the next section, you will learn about helping and hindering the marble's progress along the path.

Refining the Portal Functionality

Before jumping back into the portal code, let's make some decisions about how it should work. Right now, it sends the marble off to the specified location or, if multiple destinations have been supplied, chooses one of the locations at random. In the interest of dishing out bonuses and setbacks, you will be implementing a health system that will dictate what happens to the marble under various conditions. This way, you will be able to curb the effects of intersecting the portals.

Tracking Health

The health points will range from 0 to 20. Each time the marble intersects a portal's collider, points will be added or removed, staying within the 20-point range. Because the code for both "good" and "bad" portals is very similar, the differentiator will be the health points themselves. A negative number indicates a bad portal, while a positive number indicates a good portal.

In addition to gaining or losing health points, the player will be rewarded or penalized when the heath is above or below specified thresholds. This way, the player has the option to recover points when the health has dropped dangerously low, or to take advantage of a high health score. The functionality for extreme ends of the point span will be to move the path progress forward or backward along the path. With forward progress, the marble will be ported to the newly activated path progress position. With a backward penalty, the marble will be sent to one of the random locations already loaded into the script.

1. Open the MarbleManager script.

2. Add the `health` variable:

```
public int health = 10; // start health at half way
```

A value of 10 starts the marble with a good midpoint amount. When you implement the path position adjustments, they will work only when the health is very high or very low.

3. Save the script.

The PortalHopper script resides on both "good" and "bad" trigger objects. You could check for positive vs. negative values in the conditionals that tell the game how to react to a hit, or you could create a variable as a flag. The most economical way would be to use a simple Boolean, where `true` means *good* and `false` means *bad*. The downside is that the variable name and check box could be less than clear. If you are the one setting them up, you will probably remember the assignments, but in a studio situation, someone else could be in charge. You will often see *enums* being used in various other code, and so this is a good time to become familiar with the way they are set up.

4. Open the PortalHopper script.

5. In the same area as the regular variables, define the enum:

```
public enum HealthType {
    Good = 0, // adds health points and/or path tiles
    Bad = 1 // removes health points and/or path tiles
}
```

HealthType is the custom type you are defining, and *good* and *bad* are the two values it can have. They are assigned by element number. To use the enum, you will create a variable of type `HealthType`, named `healthType`, and then use dot notation to initialize the value. Enums are essentially custom variable types and can be marked as public, internal, or private, just as any other variable.

6. Create the variable that uses the enum and assign a value:

```
// The enum to use
public HealthType healthType = HealthType.Good;
```

> Now comes the best part about enums—the way they are displayed in the Inspector.

7. Save the script.

8. Select one of the portal objects and locate the new Health Type parameter.

9. Click the drop-down.

The two possible values, Good and Bad, are available for the author to choose from (Figure 8-3).

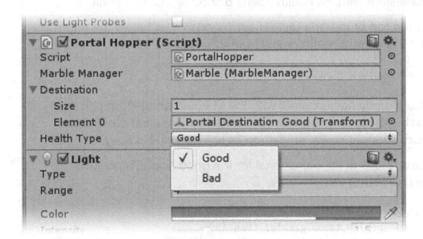

Figure 8-3. The drop-down list created in the Inspector by the enum

Next you will add a base value to add or subtract from the marble's health and an adjustment amount that will come in handy for setting ranges, changing difficult and

1. Continuing in the PortalHopper script, add the following variables:

```
public int healthPoints = 2; // amount of points to take or give
internal int adjustment = 4; // average path adjustment
```

> In case you are wondering why you couldn't just double the health points to get the path adjustment, using a second variable allows you more control in case the path length is shorter or longer. Note the use of `internal`; the `adjustment` variable will be available to other scripts, but will not be exposed to the Inspector.

2. In the Start function, add the following:

```
//  set up health points & path adjustment
if (healthType == HealthType.Good) { //good game piece
    if (healthPoints > 4) adjustment = 5;
    else if (healthPoints < 2) adjustment = 3;
}
else { // else its a bad game piece, adjust path adjustment accordingly
    if (healthPoints > 4) adjustment = -3;
    else if (healthPoints < 2) adjustment = -5;
    else adjustment = -4;
    healthPoints = healthPoints * -1; // bad health points are negative
}
```

In this code block, you are adjusting the health points and path adjustment according to the portal type of the object the script is on and the health point assignment itself. This makes the path adjustment somewhat consistent with the health points gained or lost by the hit.

3. At the top of the OnTriggerEnter function, just below the return line, get the current health points from the marble:

```
int health = marbleManager.health;
```

You already have contact with the MarbleManager through the marbleManager variable you created when you first created the PortalHopper script, so getting its health value is easy.

4. Next, block in the conditional for the good portal, a positive healthPoints value:

```
if (healthPoints > 0) { // health points are positive
    // adjust the health to no greater than 20
    health += healthPoints; // increment the health value
    if (health > 20) health = 20;
}
```

Because the health points should top out at 20, you will add them first, and then cap the value if necessary.

5. Directly beneath it, add the code for the bad portal:

```
else { // health points are negative
    // adjust the health to no less than 0
    health += healthPoints; // decrement the health value
    if (health < 0) health = 0;
}
marbleManager.health = health; // assign the adjusted value to the marble's health
```

Note that you are also *adding* the bad `healthPoints` to update the marble's health value. In this case, the points are already negative, so += is doing a subtraction.

6. Below the `marbleManager.health = health` line, add a `print` statement to keep track of the health value:

```
print (marbleManager.health);
```

7. Leave the `PortalJump` code at the bottom of the `OnTriggerEnter` function for now.

8. Save the script.

9. Activate the portal objects in the scene.

10. Locate Portal Bad and set its Health Type to Bad in the drop-down list.

11. Add or remove enough portals to have three good and three bad portals.

    Don't worry about creating extra destinations for the Good portals, as those will eventually be on the path.

12. To make testing easier at this point, set one Good portal near a corner of the board and one Bad portal near another corner of the board.

13. Set the Good portal Health Points to **3**.

14. Click Play, roll the Marble into the various portals, and watch the health value change in the console or status line. Check to make sure it doesn't go over 20 or under 0.

With the health values changing nicely, it is time to tackle the path adjustment that may go with the health point changes.

Adjusting the Path Progress

While adjusting the path progress may sound like a lot of work, you have already done something similar when you created paths for use in the game. The path tiles are managed from the PathCellManager script. Let's begin with the function that will do the adjustments. You will be passing in the base number of tiles to use for the adjustment; either a positive or negative number, so it will know which direction to go.

1. Open the PathCellManager script.

   Before calling the existing function, you will want to change the protection level on the `lastActivated` variable so it can be accessed by the PortalHopper script. Internal, as you may remember, will make it accessible but not visible to the Inspector.

2. Change the `lastActivated` variable protection level as follows:

```
internal int lastActivated = -1; // the last sequential tile visited
```

3. Save the script.

    Back in the PortalHopper script, you will add the code that calls the function. With the path adjustment functionality in place, you will differentiate the response according to the current health value.

4. Open the PortalHopper script.

5. Add the new variable to identify the PathCellManager:

```
public PathCellManager pathCellManager;
```

In the PathCellManager, you prevented the path adjustment from going too far back or forward on the path. This time, you will also make a check to prevent any path adjustment from taking place if the player has not yet started the path.

6. Add the following local variable below the `int health =` line in the `OnTriggerEnter` function:

```
int currentTile = pathCellManager.lastActivated; // current tile
```

7. Replace the *contents* of the `if (healthPoints > 0)` clause as follows:

```
// marble is stong enough to gain path tiles
if (health >= 12 && currentTile > 0){ // marble is stong enough to gain path tiles
    // increment path
    pathCellManager.PathAdjuster(adjustment);
    }
 else { // not strong enough for path boost, just increment health
    // increment health to no greater than 20
    health += healthPoints; //increment the health value
    if (health > 20) health = 20;
}
```

So now, if the health is strong (more than 11) and the player has started the marble on the path, the path position will be incremented by calling the new `PathAdjuster` function and sending it the base number of tiles to add. Health points are *not* added when the path is adjusted, as that would be like double dipping. If the health value was not high enough for a path adjustment, the `else` clause, the health value is incremented.

8. Next, replace the *contents* of the else { // health points are negative clause, where the healthPoints are a negative number for a bad portal:

```
// marble is very weak, takes a hit
if (health < 6 && currentTile > 0){
    // jump to one of the spawn places
    marbleManager.PortalJump (delay,destination[Random.Range (0,destination.Length)]);
    // decrement the path
    pathCellManager.PathAdjuster(adjustment);
}
else { // strong enough to resist path hit
    // decrement health to no less than 0
    health += healthPoints; //decrement the health value
    if (health < 0) health = 0;
}
```

If the health points to be added are negative, and the health is less than 5, the path is decremented, but no additional health points are removed. The marble is also ported to one of the spawn points. If the health value is stronger, only health points are deducted.

9. Delete the original marbleManager.PortalJump, int num = Random. Range and Transform tempDestination lines from the bottom of the OnTriggerEnter function.

10. Save the script.

11. Make sure you are not in Play mode.

12. Select the six portal objects and assign the Path Manager object to the Cell Path Manager parameter.

13. Click Play and test the new functionality. Remember to test before and after starting the Marble along the path.

The completed path is incremented and decremented according to health and portal type.

As of yet, however, the marble is not yet ported forward to the new path position after an increment. You have the means of performing the transform, but not the target position. For that, you will have to contact the PathCellManager script.

1. Open the PathCellManager script.

2. Add the following function:

```
public Transform GetCurrentTile () {
    return allPathCells[lastActivated].transform;
}
```

3. Save the script.

4. Open the PortalHopper script again.

5. Beneath the `pathCellManager.PathAdjuster` line in the `if (health >` `12` clause, add the following:

```
// jump marble to the new current tile;
marbleManager.PortalJump (delay,pathCellManager.GetCurrentTile());
```

> In this line, you are getting the transform of the current tile by calling the new function you made in the PathCellManager script, and then you are immediately passing it on to the MarbleManager's `PortalJump` function.

6. Save the script.

7. Click Play and test by rolling through enough good portals to trigger the path increment behavior.

> This time, the marble is ported to the newly assigned path progress tile.

8. Stop Play mode.

> With the good portals sending the marble to a dynamic location, you no longer have a need for the good drop points.

9. Delete the original Portal Drop Good objects from the Hierarchy view.

> You also no longer require the hot keys that you used to set up the path adjustment script.

10. Open the PathCellManager script.

11. Delete or comment out the contents of the `Update` function.

12. Save the script.

Although the game play is more interesting, it continues to be too predictable to truly engage the player. Activating the hotspots will make things a bit more challenging:

1. Select the three hotspot objects.

2. Activate them.

> The hotspots, as you may recall, temporarily increase the marble's velocity for a quick boost of speed. If approached carefully, the player may get several tiles activated at once. If hit while navigating the path, the hotspots could easily shoot the marble off track and disrupt the Marble's progress.

3. Click Play and test.

The variation in speed and predictability certainly helps the game, but it definitely lacks an element of danger. In the next section, you will be making the portal objects dynamic, both visually and in position.

Introducing Dynamic Elements

To improve both game play and visual appeal, you will replace the proxy portal objects with animated assets. The animations will be manually controlled by Mecanim, and the two types of portals will use different placement schemes, so each object will have its own script for its dynamic behavior.

Game Elements

In Chapter 4, you imported and made a start at setting up several new assets. They have had their import settings tweaked, preliminary animations set up, and materials adjusted. The prefabs you made should be ready to bring into the scene. For the game, you will use the blue gumdrops for good portals, the peppermint candies as bad portals, and the banana peels for the power boosts.

Now will also be a good time to update the cell tile textures with the atlased version, CellTiles. There's only one problem. Because the new texture contains all four cell tile textures, the mapping will be off. If you don't have access to a DCC application to change the mapping, when the texture is carefully atlased, you may be able to change the material tiling and offsets. You already have separate materials for each, so let's begin by putting the new texture in each.

Before you begin updating the materials, let's take a quick look at the game's stats to see how the draw calls are adding up:

1. Click Play and toggle on the Statistics report in the Game view.

    The draw calls are up to 210! Let's see what can be done about that. Material changes are permanent in Play mode, so you can leave the game running.

2. From the Game Assets folder, open both the Materials and Model Textures folder in the Single Column Layout so you can see the thumbnails for both at the same time.

3. Select each of the Cell materials and drag the CellTiles texture into the texture thumbnail.

    The board looks like a nice patchwork quilt. Don't panic!

4. Set the x and y Tiling to **0.5** in all four Materials.

    The draw calls remain at 210. Let's change a few materials. The Cell Activated material uses an Unlit shader. For the other three materials, you can use the Mobile/Diffuse shader.

5. Assign the Mobile/Diffuse shader to the three other cell materials.

    The draw calls drop to almost half! Removing the color that gets blended with the texture is a huge savings with this scene.

6. Set the Offsets as per Figure 8-4.

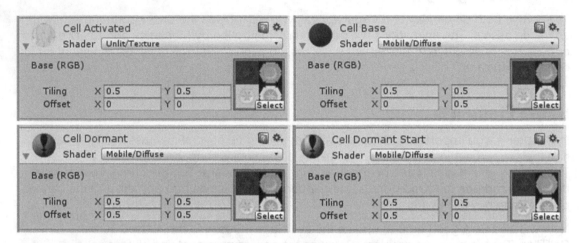

Figure 8-4. The four cell materials using the same texture, but with different offsets

7. Return to the Unity editor and inspect the new textures by clicking Play and rolling over a tile or two.

Now let's see how the new game pieces look on the updated board. You've already deactivated the hotspots and destination objects; the portals are next so you will have a clear view of the board.

1. Deactivate the six portal objects.

    The draw calls drop to eight! Clearly, there is something expensive going on there.

2. Select all six portal objects and turn off their Light components.

    Mystery solved! The Light components are the culprits. Fortunately, the new game objects will have plenty of visual effect on the game.

3. Stop Play mode and remove the Light component from the portal objects.

4. Select the Portal Good object in the Prefabs folder and remove its Light component.

    The draw calls remain at eight. You will gain more draw calls when you reactivate the mesh renderers, but it will cost only one per object. Let's bring in the new objects.

5. Deactivate the six portal objects again.

6. Drag the Popper, the Spinner, and the Banana Peel prefabs into the Scene view.

7. Position them over a tile and make sure they each sit just above the board (Figure 8-5).

Figure 8-5. The three replacement new game pieces on the new cell textures

8. Drag the three objects onto the Board Group Object.

9. Select one of the Portal Bad objects, right-click over its Portal Hopper component, and select Copy Component.

10. Select the Spinner object, right-click over any of its component labels, and select Paste as New Component.

11. Copy the Portal Hopper component from one of the Portal Good objects and paste the component onto the Popper object.

12. Select one of the Hotspot objects, copy its Hotspot Booster component, and paste it onto the Banana Peel.

The game pieces will also require a collider to catch the OnTriggerEnter events. Once again, the Sphere Collider is the least resource intensive of the colliders. To make sure the objects get a good intersection, you will use a collider that is slightly smaller than the object's mesh. That way, the marble can't just clip the outside and trigger the events. The easiest way to get a clean collider onto the imported assets is to copy one from one of the existing portal objects.

1. Select one of the portal objects.

2. Copy its Sphere Collider component.

3. Select the three game pieces and paste the Sphere Collider component onto them.

4. Set the collider's Radius to **0.65** for the Gumdrop and Peppermint, and **0.9** for the Banana Peel.

5. Click Play and make sure the new portal objects work just like the originals by rolling the marble over them and checking the health points value in the console.

6. Delete the old portal objects.

Stop Play mode. The new game pieces were imported with animation and you set up the animation clips, but nothing is animating in the scene at runtime as of yet.

Activating Mecanim Animations

With Mecanim, to see the animation play in game, you will have to set up the Animator Controller for each object.

1. Create a new folder in the Project view and name it **Mecanim**.

2. With the new folder selected, from the right-click menu, choose Create Animator Controller.

3. Name it **Spinner Controller**.

4. Duplicate it to create two more Animator Controllers.

5. Name one **Popper Controller** and the other **Booster Controller**.

6. Select the Spinner object and drag the Spinner Controller into the Animator component's Controller parameter.

7. Repeat for the other two objects, adding the appropriate controller to each.

8. Select the Spinner object and double-click the Controller's Spinner Controller.

The Animator view opens as a tab next to the Scene view with the selected controller shown in the bottom-right corner and a default Any State present.

The Any State is used in situations where any currently active state should be interrupted, such as with a character "death." For looping animations, you will add the object's animation clip as its only regular state.

1. Drag the Spinner's Spin clip from the Project view into the Animator view.

   The clip is shown as orange, the default state in the view (Figure 8-6). It takes on the clip's name, but that can be changed in the Inspector.

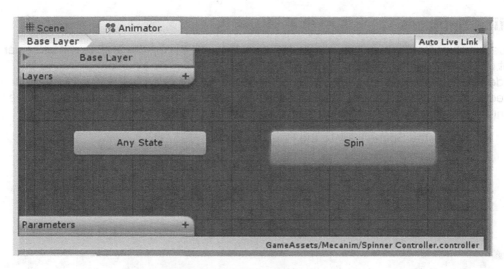

Figure 8-6. The Spin clip becoming the default state in the Animator

2. Click Play.

    The Spinner object spins happily in the viewport.

3. Stop Play mode and repeat the procedure for the Popper.

4. For the Banana Peel, drag only the B Idle clip into the Animator view.

5. Click Play and watch the imported animations play.

    The progress bar loops on the B Idle state in the Animator view, showing the animation's distance along its timeline. You will eventually bring in the other nonlooping animations and trigger them from scripting.

6. Stop Play mode and drag each of the new game pieces into the Prefabs folder.

The new game assets are ready for some secondary animation.

> **Tip** You may be tempted to deactivate Apply Root Motion in the game pieces' Animator component, but you must not do so. Root Motion refers to any *transform* on the root object, so you would lose the Spinner's *rotation* and the Popper's *scale* animations!

Shaking Things Up

To make things more interesting both visually and for game play, you will have the two types of portals exhibit different dynamic behaviors. The Gumdrops, now known as Poppers, will pop up randomly around the board, avoiding the path as landing places. The Peppermints, a.k.a. Spinners, will spin their way across the board heading for randomly chosen waypoints.

Drifting Spinners

The peppermint Spinners will be allowed to pass through all objects and so will be easier to set up. Let's begin by setting up their waypoints. Most will be positioned around the outside of the game grid, but a few will be inside the grid to provide the occasional change in direction midway. To prevent the Spinners from jumping around the outside, you will set a minimum distance for the waypoints that they can head toward.

1. Focus the Scene view to the Popper object.

2. Create an Empty gameObject and name it **Waypoint**.

3. Keeping its Y Position as is, set its X and Z Positions to **0** and focus the view to it.

4. In the Inspector, click the object icon's open arrow to open the icon drop-down.

5. Select Other and choose the Waypoint texture.

6. Drag the new Waypoint into the Prefabs folder.

Because the Waypoints don't require any scripts, you will have to find a way to identify them so you can collect them and put them into an array.

1. Click the Tag drop-down and select Add Tag.

2. Create a new tag in Element 1 and name it **Waypoint**.

3. Select the Waypoint prefab in the Project view and assign the Waypoint tag to it.

4. Create a new Empty gameObject and name it **Waypoint Group**.

5. Drag the Waypoint object into the Waypoint Group.

6. Drag the Waypoint Group into the Board Group.

7. Duplicate the Waypoint object to make 14 more copies.

8. Arrange them as per Figure 8-7.

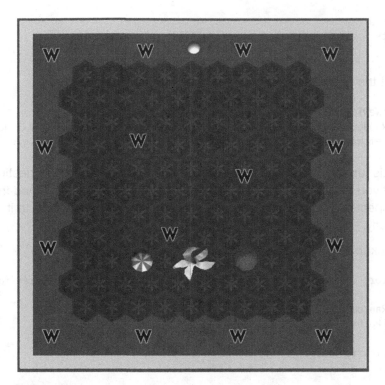

Figure 8-7. The Waypoint locations

When the Spinner gets close enough to a waypoint, it will contact the parent of the waypoint to get a new heading. The randomly chosen Waypoint must not be closer than 10 units.

1. Create a new C# script and name it **WaypointManager**.

2. Add it to the Waypoint Group object.

3. Add the following variables:

```
public Transform[] allWayPoints;
int wayLength; // length of the array;
float minDist = 10f; // closest distance to get a new target to
```

Once again you will be putting the children of the parent into an array for processing. This time, however, by searching for children with transforms, the parent will be included. It will come in as element 0, so you will have to keep that in mind when iterating through the array.

4. Load the waypoints into an array in an Awake function:

```
void Awake () {
    wayLength = transform.childCount;
    // size the array
    allWayPoints = new Transform [wayLength];
```

```
    // fill the array
    allWayPoints = gameObject.GetComponentsInChildren<Transform>();
}
```

5. Start the function that sets a destination for the Spinner:

```
public void GetNewTarget(Traveler requestedBy) {
    int num = Random.Range(1,wayLength); // get a random element number, exclude parent, 0
    Transform tempWayPoint = allWayPoints[num]; // get the object at that element number
```

> In this function, you pass in the object that is requesting a new destination.
> First you must check the distance between its current position and the
> prospective Waypoint. Then you will assign the new destination to it
> directly.

6. Check to see whether it is valid:

```
    while (Vector3.Distance(requestedBy.transform.position,tempWayPoint.transform.position)
< minDist) {
        num = Random.Range(1,wayLength);
        tempWayPoint = allWayPoints[num];
    }
    requestedBy.currentTarget = tempWayPoint.transform;
}
```

> In this while loop, you are checking the distance between the Spinner that
> requested a new destination with the randomly chosen waypoint. If the
> distance is less than the minDist, a new random Waypoint is chosen and
> checked. When the selected Waypoint is not less than the minDist, you
> break out of the while loop and directly assign the valid Waypoint as the
> target for the object that requested the new destination.

7. Save the script and ignore the errors pertaining to the missing
    Traveler; you will be creating it shortly.

Now you will create the script that tells the Spinner to move toward its current destination.

1. Create a new C# script and name it **Traveler**.

2. Add it to the Spinner object in the Prefabs folder.

Tip   If Unity does not allow you to add the new script to the Spinner because of the missing
Traveler error, perform a Build All in the script editor from the Build menu to make sure it has found
the new Traveler script.

---

3.   Add the following variables:

```
public WaypointManager waypointManager;
internal Transform currentTarget;
float speed = 8f;
```

4.   In the Start function, add the following:

```
// get first target
waypointManager.GetNewTarget(this); // request a valid target for this object
transform.LookAt(currentTarget); // turn this object to face the new target
speed = Random.Range(speed-2, speed); // randomize the speed so all are slightly different
```

5.   In the Update function, add this:

```
// move the object towards its target
float step = speed * Time.deltaTime;
transform.position = Vector3.MoveTowards(transform.position, currentTarget.position, step);
// check to see how close it is to the target
float dist = Vector3.Distance(currentTarget.position, transform.position);
print(dist);
// if it is too close, request a new destination
if(dist < 0.5f) waypointManager.GetNewTarget(this);
```

6.   Save the script.

     The errors reported by the console should disappear.

7.   Select the Spinner object in the Hierarchy view and drag the Waypoint Group into its Waypoint Manager parameter.

8.   Click Play and watch the Spinner move purposely around the board. Check the console to see the distance between the spinner and its current target destination.

9.   Stop Play mode.

10. Comment out the print statement and save the script again.

11. Update the Spinner prefab by using Apply at the top of the Inspector.

12. Duplicate the Spinner two more times and spread them out around the board.

     To be fully functional, you will have to reactivate the bad portal destination points.

13. Select the four Portal Destination Bad objects and reactivate them.

The Marble will now be at the mercy of the random destinations when struck by a marauding Spinner.

Poppers

The Gumdrops will not travel around the board like the Spinners. They will pop up in random cell/tile locations, stay for a few seconds, and then pop up elsewhere. Rather than make it too easy for the player to gain health points by rolling through them, you will be restricting them to nonpath locations. This will make it necessary for the player to leave the path if he wants to pick up points. You already have written code for porting objects, and you are more than familiar with randomizing numbers by now, so the challenge here is to restrict the destinations to nonpath tiles. Fortunately, a quick check of the target tile's active state should do the job. Let's begin with the function that finds the new base tile location.

1. Open the GridManager script.

2. Add the function:

```
public Vector3 GetBaseLocation () {
    int cLength = allBaseCells.Length;
    Transform tempLoc = allBaseCells[Random.Range(0,cLength)].transform;
    while (!tempLoc.gameObject.activeSelf) {
    tempLoc = allBaseCells[Random.Range(0,cLength)].transform;
    }
    return tempLoc.transform.position;
}
```

This function is a bit different. It is public so it can be called from other places, but instead of returning void or nothing, this one will *return* a Vector3 value. The code inside it is fairly simple; get a random base tile until you find one that is active. If it is not active, it was replaced by a path tile and cannot be used as a Popper location. Then return the valid tile's position, the Vector3 value.

3. Save the script.

Now you can create the script that operates the Popper behavior.

4. Create a new C# script and name it **Popper_Hopper**.

5. Add the following variables:

```
public GridManager gridManager; // to get the base tile locations
internal float targetTime; // for the timer
internal float onTime = 5f; // time the object is visible
internal float offTime = 1f; // time it is not visible
Animator animator; // so the animation start times can be randomized
```

With the Spinners' rotation, it didn't matter that they were all spinning with the same animation. With the Poppers, you will quickly find that they all squash up and down at the same time. To solve this visual problem, you can start the animation clip at different places along its timeline.

6. Add the following to the Start function:

```
animator = gameObject.GetComponent<Animator>();
targetTime = Time.time + Random.Range(0f,onTime);
animator.Play("Squash",0,Random.Range(0f,1f));
```

The first line identifies the Animator component. The second line starts the timer by assigning the first amount of time it will be visible. Time.time is the amount of time in seconds that has passed since the game started. The last line adjusts the start time of the animation clip/state. With Mechanim, you first tell it which state you want. Because you used the drag-and-drop method to create the states from the animation clips, the names are the same. The next argument, 0, tells what layer the state is on. Unless you are making complicated state machines for controlling your animation clips, your clip will be on layer 0. The next argument is where on the clip's timeline you want to start. The clip length is unitized, so the value of 1 corresponds to 100 percent along the timeline. You, of course, are specifying a random location on the timeline to start the animation.

Next you create the timer code that will turn the Popper off and on as well as move it around the board.

7. In the Update function, add the timer code:

```
if (visible && Time.time > targetTime - offTime){
  visible = false;
  gameObject.GetComponent<Renderer>().enabled = false; //hide popper
  gameObject.GetComponent<Collider>().enabled = false; //disable collider
  targetTime = Time.time + Random.Range(.5f,offTime); //set a new time to make visible
}

if (Time.time > targetTime){
    MoveIt(gridManager.GetBaseLocation());
    gameObject.GetComponent<Renderer>().enabled = true;//show popper
    gameObject.GetComponent<Collider>().enabled = true;//enable collider
    visible = true;
    targetTime = Time.time + Random.Range(0.5f,onTime) + offTime;// new time before hiding
}
```

The first conditional hides the Popper between pops. It first checks whether it is already hidden and if so, no further calculations are performed. If it is visible and the visible time is up, it hides the Popper, turns off the collider, and gets a new hide time. In the second conditional, if the time is up, the object is moved to a new location. That location is acquired by calling a function on the GridManager. Next, the object is made visible again, its collider enabled, and the timer set for the next hide time, once again randomizing the on time a bit so it isn't so predictable.

8. Next, create the MoveIt function:

```
void MoveIt (Vector3 location) {
    //transform it
    Vector3 newPos = new Vector3(transform.position.x,transform.position.y,transform.
position.z);
    newPos = location;
    transform.position = newPos;
}
```

This function uses the location returned by the gridManager.
GetBaseLocation call to move the Popper to its next position.

The last little function will give you a means of turning off the Popper early
if it gets hit by the Marble. This will prevent the player from double-dipping
health points from the Popper.

9. Add the following function:

```
void ForceOff () {
    targetTime = Time.time; // this forces a timer restart
}
```

Setting the targetTime to 0 forces the cycle to restart. It doesn't turn the
Popper off so much as it turns it on in a new location. You will call the
function shortly, but it is not yet hooked up to anything.

10. Save the script.

11. Add the script to the Popper prefab and then select the Popper in the
Hierarchy view.

12. Drag the Game Grid object to the Grid Manager parameter.

13. Click Play and watch the Popper wink in and out around the grid.

14. Roll through the Popper with the Marble.

The health is incremented, but you may not be able to tell whether it was a good hit.

The last little function you created will be called from the PortalHopper where the health
points are generated.

1. Open the PortalHopper script.

2. At the bottom of the OnTriggerEnter function, add the following:

```
// force time is up if this is a popper
gameObject.SendMessage("ForceOff",SendMessageOptions.DontRequireReceiver);
```

This time, you are using a `SendMessage` to call the function. A quick search of the Scripting Reference will tell you "Calls the method named `methodName` on every `MonoBehaviour` in this game object." The function (or method) is called by name, and so is a string. You may use one optional argument, and you can have it report back if there was no function of that name found. The nice thing is that you don't have to supply the component/script that the function resides on. Each of the components will be searched for the function. Obviously, you won't want to use `SendMessage` on large-scale searches where it could cost too much in terms of frame rate, but it can be quite useful on a smaller scale.

3. Save the script.

4. Click Play and roll through some Poppers to see that they disappear on intersection.

5. Stop Play mode.

6. Duplicate the Popper two more times for a total of three.

7. Place the Poppers randomly around the board.

8. Click Play and try out different strategies to complete the path.

The Poppers offer a different type of challenge. Unlike the Spinners that you have to predict their location, with the Poppers, you have to decide whether you can get to them safely and in time before they move again.

Boosters

The Banana Peels are more of a neutral game piece in that, with careful planning, you can shoot through one to gain several path tiles at a time, or, if caught unawares can be catapulted into an oncoming Spinner. At the very least, they can send the Marble quickly off course. There is already enough moving on the board so the Banana Peels will stay put, but they should at least start in different positions each time. To keep things simple, you will group them and then rotate the group in the Start function.

1. Duplicate the Banana Peel twice so you have three and rotate the duplicates for some variation.

2. Arrange them around the board, keeping in mind that they will be rotating together as a group.

3. Create a new Empty gameObject and name it **Boosters**.

4. Drag it into the Board Group and then drag the Banana Peels into the Boosters Group.

5. Create a new C# script and name it **Rotator**.

6. Add the following to its Start function:

```
transform.Rotate(0f,Random.Range(0f,360f),0f);
```

7. Save the script and drag it onto the Boosters Group.

8. Click Play several times to view the arrangement.

The Banana Peels turn up positioned haphazardly across both path and base tiles.

Although the Banana Peels are not moving around the board, you can spice up their functionality a bit more. The Banana Peel asset's animation clip was split into four separate clips. It is currently set to use the fourth clip as a looping idle clip. That leaves you three possible hit clips to fire off when the Marble intersects the peels.

1. Open the HotSpotBooster script.

   You will require an array to store the clips and will have to access the Animator states through the Animator component.

2. Add the following variables:

```
public AnimationClip[] aniClip;
internal Animator animator;
```

3. In the Start function, identify the Animator component:

```
animator = GetComponent<Animator>();
```

4. In the OnTriggerEnter function, below the return line, add the following:

```
if (animator) {
    int num = Random.Range(0,aniClip.Length);
    animator.Play(aniClip[num].name,0,0);
}
```

   You've used animator.Play before when you set the poppers to start their Squash clips in random places along their timeline. This time, you want to play their clips from start to finish, so after pulling up a clip at random, you specify 0 as the level and 0 as the place to start the clip. Note that you are using the name field of the clip because it is used as the state name by default. If you change the names of the states, you will have to make an array of the state names that can be fed into the Play function or method.

5. Save the script.

Next you will set up the rest of the Banana Peel's animation state in the Animator and learn a bit more about Unity's powerful Mecanim.

1. Select a Banana Peel object and double-click its Animator controller to load it into the Animator view.

    Currently, it contains the ubiquitous Any State and the default state, B Idle.

2. Locate the Banana Peel's clips in the Game Assets folder and drag B1, B2, and B3 into the Animator window, positioning them above the B Idle state (Figure 8-8).

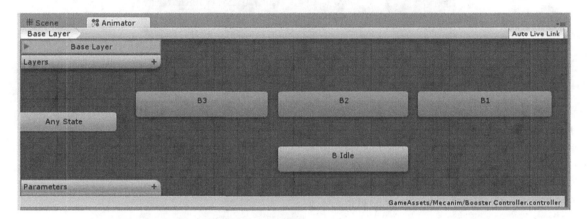

Figure 8-8. The Banana Peel's four states in the Animator view

Remember, none of the clips other than the idle were set to loop. If you triggered the clips now, they would simply stop animating when the clip was finished. With Mecanim, you can set the clips to automatically revert back to the idle clip when finished. Because Mecanim was originally developed to control character animation, you will want to prevent blending between the states. The clips you are using already start and end at the same neutral state, making blending unnecessary. Let's begin by creating transitions between the three new states and the idle state.

3. Select the B1 state, right-click, and choose Make Transition.

4. Click the B Idle state to hook up the new transition.

5. Click the new transition to see it in the Inspector.

    The Conditions for it to go from B1 to B Idle automatically default to Exit Time.

6. Reduce the blend by moving the left time marker close to the right and moving the idle to match (Figure 8-9).

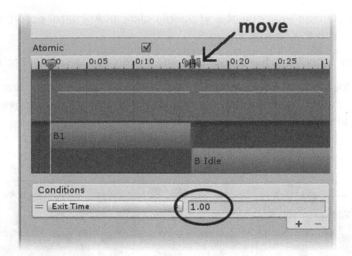

Figure 8-9. The blend reduced for the transition between B1 and B Idle

> **Tip** Moving the B Idle clip far to the right will cause it to snap back to the correct place for the adjusted transition when you let go of it.

7. Repeat the process for the B2 and B3 clips.

The new states are ready to load (Figure 8-10).

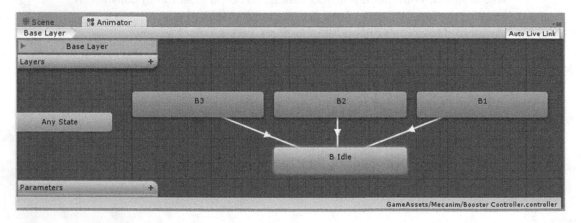

Figure 8-10. The Transitions from the one-off states back to the idle

Note that there are no transitions from the idle to the other clip states. They can be triggered only by code.

With the states set up in the Animator, you can go ahead and load them into the HotSpotBooster.

1. Select the three Banana Peel objects in the Hierarchy view.

2. Set the Ani Clips array size to **3** and load B1, B2, and B3 into the new fields.

3. Click Apply to bring its prefab up-to-date with the new parameters.

   Because the clips exist in the Project view, they are automatically included on the prefab.

4. Click Play and roll the Marble through the Banana Peels.

This time, the peels react when the marble rolls over them.

Apart from a few special effects, the components of the game are fully functional (Figure 8-11).

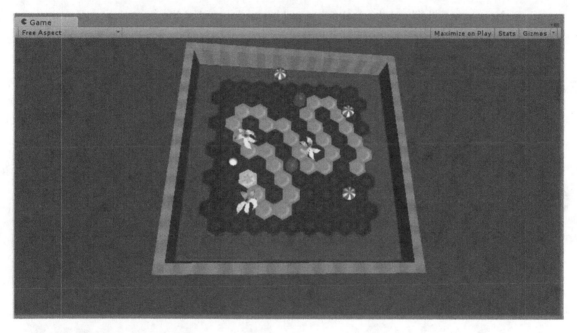

Figure 8-11. The game pieces all in play

Completing the Path

At this point, you are able to roll the Marble along the path, and, after gaining and losing health points along the way, reach the end path tile. As that is the most obvious goal, you will want to let the player know the game has ended by stopping or even hiding the other game pieces and returning the board to its upright position. The path progress is tracked in the PathCellManager script, so that is the most logical place to begin.

1. Open the PathCellManager script.

    The Toggle PathTiles function always knows where the last activated tile is. By taking the path length and subtracting 1 (the path array starts at 0, remember), you have the end tile's element number. When the lastActivated variable's value equals that, your player has completed the path.

2. Add the following at the bottom of the ToggleTileState function:

```
// check for winner
if(lastActivated >= pathLength - 1){
    ProcessWinner();
}
```

Now you will fill out the tasks that will be performed at the completion of the path in a ProcessWinner function.

3. Start blocking in the ProcessWinner function:

```
void ProcessWinner () {
    print("Winner");

    // cue the FX
```

4. Stop user input:

```
//stop input
marbleManager.repressInput = true;
```

You already have this functionality for when the board is reset.

5. Level the game board:

```
// level board
boardManager.StartBoardReset (4);
```

For the board reset at the end of the path, a 4-second reset time will be nice.

6. Stop the game pieces:

```
// stop game pieces
foreach (GameObject gp in allGamePieces) {
    gp.SetActive(false);

}
```

You will be adding the line that loads all of the game pieces in the Awake function. They will be identified by a tag. The easiest option is to deactivate them, but once you have access, you may just want to stop them from moving.

1. Hide the Marble:

```
// hide marble
marbleManager.gameObject.SetActive(false);
```

2. Show the menu:

```
// show menu
```

```
} // close the function
```

In Chapter 10, you will be handling the game GUI, so for now you will just add the place-keeper comment.

Let's see about creating the game pieces array next so you can process those objects.

3. Add the following variables to the script:

```
internal GameObject[] allGamePieces; // store the game pieces for easy processing
public MarbleManager marbleManager; // where input is turned off
public BoardManager boardManager; // where the board is re-leveled
```

4. In the Awake function, add the following:

```
//store the game piece objects
allGamePieces = GameObject.FindGameObjectsWithTag("Game Piece");
```

5. Save the script.

6. Select the Path Manager object and drag the Board Group object onto the Board Manager parameter and the Marble onto the Marble manager.

You will, of course, require the Game Piece tag before testing. You don't have to use the drop-down for the tags to gain access to them; The Tags, Sorting Layers, and regular Layers are all in the same place.

1. From the Layers drop-down at the upper right of the editor, select Edit Layer.

The Layers and Tags reside in the same place so you can access each through the Layers drop-down or from any object's Tag drop-down.

2. Open the Tags array and add Game Piece at Element 2.

3. Select the Banana Peel, Spinner, and Popper prefabs and assign the Game Piece tag to each.

To test the end, you will want to get there quickly to see whether the main functionality works.

4. Select the nine game piece objects and deactivate them.

5. Click Play and roll the Marble along the path to see the results upon reaching the end.

    The board resets, the Winner message appears in the console, the sound plays, and player input is suppressed.

    Let's check on the game pieces next.

6. Reactivate the nine game pieces.

7. Click Play and test to see the results upon reaching the end of the path.

    The game pieces disappear on cue.

    With a little more code, you can just stop them from moving by disabling the script that moves them around. As this is a different script in the Poppers and Spinners, you will make good use of SendMessage by putting the same function in both scripts. The function itself doesn't even have to have the same contents, only the same name. The Banana Peels don't have a script that moves them around during the game, but by using dontRequireReceiver, no error will be thrown.

8. In the PathCellManager script, comment out the gp.SetActive line.

9. Below it add the following:

```
gp.SendMessage("Freeze", SendMessageOptions.DontRequireReceiver);
```

10. Save the script.

11. Open the Traveler script and add the Freeze function:

```
public void Freeze () {
    this.enabled = false; // disable the script
}
```

12. Save the script.

13. Add the same function to the Popper_Hopper script.

14. Save the script.

15. Click Play and test to see the new end result.

    This time, the game objects stop moving but continue their individual animation. Feel free to use whichever end scheme you prefer.

16. Save the scene and save the project.

Either way, the ending is rather underwhelming. In the next chapter, you will be adding sound effects and special effects.

Summary

In this chapter, you merged the functionality created in Chapter 6 with the environment you created in Chapter 7 and were able to see how your marble performed with an actual path on the board.

In the interest of inspiring the player to try his skill at the little tilt-board game, you introduced a health system in which the "good" and "bad" portal interactions could help or hinder the player's progress along the path. To make the Inspector easier to read, you used *enum* to differentiate the Portal Hopper script for the two types of interaction.

With the introduction of the fledgling game pieces you started in the last chapter, you discovered that you could alter the mapping coordinates to spruce up your game tiles rather than returning to a DCC application when you received an atlased map with all four textures on it.

Before swapping out the proxy objects with some more interesting objects, you took a look at the draw calls in the game and made the discovery that not only was the Color parameter on the Diffuse shader expensive, but the little Omni lights used previously were major draw-call hogs. Remembering that interaction requires that objects contain a collider, you quickly copied an existing collider component from one of the proxy portal objects and pasted it onto the new game pieces. Upon bringing the objects into the scene, however, you discovered that Mecanim animations, with their Animator component, require a lot more work before their animations will automatically play in the scene. The key ingredient, you found, was to provide each object with its own Animator Controller. This gave you the means to introduce the clips as states. The looping clips, set as the default state, would now animate happily on startup.

Next, you introduced a waypoint system to move the Spinners randomly back and forth across the board with the help of `transform.LookAt` and the `MoveTowards` method. For the Poppers, you set a timer that allowed you to randomly relocate the objects around the board tiles. To give it a bit more intelligence, you restricted the Poppers to base tiles only by checking to see whether the randomly chosen tile was active or not.

For the Banana Peel, returning to Mecanim, you set the three hit animations to automatically return the object to the looping idle animation as soon as the clip was triggered. With scripting, you discovered how to set the Popper objects animating at different points along the animation's timeline. The same method, `Animator.Play()`, allowed you to fire off the banana hit animations at will, letting Mecanim take care of the return to the idle state.

Your last task was to block in the functionality for the player completing the path. In the function created to handle the task, you contacted various scripts to repress player input, return the board to its upright position, and stop the game pieces from performing their scripted functionality, while continuing with their imported animations.

Chapter **9**

Audio and Special Effects

Now that most of the game play is sorted out, it's a good time to look into adding some special effects to spice up the user experience. The most obvious thing that is missing is a variety of sound effects that will help your players keep tabs on the state of the marble's health while keeping their eyes on the marble and other game pieces. The other missing piece of the puzzle is a favorite of video games of all kinds: the particle system. Particle systems, a mainstay of desktop games, cannot be used with abandon for mobile applications, but with careful planning you can budget in a few for special occasions. Let's begin with audio, as it will add the most bang for the buck.

Adding Audio

As you play through your game, you've probably noticed that it is eerily quiet. In Unity, to hear sound clips, the scene must have an Audio Listener. Camera objects have an Audio Listener as a default. You probably remember removing extras anytime you added a camera to a scene. But to actually *play* the sound clip, you must use an Audio Source component.

Audio Clips

As a default, audio clips come in as 3D sounds. As an object with an Audio Source component and sound clip moves from one side of the screen to the other, the sound is played from one speaker (or earphone or earbud) to the other, enhancing the player's experience of the game. For this little game, you could probably get away with making all of the sounds 2D, but if you were playing the game with earbuds, using 3D sounds might increase your awareness of the Marble's location on the board and of the interactions of the various game pieces with the Marble.

1. From the Chapter 9 Assets folder, bring the SoundFX folder into the Project view.

2. Open the folder and click on each of the clips.

© Sue Blackman and Adam Tuliper 2016
S. Blackman and A. Tuliper, *Learn Unity for Windows 10 Game Development*,
DOI 10.1007/978-1-4302-6757-7_9

As you click on each clip, its waveform shows in the Inspector (Figure 9-1) and, if the Auto Play button is on, the clip plays once.

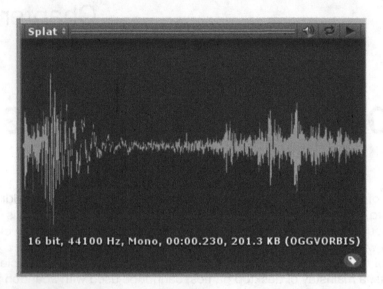

16 bit, 44100 Hz, Mono, 00:00.230, 201.3 KB (OGGVORBIS)

Figure 9-1. The waveform of the selected clip in the Inspector

At the far right, you will see the three audio icons. The first toggles autoplay off and on; when this option is off, the sound won't play when the clip is selected in the Project view. The next icon causes the clip to play looped. If you have turned off autoplay, or the looping option is not on and you want to hear the clip again, you can press the Play button at the far right.

3. Select the PongBeep clip and check it out in the Inspector (Figure 9-2).

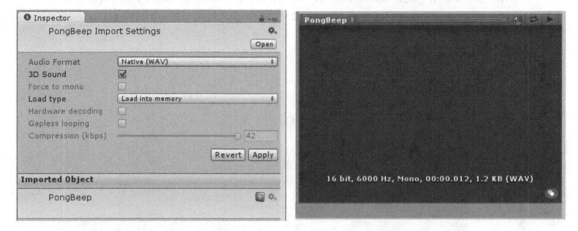

Figure 9-2. The PongBeep clip in the Inspector

Note that PongBeep doesn't show a waveform because it is in WAV format. Unity documentation recommends that short clips, especially nonlooping clips, remain in their native format. The Load Type is set to Load in Memory so that the clip is always ready to play. The downside is that it will take up memory.

4. Click the down arrow for the Audio Format (Figure 9-3).

Figure 9-3. Audio Format options on the PC

The other format option is OGGVORBIS, an open source codec similar to MPEG with a good compression rate. Most of the other clips you imported are .ogg to begin with, and most are short enough to be loaded into memory.

5. Select the Synthup clip (Figure 9-4).

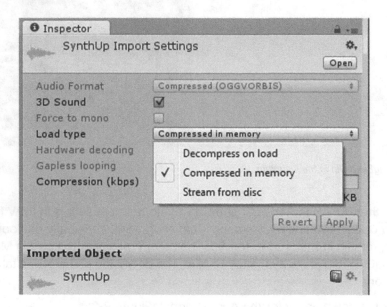

Figure 9-4. Audio load types

This clip is already in .ogg format, so there are no format options. You do, however, have some Load Type options. The clip is fairly short, but you will be playing it only when the player reaches the end of the path, so let's keep it as Compressed in Memory. Do be aware that uncompressing audio clips will suck up resources, so avoid having several uncompressing at the same time. Typically, you would be using the compressed format with background music or other ambient sounds that differ per level. Do be aware that some mobile platforms may be able to decompress only one file at a time.

The next thing to decide is whether the clip should be 2D or 3D. The interaction clips will be 3D so that the player can hear which side of the board the marble is on at the time of the intersection. The Marble reset sound, Synthup, and the pop for its landing should not be localized, so you can set them to 2D to save some runtime resources.

6. Deactivate the 3D Sound check box for the Synthup and Pop clips, clicking Apply after each change.

7. All of the sounds are short, so select each remaining sound clip and set all to Decompress on Load.

Audio Source

As mentioned earlier, to play a sound, you use an Audio Source component. The sound can be set to Play on Awake, typically used when instantiating a projectile, or it can be activated through code. Each Audio Source component can hold one sound clip. To play the default clip—unlike in earlier Unity versions, where you could use the simple accessor, `audio.Play()`—you will now have to contact the clip as you would any other component. Many times you will want to be able to choose from a variety of sounds depending upon circumstances. A character's footsteps, for instance, should change depending on the type of surface it is walking over, as well as the gait itself. Other times you will just want to break up the monotony by randomly choosing similar files.

> **Tip**   Unity has been systematically getting rid of simple accessors over the last several versions. The code is converted from `theAudio.Play()` to `GetComponent<AudioSource>().Play()` when an older script is updated. You may want to consider creating a variable to identify the Audio Source and using a replacement before allowing Unity to update the scripts automatically.

Game Pieces

The game piece objects should trigger a different sound depending on whether the health or the path is being affected. To make the setup process easier, because the good and bad game pieces are all sharing the same portal and path code, you can load the four possible sound clips and specify which to use in the conditionals for each scenario. Let's begin by adding an Audio Source to each of the game pieces.

1. Select the three game pieces, Banana Peel, Spinner, and Popper, in the Prefabs folder.

2. From the Component menu, choose Audio to add an Audio Source component.

3. With the three objects still selected, deactivate the Audio Source components' Play on Awake check box.

4. Adjust the panel so that you can see the Rolloff curve in the 3D Sound Settings section (Figure 9-5).

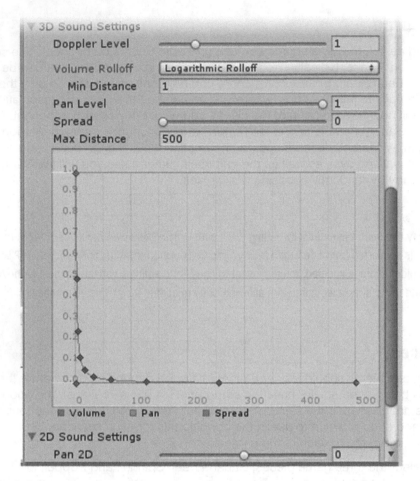

Figure 9-5. The Rolloff curve

The default Rolloff is Logarithmic. As you can see by its curve, players would be able to hear the sound only if they were very close to it. Let's select Linear and adjust the Max Distance as a more appropriate solution for the game-board environment. The distance is calculated from the camera to the object.

1. For Volume Rolloff, select Linear Rolloff.

2. Set the Max Distance to **50**.

    Besides the game pieces producing sounds when triggered, you will want to have a sound when the Marble gets reset after escaping the board.

3. Copy the Audio Source component from one the game piece objects.

4. Paste [Component as New] the Audio Source component onto the Marble object.

5. Select the Synthup sound as the audio clip for the Marble object's Audio Source component.

6. Set the Volume to about **0.5**.

Note that it shows the clip as a 2D Sound, so the 3D Clip settings will not be used. Because you could play a 3D clip from the same Audio Source component at any time, they are not grayed out.

Now let's add the code to manage the sound effects for the regular game pieces. You could use an array to store the four clips, but it might be a better choice to have individually named variables to make loading the correct clips easier. When you want to play a different sound effect, rather than loading the different clip in the Audio Source component, use theAudio. PlayOneShot().

1. Open the PortalHopper script.

2. Add the following variables:

```
public AudioClip plusHealth;
public AudioClip plusPath;
public AudioClip minusHealth;
public AudioClip minusPath;
```

3. In the OnTriggerEnter function, in the if (health >= 12 section, add the following:

```
theAudio.PlayOneShot(plusPath); // add path sound fx
```

Note that audio clips require the clip as the argument (as opposed to animation clips, which have the argument as their name, a string type).

4. In its else clause, add this:

```
theAudio.PlayOneShot(plusHealth); // add heath sound fx
```

5. In the if (health < 6 clause, for the bad game pieces, add the following:

```
theAudio.PlayOneShot(minusPath); // lose path sound fx
```

6. In its else section, add this:

```
theAudio.PlayOneShot(minusHealth); // lose heath sound fx
```

7. Save the script.

To load the clips, you can select the prefabs in the Project view. To be able to load values in a prefab, they must exist in the Project view as assets or prefabs. An object that exists only in the Hierarchy view for a particular scene or level must be loaded in the Hierarchy view. The sound clips are definitely assets that are available from the project view at any time, so you are good to go.

8. Expand the Sound FX folder in the Project view so you will be able to drag the audio clips directly into the prefab's Audio Source component.

> **Tip**   This quick-load technique works only with the Single Column Layout for the Project view.

9. Select the Popper and Spinner game pieces in the Prefabs folder.

10. Load them as follows:

```
Plus Health - ShipBellSingle
Plus Path - PortalWhoosh
Minus Health - Splat
Minus Path - buzzerSoft
```

11. Check the game pieces in the Hierarchy view to make sure each contains the newly loaded audio clips.

12. Click Play and check out the new sound effects by rolling the Marble into the game pieces.

The ship's bell clip seems to be suffering from the Doppler effect.

1. Select the Popper prefab and set its Audio Source's Doppler Level to 0.

2. Click Play and test again. This time the bell sound is not so wobbly.

    The Banana Peel booster requires only one clip, so it can be loaded directly into its Audio Source.

3. Select the Banana Peel prefab.

4. Add the AirCompressorBurst as its audio clip in its Audio Source component.

    You can trigger the sound from the HotSpotBooster script.

5. Open the HotSpotBooster script.

6. Create a new variable:

```
AudioSource theAudio;
```

7. In the Start function, add the following to assign the component to it:

```
theAudio = GetComponent<AudioSource>();
```

8. In the OnTriggerEnter function, below the Booster.Boost() line, add this:

```
theAudio.Play(); // play the loaded clip
```

9. Save the script.

10. Click Play and test the new additions.

Now, of course, you are probably thinking it would be a good time to start on the path-finished functionality.

The Marble drop event could do with a sound effect so the player will know when the Marble is in play. In the MarbleManager script, you already left a space for special effects.

1. Open the MarbleManager script.

2. Add the following variables:

```
AudioSource theAudio;
public AudioClip landed; // pop sound
```

3. In the Start function, add the following to assign the component to it:

```
theAudio = GetComponent<AudioSource>();
```

4. At the *top* of the IEnumerator DelayReset, add this:

```
theTheAudio.Play(); // play the resetting music
```

5. In both IEnumerators, under the // add some FX here line, add the following:

```
theAudio.PlayOneShot(landed); // play the pop sound
```

6. Save the script.

7. Add the Pop clip to the new Landed parameter in the Marble Manager component.

8. Click Play and test.

    You should hear the sound effects on startup anytime the Marble escapes the board.

    To hear the sound on game startup, you can reroute the Marble drop through the DelayReset function. You could set the delay to zero, but there will eventually be enough going on that a second or two will give your player a chance to get acclimated before the Marble drops.

9. In the Start function, replace SetToStart() with the following:

```
StartDelay (2f);
```

10. Save the script and test.

Now, after a brief delay and a little fanfare, the Marble drops to the board with a plop and the game is on!

Using Particles and Special Effects

Having freed up a few resources upon reaching the end of the path, you may be thinking that you could afford a particle system or two to make things even better. The trick to using particle systems with mobile devices is to severely limit the particle count, limit the life of the effect, and limit the spread if using transparency. The Shuriken particle system has tons of settings and adjustments that should help you keep the effects economical.

The Spinner's FX

Let's begin with a smoke-like effect for the Spinners:

1. Turn off Play mode.

2. From the Create menu, choose Particle System and name it **Dark Puff**.

   A particle system consisting of what appears to be slow-moving cotton balls appears.

3. Move the new object up, just above the board, to about **0.1** for its Y Position,

4. Check out the Inspector to get a peek at the possible adjustments (Figure 9-6).

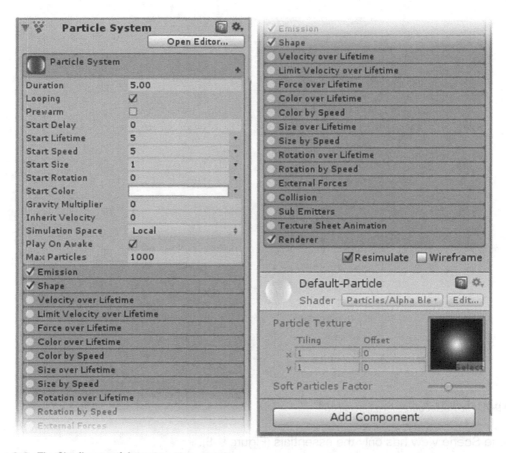

Figure 9-6. The Shuriken particle system component

Although the sheer number of parameters is rather daunting, most of the parameters make sense once you catch on to the usual type of options available.

When the particle system is selected, it will show an active preview in the Scene and Game views. The Scene view, however, has become even more cluttered with the addition of the Audio Source components. Let's clear it out a bit before jumping into particles.

5. Select the Waypoint object from the Prefabs folder.

6. Click the object icon drop-down, the custom W, and select None.

7. Repeat for the Portal Destination Bad prefab.

8. From the Scene view toolbar, open the Gizmos drop-down and toggle off the audio and any other component gizmos you wish (Figure 9-7).

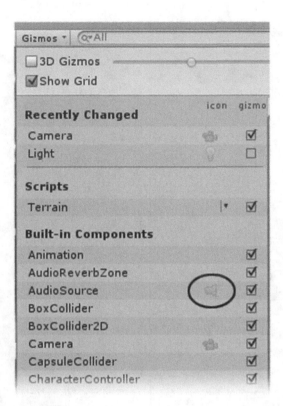

Figure 9-7. *The AudioSource icon toggled off*

Now the Scene view has only the essentials (Figure 9-8).

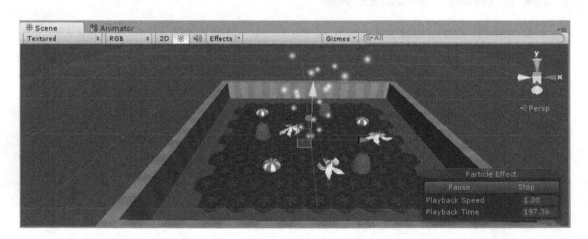

Figure 9-8. *The selected Shuriken particle system and its Particle Effect dialog box in the Scene view*

Before turning off the Loop parameter, let's adjust the spread of the emitter:

1. Select the Dark Puff again and click the rollout bar to open the Shape module.

2. Change the Angle to **0** (Figure 9-9).

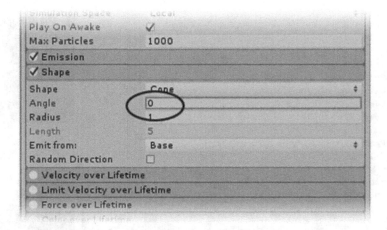

Figure 9-9. Changing the Angle of the Cone emitter

Tip   You can also grab and move the grips on the Cone emitter's gizmo in the Scene view.

---

3. Decrease the Radius to **0.5**.

    The cotton balls should be moving straight up now. Let's reduce the resource drain by limiting the duration of the particle life and the maximum number of particles next.

4. At the top of the component, set the Duration to **0.35**.

5. Set the Max Particles to **8**.

    The system is still set to Loop, but now it can't emit any new particles until the eight die out.

6. Set the Start Lifetime to **0.3**.

    Now the particles pop out sooner.

7. Set the Start Speed to **1** and the Start Size to **2**.

Most of the parameters can be randomized using various methods. Depending on the parameter, you will usually find Constant, Curve, Random Between Two Constants, and Random Between Two Curves. Let's randomize the Start Speed:

1. Click the down arrow at the far right of the Start Speed parameter.

    A menu appears with the options available for that parameter (Figure 9-10).

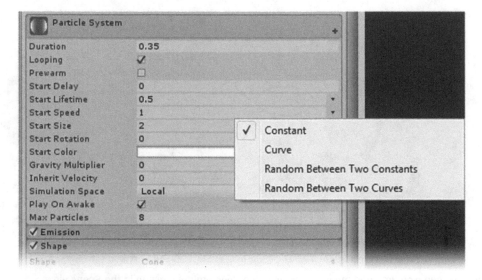

Figure 9-10. Parameter options from the drop-down menu

2. Select Random Between Two Constants and set them to **0.5** and **1**.

    If you check on Start Color, you will find that it has an option to tint the particles with a gradient. This gradient affects the particle system as a whole over the duration.

3. For the Start Color, choose Gradient.

4. Click the color swatch to open the Gradient dialog box.

    The Gradient editor appears. The top markers are for the alpha channel, and the bottom markers are for the diffuse color.

5. Double-click the lower-left marker, or click the color swatch to bring up the Color Picker and select a darkish red.

6. Double-click the marker on the lower right and select black.

7. Back in the component, set the duration to **5.35** and watch the color cycle in the viewport cover the Duration.

    Generally, you will find a gradient over the individual particle's lifetime more useful. For that, you will use one of the modules in the lower section.

8. Set the Start Color back to Color.

It should return to white.

9. Check the Color over Lifetime rollout to activate it, and then click the bar to open it.

It is set to Gradient as a default.

10. Set the Gradient up as you did with the earlier one, but this time, click just above the color bar, about 90 percent along, to create a new transparency marker.

11. Set the end transparency marker to **0** (Figure 9-11).

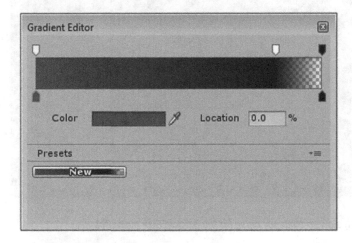

Figure 9-11. Adding a transparency marker to the gradient

12. Inspect the results in the Scene or Game view.

The particles are now going through the gradient individually.

The particles are using the default particle system material. It uses an alpha channel texture to get the soft, blobby falloff to transparency. While transparency costs in mobile applications, it is less of an issue if it doesn't use much pixel space onscreen. So far, this one is fairly small, so let's increase the size of the particles over their lifetime.

1. Locate the Size over Lifetime, activate it, open it, and click the curve (the default option for size) thumbnail to see the curve at the bottom of the Inspector.

On the upper left, the Size, 1.0, represents 100 percent of the Start Size you set earlier. Let's grow this one larger over time. You could work backward and change the Start Size, but it will be just as easy to increase the percent.

2. Change the 1.0 to **2.0** and move the left curve node down to **1**.

Instead of fiddling with the tangency handles, you can use a preset from the bottom of the mini-curve editor.

3. Select the fast-out, slow-in curve, and move the left node back up to 1 again (Figure 9-12).

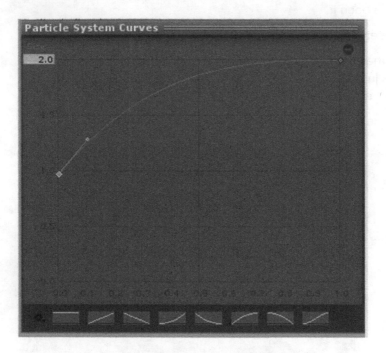

Figure 9-12. A fast-out, slow-in tangency curve for the particle Size over Lifetime

4. Set the Duration back to **0.35**, deactivate the Play on Awake check box (just above the Max Particles parameter) and deactivate Looping.

    With Looping turned off, you will have to click the Simulate button in the Scene view to see the particle system in action. If the simulation was running, be sure to click Pause a couple of times first.

5. Click the Simulate button a few times to see what the particle system will look like in action.

6. Select one of the Spinners and focus the viewport to it.

7. Select the Dark Puff particle system and use Move to View from the GameObject menu to align it with the Spinner.

8. Drag the particle system onto the Spinner and then move it up a little so the puffs are above the peppermint.

9. Click Play and click the Simulate button.

    The particles spin with the parent, but the duration is so brief that they look lopsided.

10. Stop Play mode and decrease the Radius in the Shape module to **0.2** and set the Start Size to **3**.

11. Click Play and click Simulate again.

    This time the puffs stay closer to the Spinner and look suitably toxic.

12. For fun, while you are still in Play mode, locate the particle system's Simulation Space parameter and change it from Local to World Space.

    Now the particles are left where they were born as the Spinner moves away.

13. Stop Play mode and drag the Dark Puff object into the Prefabs folder.

The other two Spinners now sport a Dark Puff of their own. You might think it would make more sense to update the Spinner to include the particle system, but you will be experimenting with another means of limiting the asset usage with the particle systems.

The Popper's FX

For the Poppers, you will create a confetti-like effect. This time, you will switch to a mesh particle and do away with the transparency by using Default-Particle material. The Max Particles count will be higher, but it will not have to be constantly turned to face the viewport, or billboarded, either. A downside it that it will have to use a two-sided shader or you will be wasting resources by calculating its position when it is back-face culled.

1. Create a new Particle System and name it **Confetti**.

2. Set its Duration to **0.5** and its Start Size to Random Between Two Constants, **0.5** and **1**.

3. Set its Start Color to Random Between Two Colors and set the second color to a nice blue to match the gumdrops.

4. At the bottom of the module rollouts, click to open the Renderer rollout.

5. For Render Mode, select Mesh and change the Mesh from Cube to Quad via the Browse icon.

6. Deactivate the Cast Shadows and Receive Shadows options.

    The billboard particles will not cast or receive shadows if the options are left on. Your Directional Light is not set to cast shadows, but if it was, these mesh particles would be included, sucking up resources. So you don't really have to turn off the options in this case, but it is a good habit to develop.

7. In the game assets' Materials folder, right-click and choose Create Material. Name the material **Simple Particles**.

8. Change the shader to Mobile, Particles, Alpha Bended.

9. Select the Confetti object again. In the Renderer rollout, assign the new material.

You should be able to see the material on both the top side and the bottom side of the particles if you tip the Scene view up and then down.

Now you will make the particles a bit more interesting. They will come up in a narrow stream, and then, overcome by gravity, will fall back down, fluttering all the way.

1. Set the Start Lifetime to Random Between Two Constants, **0.5** and **1**.

2. Change the Start Size from **0.1** to **0.4**.

3. Set the Start Speed to **10** and the Gravity Multiplier to **0.1**.

4. In the Shape module, set the Radius to **0.2** and the angle to **4**.

    The effect is improving, but the particles could use some spin.

5. Set the Start Rotation to Random Between Two Constants, **0** and **180**.

6. Activate and open the Rotation over Lifetime module.

7. Set the Angular Velocity to Random Between Two Constants, **360** and **1080**.

The particles are happily tumbling down now.

There is a bit of a mystery remaining, however. The Max Particles are set to 1000, yet very few are created in the viewport. The answer lies in the Emission section.

1. In the Emission section, change the Rate to **40**.

2. Set Max Particles to **40**.

3. Deactivate the Looping check box, and then click Simulate a few times to see the result.

4. Select one of the Poppers and focus the view to it.

5. Select the Confetti object and use Move to View to position it to the Popper.

6. Move it to the top of the Popper and then drop it onto the Popper in the Hierarchy view.

7. Click Play and then press the Simulate button regularly to see the Confetti in action.

    Note how the particle system inherits the Popper's squashing animation (Figure 9-13).

Figure 9-13. The Confetti particle system inheriting the gumdrop's animated scale transform

8.   Stop Play mode and drag the Confetti object into the Prefabs folder.

The Booster's FX

For the Banana Peels, you will be creating a vapor trail as the Marble is shot across the board. This time, the particle system will stay with the Marble and be cued when the Marble receives the physics boost.

1.   Create a new Particle System.

2.   Set its Duration to **0.5**, its Start Lifetime to **0.5**, and its Start Size to **2**.

3.   Change its Start Color to Gradient and set the alpha value to go from **255** at 85 percent to **0** at 100 percent.

4.   Set Simulation Space to World, and the Start Speed to **0** so the particles will be left behind when the Marble rolls.

5.   Set the Max Particles to **50**.

     To work with the boost effect, you will require a higher emission rate at the start and a lower one toward the end of the duration. To do that, you can use a curve.

6.   Open the Emission section and change the Rate from Constant to Curve. Click the curve's thumbnail to view it in the preview window at the bottom of the Inspector.

7.   Change the curve to the fast-out, slow-in preset and set the Rate to **100** (Figure 9-14).

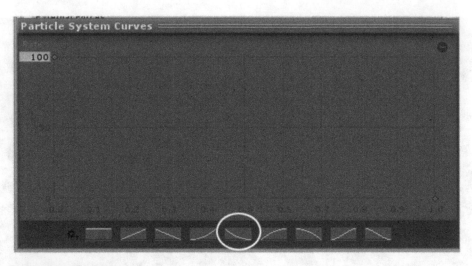

Figure 9-14. The Emission's Rate curve

8.   For Shape, set the Cone to an Angle of **25**, and a Radius of **0.22**.

9.   Activate Color over Lifetime and change the gradient to an orangish yellow at the start and a greenish yellow at the end. Set its alpha to fade toward the end as well (Figure 9-15).

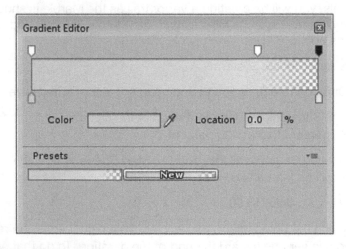

Figure 9-15. The Color over Lifetime gradient

If you had multiple particles that you wanted to use the same gradient for, you could click the New button in the Preset section to make the gradient available for reuse.

To create a proper vapor trail, you will want the size of the particles to shrink over their lifetime as well as fade.

10. Activate the Size over Lifetime module. Set the Curve to a linear
    curve from 1.0 to 0.4 (Figure 9-16).

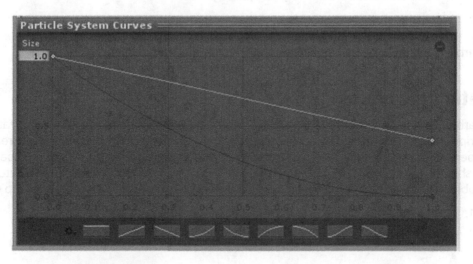

Figure 9-16. The Size over Lifetime curve

11. Align the particle system with the Marble and then drag it onto the
    Marble in the Hierarchy view.

12. Click Play and roll the Marble through the Banana Peels to see
    the effect.

13. Stop Play mode.

To be more efficient, you will fire off the particle system only when the Marble goes through
a Banana Peel. Because it will always be on the Marble and will be triggered to play at will,
you can put the Particle System component directly onto the Marble. This makes it a lot
easier to trigger as well.

1. Copy the Particle System's Particle System component.

2. Select the Marble and use Paste as New to add it to the Marble.

3. Delete the original Particle System.

4. In the Particle System component, deactivate Looping and Play
   on Awake.

   To trigger the effect, you will add a few lines of script.

5. Open the Marble's Booster script.

6. In the Boost function, above the rigidbody line, add the following:

```
particleSystem.Play();
```

The ParticleSystem class, just like the Camera, RigidBody, and several other component classes, already has a defined variable in the Component class, so you don't have to identify it expressly.

7. Save the script and click Play.

The Marble now leaves a trail after shooting through the Banana Peels.

Updating the Marble

The Marble itself is beginning to look rather bland. The Game Pieces material has a rather nice striped area in its upper-left corner, but the Unity-generated sphere would require a remapped version. This time, you can try another method of updating: you will replace just the mesh in the Sphere(Mesh Filter) component. That way, you won't have to re-create the entire object.This will also allow you to use a lower-poly sphere, as it is never seen up close.

1. From the right-click menu in the Game Assets folder, use Import Asset to bring in the new Marble asset from the Chapter 9 Assets folder.

   The Marble locates the correct material on import.

2. Select the original Marble in the Hierarchy view.

3. In the Sphere(Mesh Filter) component, select the Browse button next to the Mesh field.

4. Select the Marble mesh from the available meshes in your project (Figure 9-17).

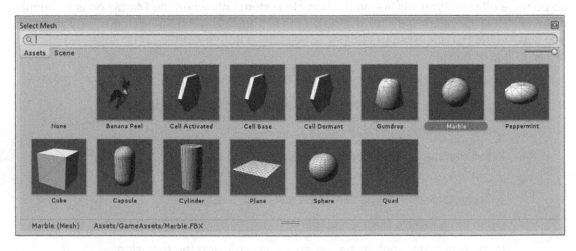

Figure 9-17. Substituting a different mesh from those available in the projects

The Marble mesh replaces the original Sphere mesh (Figure 9-18).

Figure 9-18. The Marble mesh replacing Unity's Sphere mesh in the Marble object

    5.   Drag and drop the Game Pieces material onto the marble.

    6.   Click Play and make sure the Marble functions as before.

    7.   Stop Play mode.

Although updating a mesh with this method is not something you will have to do often, you may occasionally have to find meshes that have gone missing for no apparent reason.

Managing the Portal Particles

You've blocked in the Spinner and Popper particle systems as children of the game pieces themselves. In the case of the Spinner, where the Dark Puff looks good following its parent, the result is quite good. For the Poppers, however, when the object is ported to another location, the particle system goes with it, making it visually confusing. You could unparent the particle system just before the Popper was ported, but then you would have to move it back to the Popper after it was finished and reparent it. If you are going to do that much work, you may as well create a simple pool system to manage the particle systems.

Drawing from a Pool

You've already made a sort of static pool system for using the path tiles. The tiles were pulled from the array until the path was built for each path configuration. For a true, dynamic pool, objects will be returned after use so they can be reused during the game. The Popper particle system is a perfect test subject for a very simple pool system.

The new ingredient you will use is a *stack*. As with a *list*, you will have to include System. Collections.Generic. The two methods you will use are Push and Pop. Push() "pushes" an object onto the "top" of the stack. and Pop() "pops" an object off the top of the stack (Figure 9-19). The benefit of the stack is that you do not have to parse an array to see whether an object is available. If it is on the stack, it is available. When you pop it, you will also activate it; and when you push it, you will deactivate it.

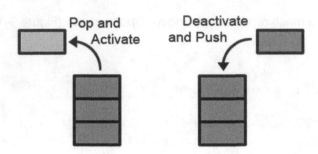

Figure 9-19. Popping an object off the Stack (left), and pushing an object onto the stack (right)

The first step is to feed the objects from an array into the stack. For the Poppers, because the particle systems will get left behind, you might possibly require up to double the number of them in the scene. Let's consider six to be plenty. If you were going to increase the number of game pieces for increasing levels of difficulty, you might want to instantiate the correct number at the beginning of each level, but this is a very simple little game, so you will just have a set number to draw from.

1. Turn on Play on Awake in the Confetti prefab in the Project view.

2. Delete the Confetti object from the Popper.

3. Create an Empty gameObject; set it at **0,0,0** and name it **Popper Pool**.

4. Drag the Confetti prefab into the hierarchy, directly into the Popper Pool object.

5. Duplicate the Confetti object five times so you have a total of six Confetti objects in the Popper Pool.

   And you will use the same procedure for the Dark Puff pool.

6. Turn on Play on Awake in the Dark Puff prefab in the Project view.

7. Delete the Dark Puff object from the Popper.

8. Create an Empty gameObject; set it at **0,0,0** and name it **Spinner Pool**.

9. Drag the Dark Puff prefab into the hierarchy, directly into the **Spinner Pool**.

10. Duplicate the Dark Puff object five times so you have a total of six Dark Puff objects in the Spinner Pool.

11. Create a new C# Script and name it **SimplePool**.

12. Add the new script to the Popper Pool and Spinner Pool objects.

In this script, you will load the objects that are children of the Pool parents. To keep it more generic, you can find them by their transforms rather than their Particle System components.

1. Add the following include at the top of the script:

```
using System.Collections.Generic;
```

2. Add the following variables:

```
public Stack<GameObject> availableGameObjects; // the objects that are available for use
public Transform[] allGameObjects; // the objects that could be in the pool
```

3. Start an Awake function and load the particle systems into the array by using their Transform component:

```
void Awake () {
    // set the size of the array
    allGameObjects = new Transform [transform.childCount];
    // find all the children containing the Transform component & put them into the array
    allGameObjects = gameObject.GetComponentsInChildren< Transform >();
```

4. Load the contents of the array into the stack:

```
availableGameObjects = new Stack<GameObject>();
for (int x = 1; x < allGameObjects.Length; x++) {
    availableGameObjects.Push(allGameObjects[x].gameObject); // add the objects to the stack
    allGameObjects[x].gameObject.SetActive(false);
}
```

Note that the counter starts at 1 because the parent, having a Transform component, was added to the array first. Also note that your stack is for gameObjects, so you must cast the transforms up to the gameObject before putting the array contents into the stack.

5. Add the curly bracket to close the Awake function:

```
}
```

You will require two main functions for your simple pool system: one to pop an object off the stack and position it in the scene, and another to push it back onto the stack when it has finished. If you had something like a projectile, where you cannot predict when it will have to be destroyed, you would have the object itself report back to the pool manager script to be pushed back on the stack. With the particle systems, you already know the duration and the maximum particle lifespan, so you can take advantage of an IEnumerator to tell the script when to push the newly activated article back on the stack.

Let's begin with the pop functionality. It will be responsible for transforming the particle system to the correct location, parenting it to the correct object, and activating it. You will pass in two arguments: the parent object and the location to set the object.

1. Create the function and assign the "popped" object to a temporary local variable:

```
// remove & use pool object
public void PopAndUse (Transform newParent, Vector3 location) {
    GameObject stackObj = availableGameObjects.Pop ();
```

2. Move the stack object to its new location:

```
//transform it
Vector3 newPos = new Vector3(stackObj.transform.position.x, stackObj.transform.
position.y,stackObj.transform.position.z);
newPos = location;
stackObj.transform.position = newPos;
```

3. Parent the stack object and set it as active:

```
// parent the object
stackObj.transform.parent = newParent;
stackObj.SetActive (true);
```

> With the Spinners, the Spinner itself will be the parent, but with the Poppers, the parent will be the Board Group. Passing in the parent allows the code to be more reusable.

4. At the bottom of the PopAndUse function, start the co-routine and then close the function:

```
    // make arrangements to return the object
    StartCoroutine(ReturnWhenFinished (stackObj));
 } // close the PopAndUse function
```

5. Create the IEnumerator as follows:

```
IEnumerator ReturnWhenFinished (GameObject toBeReturned) {
    float targetDelay = 3f;
    yield return new WaitForSeconds(targetDelay);
    toBeReturned.transform.parent = null;
    // put it back in the pool
    ReturnAndPush(toBeReturned);
}
```

> After the time has passed, the object is removed from the parent and returned to the stack. The object in question was passed into the IEnumerator as an argument. You could calculate the delay time withtoBeReturned.particleSystem.duration + toBeReturned. particleSystem.startLifetime if you wish, but a flat time of 3 seconds should be fine for either of the particle systems because neither is set to loop.

6.   Add the ReturnAndPush function:

```
// put it back in the pool
void ReturnAndPush (GameObject returnedObj) {
    returnedObj.SetActive (false);
    availableGameObjects.Push (returnedObj);
}
```

7.   Save the script.

Using the Pool

With your simple pool system set up, you will make use of it through the PortalHopper script:

1.   Open the PortalHopper script.

2.   Add the following variables:

```
// particle system variables
public SimplePool plusFX;
public SimplePool minusFX;
public bool dontParent = true; // flag to parent to the board or this gameObject
Transform fxParent;
```

As the script handles both the good and bad game piece functionality, the variables will hold both pool objects and the instructions about which parent to use. You could just as easily hard-code the correct parent, but this gives you the flexibility to use particle systems with different behaviors on your game pieces. For the Poppers, on which you don't want the particle systems parented, dontParent is set to true. For the Spinners, you will set this option to false.

3.   At the bottom of the Start function, finalize which object is to be the parent of the pool FX object:

```
if (dontParent) fxParent = transform.parent; // the object's parent, the Board Group
else fxParent = transform; // the object this script is on
```

4.   In the OnTriggerEnter function, just under the if (healthPoints > 0) line, add the following:

```
plusFX.PopAndUse(fxParent, transform.position);
```

5.   Just under the else { // health points are negative line, add this:

```
minusFX.PopAndUse(fxParent, transform.position);
```

6.   Save the script.

7. Select the three Popper objects and three Spinner objects in the Hierarchy view.

8. Drag the Popper Pool object into the new Plus FX parameter.

9. Drag the Spinner Pool into the new Minus FX parameter.

10. Deactivate the Don't Parent check box for the Spinners (Figure 9-20).

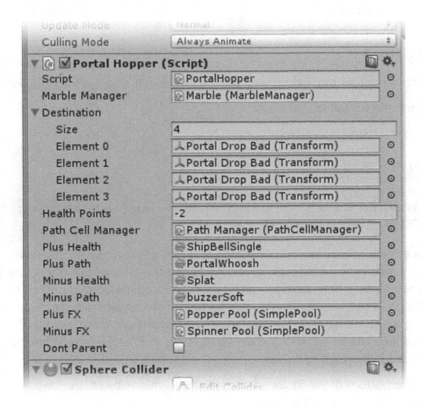

Figure 9-20. The Portal Hopper parameters

11. Click Play and test the new functionality.

You should be able to see the particle system objects moved in and out of the various parents as they are used and returned. Note that they aren't parented back to their pool objects when finished, but are merely left unparented until used again.

The Path End FX

For the grand finale effects, you will be importing a Unity package with a prefab. The difference here is that you will be using a *particle effect*, or more simply put, a hierarchy of both particle systems and other objects. One of the great features of the Shuriken particle system is the ability to see all particle systems in the effect working at the same time and be able to edit them concurrently as well.

1. From the right-click menu, select Import Package ➤ Custom Package. From the Chapter 9 Assets folder, select FX_Finale. unitypackage.

   The package contains a prefab with a Particle Effect.

2. Drag the Particle Finale prefab into the Hierarchy view and click Play to see and hear it in all its glory.

   It consists of three particle systems, an Audio Source component, and a light with an animated intensity, all of which are set to Play on Awake.

3. Select the Particle Finale prefab in the Hierarchy view.

   To create a Particle Effect, the topmost parent must have a Particle System component. To view it and its children, you will open the Particle Effect editor.

4. At the top right of its Particle System component, click the Open Editor button (Figure 9-21).

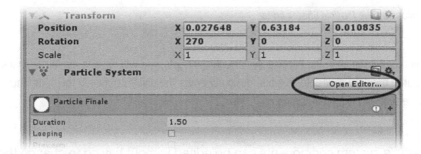

Figure 9-21. Accessing the Particle Effects editor

The editor opens to reveal the Particle System components of the parent and children, along with the preview window for the mini-curve editor (Figure 9-22).

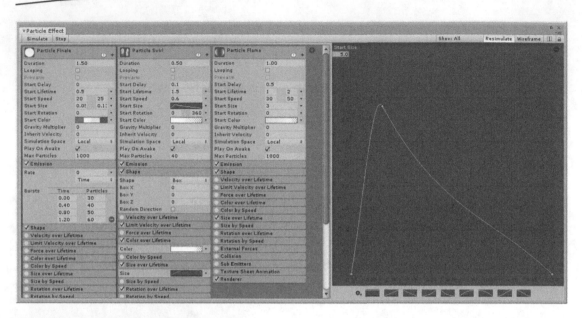

Figure 9-22. Accessing the Particle Effects editor

> **Tip** If you don't see all of the Particle System components, you will have to move the divider to the right until they are all visible. Position the cursor over the divider between the component and the curve editor and drag it to the right.

The three particle system components can be edited without having to change the selection in the Hierarchy view. Additionally, if you click the Simulate button in the viewport, you will see all three of the effects play out as designed.

A few interesting things have been used to create the finale effect. The parent effect is using a combination of Bursts and a gradient Start Color. In the Emissions section, the Bursts set the particles off in the specified intervals. The colors are synchronized to fall within a single Burst, giving the illusion of being four separate particle systems. Under Renderer, instead of the default Billboard Render Mode, it uses Stretched Billboard to give a streaky effect.

The second effect, the swirls, makes good use of Start Rotation and Rotation over Lifetime, but more important, this effect suppresses upward movement with Limit Velocity over Lifetime, where the z velocity is set to 0. In Shuriken, z is up in the world, so you will see some transform settings that are related to that coordinate system.

The third effect is similar to some of your earlier particle systems. It uses a higher number of particles to give a more solid look that is shaped with Size over Lifetime. It also uses a Gradient in both Color and Color over Lifetime to achieve a nice fade-out.

In keeping with the guidelines for keeping overdraw to a minimum, the Particle Finale effect is kept fairly localized, so you will want to fire it off at the location of the final path tile when the Marble has completed the course. Let's revisit the PathCellManager script, where the winner code lives.

1. Deactivate the Particle Finale in the Hierarchy view and drag it into the Board Group.

2. Open the PathCellManager script.

3. Add the following variable:

```
public GameObject finalFX; // the particle effect for the end of path
```

Because the end of the path is set before the game starts, you can position the effect in the LoadPath function. The last tile element number is the path length minus 1.

4. At the bottom of the LoadPath function, add the following:

```
// position the particle fx at the path end
Vector3 newPos = new Vector3(finalFX.transform.position.x,finalFX.transform.
position.y,finalFX.transform.position.z);
newPos = allPathCells[pathLength-1].transform.position;
finalFX.transform.position = newPos;
```

Now you can activate the final effect from the ProcessWinner function.

5. In the ProcessWinner function, under the // cue the FX line, add this:

```
finalFX.SetActive(true); // turn on the final effects
```

6. Save the script.

7. Drag the Particle Finale object into the Path Manager's new Final FX parameter.

8. Click Play and play though to the end of the path.

The end path effects definitely signal the path's completion. The Particle Finale is still active, however, so it would probably be a good idea to turn it off after it finishes and you are waiting for player input. Let's create a small IEnumerator to handle its deactivation.

1. Under the finalFX.SetActive(true) line, add this:

```
StartCoroutine(Deactivate(finalFX ,2.5f)); // send the object off to be deactivated
```

You could have customized the IEnumerator to deactivate just finalFX, but deactivating an object after a short pause is a good generic bit of code. The Destroy method, the code you would use in a nonmobile game, even has a delay built in as one of its arguments.

2. Create the IEnumerator:

```
IEnumerator Deactivate (GameObject target, float pause) {
    // pause before reactivation
    yield return new WaitForSeconds(pause);
```

```
    // deactivate the object
    target.SetActive(false);
}
```

3. Save the script.

4. Click Play and play though to the end of the path.

5. Check the state of the Particle Finale in the Hierarchy view.

This time, the Particle Finale is deactivated after it has done its job.

Conspicuously missing from your game at this point is a nice heads-up display (HUD) to inform the player of the Marble's health as well as the amount of time that has passed. Once the path has been completed, the player will be faced with some options before being able to restart the game and play again. In the next chapter, you will add the GUI elements that will round out your game.

Summary

In this chapter, you spiced up the action with the addition of sound effects and particle systems.

Sound effects, you discovered, could be handled in several ways, but the main takeaway is that very short sounds that are played often are best loaded into memory, while longer sounds that play in the background or are played infrequently are better off streamed.

Next, you learned that besides having the one Audio Listener in a scene, you require an Audio Source to actually play a clip. When the sound effect was set to 3D rather than 2D, you discovered that a falloff curve controls the distance to the object with the Audio Source the player (for *player*, read *camera*) had to be. The two main means of causing the sound to be played, you found, were AudioSource.Play() that plays the default clip loaded in the Audio Source component, and AudioSource.PlayOneShot(), which could temporarily take over an Audio Source and play a specified sound clip.

With the addition of particle systems to your game, you had a first look at Shuriken, the complex particle system implemented in Unity. With its generous options for setting up your particle systems, you found that most options involved either a change over the duration of the particle system, or, a change over the individual life of the particles. Most effects, you found, had numerous options, beginning with a single constant value and extending to random values between two curves or gradients depending on the parameter type.

With a few particle systems to work with, you then implemented a simple pool system to use and reuse a limited number of particle systems. The pool system is a mainstay of mobile games for which instantiating and destroying objects is too costly. By "popping" and "pushing" items off a stack, you were able to determine which objects were available for use, while preventing overuse that would bring a mobile game to a crawl.

Finally, after building a few effects from scratch, you imported the finished final effect, where you learned that you could group particle systems and other FX (lights, audio, and so forth) into particle effects that could be opened and edited together in the Shuriken editor. With the newly imported special effect, you made a start at triggering various tasks associated with the completion of the Marble's progress on the path.

Chapter 10

GUI and Menus

With the inclusion of Unity's long-awaited Unity UI, graphical interfaces have become both more powerful and more complex. The trade-off is that you no longer have to code everything for location and interaction. In this chapter, you will be filling in a few last parts of your game by providing a heads-up display (HUD) for your in-game play statistics to put a bit more pressure on the player. You will also be creating a simple menu. Although your game has only one level, you will allow your player to adjust the difficulty at the beginning of each session.

Working with the Unity UI

Designed with a strong leaning toward the special requirements for mobile devices, the Unity UI has gone a long way toward making menus and HUD less painful to author. The legacy GUI Text and GUI Texture objects have been removed from the menu options, but the fully scripted Unity GUI system remains. The two biggest downsides of the earlier Unity GUI system are that it must be fully scripted (there are no gameObjects directly associated with it) and it is extremely inefficient as far as resources go, for mobile devices.

Layout

One of the most appreciated aspects of the Unity UI system is its layout capabilities. Not only do elements snap to align nicely, but you also have control over whether they should shrink with a window resizing, or retain their relative positions and size. The key to this scheme is an anchoring system and the concept of a canvas that it is built upon, in particular, the canvas's Canvas Scaler component.

© Sue Blackman and Adam Tuliper 2016
S. Blackman and A. Tuliper, *Learn Unity for Windows 10 Game Development*,
DOI 10.1007/978-1-4302-6757-7_10

For this project's UI, you will be working in 2D space. Do be aware, though, that the Unity UI objects, though essentially 2D, exist in 3D space. While generally flat to the viewing screen, you do have the option of skewing the canvas to present the player with a true perspective view of the GUI. Let's begin by creating a new scene for a few experiments:

1.   Create a new folder and name it **Scenes**.

2.   Drag all of the scenes into it to tidy up the Project view.

3.   Create a New Scene in the Scenes folder and name it **Start Menu**.

4.   Double-click it to open the new scene and delete the Directional Light.

5.   Select the Main Camera and set its Clear Flags to Solid Color.

6.   If it isn't already, turn off the Camera icon in the Scene view's Gizmos drop-down list.

As mentioned earlier, all Unity UI objects must be children of a *Canvas* object. Creating a UI object, however, will automatically generate the Canvas for you.

1.   From the GameObject menu, choose UI ➤ Button.

     In the Hierarchy view, you will see that the Button has been added as a child of the Canvas automatically (Figure 10-1).

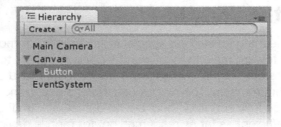

Figure 10-1. The Canvas and EventSystem automatically generated with the first UI object

     The Button is currently in the lower-left corner of the Game view. To set up its location, you will want to switch the Scene view to 2D display.

2.   Toggle the Scene view to 2D (Figure 10-2).

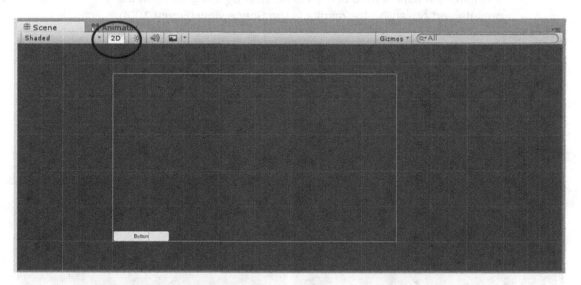

Figure 10-2. The Scene view using 2D display

The 2D display is essentially an iso (or flat) view from the back of the z direction (Figure 10-3).

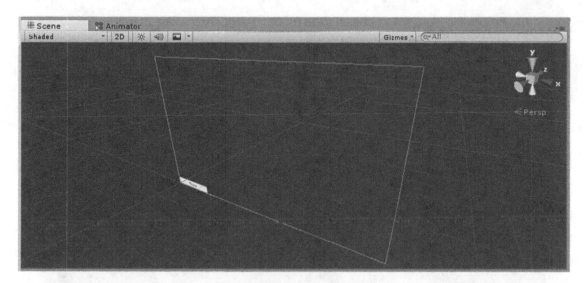

Figure 10-3. The Scene view with 2D display toggled off

The Canvas reflects the size dictated by the Game view. It is not a gameObject that can be adjusted, but keeping it from changing unintentionally during your GUI setup is essential.

3.   With 2 × 3 layout, or with the Scene or Game view floating, try changing the aspect ratio of the Game view by using some of the presets and observing the results in the Scene view (Figure 10-4).

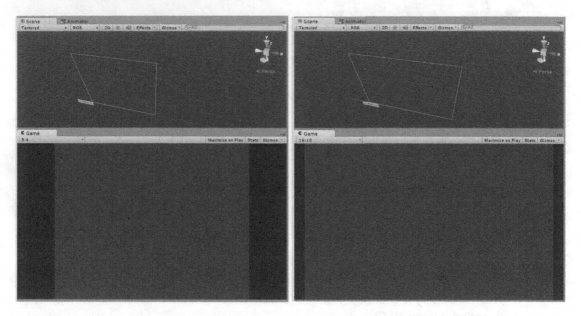

Figure 10-4. The aspect ratio affecting the Canvas bounds, 5:4 (left) and 16:10 (right)

4.   Select the Button and observe the four anchor corner icons in the center of the Canvas (Figure 10-5).

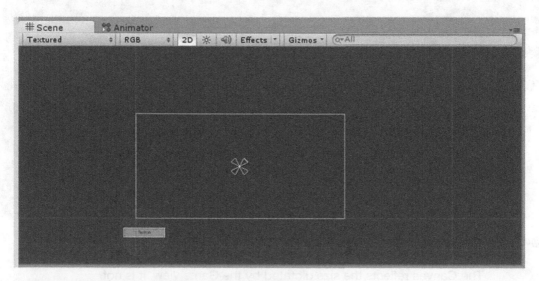

Figure 10-5. The Button's anchor points in the center of the Canvas

As the aspect ratio of the Canvas is changed, the Button retains its distance from its anchor, causing it to move off and on screen.

5. Set the Game view back to Free Aspect.

6. Click and drag the Button up toward its anchor points (Figure 10-6).

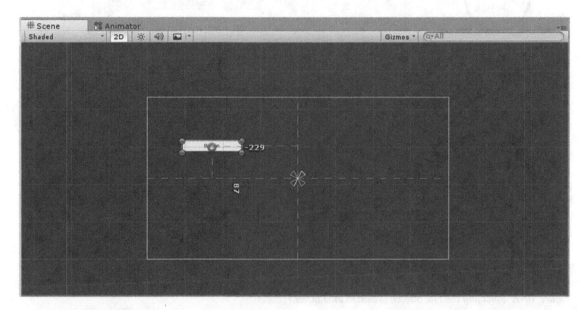

Figure 10-6. Moving the Button around the anchor points

As you move the Button, the guidelines report the offset from the anchor points. When you reach the center position, the lines turn blue. The offset from the anchor points is reflected in the inspector as the Pos X, Pos Y, and Pos Z. When the Button is centered, they will show as 0,0,0. The size of the Button is its Width and Height. The anchor's positions are *unitized*, where 0,0 is the lower left and 1,1 is the upper right. The X and Y Min and Max are currently all 0.5.

7. Move the Button so it is centered on the anchors, watching for the blue guidelines to indicate when the Button is centered.

8. Try adjusting the aspect ratio of the Game view.

    This time the Button retains its central location. It also retains its size and aspect ratio.

    The four anchor points can be moved manually or into preset locations. Let's do a few experiments with both methods.

9. With the Button selected, click the Anchor Presets button at the top-left corner of the Inspector and select the Full Stretch option in the lower-right corner (Figure 10-7).

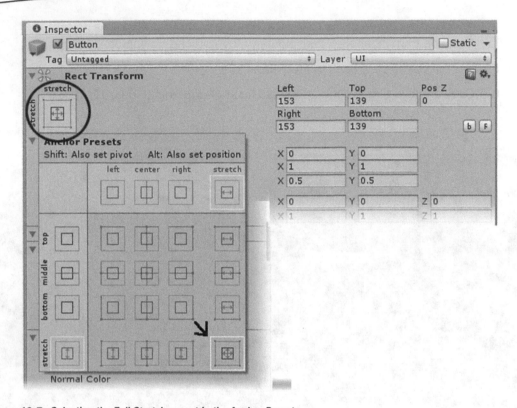

Figure 10-7. Selecting the Full Stretch preset in the Anchor Presets

The Anchor Presets icon changes to reflect the selected preset.

10.   Change the Game view window size to see the full stretch in action (Figure 10-8).

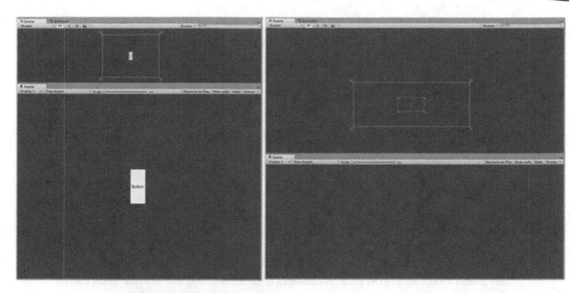

Figure 10-8. The Button stretching along with the window

You will notice that if the window's aspect ratio is too extreme, the Button will sport a red X, indicating that it will not be visible. Clearly, this could be a serious problem. Worse yet, if you correct the size in one, it will adversely affect the size in other resolutions or aspect ratios.

11. Try some of the other anchor presets and adjust the Game view's aspect ratio.

The Top/Bottom and Left/Right presets can be useful for HUDs where the elements are kept off to the sides, but scaling may continue to be a problem. Now is the time to set the Canvas gameObject's Canvas Scaler component. This is what will help you set up your UI in such a way that it will work with multiple screen resolutions with a minimum of additional work. As a default, its UI Scale Mode is set to Constant Pixel Size. Because you won't be worrying about pixel perfect for this project, you will change it to a more flexible choice.

1. Select the Canvas object and set its UI Scale Mode to Scale With Screen Size (Figure 10-9).

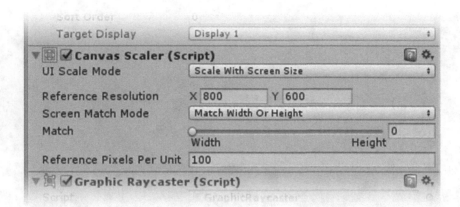

Figure 10-9. The Scale With Screen Size option

The first thing to set is a resolution. A good place to start is with the smallest resolution you plan on supporting. Currently, the Lumia 520 phone, a Windows phone and one of the top-selling phones of any OS, supports 854 × 480 pixels. This resolution is roughly a 16:9 aspect ratio, which will leave space on either side of the playing board for some UI elements.

2.   Set the Reference Resolution to **854 × 480**.

3. Set the Game view to 16:9 (Figure 10-10).

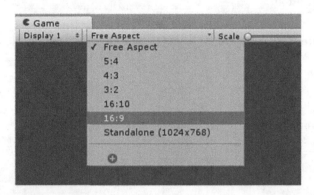

Figure 10-10. Setting the Game view's aspect ratio

You will be using the Screen Match Mode's default, Match Width or Height. The next decision point comes with whether to match the Width, Height, or something halfway between. This is done with the slider below the Screen Match Mode. The background image you will be using will look better cropped on the sides rather than top and bottom, so you will choose to keep the Height the driving parameter.

4. Move the Match slider all the way to the right for a value of **1**.

For now, with the start screen, you will just use the centering option and there should be no problems.

5. Select the Button and set its anchors back to the center preset (Figure 10-11).

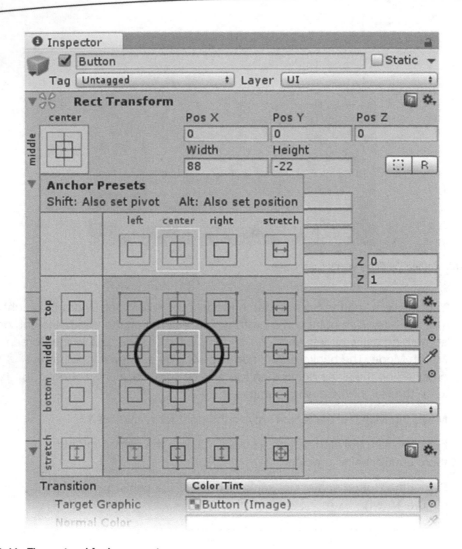

Figure 10-11. The centered Anchors preset

With the anchors centered, the Button, the most important element, will be the same size regardless of screen resolution. Let's see about fixing the Button size.

To manipulate the Button, you will see that, once selected, it has a Rect (as in *rectangle*) Transform gizmo (Figure 10-12).

Figure 10-12. The Rect Transform gizmo

With the bars, you can click and drag to change the size of the Button on the selected side. By clicking and dragging on a corner blue dot, you can change the size on two axes. The center blue ring is the pivot point and can be relocated by clicking in its center and dragging it. And, if you position the cursor just outside of the corner dots, you can rotate the object on its z axis. As expected, alignment snaps are well implemented to help you with your layout.

Tip Be careful when transforming UI gameObjects that an extra pick hasn't selected one of its children. The Button, for example, has a Text child object.

---

6. If your button is showing a red X, drag the top or bottom of the Button's gizmo, make sure it is right-side-out again, and recenter it on the anchor points.

7. Hover the pivot point circle until it highlights. Then click and drag it to down to the Button's lower edge.

8. In the Inspector, set the Button's Pos Y to **30** to offset it that far above the anchor points.

9. Drag the *top* of the Button's gizmo and resize the button to a Height of **40** (watch the Height in the Inspector as you pull the top upward).

10.   To get an even width, type the value of **250** directly into the Width
       parameter in the Inspector (Figure 10-13).

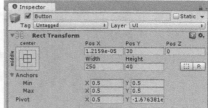

Figure 10-13. The Button sized and relocated using the Inspector and the Rect Transform gizmo

11.   Rename the Button to **Play Button**.

Along with a Play button, you will offer the player a chance to adjust the game's difficulty.
For that you will use a slider:

1.   Double-click the Button in the Hierarchy view to focus the view.

2.   From the GameObject menu, choose UI ➤ Slider and name it
      Difficulty Slider.

      The Slider's anchors should already be centered in the Canvas so it too will
      retain its size with respect to the Canvas. Also, when a parent's anchors are
      set, all of the children will inherit from those anchors as well.

3.   Set its Width to **250** and its Height to **40**.

4.   Move it down to a Y Position of about **-88**.

      With its new measurements, the Slider looks rather chunky. Let's see what
      can be done to it.

5.   Set the Slider component's Value to **0.9** so you will be able to see the
      various parts of the slider.

6.   Next, open the Difficulty Slider to inspect its hierarchy.

      Besides a Background, it has two other children: a Fill area and a Handle
      Slide area. The Background can increase the pick area for the Slider's
      handle, a useful behavior for a small mobile screen and large player fingers.

7.   Deactivate the Background object for now.

8.   Select the Handle and for its Image component's Source Image, click
      the Browse icon, and select the UISprite instead of the Knob.

The Slider is looking more like a regular slider (Figure 10-14).

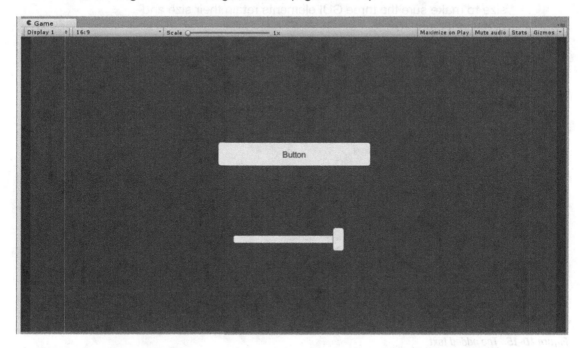

Figure 10-14. The reworked slider

You will also want to add a label for the slider:

1. Create a new Text object and name it **Slider Label**.

2. Position it between the Play Button and Difficulty Slider.

3. In the Text component, set its Alignments to centered, its Font Style to Bold, and its Font Size to **30**.

4. Set the Text to **easy med hard**.

    The text Size is too large for its bounding rectangle and does not show. You could adjust its size, or, allow the text to overflow.

5. Set the Horizontal and Vertical Overflows to Overflow.

6. Set its Color to a saturated green.

7. Drag the Slider Label into the Difficulty Slider group so it inherits the centered anchors.

8. Switch to Free Aspect on in the Game view, and change the view
    size to make sure the three GUI elements retain their size and
    position (Figure 10-15).

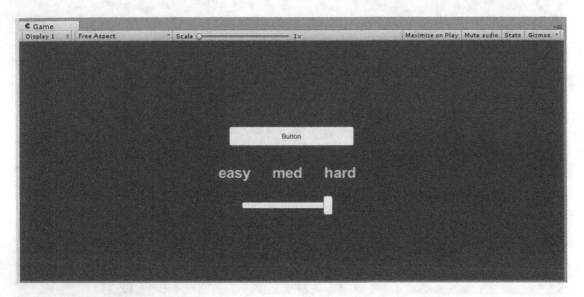

Figure 10-15. The added text

Processing Sprite Textures

Now let's look at a few of the more visual aspects of the UI objects. The Button consists of
two components: an Image component and a Button component. The Image component
is set up to take a Sprite type image, and its Image Type is set to Sliced. This means the
texture can be set up to stretch only the inner part of the texture, leaving the corners intact.

Before importing the UI textures, you will take advantage of 2D mode. This will speed up the
processing of the textures that will be used only for the UI, setting them to Sprite type on
import instead of the Texture type you saw in Chapter 4.

1. From the Edit menu, choose Project Settings ➤ Editor.

2. Change the Default Behavior Mode to 2D (Figure 10-16).

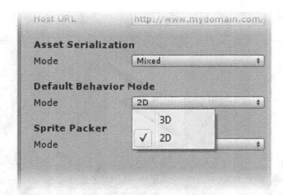

Figure 10-16. Changing the Default Behavior Mode

Besides importing the textures set to Sprite type, this setting will also change the Scene view to 2D. You are already using the 2D display for the Scene view, but this will definitely save time with the textures. Be aware, however, that it will also set new cameras to orthographic rather than perspective.

3. Drag the UI Textures folder into the project from the Chapter 10 Assets folder.

    It contains several new textures for your menu and HUD (Figure 10-17).

Figure 10-17. The new GUI textures in the Two Column Layout

The first thing you will notice is that the sprite textures all have expand arrows in the Two Column Layout. Unlike 3D objects that have their mapping built in, for 2D objects that share an atlased texture, you must specify how the texture sheet is divided. The second thing that you will see is that the transparent backgrounds of sprites are shown in the familiar gray checkered pattern (Figure 10-18).

Figure 10-18. The Sprite type showing its transparency (left), and the Texture type showing its solid background (center), and alpha channel (right)

Let's go ahead and customize the Start Menu's GUI objects.

1. Select the Play Group object from the UI Textures folder.

2. From the Sprite Mode drop-down, select Multiple (Figure 10-19).

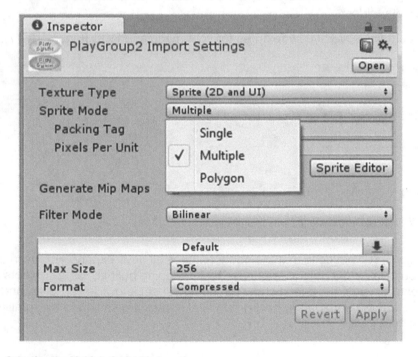

Figure 10-19. Selecting the Multiple Sprite Mode option

For the Play button, you will be using multiple sprites.

3. Click the Sprite Editor button (it is located halfway down on the right).

4. In the Sprite editor's top left corner, click Slice and select the Grid By Cell Count option.

5. Set the Column & Row counts to *2* and press Slice (Figure 10-20).

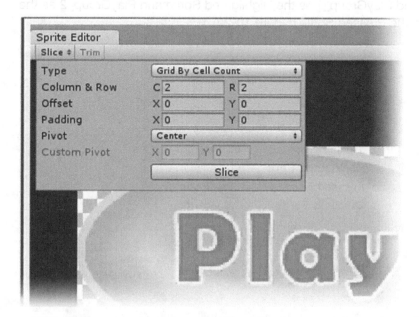

Figure 10-20. Using the Grid By Cell Count option to separate the atlased texture sheet

Fine gray lines appear indicating the slice locations.

6. Click the Apply button from the upper left of the Sprite Editor and then close it.

7. Click the expand arrow for the PlayGroup texture in the Project view.

The new sprites generated from the texture sheet are now available for use (Figure 10-21).

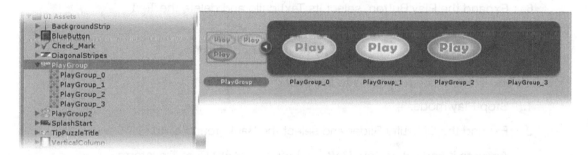

Figure 10-21. The sprites generated from the atlased texture sheet, One Column Layout (left), and Two Column Layout (right)

Let's load the new sprite textures onto the Play Button.

1. Select the Play Button and load PlayGroup_0 as the Image component's Source Image.

2. In the Button component, change the Transition to Sprite Swap.

3. Load PlayGroup_1 as the Highlighted Sprite and PlayGroup_2 as the as the Pressed Sprite (Figure 10-22).

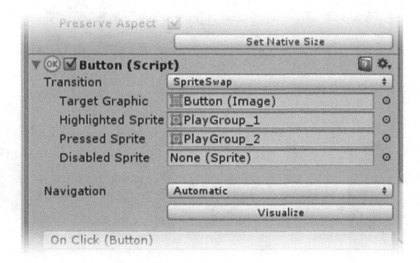

Figure 10-22. The sprites loaded in for the Button transitions

With the Button image in place, you can see that the button will have to be adjusted to match the image.

4. In the Button's Image component, click Preserve Aspect Ratio.

5. Click Set Native Size.

With the texture providing the text, you can get rid of the default Text object.

6. Expand the Play Button, select its Text child and delete the Text gameObject.

7. Click Play and test the Button by hovering and clicking.

Now let's add some custom textures to the Slider:

1. Stop Play mode.

2. Expand the Difficulty Slider and select the Background child.

3. Activate it and set its Top, Bottom, Left, and Right Rect Transform parameters to **-5**.

4. Set its Color to r, **24**; g, **65**; b, **255**.

    The background image is a flat blue.

5. Select the Fill Area's Fill child and the Handle Slice Area's Handle
    child and assign the BlueButton sprite texture as their Source Image.

The texture is stretched across the Fill image and squished on the Handle (Figure 10-23).

Figure 10-23. The stretched BlueButton sprite

For this image, you will use Unity's slicing feature. Also known as *9 slice*, it defines the region of
the image that will be allowed to stretch, allowing the corners to retain their original pixel size.

1. Select the BlueButton sprite in the Project view.

2. Open the Sprite Editor.

    Because Sprite Mode is set to Single, the editor opens with the slice
    guides, thin green lines, around the outside the image.

3. Click and drag on the guide grips to adjust their positions so that the
    Borders are all 12 pixels each (Figure 10-24).

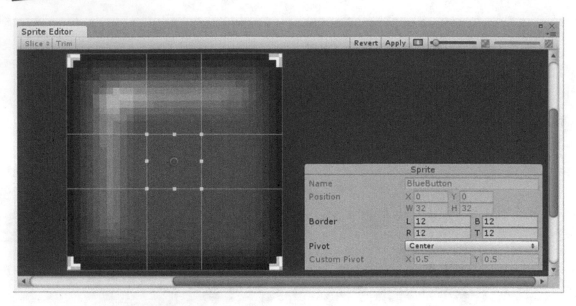

Figure 10-24. The sliced BlueButton sprite

4. Click Apply and close the editor.

    Before you can see the changes, you will have to update the Image Type in the Image components.

5. Select the two objects and set their Image Type to Sliced.

6. Inspect the changes in the Scene or Game view.

This time, the corners are held and the center is stretched (Figure 10-25).

Figure 10-25. The Slider parts with the sliced texture holding the corners

In case you are wondering why the Handle remains squashed looking, consider the sprite's size, 32 pixels. If the borders take up 24 pixels (12 and 12), and the handle uses less than 24, the remaining pixels must be squashed to fit.

Let's put a more interesting texture on the Fill image to see how the Slider behaves at runtime.

1. Select the Fill child and assign DiagonalStripes sprite texture as its Source Image.

   This image also stretches, but slicing will not solve the problem. This time you will set it to tile.

2. In the Image component, change its Image Type from Simple to Tiled.

   The texture is tiled to fit the object.

3. Click Play and move the Slider.

   The Fill image changes size, but the mapping remains intact (Figure 10-26).

Figure 10-26. The Difficulty Slider's Fill holding its mapping as the value changes

Background Management

Next you will add a background image to give the Start Menu a bit more appeal by hinting at the game play and environment. Once you move away from the centered anchor option, it becomes more important to do your initial setup in your target aspect ratio.

1. Stop Play mode.

2. Set the Game view to the 16:9 aspect ratio.

3. From the UI section, create a new Image object and name it **Menu Background**.

4. Drag the new image up to the top of the Canvas group so it will be drawn first, or in back of the rest of the objects.

5. Load the SplashStart sprite in as its Source Image.

6. Snap its sides to the Canvas's sides.

7. Leave the Anchors at Middle/Center.

8. Try adjusting the Game view to see how the background holds up in a few different aspect ratios (Figure 10-27).

Figure 10-27. Three different Game view aspect ratios: 6:9 (left), 3:2 (center), 5:4 (right)

The background scales to fit the height as per the Canvas Scaler, and the sides are cropped.

Adding a title will be more challenging. The place to start is with the smallest resolution you plan on supporting. Currently, the Lumia 520 phone, one of the top-selling phones of any OS, supports 854 × 480 pixels. To make testing easier, you will set up a couple of custom resolutions for the Game view. Be aware that these custom resolutions will be a new part of your editor layout and are not stored in the project.

1. Click the plus icon at the bottom of the Game view's aspect drop-down and add the following (Figure 10-28):

   Lumia 520, 854 × 480

   720p, 1024 × 720

   1080p, 1920 × 1080

   Surface Pro, 3:2, 2160 × 1440

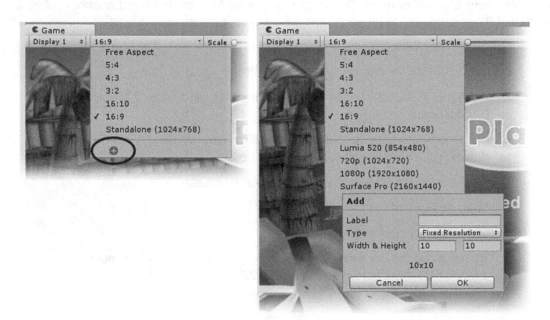

Figure 10-28. Adding custom resolutions to the Game view

> **Tip**   The Asset Store has many useful items, including one made specifically for testing different sizes and resolutions. If you plan on seriously getting into the mobile market, be sure to check out Flying Whale's xARM.

Next you will want to float the Game window so you can adjust the size and change the settings unimpeded. To make it easier to return to your favorite layout, you can save a custom layout first.

2. From the Layout drop-down at the upper right of the editor, select Save Layout.

3. Name it something meaningful.

4. Click the Game view tab and drag it off the editor until it no longer tries to dock itself.

5. Select your new layout from the Layout drop-down to see your saved layout reset.

6. Tear off the Game view again.

For the title image, you will arrange the anchors halfway between center and full stretch. This will allow for some increase of size, but not to the point of overpowering the Button and Slider, which are retaining the same size independent of screen size.

1. Select the Lumia 520 resolution and make the view large enough to see the correct resolution.

2. Create a new Image and name it **Title Image**.

3. Load the TipPuzzleTitle image in as its Source Image and set it to Preserve Aspect.

4. In the Rect Transform, set the Z Rotation to **13.5**.

5. Adjust the size until the image fits in the top-left corner (Figure 10-29).

Figure 10-29. The title image, crowded into the view

The image, the title of your little game, just isn't as big and important as you'd like to see it. Let's use the Canvas Scaler to gain a bit more real estate for the title.

6. Select the Canvas Scaler and set its Reference Resolution to **1024 × 720**.

    The background image will require adjustment to compensate.

7. Set the Game view to the Lumia size and snap the background image to the new Canvas borders.

    The logical move might be to anchor the image to the top-left corner of the Canvas at this point. but by pushing the anchors out to the bottom corner of the existing UI elements, you can gain a little bit of scaling and keep the picture larger.

8. Set the size, location, and anchors as per Figure 10-30.

Figure 10-30. The title image with custom adjustment

9. Check using the other resolutions to see how the title holds up (Figure 10-31).

Figure 10-31. Slight scaling of the Title image between the Lumia (left), 720p (center), and Surface Pro (right) screen presets

The anchors on the left are lined up with the left side of the Canvas, anchoring the image to the left side as it scales. The right side anchors are a bit over halfway, so the image will scale only about half of what it would if the anchors were all the way to the right side. With Preserve Aspect turned on, the exact top/bottom numbers aren't crucial as long as the Max Y is near the top to anchor it from the top.

Let's investigate how order in the Hierarchy view affects interaction.

1. Click Play and test the UI.

    The Difficulty Slider works, but the Play button does not respond. The title image, though transparent beyond the text, is blocking the button.

2. In the Hierarchy view, move the Title Image above the Play Button, but below the Menu Background.

3. Click Play and test again.

    With the button and slider scaled down for the title image, it will be important to increase the slider's pick area.

4. Select the Difficulty Slider and create a new Image GameObject inside it

5. Name it **Background Pick** and move it above the original Background object.

6. Adjust its size so it is larger than the other parts of the slider on the sides and bottom and reaches almost to the Start Button at the top (Figure 10-32).

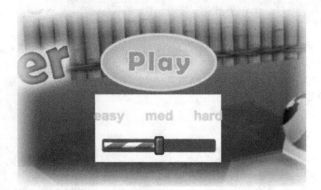

Figure 10-32. Increasing the slider's pick area with an Image

7. In its Color parameter, turn its Alpha value to **0**.

    Before you can script the button to open the Board Level, both scenes must be added to the build. The first will go in at position 0 and will be the first scene loaded when the built game is run. Scenes can be added, removed and re-ordered from the build.

8. Save the scene.

9. From File menu, select Build Settings and click Add Current.

10. Close the Build Settings window.

The Start Menu has been added to the build.

Game Level GUI

With a few exceptions, the Game Level GUI is technically similar to the Start Menu's GUI, so you will be importing it as a Unity package.

1. Open the Board Level scene.

2. Import the GameLevelGUI.unitypackage from the Chapter 10 Assets folder.

3. Drag the Game Level GUI prefab from the Assets/Prefabs folder into the Hierarchy view.

The new UI is nothing special, but it includes a check box and it also gets deeper into Text component functionality. Just as with some of the Start Menu elements, these are anchored to the sides. Some of the elements are allowed to scale slightly differently than the Canvas Scaler handles. Let's begin by checking the GUI at the target resolutions.

1. Set the Game view to the Lumia 520 setting.

2. If necessary, adjust the camera's x, y, and z positions. Center the game board in the viewport (Figure 10-33).

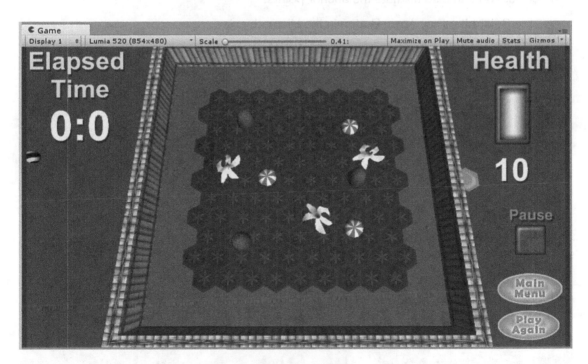

Figure 10-33. The imported Game Level GUI at the Lumia 520 resolution

As with the Start Menu, the smallest resolution should be where your controls take up the most screen space.

3. Try the other preset screen sizes (Figure 10-34).

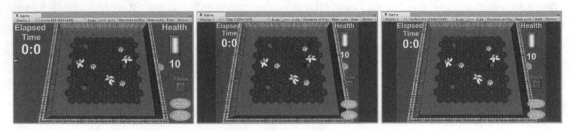

Figure 10-34. The Game Level GUI at three of the target size/aspect ratios

The GUI elements are a bit crowed at the narrower aspect ratios, but the controls have shrunk just enough that they shouldn't interfere with the board area where the action happens. Before rushing off to shrink controls, remember that some are meant to be pressed and must not be so small as to make touching ambiguous.

Before hooking up the Button functionality, you will create an animation with the Play Again button to mark the Marble reaching the end of the path. Besides animating the usual transforms, you can also animate the anchor points.

1. Select the Play Again Button in the Hierarchy view.

2. From the Window menu, open the Animation window and click the Create button (Figure 10-35).

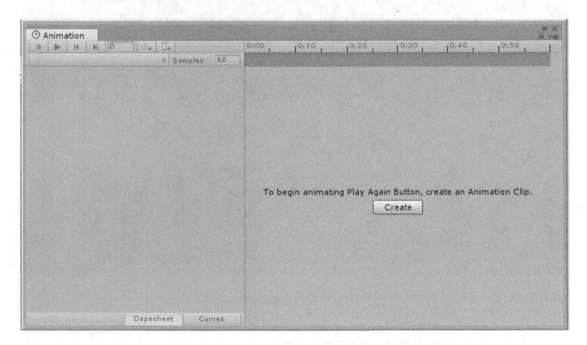

Figure 10-35. Creating a new Animation clip for the UI object

3. Name the new clip **ButtonAni** and create a new folder named **Animation Clips** to store it in.

4. Click the time indicator up at the timeline and drag it to **1:00**.

5. In the Scene view, move the Button to the center (watch for orange guide lines) and in the Inspector, set its X and Y Scale to **2**.

6. Now set its Anchors to the Middle/Center preset.

7. Drag the time indicator from 0:00 to **1:00** to see the animation.

8. Click the Animation's Play button and observe the speed.

   It is a bit slow.

9. Drag the top key (that will move all at that time location) at the 1:00 time to **0:4** and click Play again.

   The animation is quicker.

10. Close the Animation window and check out the Play Again's new Animator component in the Inspector.

Creating the animation automatically added the Animator component and created an Animator Controller for it named after the Button, Play Again Button.

Let's continue the button's animation.

1. Click Play.

   The Button animates to the center, over and over. Besides preventing a looping animation, you will also have to stop the Button from animating on startup.

2. Locate and select the ButtonAni clip in the Project view and deactivate the Loop Time check box in the Inspector

3. With the Play Again Button selected, open the Animator tab, right-click, and choose State ➤ Empty to create a new state.

Tip   Double-clicking the Controller in an object's Animator component will also open the Animator view.

---

4. Right-click over it and choose Set As Layer Default State. Then name it **Default** in the Inspector.

5. Click Play.

Now the Button will no longer play automatically on star up.

There's one last graphical thing to do. Let's put a nice gradient into the background of the Board Level. You will use a second Canvas so you can set it to draw behind the 3D scene:

1. Create a new Canvas object and name it **Canvas Background**.

2. Add an Image object to it and name it **Background**.

3. Drag BackgroundStrip in as its Source Image.

4. Set the anchors to the edge of the Canvas (Stretch/Stretch) and scale the image out to them as well.

5. Set the Canvas Render Mode to Screen Space Camera.

    The background drops behind the other UI objects.

6. Load the Main Camera in as the Render Camera.

    In the Game view, the background drops behind the 3D objects.

7. Test the different screen sizes and aspect ratios to assure yourself that it behaves well with any preset.

Hooking Up the Functionality

With the GUI elements in place and sizing correctly, it's time to hook them up to the code that feeds the displays. The health parameter is already in place but the game timer itself will require a bit of scripting. Let's take care of it first. From this point out, a lot of scripts will be talking to each other, which means, of course, a lot of introductions as you identify them to each other.

While manually doing a drag-and-drop into a parameter isn't bad occasionally, it gets old fast. Using GameObject.Find() is not bad if it happens only on load, but you can improve upon it by using FindWithTag so it doesn't have to go through all of the scene's objects. Creating a separate tag for each of the communicating objects would be overkill, but you can improve efficiency with a few extra tags. You've already tagged the game pieces as Game Piece. Let's create a new tag for the script that will manage the Board Level UI:

1. Select any object.

2. At the top of the Inspector, open the Tag drop-down and select Add Tag. Click the plus twice to create two new tags.

3. Name them **HUD** and **Holder**.

Making the Game Timer

The little game is already full of rewards and pitfalls to keep the player engaged during the game, so your next task is to entice the player to want to play the game again and again. A scoring system could be introduced by letting the player try to roll the Marble through yet another type of game piece, but a better solution would be to use the time it takes to complete the path as the incentive to Play Again. The timer itself is relatively easy. Remember, Time.time returns the amount of time in seconds since the game was started.

In this case, you will be using `Time.timeSinceLevelLoad` because `Time.time` would be returning time from the start of the entire game—that is, since the Start menu (once you have it hooked up). You will also want to be able to start and stop the timer for various reasons, so there will be a bit more scripting involved.

Let's begin by creating a script to manage all of the game HUD:

1. Open the Board Level scene.

2. Create a new C# script in the Game Scripts folder and name it **GameHUD**.

3. Add the following to access the Unity UI elements:

```
using UnityEngine.UI;
```

4. Add the following variables beneath the class declaration:

```
// timer variables
float elapsedTime; // need for starting and stoping timer
float startTime; //
bool ticking = false; // flag for timer active
string formattedTime; // float converted to nice string for display
public Text currentETime; // the elapsed time GUI

//health variables
internal int health = 10; // tracking health
```

> The last line is for the health variable. Although it is tracked in the MarbleManager script, as soon as the path is completed, the Marble is deactivated, leaving the health variable inaccessible. Health is adjusted in the PortalHopper script, so it will be easy to send updates to the GameHUD script at the same time.

5. Create the function that will handle the timer's state:

```
public void ToggleTimer (bool state) {
    ticking = state;
    if (state) startTime = Time.timeSinceLevelLoad - elapsedTime;
    else elapsedTime = Time.timeSinceLevelLoad - startTime;
}
```

> This function is in charge of setting the state of the timer. Passing `true` starts the timer, and passing `false` stops the timer. When you initially start the timer, `Time.timeSinceLevelLoad`, the amount of time that has passed since the level was loaded, is 0. As this is the first time it is started, `elapsedTime` is also 0, so the first `startTime` will be 0. The current elapsed time can always be calculated with `Time.timeSinceLevelLoad - startTime`. After a pause, the game is started up again and the `startTime` recalculated. The new `startTime` is the current `Time.timeSinceLevelLoad` *minus* the elapsed time. Figure 10-36 may help you visualize the functionality.

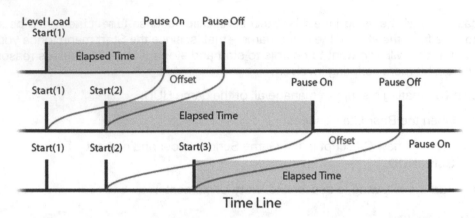

Figure 10-36. *An example of the time code's functionality*

6. Start the timer from the Start function:

```
ToggleTimer (true); // call the function & start the timer
formattedTime = string.Format("{0:0}:{1:00}", 0, 0);
```

The second line initializes the time for use with the GUI. Using string.Format, you define within the curly brackets, and the arguments 0, 0 replace the placeholders inside the brackets. Later, when you allow the player to pause the game at will, that pause will be added in as well.

In the Update function you will break the time into seconds and minutes and feed it into the same string format.

7. In the Update function, calculate the current elapsed time if the timer is running:

```
if (ticking) {
    float timer = Time.timeSinceLevelLoad  - startTime;
    int minutes = Mathf.FloorToInt(timer / 60F);
    int seconds = Mathf.FloorToInt(timer - minutes * 60);
    formattedTime = string.Format("{0:0}:{1:00}", minutes, seconds);
    currentETime.text = formattedTime; // update the GUI text
}
```

This code breaks the current elapsed time into seconds and minutes, and then feeds the values into a string so that can be displayed by the GUI in the Text component.

8. Save the script.

9. Create a new Empty gameObject and name it **HUD Manager**.

10. Drag the GameHUD script onto it and assign the HUD tag to it.

11. From the Canvas, locate the Timer Label's Elapsed Time Value object and drag it into the HUD Manager's Current E Time parameter.

12. Click Play.

The timer ticks happily away but does not yet stop when the path has been completed.

The PathCellManager script contains the code that is played when the path is completed, so it will have to tell the timer to stop at that time.

1. Open the PathCellManager script.

2. Add the following variable to identify the GameHUD script:

```
GameHUD gameHUD; // so the timer can be turned off at game end
```

3. In the Start function, add the following:

```
gameHUD = GameObject.FindWithTag("HUD").GetComponent<GameHUD>();
```

4. Near the top of the ProcessWinner function, add this:

```
// turn off timer
gameHUD.ToggleTimer(false);
```

5. Save the script.

6. Click Play and complete the path.

The timer stops nicely when the path is completed.

Now you will see about pausing the timer when the Marble escapes the board. Because the player can trigger the event with wild board tipping, a little time penalty might be a good deterrent, but because the physics may fail while the player is being careful, you wouldn't want to "charge" for the entire reset time. In this case, there will be a short lag time when the Marble escapes until the reset is triggered, so the penalty will automatically be very small. The reset is triggered in the DeathZoneReset script, but is actually handled in the MarbleManager script.

1. Open the MarbleManager script.

2. Add the variable to identify the GameHUD:

```
GameHUD gameHUD; // so the timer can be turned off while resetting
```

3. At the top of the Start function, add the following:

```
gameHUD = GameObject.FindWithTag("HUD").GetComponent<GameHUD>();
```

4. At the top of the IEnumerator DelayReset, add this:

```
// turn off timer
gameHUD.ToggleTimer(false);
```

5. At the bottom, below the SetToStart() line, add this:

```
// turn on timer
gameHUD.ToggleTimer(true);
```

6. Save the script.

7. Click Play and tip the board until the marble escapes.

The timer should now pause while the marble is being reset and start up again as it pops into play.

Adding Health

Before hooking up health to the new GUI, you will want to have the PortalHopper script update the value in the GameHUD script so it will be available even after the Marble has been deactivated.

If the health had to be updated every frame, you could update the variable directly and add the code to the Update function. But it has to be updated only after each score adjustment, so you will call a function to handle the value change.

1. Open the PortalHopper script.

2. Add the variable to identify the GameHUD:

```
GameHUD gameHUD; // so the HUD can track health
```

3. In the Start function add the following:

```
gameHUD = GameObject.FindWithTag("HUD").GetComponent<GameHUD>();
```

4. In the OnTriggerEnter function, below the print(marbleManager.
   health) line, add the following:

```
gameHUD.UpdateHealthGUI(health); // update and process health in HUD
```

5. Comment out the print line.

6. Save the script.

With the health now being updated in the GameHUD script, you can hook up its value to both the Health Value and Health Bar objects:

1. Open the GameHUD script.

2. Add the following variables:

```
public RectTransform healthBar; // the Health Bar image's Rect Transform
public Text healthText; // The health value label
public Image imageColor;
```

> For the Health Bar, you will be adjusting the Y Scale and changing the image color. Because Scale is a transform, you will have to use the usual process for setting its value. Note that you are asking for its *local* scale values.

3. Create the UpdateHealthGUI function:

```
public void UpdateHealthGUI(int newHealth) {
    // health bar value
    health = newHealth;
    Vector3 tempScale = new Vector3(healthBar.localScale.x,healthBar.localScale.y,healthBar.
    localScale.z);
    tempScale.y = health/20f;
    healthBar.localScale = tempScale;
    healthText.text = string.Format("{0}%", health);
}
```

4. Save the script.

5. Drag the Health Value object into the new Health Text parameter.

6. Drag the Health Bar into both the Health Bar and Image Color parameters.

7. Click Play and test.

The text is kept up-to-date, and the bar scales according to that value.

Calculating the color change will be fairly easy. Out of a maximum of 20, if the Health is 5 or less, the color will be red, warning the player that a hit by a Spinner will lose path progress. If the value is over 15, the color will be green, indicating that path progress will be gained when a gumdrop is hit.

Rather than hard-coding the colors, you will create a gradient and sample the color from the corresponding location on it.

1. Continuing with the GameHUD script, add the following variable:

```
public Gradient gradient; // the Health Bar image's color source
```

2. At the bottom of the `UpdateHealthGUI` function, add the following:

```
// Health bar color
imageColor.color = gradient.Evaluate(tempScale.y);
```

3. Save the script.

4. In the Game HUD component, double-click the gradient's color bar to open the Gradient editor.

    The top side of the bar is for alpha values, and the bottom side is for color.

5. Set the first and last alpha channel markers to white, or 255, by clicking them and then adjusting their values.

    For the colors, click just above the bottom side of the color bar to create new markers. You can move the newly created marker by dragging it or typing in a location. You can set a different color by clicking the color swatch for the selected marker and setting it in the usual Color Editor. Unity limits you to eight markers for color and eight for alpha channel.

6. Set the colors as per Figure 10-37.

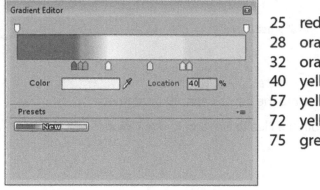

25	red	(255,40,40)
28	orange	(255,145,0)
32	orange	
40	yellow	(255,255,0)
57	yellow/green	(200,255,60)
72	yellow/green	
75	green	(0,255,0)

Figure 10-37. The health gradient, locations, colors, and their RGB values

7. In the GameHUD, initialize the new health display values in the `Start` function:

```
UpdateHealthGUI(health); //initialize the health GUI
```

8. Save the script.

To test the functionality at this point, you could easily spend extra time avoiding spinners and getting blown off course by the boosters. To be more efficient, you can turn off the game pieces that will impede your testing.

1. Deactivate the Spinners and Boosters.

2. Click Play and accumulate enough points to register 20.

3. Turn on the Spinners and Boosters.

4. Test the bar's behavior as the points go up and down.

The Health Bar provides improved feedback to keep the player apprised of the Marble's health.

Pausing the Game

For the Pause toggle, you will be altering time with Time.scale in the GameHUD script. Setting the time scale to 0 effectively stops game play, but at the same time allows the player interaction with GUI controls.

There are some serious side effects of stopping Play mode while the timescale, is at 0 as it does not automatically reset to 1 when you stop Play mode. This can prevent collider states from resetting, yield statements from ending, and play havoc with anything using the system clock. Fortunately, you will add a bit of code to prevent testing from being a painful experience.

1. Open the GameHUD script.

2. Create the following variable:

```
// flag for pausing game
bool isPaused;
```

3. Add the following function to toggle time:

```
public void PauseToggle () {
   if (isPaused) {
       print("Unpaused");
       Time.timeScale = 1.0f;
       isPaused = false;
   }
   else {
       print("Paused");
       Time.timeScale = 0.0f;
       isPaused = true;
   }
}
```

To turn the timescale back on in case you stop Play mode during a pause, you will use OnApplicationQuit, and then check to see whether it was the editor.

4.   Add the following function to make sure timescale gets reset:

```
public void OnApplicationQuit() {

    Time.timeScale=1; // always reset timeScale on exit

}
```

5.   Save the script.

With the previous UI objects, you used scripting to update their various parameters to match the game's state. This time, because the toggle is interactive, the player will change the game's state. To call a function from a UI object, you will make use of the Toggle component's On Value Changed flag. Unlike most of Unity, where you would have to create a script to hold an OnValueChanged function, the UI system lets you create the event in the object's GUI component, select the object with the script component you want to call, and specify the method or function within it.

Tip   Any functions or methods called from an On Click event must be made public.

---

1.   Select the Pause toggle/check box object.

2.   In the Toggle script component, deactivate the Is On parameter (just above the Toggle Transition parameter) so it will be off on startup.

3.   In the Toggle component, at the bottom, click the plus icon to create a new On Value Changed event if there isn't one already there from the package import (Figure 10-38).

Figure 10-38. Creating an event for a Unity UI component

4.   If it isn't already set to Runtime Only, change that option now to avoid future problems with TimeScale and other issues.

5.   Drag the HUD Manager object from the Hierarchy view to the Object field of the new event. Warning: do not drag this from your Project view. This must be from the Hierarchy window as you need an actual game object instance in your scene to call this code on.

6. From the Functions drop-down, choose GameHUD ➤ PauseToggle( ) (Figure 10-39).

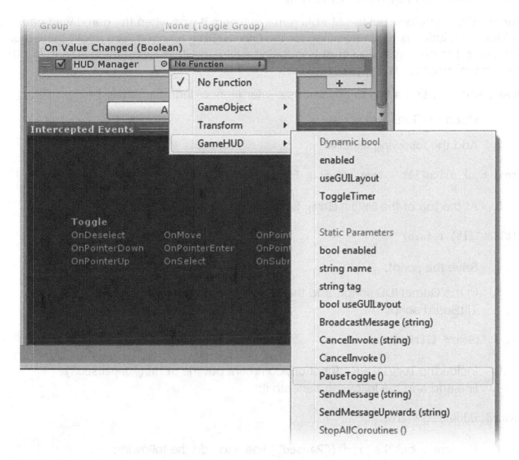

Figure 10-39. Loading the method to call when the toggle's state is changed

7. Click Play and tilt the board.

8. Click the Pause toggle.

   The timer stops, and the animations and physics stop.

9. Click the Pause toggle again.

   Everything picks up where it left off. In case you hadn't noticed, however, player input was *not* paused. This makes sense if you think about it. If the player couldn't interact with the GUI, how could he start the game up again? The problem appears when you try to drag in the view to tip the board. Because click-and-drag is more of a UI-type input, it is still active! Not only that, but now the game may freeze up if the board is tipped.

10.   Pause the game again.

11.   Click and drag in the Game view.

The board tilts as before, but the Marble remains where it was when the game was paused. The simplest solution is to create a flag for the OnMouseDrag function. You might think that you can stop the contents of a script from being evaluated if you were to disable it, but the only thing that disables is its Start function.

Let's see about setting a flag to prevent user interference during a pause.

1.   Open the TiltBoard script.

2.   Add the following variable:

```
internal bool allowTilt = true; // flag for pausing tilt
```

3.   At the top of the OnMouseDrag function, add the following:

```
if (!allowTilt) return;
```

4.   Save the script.

5.   In the GameHUD script, add the following variable to access the TiltBoard script:

```
public TiltBoard tiltBoard;
```

6.   Inside the TogglePause function, comment out the print("Unpaused") line and add the following beneath it:

```
tiltBoard.allowTilt = true;
```

7.   Comment out the print("Paused") line and add the following beneath it:

```
tiltBoard.allowTilt = false;
```

8.   Save the script.

9.   Assign the Board Group object to the HUD Manager's new Tilt Board parameter.

10.   Click Play and test the tilt blocking during a pause.

This time, the board doesn't budge during the pause. Blocking user input during a pause also prevents issues with pausing during a reset.

With the Board Level fairly functional, it is time to add it to the build and think about changing levels or scenes.

11.   Stop Play mode and save the scene.

12.   Open the Build Settings window and click Add Open Scenes.

With both scenes added to the build, you are ready to let the player restart the game either during or after completion of the path.

Encouraging Another Game

To entice the player to restart the game, you will trigger the Play Again Button's animation when the player has completed the path. The PathCellsManager script knows when that happens. It will have to have contact with the Play Again Button's Animator component so it can trigger the animation.

1. Open the PathCellManager script.

2. Add the following variable:

```
public Animator buttonAni; // button's animator component
```

3. In the ProcessWinner function, under the // show menu line, add this:

```
buttonAni.Play("ButtonAni");
```

4. Save the script.

5. Drag the Play Again Button onto the Path Manager's new Button Ani parameter.

6. Click Play and complete the path.

The Button zips to the middle of the screen and comes to a stop.

When the player clicks the button, the Start Menu scene should load. It doesn't matter where you add this code, as it will be accessed through the Button's event system. Logically, it will make the most sense to put it with the rest of the HUD code.

In older versions of Unity, you changed levels by using Application.LoadLevel. This has been changed to SceneManager.LoadScene and requires another library.

1. Open the GameHUD script and near the top, add the following:

```
using UnityEngine.SceneManagement;
```

2. Add the following functions:

```
public void StartMenu () {
    // restart
    SceneManager.LoadScene ("Start Menu");
}

public void PlayAgain () {
    // restart
    SceneManager.LoadScene ("Board Level");
}
```

3. Save the script.

With `SceneManager.LoadScene`, you can use either the scene's build index number or its name. You've already added the two scenes to the build, but will eventually add a preload scene to make data retention go smoother. By using the level name, you can add an earlier level without having to change the script. To call the function, you will add an event to the Button's On Click behavior.

1. Select the Play Again Button in the Hierarchy view.

2. Create a new On Click event and drag the HUD Manager in as the Object.

3. Select the GameHUD's `PlayAgain()` as the function.

4. Save the scene.

5. Click Play and pick the button when the path has been completed.

    The Board Level is loaded.

6. Stop Play mode and repeat the procedure with the Main Menu button calling the `StartMenu` function.

7. Test the Main Menu button.

Now, of course, you will want to head back to the Start Menu and hook its Play button up to the Board Level.

Finishing the Start Menu

Earlier in the chapter, you created a simple start screen. It currently consists of a Play Game button and a Difficulty Slider. When the game has ended, the player can return to the Start menu when the Play Again button is pressed. This allows the player to change the difficulty if desired.

Loading the Board Level

As you know already, loading the Board Level is easy. Retaining data between levels is a bit trickier than it sounds. Let's begin by creating a script to manage the Start Menu's GUI.

1. Open the Start Menu scene.

2. Create a new Empty gameObject named **Game Manager**.

3. Create a new C# script named **GameManager**.

4. Add it to the new gameObject.

5. Add the following at the top of the script:

```
using UnityEngine.SceneManagement;
using UnityEngine.UI;
```

6. Add the following function for the Play Button:

```
public void LoadGameLevel () {
SceneManager.LoadScene ("Board Level");
}
```

7. Save the script.

8. Select the Play Button and click the plus sign to add a new On Click event to it.

9. Drag the Game Manager in as the object and from GameManager, select the LoadGameLevel() function.

10. Save the scene.

11. Click Play and press the Play button.

The Board Level scene starts.

12. Stop Play mode to return to the Start Menu scene.

Retaining Data Between Levels

For the Difficulty Slider, you will have to retain the setting the player has chosen when the level changes. To do this, you add an Awake function with DontDestroyOnLoad(). The problem is that if you are going back and forth between level and menu, you will soon have several duplicates of the object. The trick is to check for the existence of the object you want, and to either delete extras or instantiate a new one depending on what was found. The code is a bit confusing, but keeping data persistent between levels/scenes is a necessity in most games.

1. In the Start Menu scene, create an Empty gameObject and name it **Holder**.

2. Assign the Holder tag to it.

3. Create a new C# script, name it **Persistent**, and add it to the Holder object.

4. Add the following variables:

```
private static Persistent instanceRef;
```

5. Add the Awake function:

```
void Awake () {
   if(instanceRef == null) {
      instanceRef = this;
      DontDestroyOnLoad(gameObject);
   }
   else {
      DestroyImmediate(gameObject);
   }
}
```

This code checks to see whether it already exists in the scene and if so, deletes itself (its parent object).

6. Drag the Holder gameObject into the Prefabs folder to create a prefab of it.

Next you will create the script that will pull in the prefab if it is not there already:

1. Create a new script and name it **PersistentChecker**.

2. Add the following variable:

```
public GameObject holder;
```

3. Add the Awake function:

```
void Awake () {
   if (!GameObject.FindWithTag("Holder")) {
      holder = Instantiate(holder);
      holder.name = "Holder";
   }
}
```

4. Save the scripts and the Start Menu scene and open the Board Level.

Now you will create the means of checking for the presence of the Holder object.

1. Create a new Empty gameObject and name it **Check for DDLs**.

2. Drag the new PersistentChecker script onto it.

3. From the Prefabs folder, load the Holder prefab into its Holder field.

4. Drag the Check for DDLs object into the Prefabs folder and save the scene.

5. Click Play and go back and forth in the levels, watching for the Holder object.

The Holder object appears in each scene as an addition to the regular scene (Figure 10-40).

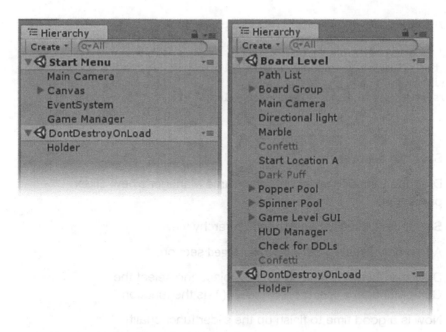

Figure 10-40. The Holder object persistent through both levels

Now you can add the slider data to the Persistent script, share it with the GameManager script, and then make use of it in the Board Level:

1. Add the following variable to the Persistent script and save the script:

```
// make this data available to all levels
internal int difficulty = 3; // the level of difficulty value
```

2. Open the Start Menu scene and open the GameManager script.

3. Add the following variables:

```
public Slider slider; // access for the slider
Persistent persistent; // object that carries the difficulty values throughout levels
```

4. In the Start function, locate the Holder object and its Persistent component:

```
persistent = GameObject.FindWithTag("Holder").GetComponent<Persistent>();
```

5. Apply the stored difficulty value to the slider value in the Start function:

```
slider.value = persistent.difficulty;
```

So far, the player can change the Slider's value, but it has yet to be associated with the difficulty variable. To track when it has been changed, you will create an UpdateSliderValue function and access it from the Slider's event system.

1. Add the following `UpdateSliderValue` function:

```
public void UpdateSliderValue () {
    // get the slider value and update difficulty in the Persistant script
    if(persistent) {
        persistent.difficulty = (int)slider.value;
    }
}
```

2. Save the script.

3. Drag the Difficulty Slider onto the Game Manager's new Slider parameter.

4. Select the Difficulty Slider in the Hierarchy view.

5. Add a new event to the `OnValueChanged` section.

6. Drag the GameManager in as the Object and select the GameManager's `UpdateSliderValue()` as the function.

    Now is a good time to finish up the slider functionality.

7. Set the Min Value to **1**, the Max Value to **5**, activate the Whole Numbers check box, and set the (starting)] Value to **3**.

8. Save the scene and then test to see that the slider retains the values you set between levels.

The `difficulty` value will be used in the Board Level when that level has been loaded. It will be used to change the Spinner and Hopper settings to make game play more interesting. Here, you will begin to use the Difficulty Slider's value to affect the game play:

1. In the Traveler script, add the following variable:

```
Persistent persistent; // holds difficulty settings
```

2. At the top of the `Start` function, use the `difficulty` value to adjust the Spinner speed according to difficulty:

```
persistent = GameObject.FindWithTag("Holder").GetComponent<Persistent>();
speed = 3 * persistent.difficulty + Random.Range(0,3);
```

    With the new adjustment, speed as an integer will provide a more noticeable variation when used in `Random.Range`.

3. Change the speed variable to an int, also removing the f from the 8, and save the script.

If you wish, add a `print` statement at the bottom of the `Start` function to see the assignments each time the Board Level is started.

In the Popper_Hopper script, the difficulty value will be used to affect the amount of time the gumdrops will be present before popping to another location.

1. Open the Popper_Hopper script.

2. Add the following variable:

```
Persistent persistent; // holds difficulty settings
```

3. At the bottom of the Start function, add the following:

```
persistent = GameObject.FindWithTag("Holder").GetComponent<Persistent>();
onTime = (6 - persistent.difficulty) + Random.Range(0,3);
```

4. Once again, test the equation with the range of possible difficulty values.

5. Save the script.

6. Click Play and test the game. Change the difficulty value to the extremes on each replay.

7. Tweak the adjustments in either script if you feel the results could be improved.

Interacting with the GUI by Using a Gamepad

In case you have been worrying about how you are going to let your gamepad users interact with your new GUIs, you will be happy to hear that Unity has already incorporated the functionality for you. As you have seen in Chapter 5, many of the preset "virtual" input controls already have a joystick version or, in the case of buttons (both keyboard and mouse), "alternate" inputs. As a default, Unity has mapped the x and y (left stick) axes to GUI navigation by using the Horizontal and Vertical inputs.

Let's begin by checking out the default mapping to see how it behaves with your UI. The first task is, of course, to plug in or activate (for Bluetooth) your gamepad.

1. Turn on or plug in your gamepad.

2. Open the Start Menu and click Play.

3. Tip the left stick up and down to see if anything happens.

    No reaction is apparent. It turns out that there is one little setting you must use to get the gamepad navigating the UI elements.

4. Stop Play mode and in the Hierarchy view, select the EventSystem object.

    Note the First Selected parameter's value field. It requires a gameObject.

5. Open the Canvas and drag the Play Button into the EventSystem's First Selected field.

6. Click Play and tip the left stick up and down.

   You should now see the Play Button highlight going off and on as the focus changes.

7. When the Play Button is not highlighted, test the left and right directions with the left stick.

   This time the slider works. In case you are wondering at the choppy movement, remember that its value maxes out at 5 and it is set to use whole numbers.

   The most obvious thing you have probably realized is that with gamepad navigation, it will be quite important to set the Highlight parameter to something other than white. Color Highlights are additive, whereas white is ignored.

8. Stop Play mode and select the Difficulty Slider.

9. Set its Highlighted Color to something other than white.

10. Click Play and test the results.

The effect is pretty ugly. Let's try using a different image for the Highlighted Color.

1. Stop Play and set the Difficulty Slider's Transition to Sprite Swap.

2. Select the UI Assets folder, right-click, and choose Import Package Custom ➤ Package.

3. From the Chapter 10 Assets folder, select RedButtonSprite and click Import.

   A nice, shiy, red version of the BlueButton is 9-sliced and ready to use.

4. Add the new RedButton as the Highlighted Sprite in the Difficulty Slider component.

5. Click Play and test with the gamepad.

   The new addition looks much nicer. It's always a good idea, however, to check the original functionality after a change.

6. Switch to the mouse, hover, and then drag the handle.

   The handle reverts to blue during the drag.

7. Stop Play mode and add the RedButton to the Pressed Sprite field.

8. Click Play and test both navigation methods.

   This time both methods work nicely. Now, of course, you are probably wondering how to "press" a highlighted button. A quick check of the Input Manager will reveal that Unity has mapped one of its two Submit inputs with the Joystick 0 button, the A button on the gamepad.

9. Cycle over to the Play button and press the gamepad's A button.

   The Game Level is loaded, but not yet hooked up to use the gamepad.

10. Stop Play mode and save the scene.

Now you will activate gamepad navigation with the Board Level and see whether it holds any surprises.

1. Open the Board Level scene.

2. Select the EventSystem object, and from Game Level GUI ➤ Canvas ➤ Pause Label, drag the Pause object into the First Selected field.

3. Click Play and test the gamepad navigation.

4. While you are there, try using the up and down arrow keys.

It turns out, the Horizontal and Vertical axes that Unity uses for the UI navigation are already being used to tip the board (from Chapter 6) . At this point, you need to make an executive decision about the controls. Unity's defaults will usually be fairly standard, but you should change them if your game play will benefit from better controls. The board tilting requires infinitely more finesse than cycling through UI elements, so you will switch the UI navigation to the secondary stick, axes 4 and 5, and create a couple of new virtual inputs for the board tipping.

1. Open the Input Manager.

2. Duplicate the second Horizontal element by right-clicking it and selecting Duplicate Array Element.

3. Rename one of them **Horizontal2**.

4. Duplicate the second Vertical element the same way.

5. Rename one of them **Vertical2**.

6. In the Horizontal input, change the Axis from X Axis to 4th Axis (Joysticks).

7. In the Vertical input, change the Axis from Y Axis to 5th Axis (Joysticks).

Tip   The UI assignments for using the Vertical and Horizontal axes can be found in the EventSystem's Standalone Input Module component.

Having changed the names of the X and Y inputs, you will have to update the Tiltboard script to match.

8. Open the Tiltboard script.

9. In the Update function, change "Horizontal" to "Horizontal2" and "Vertical" to "Vertical2":

```
float xRotation = Input.GetAxis("Vertical2")  * speed * Time.deltaTime;
float zRotation = -Input.GetAxis("Horizontal2")   * speed * Time.deltaTime;
```

10. Save the script and test the new assignments.

Now the left stick controls the board tip, and the right-click controls the UI navigation.

The Pause check box/toggle should have a highlight, but using the RedButton for the Highlighted state won't be as good a choice visually as it was for the slider. This time, you can try a simple opacity change for the check box.

1. Stop Play mode and select the Pause toggle.

2. Set its Normal Color to a medium darkish grey, RGB, **80**, **80**, **80** with full opacity, **255**.

3. Set its Highlighted Color to White with full opacity, **255**.

4. Click Play and test by navigating off and on the Pause check box.

    Now the Pause UI element is easier to identify when it has the focus. In case you are wondering why Pause was selected as the First Selected, it is so the player can toggle it off and on without having to first navigate to it. The Main Menu and Play buttons don't involve the same urgency as being able to pause the game before getting hit by a marauding peppermint.

5. Stop Play mode and save the scene and the project.

With the simple GUI, the Start menu and the game controller working, in the next chapter you will add a reward system that should entice the player to spend money to improve his chances of an easy win.

Summary

In this chapter, you were introduced to Unity's latest UI system, where you discovered that GUI objects are similar to 3D objects in that they are made of components and actually exist in 3D space. Upon switching the Scene view to the 2D option, you found that the GUI objects can easily be snapped and aligned. A key feature, you discovered, is the anchoring system, where the location of the four corner points dictate whether the object scales or retains its location relevant to one or more of the screen's borders. The Canvas Scaler component, you learned, is a key factor in gracefully handling resolution and aspect ratio changes.

After changing the editor's Default Behavior Mode to 2D, you were able to import the GUI textures as Sprite types and learned that they can be singular or sliced into multiple images for use with the various Unity UI components. As with previous Unity GUI systems, you discovered that images for buttons and other backgrounds can take advantage of the 9-slice technique that enables the borders of images to remain correct while the centers are scaled to fit. With background images, you learned that it was advantageous to lock either the width or height in the Canvas Scaler to crop rather than allow a nonuniform scaling.

After importing a Unity package for the Board Level's GUI, you got some firsthand experience with using the GUI component's built-in event system to call existing functions. With the game GUI in place, you proceeded to create a timer to put a bit of pressure on your player, and then to expose the health point system to provide encouragement.

With the mobile platform in mind, you created a means to pause the game, discovering that a pause does not affect the player's input, only game physics and animation. Next, you brought the Start Menu scene and Board Level together through SceneManager.LoadScene, where you also learned how to make data persistent between menus and levels. And finally, you got a first look at how Unity's UI system can adapted for use with a game controller.

Chapter 11

Rewards and Monetization

As it stands, your little game could be considered to be complete. In the early days of computer games, you would shop it around and find a publisher who would then take care of the box, marketing, and retailers to sell your game. You, as the developer, might see around 5 percent of the retail price; for a $20 game (typical for an indie developer), that meant 50 cents, or at most, a dollar. As the Internet became ubiquitous, it became possible for indie developers to sell their own games online for half the retail price and cut out the publishers. That also meant cutting out the marketing, so the number of units sold dropped accordingly. Filling a need, Valve came up with Steam, an online publisher, or store, for both their own games and *approved* games (meaning, they monitor the quality) from indie developers as well.

When the *mobile* market became viable for indie developers, things changed once again. The price for a game dropped, so our indie developer was back to that 50 cents or a dollar or two per game. The difference, of course, was the market size itself being exponentially larger. The publisher gave way to the "Store," with Apple, Google, and Microsoft as the shopkeepers for their respective platforms.

And then something interesting happened. Developers started to give their games away for free and look for other ways to derive income from them. At first, it was as simple as giving the first level away for free and then charging for subsequent levels. And then came *in-app purchases*, or *IAPs*. The purchases could be anything from a new outfit for the character, a better weapon, a more powerful spell, or even in-game currency to buy items as part of the game play itself. The third monetization scheme, in-app advertisements in the form of video ads, became possible when third-party companies saw the opportunity for ongoing management of the placement and content of paid advertisements. If players watch the complete ad, they usually get a reward. Better yet, the developer earns money for the player watching and/or clicking though to act upon the advertisements.

The bottom line is that you, as the game *designer*, now must think about how monetization is incorporated into your game. In this chapter, you will create an in-game store enabling players to make purchases that make the game easier to win.

© Sue Blackman and Adam Tuliper 2016
S. Blackman and A. Tuliper, *Learn Unity for Windows 10 Game Development*,
DOI 10.1007/978-1-4302-6757-7_11

In-App Purchases

To entice players to use your in-game "store," you will make two perks available. The first gives players the ability to move the banana boosters to a location of their choosing. Because the boosters often are a hindrance as much as a help, this feature will be fairly inexpensive. The big-price item will be a means for removing the peppermints from the board. And, along with the two item-type purchases, you will also let players purchase the game's currency, tipCoins. To encourage players to keep playing, they will be rewarded with tipCoins each completion of a game board. Bonus coins will be awarded for fast completion times.

Persistent Data

Although storing player stats, purchases, and high scores (or low times, in this case) somewhere on a server is beyond the scope of this book, you will at least be keeping track of the current totals for the three items: the number of tipCoins in the player's account, the number of banana-moving opportunities the player has purchased, and the number of peppermint removals purchased, The latter two will have to be adjusted as they are used.

Managing the New Data

The reward system will require several variables to keep track of the additional data. To give the player a fun visual, the banana-moving functionality will be represented as a wheelbarrow loaded with a banana peel. The peppermints will be crushed (destroyed) by the weapon-wielding guard character from Chapter 4.

1. Open the Persistent script.

2. Add the following variables:

```
// keeping track of:
    internal float cash = 0f; // cash in pocket
    internal int wheelbarrows = 3; // usable banana movers
    internal int candyCrushers = 3; // usable peppermint crushers

    // rewards
    internal float winCash = 10f; // default win cash
    internal float timeBonus = 5f; // bonus for fast time
    private float timeThreshold = 100; // maximum seconds allowed for speed bonus

    // prices
    internal float wbPrice = 10f; // price per wheelbarrow/banana mover
    internal float crusherPrice = 75; // price per peppermint crushed
    internal float coinPrice = 0.99f; // the purchase price of tipCoins
    internal int coinAmount = 50; // how many coins you get
```

3. Add a function to calculate the tipCoins earned for winning the game:

```
public void CalculateWinCash (float winTime) {
    // a game has been won
    float bonusCash = 0;
    print (winTime + " < ? " + timeThreshold);
    if (winTime < timeThreshold) bonusCash += timeBonus;
    cash = cash + winCash + bonusCash;
    print ("cash in account = " + cash);
}
```

You will call the function each time the game is completed. In the function that handles a completed game, the PathCellManager's ProcessWinner function, you will get the time from the GameHUD just after it stops the timer. Then you will send it to be processed back in Persistent, where the bonus will be added if the time was fast enough. The PathCellManager script will need to be able to contact the Persistent script.

4. Open the PathCellManager script and add the following variable:

```
private Persistent persistent;
```

5. Assign the variable in the Start function:

```
persistent = GameObject.FindWithTag("Holder").GetComponent<Persistent>();
```

6. In the ProcessWinner function, under the gameHUD.ToggleTimer line, add the following:

```
persistent.CalculateWinCash(gameHUD. GetGameTime ());
```

7. In the GameHUD script, create the new GetGameTime function that returns the current elapsed time:

```
public float GetGameTime () {
    float endTime = Time.timeSinceLevelLoad  - startTime;
    return endTime;
}
```

8. Open the Board Level scene.

9. Save the scripts and deactivate the Spinners and Boosters if you wish.

10. Test by winning a few games both slowly and quickly, checking the status line when you do so.

Tip   Remember, the bonus time threshold is 100 seconds, and the game is showing minutes and seconds, so a slow speed would be over 1:40.

The player should be encouraged to play again, so you will want to show him his current stash of tipCoins, and later, the number of wheelbarrows and crushers he has available.

1. From the Chapter11 Assets folder, import the GUIExtras. unitypackage.

2. In the Hierarchy view, expand the Game Level GUI so you can see the Canvas object.

3. From the Prefabs folder, drag the Rewards Panel prefab onto the Canvas.

You should now have a nice little collection of labels, buttons, and toggles to keep your player up-to-date (Figure 11-1).

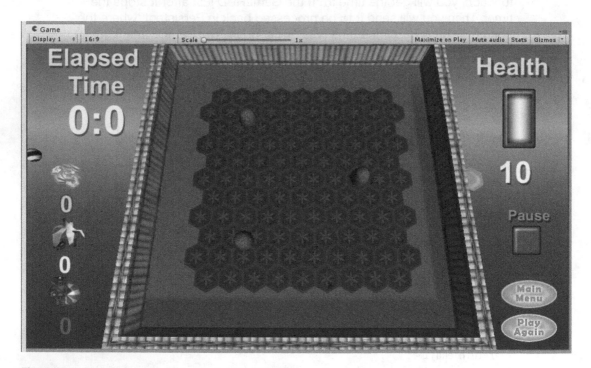

Figure 11-1. The new rewards and monetization GUI objects

The new GUI objects will be managed from the HUD Manager's GameHUD script.

4. Add the following variables to the GameHUD script:

```
//GUI
public Text cashValue;
public Text barrowCount;
public Text crusherCount;

Persistent persistent;
```

5. Find and assign persistent in the Start function:

   ```
   persistent = GameObject.FindWithTag("Holder").GetComponent<Persistent>();
   ```

6. Save the script and assign the corresponding GUI objects (TC Value, Count B, and Count C) to the Game HUD's new parameters.

7. In the PathCellManager script, in the ProcessWinner function, under the persistent.CalculateWinCash line, add this:

   ```
   gameHUD.UpdateTipCash();
   ```

8. Back in the GameHUD script, add this function:

   ```
   public void UpdateTipCash () {
       cashValue.text = persistent.cash.ToString();
   }
   ```

   As long as you're in gameHUD, let's update the cash label on start of the level as well.

9. In the Start function, after persistent has been assigned, add a call to the new function:

   ```
   UpdateTipCash();
   ```

10. Comment out the print statement in Persistent's CalculateWinCash function.

11. Save the scripts and the scene and test the number of tipCoins the player is earning on completing the path.

Creating the Purchased Functionality

Before creating the store, you will add the functionality that lets the player move the bananas and call the guard out to get rid of peppermints. For the two scenarios, you will have a chance to use a couple of valuable Unity techniques. The banana movers will make use of converting cursor position to world space. The Guard will give you a chance to direct an animated character.

Moving Bananas

The bananas will be moved around the board with a click and drag by the user. The first thing to do is to try some test picks on the bananas. You can begin by using a Destroy as it is the quickest and most obvious way to see whether the pick is working (and more fun than a print statement).

1. Open the Board Level scene and activate the Banana Peels if you had turned them off.

2. Open the HotSpotBoosters script.

3. Add an OnMouseDown function:

```
void OnMouseDown () {
    Destroy(gameObject);
}
```

4. Save the script and try picking the bananas.

   Nothing happens.

   Realistically, rearranging game pieces should probably be done with the pause on.

5. Hit Pause, and try picking again.

   Again, no response.

   The issue here is that you have two big colliders intercepting the picks. Let's identify the colliders.

6. Turn off 2D mode and select the Board Group.

   The blue gizmos are audio, so you can ignore them or turn the icons off under Gizmos. The Board Group has a large Sphere Collider for tilting the board and the Live Zone (a child of the Board Group) also covers quite a bit of real estate.

7. Stop Play mode, turn off the two object's, colliders, and test again.

   This time, the picked bananas disappear. Pick works when the Board Group and Live Zone colliders are off. You can turn them off in the GameHUD's PauseToggle function.

1. Delete the OnMouseDown function.

2. Open the GameHUD script.

3. Add the two variables:

```
public Collider boardGroupCollider;
public Collider liveZoneCollider;
```

4. In the PauseToggle function, turn them on at the top of the if clause
    (where the pause is turned off) and on at the bottom of the Else
    clause:

```
public void PauseToggle () {
    if (isPaused) {
        boardGroupCollider.enabled = true;
        liveZoneCollider.enabled = true;
        //print("Unpaused");
        tiltBoard.allowTilt = true;
        Time.timeScale = 1.0f;
        isPaused = false;
    }
    else {
        //print("Paused");
        tiltBoard.allowTilt = false;
        Time.timeScale = 0.0f;
        isPaused = true;
        boardGroupCollider.enabled = false;
        liveZoneCollider.enabled = false;
    }
}
```

5. Save the script and assign the two objects to the two new variables
    and turn their colliders back on.

6. Test and try picking some of the tiles on the board.

Back in Chapter 7, when you were creating the paths, the tiles responded to picks. You
added FIXME comments to remind yourself to address this functionality later. The BaseCells,
PathCells, and PathCellManager scripts all have FIXMEs. Fixme (case is unimportant in the
keyword) can be used to store tasks through // Todo and // Fixme, which then will appear
in the task view of MonoDevelop, Xamarin Studio, and Visual Studio. Let's see about finding
the FIXME commented code and disabling it.

1. Open the scripts and use the Search option to look for FIXME.

2. Comment out the sections marked with FIXME in the
    PathCellManager script and the entire OnMouseDown functions in the
    other two.

The next issue that may crop up is an odd one. If you stopped Play mode while Pause was
on, the colliders you had turned off during the pause have not been reset! If you start the
game again, the board will not tilt. Whether it is related to the timescale code or something
else, for testing purposes, you will want to make sure the colliders are properly reset.

The most logical solution would be to initialize the objects in the Start function of the same
script that turns them off and on during game play, the GameHUD script. But there's a
problem with that. If the object with the collider has not yet been loaded into the scene, its
state will not be changed.

Although you could add the code to the objects individually, keeping it on the GameHUD script will give you a chance to investigate the script execution order. If the GameHUD script was evaluated last, the other objects should have time to load. Let's test the collider states to see what is happening:

1. Click Play and then stop while in pause mode.

   The two colliders, from Board Group and Live Zone, will probably be off.

2. Click Play and check the two colliders.

   Their states have not been reset. You are not able to tip the board.

3. At the bottom of the GameHUD script's Start function, add the following:

   ```
   //reset collider states
   boardGroupCollider.enabled = true;
   liveZoneCollider.enabled = true;
   ```

4. Save the script.

5. From the Edit menu, choose Project Settings ➤ Script Execution Order.

6. Drag the GameHUD script onto the Default Time box.

   The GameHUD script automatically is assigned a time of 100 milliseconds after the default time (Figure 11-2).

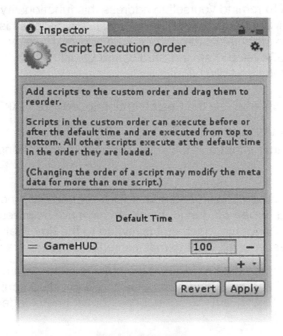

Figure 11-2. The GameHUD script set to execute after the default time

7. Change the time to **-100** and watch the result (Figure 11-3).

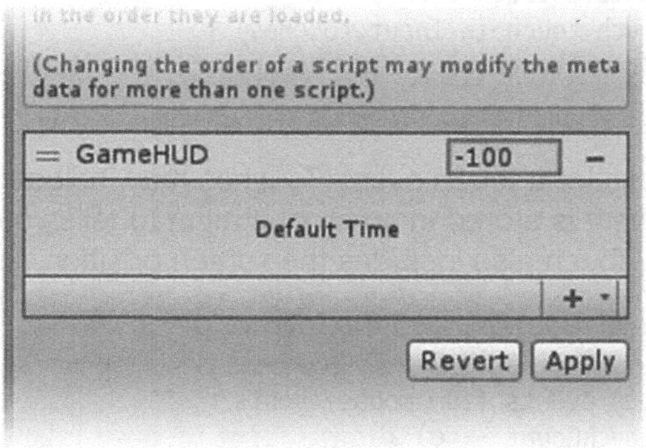

Figure 11-3. The GameHUD script set to execute before the default time

Now the script shows above the Default Time so it will be executed first.

8. Set the time back to **100** and click Apply.

9. Test the results by stopping the game in Play mode, and checking the two colliders.

   They probably will be off when you exit Play mode.

10. Click Play again and check the two colliders after the marble has dropped.

   This time they should be properly turned on.

Now would be a good time to once again start thinking about the differences between mobile and desktop platforms. With no mouse in mobile platforms, you might think that there is no OnMouseDown. Unity actually implemented functionality to allow touch to work with mouse down, but does not recommend it. In keeping with Unity's recommendation, you will use the mouse while authoring, but the code will also be able to handle touch. Rather than using OnMouseDown, you will detect mouse button activity in the Update function and send it on to a touch-handling function.

1. Create a new script, **PlayerMovable.**

2. Add the following variables:

   ```
   private bool isDragging = false;
   private Camera theCamera;
   private Transform currentBananaPeel;
   ```

3. In the Start function, find the camera:

   ```
   theCamera = Camera.main;
   ```

4.   In the Update function, add the preliminary touch code:

```
// Handle native touch events
foreach (Touch touch in Input.touches) {
    HandleTouch(touch.fingerId, touch.position, touch.phase);
}
```

This code checks for a touch event. Touches may include more than one finger, so the event is stored in an array. fingerId tells you the finger (ID 0 is the first touch). Touch also includes the screen position, touch.position.

5.   Also in the Update function, add the following:

```
// Simulate touch events from mouse events
    if (Input.touchCount == 0) {
}
```

On a desktop, unless you are using a touchscreen-enabled monitor, touch.count will always equal 0, so now you can check for mouse button events.

6.   Add the mouse button code inside the conditional:

```
if (Input.GetMouseButtonDown(0) ) {
    HandleTouch(10, Input.mousePosition, TouchPhase.Began);
}
if (Input.GetMouseButton(0) ) {
    HandleTouch(10, Input.mousePosition, TouchPhase.Moved);
}
if (Input.GetMouseButtonUp(0) ) {
    HandleTouch(10, Input.mousePosition, TouchPhase.Ended);
}
```

Button 0 is the left mouse button. Note that the code is all redirected to the touch-handing function, HandleTouch, along with the equivalent TouchPhase type, Began, Moved, and Ended.

7.   Add the HandleTouch function:

```
private void HandleTouch(int touchFingerId, Vector2 touchPosition, TouchPhase
touchPhase) {
    switch (touchPhase) {
        case TouchPhase.Began:
            // mouse down or finger touch
            print("touch down");
            break;
        case TouchPhase.Moved:
            // mouse or finger moving
            print("moving");
            break;
```

```
        case TouchPhase.Ended:
            // mouse or finger up
            print("mouse up");
            break;
    }
}
```

The switch statement allows you to avoid using nested if statements.

8. Save the script and add it to the HUD Manager.

9. Click Play and test the pick, checking the status line or console as you do so.

So far, the code is quite generic. The next step is to get it to react only when there is a Banana Peel under the initial pick or touch. For that, you will use a raycast. The HandleTouch function will be casting rays into the scene from the screen-space mouse or touch location.

In the TouchPhase.Began case, the raycast looks for an object named Banana Peel. When it finds one, it assigns it as the current dragging object and turns on the isDragging flag.

In the TouchPhase.Moved case, the raycast looks for the Board Surface object (you will create it shortly). If it finds it, the Banana Peel is moved to the intersection of the raycast and Board Surface.

In the TouchPhase.Ended case, the isDragging flag is set to false.

1. At the top of the HandleTouch function, declare the raycast variables:

```
Ray ray = theCamera.ScreenPointToRay(touchPosition);
RaycastHit[] hits;
int i = 0;
```

The first line also calculates the ray by using the mouse down or touch location passed into the HandleTouch function.

2. In the TouchPhase.Began case, identify the Banana Peel hit and start the isDragging flag:

```
case TouchPhase.Began:
    // mouse down or finger touch
    print("touch down");
    hits = Physics.RaycastAll(ray);
    while (i < hits.Length) {
        RaycastHit hit = hits[i];
        if (hit.collider.name == "Banana Peel") {
            isDragging = true;
            currentBananaPeel = hit.collider.transform;
            return;
        }
        i++;
    }
    break;
```

3. At the top of the TouchPhase.Moved case, add the following   :

   ```
   if(!isDragging) return;
   ```

4. At the top of the TouchPhase.Ended case, add this:

   ```
   isDragging = false;
   ```

5. Due to a change in Unity's duplication naming, make sure all three of your Banana Peels are named **Banana Peel**.

Tip   Alternatively, you could use hit.collider.name.StartsWith("Banana Peel") or .Contains("Banana Peel").

---

6. Save the script and test.

   If you were over a Banana Peel when you clicked, the console should show the "moving" printout. Otherwise, there will be no message until you mouse-up.

   Now that you can see your code recognizing the Banana Peels, you can reposition them. The raycast code is similar, but this time it looks for an intersection with the Board Surface object (you will create it shortly) and then moves the Banana Peel to the hit point.

7. In the TouchPhase.Moved case, below the return line, add the following:

   ```
   hits = Physics.RaycastAll(ray);
      while (i < hits.Length) {
      RaycastHit hit = hits[i];
      if (hit.collider == boardSurfaceCollider) {
         Vector3 temp = new Vector3 (currentBananaPeel.position.x
   ,currentBananaPeel.position.y, currentBananaPeel.position.z);
         temp = hits[i].point;
         currentBananaPeel.position = temp;
      }
   i++;
   }
   break;
   ```

   Each *hit* is checked for a collision with the Board Surface object's collider (one of the pieces of info stored by RaycastHit). A temporary Vector3 variable is created to hold the current transform of the object that has this script.The hit point location is assigned to the temp variable, and the object is set to the new location. The While loop continues through the array incrementing the i variable.

8. Feel free to comment out any leftover print statements.

Before you test the new code, you will have to create the Board Surface. The board is actually lower than the board tiles, so you will create a simple quad to intercept the rays. It will have a Mesh Collider and, as a bonus, it will also prevent the player from moving the bananas off the tile grid. The quad's collider will have to be turned off during regular play, or the Marble will not be able to roll smoothly across the board.

1. From the 3D Object submenu, create a quad and name it **Board Surface**.

2. Rotate it 90 degrees on its x axis to align with the board and then scale it to match the tiled area (about 20 × 20).

3. Position it about the same height as the top of the tiles (Figure 11-4).

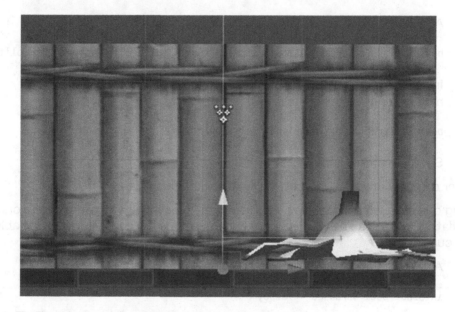

Figure 11-4. The Board Surface object aligned with the top of the tiles

4. Turn off its Mesh Renderer component and put it into Board Group.

5. In the GameHUD script, add a variable for the Board Surface's collider:

```
Collider boardSurfaceCollider;
```

6. Find and assign it in the Start function:

```
boardSurfaceCollider = GameObject.Find("Board Surface").GetComponent<Collider>();
```

7. Turn it off in the TogglePause's if(isPaused) clause:

```
boardSurfaceCollider.enabled = false;
```

8. And turn it on in the `else` clause:

    ```
    boardSurfaceCollider.enabled = true;
    ```

9. Save the script.

    The Board Surface's collider also has to be added to the PlayerMovable script.

10. In the PlayerMovable script, add a variable to hold the Board Surface's collider:

    ```
    public Collider boardSurfaceCollider;
    ```

11. And Find and assign it in the `Start` function:

    ```
    boardSurfaceCollider = GameObject.Find("Board Surface").GetComponent<Collider>();
    ```

12. Initialize it with the other two colliders in the GameHUD script to make sure its state has been reset at start-up:

    ```
    boardSurfaceCollider.enabled = false;
    ```

13. Save the scripts and test.

The player can now drag the Banana Peels around the board.

By adding one more conditional, you can restrict the functionality to pause mode only. The entire `Update` function can be ignored if not in pause mode, so you will want a variable that stores is current state.

1. Add the following variable to the PlayerMovable script:

    ```
    internal bool isPaused = false;
    ```

2. At the top of the `Update` function, add the following:

    ```
    if(!isPaused) return;
    ```

    The GameHUD script manages the pause state, so it will have to tell the PlayerMovable script anytime the pause state is changed. Both scripts are on the HUD Manager object so it will be a quick find.

3. In the GameHUD script, add the following variable:

    ```
    PlayerMovable playerMovable;
    ```

4. Assign it in the `Start` function:

    ```
    playerMovable = GetComponent<PlayerMovable>();
    ```

5. In the PauseToggle function's isPaused clause, add the following:

```
playerMovable.isPaused = false;
```

6. In the PauseToggle function's else clause, add this:

```
playerMovable.isPaused = true;
```

7. Save the scripts and test.

The Touch/mouse-down action is working well.

The next task is to allow only one "move" episode for each Barrow (Banana Peel move event) purchased. As soon as the player clicks a banana, the available count is decremented. The PlayerMovable script will need to make contact with Persistent to update the count and to the GUI objects to update the count in the UI. Picks once the count has dropped to 0 must be blocked.

1. At the top of the PlayerMovable script, add the following:

```
using UnityEngine.UI;
```

2. Add the following variables:

```
private Persistent persistent;
private Text barrowCount;
```

3. Assign them at the bottom of the Start function:

```
persistent = GameObject.Find("Holder").GetComponent<Persistent>();
barrowCount = GameObject.Find ("Count B").GetComponent<Text>();
```

4. In the TouchPhase.Began case, above isDragging = true, add this:

```
if(persistent.wheelbarrows == 0) return; // no more perks
```

5. Below isDragging = true, add this:

```
persistent.wheelbarrows --; // decrement the perks
barrowCount.text = persistent.wheelbarrows.ToString();// update the UI
```

6. Test the new pick functionality.

The count goes down, but still needs to be initialized in the GUI when the level starts. Let's handle that in the GameHUD.

7. In GameHUD, add the following:

```
public void UpdateBarrow () {
   barrowCount.text = persistent.wheelbarrows.ToString();
}
```

8. And call it from the Start function:

    ```
    UpdateBarrow ();
    ```

9. Play and test the new functionality.

10. Feel free to test different numbers in the Persistent script.

Next you will want to prevent the player from accidently moving a banana. When the player activates the banana-moving button (toggle, in this case), the "checkmark" (an outline) should go *on*, indicating he is in moveable mode. Once you have access to the outline, you can also disable the toggle and block the player from moving more banana peels if the count reaches 0. The graphic for toggle objects is managed in the parent object's Toggle component, Wheelbarrows.

1. In the PlayerMovable script, *and* the Game HUD script, add the following variable:

    ```
    private Toggle barrowToggle;
    ```

2. Find and assign it in both Start functions:

    ```
    barrowToggle = GameObject.Find("Wheelbarrows").GetComponent<Toggle>();
    ```

3. In the TouchPhase.Began case, change the first condition to include a check of the toggle's state:

    ```
    if(persistent.wheelbarrows == 0 || barrowToggle.isOn == false)
    return; // no more perks or not activated
    ```

    Once all of the bananas have been picked, the toggle should be disabled.

4. Just above that section's final return statement, add the following:

    ```
    if (persistent.wheelbarrows == 0) barrowToggle.interactable = false;
    // disable the toggle
    ```

    And the toggle's interactive state should be disabled if not in pause mode.

5. In the GameHUD script, PauseToggle's isPaused section, add the following:

    ```
    barrowToggle.interactable = false; // disable the toggle
    ```

6. In the else section, add this:

    ```
    if (persistent && persistent.wheelbarrows != 0) barrowToggle.
    interactable = true; // enable the toggle if count not 0 and
    persistent is in scene
    ```

The check for `persistent` was added to prevent an error on exit when the line threw an error because the `Holder` object (with the Persistent script) had already been removed from the scene.

7. Disable the toggle in the `Start` function as well:

```
barrowToggle.interactable = false; // disable the toggle
```

8. Save the scripts and test. Remember that you must turn the button on before moving the Banana Peels.

9. Change the initial Wheelbarrow count in the Persistent script and test again to make sure it works in several scenarios, and then leave it set to **3**.

The banana functionality is reasonably well behaved under most situations. The trick now will be adapting it for use with a gamepad.

Adapting the Banana Peel Move for a Gamepad

Let's begin by assessing the gamepad's functionality and then see what can be fed into the touch code so you won't have to duplicate the rest of the code. You will also want to take care not to interfere with the basic UI navigation.

Touch or mouse-down is easy; you can use a button-down. The gamepad buttons 0 and 3 are already used for Submit/Enter and the Marble jump, respectively. Unity also premaps button 1 as Cancel. Mouse-up signals a release of the Banana Peel and as such is key functionality. For the drag functionality, you will be using the right bumper, or RB.

The main challenge is that there is no pointer, so there is no way get a position for either clicking *or* dragging. For that, you will be creating a custom cursor, or pointer, that can be moved around by the left stick. The board is already frozen during the banana move, so the left stick is freed up for this additional functionality while the right stick continues to manage the UI navigation.

The starting point for the mode occurs when the player clicks the Wheelbarrows button. While the custom cursor is being moved around, you will use one image, and while it is dragging a Banana Peel, you will use a version that is less opaque. This will help the player to know when he has successfully picked up a Banana Peel.

1. Make sure your gamepad is active.

2. Choose GameObject ➤ UI ➤ Image to create an image.

3. Name it **Pointer**. From the Rewards asset, load the WB_Pointer in as its Sprite.

4. Click Preserve Aspect and set the Width and Height of the Rect Transform to **70**.

5. Duplicate Pointer, name it **PointerWorking**, and then drag it onto Pointer so it becomes a child of Pointer.

6. Load the WB_Pointer Faded sprite in as its Sprite.

Now let's see about making it move by using the gamepad.

1. Create a new script and name it **CustomPointer**.

2. Add the variable for adjusting the speed:

```
public float speed = 200f;
```

3. In the Update function, add the code that moves the image:

```
transform.Translate (Vector2.right * speed * Time.deltaTime * Input.GetAxis
("Horizontal2"));
transform.Translate (Vector2.up * speed * Time.deltaTime * Input.GetAxis
("Vertical2"));
```

4. Save the script and add it to the Pointer object.

5. Click Play and manipulate the left stick.

   The sprite moves, as does the board. Let's try moving it during a pause.

6. Navigate to the Pause toggle and click the A button to pause the action.

7. Now use the left stick to try to move the sprite.

   Nothing happens because you are using Time.timeScale = 0 in the GameHUD script to pause most of the action. Time.deltaTime is affected because a 0 timescale means there *is* no delta (change). Fortunately, there is an easy way to override it.

8. In the two transform.Translate lines, change Time.deltaTime to Time.unscaledDeltaTime.

9. Save the script and test the sprite move during a pause.

This time, the board stays still and the sprite moves around when you use the left stick.

You may now be wondering whether there are also ways to override the 0 timescale pause on animations. It turns out that there is a way to do so, and it is incredibly simple. Because the animations on your game pieces are independent of the transforms you have scripted, you can keep them animating during a pause.

1. Stop Play mode and open the Prefabs folder.

2. Select the Spinner and, in the Animator component, change Update Mode to Unscaled Time.

3. Click Play and pause.

   Now the game pieces happily animate in place.

4. Stop Play mode and set the Popper, Banana Peel, and Guard prefabs to Unscaled Time if you wish.

Let's get back to the pointer. Now that you know it can be moved with gamepad input, there is another little issue that could use some attention. Using a 0 Dead value for the left stick is great for the board tipping, but allows the Pointer to wander off when not in use. Increasing the Dead value will stop the wandering, but cause lags while the input is in the Dead zone. Ideally, you want to smoothly ramp up the speed that you are multiplying the input with, so that it is smaller when the numbers are in the Dead zone and faster when they are not. If the math involved in that type of calculation makes your head hurt, you're in luck. Josh Sutphin of Kickbomb Entertainment has a wonderful blog from his Triple Helix days explaining the dead zone problem, a history of solutions, and, best of all, a nice bit of code that will improve the gamepad stick experience in a few extra lines of code.

1. In the Custom Pointer script, change the two `transform.translate` lines in the Update function to the following:

```
float deadzone = 0.25f; // this will override the 0 value set in the Input
Manager
Vector2 stickInput = new Vector2(Input.GetAxis("Horizontal2"),
Input.GetAxis("Vertical2"));
if(stickInput.magnitude < deadzone)
    stickInput = Vector2.zero;
else
    stickInput = stickInput.normalized * ((stickInput.magnitude -
    deadzone) / (1 - deadzone));

transform.Translate (Vector2.right * speed * Time.unscaledDeltaTime
* stickInput.x);
transform.Translate (Vector2.up * speed * Time.unscaledDeltaTime *
stickInput.y);
```

2. Save the script and check out the huge improvement in Pointer movement.

Let's continue by hooking the Pointer functionality into the rest of the GUI.

3. In the Custom Pointer script, at the top, add the following:

```
using UnityEngine.UI;
```

4. Add a few more variables:

```
public Image pointer;
public Image pointerWorking;
public Toggle wheelbarrows;
bool isActive = false;
internal bool usingGamepad = false; //  no gamepad available
```

The isEnabled flag is public, so the top-level functionality can be controlled by the GameHUD's pause functionality. The only time the pointer should be visible and moving is during a pause.

5. In the `Start` function, check for a gamepad:

    ```
    if (Input.GetJoystickNames().Length > 0)
            usingGamepad = true;
    ```

6. At the top of the `Update` function, check for an active gamepad:

    ```
    if (!usingGamepad || !isActive) return;
    ```

7. Create the function that will manage the sprites' visibility:

    ```
    public void SetPointerState (int state) {
        switch (state) {
            case 0: // neither image rendered
                pointer.enabled = false;
                pointerWorking.enabled = false;
                break;
            case 1: // pointer rendered
                pointer.enabled = true;
                pointerWorking.enabled = false;
                break;
            case 2: // pointerWorking rendered
                pointer.enabled = false;
                pointerWorking.enabled = true;
                break;
        }
    }
    ```

8. Initialize the sprites to off in the `Start` function:

    ```
    SetPointerState(0); // turn off both pointer images
    ```

9. Create a function for the Wheelbarrow button to call when picked:

    ```
    public void ActivatePointer (){
        if(!usingGamepad) return;
        isActive = true;
        SetPointerState(1); //temporary
    }
    ```

The Wheelbarrow button can be picked only if the game is paused, so if the gamepad is in use, for now, you can turn on the pointer here.

1. Save the script and assign the Wheelbarrows toggle to the Pointer's new Wheelbarrows parameter.

2. Select the Wheelbarrows toggle.

3. Create a new `OnValueChanged` event.

4. Drag the Pointer in as the Object.

5. Select the `CustomPointer` script and its `ActivatePointer()` function.

6. Click Play and test by pausing the board, navigating to the Wheelbarrows toggle, and pressing the A key.

   The Pointer sprite should now appear in the center of the screen.

7. Use the left stick to move the sprite over a Banana Peel.

Having gotten this far into the process, your next task will be to use the A button on the gamepad to pick up and drop Banana Peels. The two pointers' Image components will be turned off and on to let the player know the state of the Banana Peel.

1. Open the PlayerMovable script.

2. Add the following variables:

```
public bool usingGamepad = false;
public Transform pointer;
private Vector2 pointerPosition;
```

   The pointer variable is so you can get its transform, and the pointer position is the (x, y) format required by the touch code. In order to keep the touch, mouse, and gamepad code from interfering, you can use a low-tech means of checking to see whether the player is using a gamepad. Because a desktop system can have a gamepad on and active while the player is using a mouse, checking for the existence of a gamepad is not enough.

   The logic is as follows: The focus starts on the Pause toggle. To get to the Wheelbarrow toggle, the gamepad user must use the Horizontal2 axis to get there. The check is performed only during the pause, so the impact is minimal.

3. At the top of the `Update` function, just below the `if(!isPaused)` line, add the following:

```
if(Mathf.Abs(Input.GetAxis("Horizontal")) > 0.2f) {
    usingGamepad = true; //
}
```

   Using `Mathf.Abs` gets the absolute value of the input, so both negative and positive directions are checked at the same time. Remember, `Horizontal`, not `Horizontal2`, input is used for GUI navigation.

4. At the bottom of the `Update` function, add the code that finds the location of the sprite cursor if the gamepad is in use:

```
if (usingGamepad) {
    pointerPosition = new Vector2 (pointer.position.x,pointer.position.y);
    if (isDragging) HandleTouch(10, pointerPosition, TouchPhase.Moved);
```

The pointer's position is converted to a `Vector2` value. If a Banana Peel object is "picked up," the location is sent on to the touch code's `Moved` case. The gamepad code makes use of the `isDragging` flag that is already being used in the Touch code for dragging the Banana Peels.

5. Below that, add the code that handles the gamepad button pushes:

```
if(Input.GetButtonDown("Submit")) {
    HandleTouch(10, pointerPosition, TouchPhase.Began);
    pointer.GetComponent<CustomPointer>().SetPointerState(2);
// turn on working pointer
}

if(Input.GetButtonUp("Submit")) {
    HandleTouch(10, pointerPosition, TouchPhase.Ended);
    pointer.GetComponent<CustomPointer>().SetPointerState (1);
// turn on regular pointer
}
```

6. And finally, close the `usinggamepad` conditional:

```
} // close usingGamepad conditional
```

The working pointer sprite should not be turned on before a valid pick is confirmed, so you will turn it on inside the `TouchPhase.Moved` case.

7. Inside the `TouchPhase.Began` case, under the `currentBananaPeel.position = temp;` line, add:

```
if (usingGamepad) pointer. GetComponent<CustomPointer>().
SetPointerState(2); // turn on working pointer
```

8. Save the script and assign the Pointer to the GameHUD's Player Movable component.

9. Click Play and test the pick up, move, and drop functionality.

The functionality is a bit hit-or-miss because the Submit button-down is also repicking the current GUI focus, the Wheelbarrow toggle. You will address that issue a bit later.

The player has two options at this point. He can continue moving Banana Peels around until he has run out of Wheelbarrows, or he can cancel the mode at any time. Both scenarios will require the Pointer being reset and hidden, and the focus set on the most logical candidate, the Pause toggle. Let's create the function that will be triggered if the virtual Cancel button is triggered. A quick look at the Input Manager will show that one of the Cancel inputs is mapped to the joystick button 1, the B button on the gamepad.

1. In the PlayerMovable script, add the following variable to identify the GameHUD script:

    ```
    GameHUD gameHUD;
    ```

2. Assign it in the Start function:

    ```
    gameHUD = GameObject.Find("HUD Manager").GetComponent<GameHUD>();
    ```

3. In the Update function add the line that catches the Cancel just above the usingGamepad conditional's closing curly bracket:

    ```
    if(Input.GetButtonDown("Cancel")) {
        StopMovable ();
    }
    ```

4. And create the new function:

    ```
    void StopMovable () {
        // turn off and reset pointer
        pointer.GetComponent<CustomPointer>().ResetPointer();
        // reset GUI focus
        gameHUD.ResetFocus();
    }
    ```

5. In the CustomPointer script, create the ResetPointer function:

    ```
    public void ResetPointer(){
        isActive = false;
        SetPointerState(0); // turn off both pointer images
    Vector3 tempPos = new Vector3(transform.position.x, transform.position.y,
    transform.position.z);
        tempPos.x = Screen.width/2;
        tempPos.y = Screen.height/2;
        transform.position = tempPos;
    }
    ```

To reset the focus, you will create the ResetFocus() function in the GameHUD so it can be used by other scripts. This little task is not as simple as you might think, but is a crucial part of game flow. The first thing you require is a new using statement.

1. Open the GameHUD script.

2. At the top of the GameHUD script, add the following:

    ```
    using UnityEngine.EventSystems;
    ```

3. Next, add the following variables:

    ```
    public EventSystem theEventSystem; //
    public GameObject newFocus; // in case a UI element is disabled
    ```

4. Add the `ResetFocus()` function:

    ```
    public void ResetFocus () {
        theEventSystem.SetSelectedGameObject(newFocus);
    }
    ```

> **Tip** You could check for missing focus by using `if(theEventSystem.currentSelectedGameObject == null)`.

5. Save the the scripts and, in the GameHUD, assign the EventSystem to the Event System parameter and the Pause toggle to the New Focus parameter.

6. Click Play and test the cancel functionality by pressing the B (Cancel) button on the gamepad while you are in banana movable mode.

The Pointer disappears, and the focus is set to the Pause toggle, allowing the player to continue the game.

Closely related to this functionality is being able to turn focus off. By doing so during the movable mode, you can prevent the player from "un-pausing" the game in the midst of moving Banana Peels.

7. Back in the GameHUD, create another function to remove focus:

    ```
    public void RemoveFocus () {
        theEventSystem.SetSelectedGameObject(null);
    }
    ```

    This one you will want to call as soon as the Wheelbarrows button is pressed, but only if there is an active gamepad.

8. In the CustomPointer script, add a variable for the GameHUD script:

    ```
    public GameHUD gameHUD;
    ```

9. At the bottom of the `ActivatePointer` script, after it has checked for an active gamepad, call the `RemoveFocus` function:

    ```
    gameHUD.RemoveFocus();
    ```

10. Save all scripts and assign the HUD Manager object to the Pointer's Game HUD parameter.

11. Click Play and test.

With the movable mode in progress, the player can no longer navigate the GUI until he presses the Cancel button. This also fixes the problem so the Banana Peels are reliably picked up on button-down.

The next bit of functionality is to turn the Pointer off when the player finishes using the last of the Wheelbarrows. For that, you will set a flag when the Wheelbarrow count is updated, and then turn the Pointer off when the player drops the current Banana Peel.

1. In the PlayerMovable script, add the following variable:

    ```
    bool empty = false; // flag for turning off pointer if no more Wheelbarrows
    ```

2. In the case TouchPhase.Began section, change the if (persistent. wheelbarrows == 0) line to the following:

    ```
    if (persistent.wheelbarrows == 0){
        barrowToggle.interactable = false; // disable the toggle
        empty = true;
    }
    ```

3. In the case TouchPhase.Ended section, add this:

    ```
    if (empty) pointer.GetComponent<CustomPointer>().ResetPointer();
    ```

4. Click Play and test by using all of the Wheelbarrows.

    The Pointer disappears as the last Banana Peel is dropped.

    The next test is to see whether you can cancel and then return to use the remaining Wheelbarrows.

5. Click Play, move a Banana Peel, press the Cancel button, and return and try again.

    As soon as you reenter movable mode, the Pointer becomes visible. Let's reset the usingGamepad flag in the PlayerMovable script when the player cancels the mode.

6. In the PlayerMovable script, at the bottom of the StopMovable function, add the following:

    ```
    usingGamepad = false;
    ```

7. Because it will make one last pass through the Update function, change the if(Input.GetButtonUp("Submit")) conditional to the following:

    ```
    if(Input.GetButtonUp("Submit")) {
        HandleTouch(10, pointerPosition, TouchPhase.Ended);
        if(empty) return;
        pointer.GetComponent<CustomPointer>().SetPointerState (1);
        // turn on regular pointer
    }
    ```

8.   Save the script and test again.

This time, the procedure goes smoothly. Before checking it by using the mouse, you will want to filter out turning on the Pointer if the axis is not being used. Clicking the Wheelbarrow toggle calls the `ActivatePointer` function in the CustomPointer script. Let's add the check in there:

1.   Add one more variable to the CustomPointer script:

```
public PlayerMovable playerMovable;
```

2.   At the top of the `ActivatePointer` function, change the if(!usingGamepad) line to:

```
if(!playerMovable.usingGamepad) return;
```

3.   Save the script and assign the HUD Manager to the Pointer's Player Movable component's new parameter.

4.   Click Play and test the Banana Peel–moving procedure using the mouse.

5.   Check the gamepad usage one more time.

Both workflows behave as designed.

Crushing the Peppermints

With the bananas taken care of, it's time to see about reducing the peppermint threat. Because the peppermints (the Spinners) are always on the move, it really doesn't matter which one is neutralized. The quickest solution is to just let the player click a peppermint. But he will have spent a lot of tipCoins to get rid of a peppermint, so you will want to do something a bit more interesting (rewarding).

Neutralizing the Spinner

Let's start with the basics by turning off the collider and renderer of the picked peppermint (Spinner).

1.   Create a new C# script and name it **Neutralizer**.

It will have to be able to contact the corresponding UI objects and Persistent. You will be able to copy much of the code from the PlayerMovable script, changing from `barrow` to `crusher`.

2.   Add the path for the UI:

```
using UnityEngine.UI;
```

3. Add the variables:

    ```
    private Persistent persistent;
    private Text crusherCount;
    private Button crusherButton;
    private AudioSource theAudio;
    public AudioClip crushFX;
    ```

4. Find and assign them in the Start function:

    ```
    persistent = GameObject.Find("Holder").GetComponent<Persistent>();
    crusherCount = GameObject.Find("Count C").GetComponent<Text>();
    crusherButton = GameObject.Find("Crushers").GetComponent< Button>();
    theAudio = GetComponent<AudioSource>();
    ```

5. Add a temporary OnMouseDown function:

    ```
    void OnMouseDown() {
      NukeIt();
    }
    ```

    This will make it easier to test.

6. Now add the NukeIt function where all of the work is done:

    ```
    public void NukeIt () {
        if(persistent.candyCrushers == 0 || crusherButton.
        interactable == false) return; // no more perks or not activated
        theAudio.PlayOneShot(crushFX);
        //disable the collider and renderer
        GetComponent<Collider>().enabled = false;
        GetComponent<Renderer>().enabled = false;
        persistent.candyCrushers --; // decrement the perks
        crusherCount.text = persistent.candyCrushers.ToString();
        // update the UI
    }
    ```

7. Save the script and add it to the three Spinner objects and activate them if they were turned off.

8. Load the Crush sound clip into their Crush FX parameter.

9. Open the Gamel IUD script and add the following to the Start function:

    ```
    UpdateCrusher ();
    ```

10. Create the new function:

    ```
    public void UpdateCrusher () {
    crusherCount.text = persistent.candyCrushers.ToString();
    }
    ```

11. Save the script and test.

The peppermints disappear from the scene on pick, and the count goes down. You will refine the functionality later.

Hiring Some Help

To give the player his money's worth for purchasing a means of getting rid of those pesky peppermints, you will bring in a character to make the task more interesting. The weapon-wielding Guard character from Chapter 4 will spice things up nicely.

1. Import the Guard.unitypackage from Chapter 4 or from the Chapter 11 Assets folder.

2. From the 3D Assets folder, select the Guard and in the Model section, set the Scale Factor to **.012**. Click Apply.

3. In the Rig section, note that the Guard is set up as Humanoid.

4. Check out the Animation Section to see the animation clips you set up in Chapter 4.

5. Click each clip and press the preview window's Play button to see the animations.

6. Create a new clip and name it **Guard Quick Block**.

7. Set its start to **218** and its End to **222**.

Note the difference between the Guard Run and Guard Walk animations vs. the Guard WIP. *WIP* stands for *walk in place*. With Mecanim, you can use the transform baked into the root animation to move the character, or let scripting move him. There is also an option not to use root motion if the animation has it. In this case, you will let the animation move the character.

For this little game, setting up full-blown Mecanim controls is hardly worth the time, so you will be calling the animations directly from scripting and using just a few of the Mecanim features. The first thing you will require is an Animator Controller for the state machine:

1. Create a new Animator Controller in the Project view's Mecanim folder.

2. Name it **Guard Animator Controller**.

3. Drag the Guard into the scene view so he is at the top-center area of the tilt board (Figure11-5) and rotate him 180 degrees so he is facing forward.

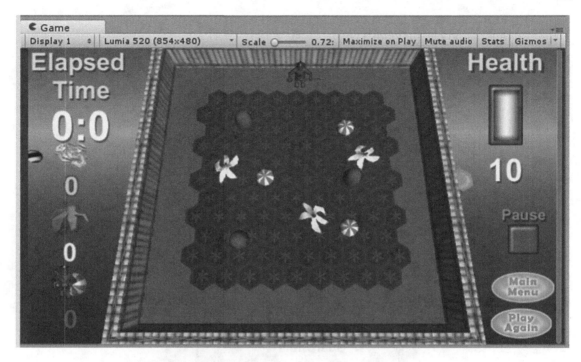

Figure 11-5. The Guard at the top center of the board

4. From the Components menu or Add Component button, in the Physics submenu, give the Guard a Character Controller component.

    The Character Controller is a collider and physical object respecting only the basics of physics rolled into one, with a few extra parameters that are useful for characters. It is a good, quick way to set up a very simple character but does not actually use Rigigdbody physics and as such is somewhat limited.

5. In the Character Controller component, if it was not the default, set the (collider) Center Y to **1.4**, the Radius to **0.5**, and the Height to **2.75**.

6. Add the Guard Animator Controller to the character by dropping it directly onto him in the Hierarchy view. You will see that it automatically goes to the Animator component's Controller field.

7. Drag the Guard into the Board Group so he will move with it when it tips.

8. From 3D Assets folder, expand the Guard asset until you can see the animation clips (Figure 11-6).

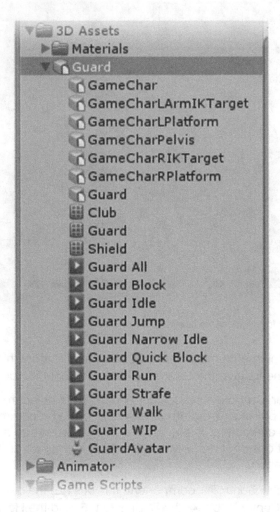

Figure 11-6. *The expanded Guard asset*

9. Select the Guard in the Hierarchy view and click the Animator tab, or, if it is not yet visible, open it from the Window menu.

10. Now drag the Guard Idle, Guard Narrow Idle, Guard Run, Guard Walk, and Guard Quick Block (drag it in twice) animation clips into the Animator window.

The first one in is set as the Default (it is an orange color). For the first tests, you will want him to start at a run.

1. Right-click over the Guard Run state and choose Set as Layer Default State.

2. Save the scene and play.

   The Guard runs to the other side of the board.

   You will use a couple of transitions to make use of the quick blocks.

3. Right-click over the Guard Quick Block state and choose Make Transition.

4. Drag and drop the connection onto Guard Run.

5. Right-click over the Guard Quick Block 0 state and choose Make Transition.

6. Drag and drop the connection onto Guard Walk (Figure 11-7).

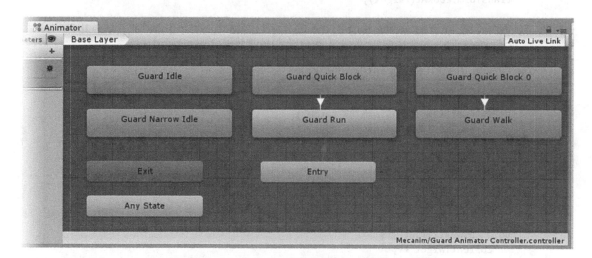

Figure 11-7. The Guard animation clips/states with the two Guard Quick Block transitions

The default transition uses the first clip's end time as its condition to blend to the next state. You will trigger the first state, and it will automatically blend to the second state where it will start looping.

You will use a Look At to point him in the direction of his target peppermint. Because they are constantly on the move, it won't matter which one he goes toward, so you will create an array to hold the peppermints and set him to go after them in order.

1. Create a new C# script and name it **Crusher**.

2. Add the following variables:

    ```
    public Transform[] targets; // the peppermints
    internal int maxCrushers = 3; // the max number of crushers per game
    int currentTarget = 0; // index number of current target
    Transform target; // location of the current target
    ```

3. In the Start function, initialize the target to the first array element:

    ```
    target = targets[0]; // set the first target
    ```

4. In the Update function, add the following:

    ```
    transform.LookAt(target);
    ```

    When he intersects the target, the GUI will have to be updated through the peppermint's Neutralizer script, and the next target assigned.

5. Create the OnTriggerEnter function:

    ```
    void OnTriggerEnter (Collider collider) {
        if (collider.transform == target){
            collider.GetComponent<Neutralizer>().NukeIt();
            GetNextTarget();
        }
    }
    ```

6. And the function to get the next target:

    ```
    void GetNextTarget() {
        currentTarget ++;
        if (currentTarget < maxCrushers) {
            target = targets[currentTarget];
        }
    }
    ```

7. Save the script and add it to the Guard.

8. Set the Targets array size to **3** and drag the three Spinners into the slots.

9. Save the scene.

10. Click Play and watch the Guard clean up the peppermints.

When his mission is completed, he spins wildly and ricochets around the board.

Next, the Guard will need a base point to return to and a means of telling him he's finished.

1. For the base point, create an Empty gameObject and add a Sphere Collider to it.

2. Set the collider to Is Trigger.

3. Name it **Guard Base Point** and add it to the Board Group.

4. In the Scene view, move it to the guard's feet.

    It will always be the last target, so you can add it to the Guard's Target array.

5. Set the Target array to **4** and add the Guard Base Point to it as Element 3.

6. In the Crusher script, create the following variables:

```
internal bool hunting = true;
Animator animator;
```

The hunting flag will allow you to turn the LookAt off and on in the Update function. The finished flag will stop the LookAt before it cycles again. The animator will let you communicate with the state engine to change the animations. Once he is finished, you will also disable the Crusher button.

1. In the Start function, assign the animator:

```
animator = GetComponent<Animator>();
```

2. Use the hunting flag in the Update function:

```
void Update () {
    if (hunting) {
        transform.LookAt(target);
    }
}
```

3. In the OnTriggerEnter function, at the top, add the following:

```
if(!hunting) return;
```

4. And above the <Neutralizer>().NukeIt() line, add this:

```
animator.CrossFade("Guard Quick Block",0.1f);
```

5. In the GetNextTarget function, add an else:

```
else {
    currentTarget = 3;
    target = targets[currentTarget];
    animator.CrossFade("Guard Quick Block 0",0.1f);
}
```

6.   Save and test.

Now, after he's destroyed the peppermints, he walks calmly to the base point and spins because the code throws an error when it tries to neutralize a non-peppermint object. One more condition will avoid that problem.

7.   In the OntriggerEnter function, just below the if (!hunting) line, add this:

```
if (collider.transform == target && currentTarget == 3) {
    hunting = false;
    animator.CrossFade("Guard Narrow Idle",.5f);
    return;
}
```

8.   Save and test.

If he finishes his task and has a long walk to get back to the base point, you are probably thinking his walk is painfully slow. That can be fixed in the Animator view:

1.   Select the Guard.

2.   In the Animator tab, select the Guard Walk state.

3.   In the Inspector, set the Speed to **3**.

4.   Change the run speed to **1.25** while you are there.

Now it would be nice if he turned around after reaching the base point. You will have him turn to face the center of the board (the place where the ball drops in). Note the CrossFade time of 0.75 seconds for the transition to idle.

1.   Create a new variable:

```
public Transform theBoard;  // board centre
```

2.   Below the CrossFade("Guard Narrow Idle line, add the following:

```
transform.LookAt(theBoard);
```

3.   Save the script and assign the Board object to the new parameter.

4.   Save the scene and test.

Now the Guard is beginning to be quite well behaved.

You may have noticed that the number of crushers has been going down but has not yet been initialized at the start of the scene. Now is a good time to hook up the guard to the rest of the reward system.

1. In the Animator view, set the Guard Narrow Idle as the default state.

2. In the Crusher script, set the `hunting` variable's value to `false`.

   The player may or may not want to use up his crushers, so the guard should not be activated until the player presses the Crusher button. That means you will also have to have access to the UI.

3. At the top of the Crusher script, add the following:

   ```
   using UnityEngine.UI;
   ```

   And you will have to contact the Persistent script to see how many crushers have been purchased.

4. Add the following variables:

   ```
   Persistent persistent;
   Button crusherButton;
   ```

5. Find them in the `Start` function:

   ```
   persistent = GameObject.FindWithTag("Holder").GetComponent<Persistent>();
   crusherButton = GameObject.Find("Crushers").GetComponent<Button>();
   ```

6. Create the function that will be called from the button press:

   ```
   public void Activate() {
   // Get max crushers available
   maxCrushers = persistent.candyCrushers;
   if (maxCrushers > 3) maxCrushers = 3;
   if (maxCrushers == 0) return;
   hunting = true;
   animator.CrossFade("Guard Run",.2f);
   }
   ```

   On activation, the number of crushers is updated from the Persistent script. The number is capped to 3, the max number of peppermints in the scene. If none are available, the activation is ignored.

7. Save the script.

8. Select the Crusher (the UI button). In its Button component, add an On Click event using the Guard object and the Activate function.

   You can deactivate the button when the guard has finished and block repeated activation once hunting has been activated so the player can't press it again before the guard has finished.

9. At the bottom of the `GetNextTarget`'s `else` clause, add the following:

   ```
   crusherButton.interactable = false;
   ```

10. At the top of the `Activate` function, add the following:

    ```
    if (hunting) return;
    ```

11. In the Persistent script, set the Crushers number to **2**. Test, and then set the number to **5** to make sure the correct numbers of peppermints are removed from the scene and the correct number of crushers persist through the next game.

Because the Guard procedure is just a one-shot deal, the gamepad additions will be simple. GUI navigation is already in play, so the only task will be to reset focus to the Pause toggle when the Crusher's toggle is pressed.

1. Open the Crusher script.

2. Add a variable for the GameHUD:

   ```
   public GameHUD gameHUD;
   ```

3. In the `Activate` function, below the `if(hunting) return` line, add the following:

   ```
   gameHUD.ResetFocus();
   ```

4. Save the script and assign the HUD Manager to the Guard's Crusher component's new GameHUD parameter.

5. Click Play and test using the gamepad.

Hiding the Guard

The guard is working well, but unless the player has forked out some tipCoins for some crushers, the guard shouldn't be on the board. To spice up the purchase even more, you can bring in the Guard House asset from Chapter 4 so he will have a better place to hang out. If this is purely a desktop application, you could toss the Guard and Guard House into an empty gameObject and deactivate them all at the same time. Unity, however, recommends turning off the Mesh Renderers and colliders as more-efficient means of temporarily having objects go in and out of the scene. The Guard-related objects are renderers for the Guard House, Guard, Club, and Shield. For the colliders, you have one for the Guard and two for the Guard House.

1. Import the GuardHouse.package from Chapter 4 or the Chapter 11 Assets folder.

2. Drag its prefab (it already has colliders) into the scene and position it in the top-left corner of the board, setting its Y Rotation to **130**.

3. In the Hierarchy view, drag it into the Board Group.

4. The Guard is a little bit too wide to be able to fit nicely through the door, so move him slightly out in front of it.

5. Move the Guard Base Point object there as well.

6. Click Play and test.

   You may notice that the Marble can force its way under the Guard on its way into the corner.

7. Make sure the Guard is far enough in front of the structure to roll it out again.

   You can control the visibility and colliders from the Crusher script.

1. Add the following variables to the Crusher script:

```
//To toggle on/off
public Renderer guardHouse;
public Renderer guard;
public Renderer club;
public Renderer Shield;
public CharacterController guardCollider;
public Collider gHWallLeft;
public Collider gHWallRight;
```

2. Create the following function to do the work:

```
void ToggleGuardStuff(bool state) {
    crusherButton.interactable = state;
    guardHouse.enabled = state;
    guard.enabled = state;
    club.enabled = state;
    Shield.enabled = state;
    guardCollider.enabled = state;
    gHWallLeft.enabled = state;
    gHWallRight.enabled = state;
}
```

3. At the bottom of the Start function, toggle the Guard objects off or on depending on the Crusher count:

```
if(persistent.candyCrushers > 0) ToggleGuardStuff(true);
else ToggleGuardStuff(false);
```

4. Save the script and assign the new objects, making sure that you use the Guard mesh object for the renderer object (Figure 11-8).

    Note, you can expand the Guard object to locate the child objects easier.

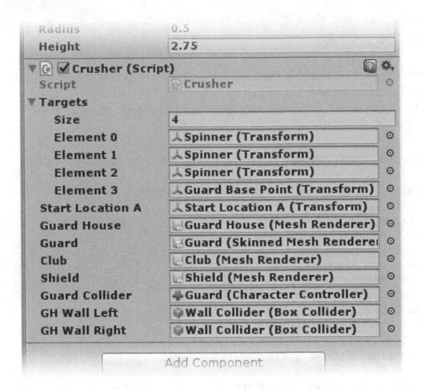

Figure 11-8. The new parameter assignments

5. Click Play and test the functionality by using up the crushers and playing another game.

    The Guard (and Guard House) appear only when the player has purchased at least one Crusher.

Making the Store

With the reward system working, it's time to make the Store. This is where the player will go to spend his tipCoins, purchase more coins, and purchase the functionality to win the game easier. If the store is a separate level or scene, and you let him visit it during the game, you would have to store the transforms of just about everything in the Board level so it would be the same when he returned. If you blocked the Board Level scene with a second Canvas, it could contain your store while the rest of the scene is running. The downside of this scenario is that the player may want to check the store before he commits to the Play button. A simple alternative to the first scenario is to give him access to it only from the main level or start screen. This has the added advantage of making him more likely to purchase the helper services before he sees whether the path looks easy or hard.

1. Create a new scene and save it as **Store Level**.

2. Select the Camera and set its Clear Flags to Solid Color and delete the Directional Light, if there was one by default.

3. Set the window size to 16 × 9 or one of your presets.

4. Import the Store.unitypackage from the Chapter 11 Assets folder.

5. In 2D viewport mode, drag the blue rect corners out to meet the anchors and canvas border if they are not already in place.

    The GUI has been set up for you, but not yet hooked up to the game (Figure 11-9). The Canvas is set to Scale With Screen Size, Match Width Or Height, and uses the Nokia Lumia's size as the Reference Resolution centered between Width and Height. The center panel is anchored to the center, the title to the top, and the price panel to the bottom. The two navigation buttons are anchored to their respective corners. Feel free to check out the screen in your preset sizes.

Figure 11-9. The Store prefab

    Before hooking anything up, let's add it to the Build Settings to make it accessible from the Start menu.

6. Save the scene and choose Edit ➤ Build Settings ➤ Add Open Scenes.

7. Close Build Settings.

8. Add the Check for DDLs prefab to the scene and save the scene.

To activate gamepad functionality, you will, of course, have to supply a first-selected GUI object. To encourage the player to spend money, that will be the Buy Coins button.

1. From the GameObject menu ➤ UI sub-menu, add an EventSystem object.

2. Drag the Buy Coins object into the First Selected field.

3. Click Play and test the store functionality by using a gamepad.

4. Save the scene.

The Start Menu was set up for the gamepad navigation in Chapter 10, so you should now be good to go for the gamepad after hooking up the functionality.

Finishing the Start Menu

To access the store level, you will be updating the Start Menu and finishing its functionality.

1. Open the Start Menu.

2. Import the StartGUIextras.unitypackage.

3. Set the Game view to the 16:9 setting.

4. Drag the Start GUI Extras prefab directly into the scene's Canvas.

5. Drag the blue rect corners out to meet the anchors and canvas border if they are not already in place.

6. Check your various preset screen sizes to make sure the elements maintain good placement and scale.

   The extras include a Store, Credits, and Extras button as well as a few simple instructions (Figure 11-10).

Figure 11-10. The new additions to the Start menu

1. Import the CanvasCredits,unitypackage.

2. Drag the Canvas Credits prefab into the Hierarchy view.

3. Drag it into the Hierarchy view, *not* into the existing canvas (Figure 11-11).

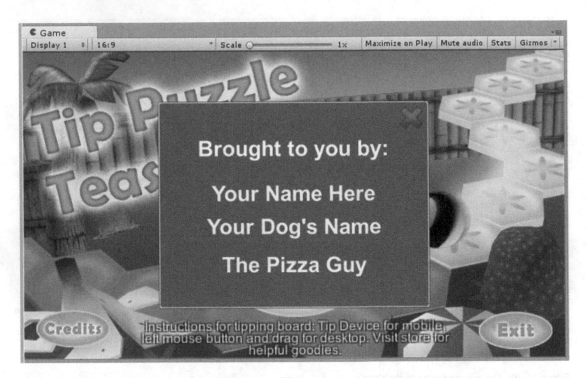

Figure 11-11. The credits Canvas—everybody gets credit!

The Canvas Credits is a second Canvas object in the scene. Just as with regular gameObjects, activating and deactivating GUI Canvases will cost battery life, so once again you will be hiding the graphics and disabling picks to economize. Using a second Canvas allows you to deal with all of its components at the same time, but there are a few gotchas.

1. Click Play.

   The new canvas goes behind the contents of the first canvas. Changing the Canvas Credits' location in the hierarchy will not fix the problem. The answer is to change the Sort Order.

2. In its Canvas component, set its Sort Order to **1**(Figure 11-12) and click Play.

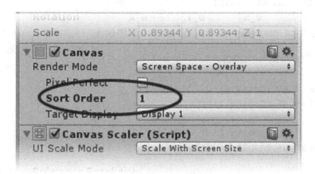

Figure 11-12. Adjusting the Sort Order—lower numbers are drawn first

This time it stays on top.

> **Tip**   You can bring a canvas forward to work on in Edit mode by turning the Canvas component off and then on.

3. Hover over the Exit or Credits button.

    The buttons respond, and shouldn't, so you will want a way to block interaction with the Main Canvas while the credits are up. The simplest thing to do is to cover it with a full-sized Panel object.

4. Exit Play mode and from the gameObject menu choose UI ➤ Panel to add a Panel to the Canvas Credits group and scale it to full size if it hasn't done so automatically.

5. In Play mode, try hovering the buttons again.

    This time there is no response.

6. Stop Play mode and move the blocker Panel up to the top of the Canvas so it won't block the credits panel close button and set its Color's alpha value to **0**.

7. Set the Canvas component's Sort Order to **1**.

    To hide and show the credits, you will disable the Canvas. In doing so, the credit's Close button will also be disabled. Let's do that in the GameManager script.

8. Open GameManager script.

8. Add the following variables:

```
public Canvas creditsCanvas;
public Button closeCredits;
```

9. Save the script and assign the objects to them.

10. Add the following functions:

```
public void OpenCredits () {
   creditsCanvas.enabled = true;
}
public void CloseCredits () {
   creditsCanvas.enabled = false;
}
```

11. Add the call to CloseCredits from the Start function to make sure it is off at startup:

```
CloseCredits ();
```

12. Save the script and disable the Canvas Credits' Canvas component.

Now you are ready to connect the buttons with the new functions via their On Click events.

1. Select the Credits button from the main Canvas and create an On Click event.

2. Load the Game Manager as its Object and assign the Game Manager's OpenCredits() function to it.

3. Select the Close Button from the Canvas Credits and create an On Click event

4. Load the Game Manager as its Object and assign the Game Manager's CloseCredits() function to it.

5. Click Play and test by opening and closing the credits panel.

The application Exit button is fairly easy to code, but doesn't actually stop play in the editor without special editor code. A few lines of specialized code are well worth the effort.

1. In the GameManager, add the following function:

```
public void EndGame (){
   Application.Quit(); // end the application
   #if UNITY_EDITOR
      UnityEditor.EditorApplication.isPlaying = false;
   #endif
}
```

For some mobile platforms, you may not be able to let the game close itself. This is addressed in Chapter 12.

2. Save the script and select the Exit Button from the main Canvas; create an On Click event.

3. Load the Game Manager object into it and assign the GameManager's EndGame() function to it.

    Loading the Store will be easy.

4. Add the following function to the GameManager script:

    ```
    public void LoadStoreLevel () {
        SceneManager.LoadScene("Store Level");
    }
    ```

5. Select the Store Button and create an On Click event.

6. Load the Game Manager object into it and assign the Game Manager's LoadStoreLevel() function to it.

7. Save the scene and play to test.

Hooking Up the Store

With the remainder of the Start menu's functionality taken care of, it's time to work on the store functionality. As you may have guessed, the store will be in contact with the Persistent script, where all of the important data is kept.

1. Open the Store Level scene.

2. Create a new empty gameObject and name it **Store Manager**.

3. Create a new script and name it **StoreManager**.

4. Add the StoreManager script to the Store Manager object.

5. Add the following paths at the top:

    ```
    using UnityEngine.UI;
    using UnityEngine.SceneManagement;
    ```

6. Add the following variables:

```
Persistent persistent;

//GUI
public Text CurrentCoins;
public Text CurrentWheelbarrows;
public Text CurrentCandyCrushers;

// purchase prices
private float wbPrice;
private float crusherPrice;
private float coinPrice;
private float coinAmount;

// price labels
public Text wbPriceLabel;
public Text crusherPriceLabel;
public Text coinPriceLabel;
public Text coinAmountLabel;
```

7. In the Start function, make sure time is running:

```
Time.timeScale = 1;
```

You added code in the Board Level to reset time on exit, but to make sure
your yield statements will execute properly, it is safest to reset time in this
scene as well.

8. Find and assign the Holder object:

```
persistent = GameObject.Find("Holder").GetComponent<Persistent>();
```

9. Then get the purchase prices (in case they have been changed):

```
//update prices
wbPrice = persistent.wbPrice;
crusherPrice = persistent.crusherPrice;
coinPrice = persistent.coinPrice;
coinAmount = persistent.coinAmount;
```

The Store Level came in with the text already set, but in using variables for the amounts, you
will can update the text in case you want to change the amounts.

1. Below that, update the pricing in the GUI:

```
//load into price labels
wbPriceLabel.text = wbPrice.ToString() + " each";
crusherPriceLabel.text = crusherPrice.ToString() + " each";
coinPriceLabel.text = coinAmount.ToString() + " for $" + coinPrice.ToString();
```

2. Save the script and assign the corresponding text components in the Price Panel objects (Figure 11-13).

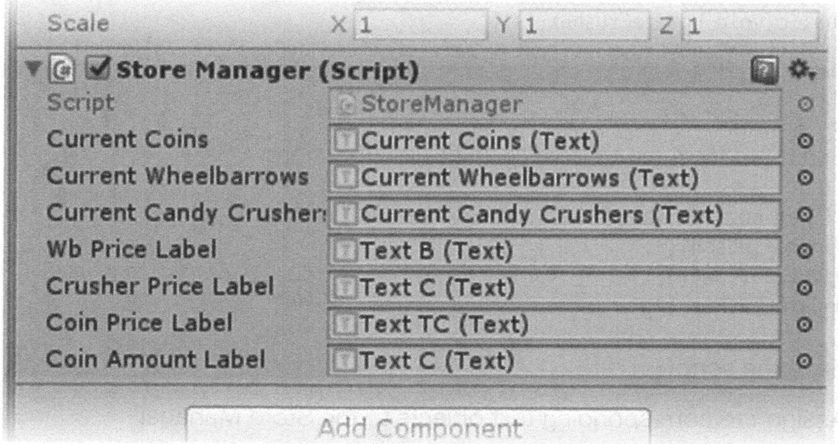

Figure 11-13. The Store Manager assignments

3. Add the function to return to the main menu (a.k.a., the Start Menu):

```
public void LoadStartMenu () {
// go to the main menu
    SceneManager.LoadScene("Start Menu");
}
```

4. Create the function to play the game:

```
public void LoadBoardLevel () {
    // play the game
    SceneManager.LoadScene("Board Level");
}
```

5. Save the script.

6. Create new On Click events for the Play and Main Menu buttons and assign the new StoreManager functions, LoadBoardLevel() and LoadStartMenu() to them.

As soon as the scene loads and the Persistent script is found, you will want to update the current totals. As in the GameHUD, you will grab them from the Persistent script and load them directly into the GUI text.

1. Add the following functions:

```
public void UpdateTipCash () {
    CurrentCoins.text = persistent.cash.ToString();
}
```

```
      public void UpdateBarrow () {
         CurrentWheelbarrows.text = persistent.wheelbarrows.ToString();
      }

      public void UpdateCrusher () {
         CurrentCandyCrushers.text = persistent.candyCrushers.ToString();
      }
```

2. Call them from the bottom of the Start function:

```
// get current values and update them in the UI
UpdateTipCash ();
UpdateBarrow ();
UpdateCrusher ();
```

3. Save the script.

4. Assign the corresponding text objects to the Store Manager component's parameters.

5. Save the scene and play through from the Start Menu scene.

6. Test the menu and Play buttons while you are there.

For the purchase buttons, there will be a little math involved. At this stage, you will magically get tipCoins from the click of a button. You will probably want a message that tells whether the transactions were completed.

1. Reload the Store Level.

2. In the StoreManager script, add the following function to purchase tipCoins:

```
public void BuyCoins () {
   // do the real purchase here...

   //add the coins
   persistent.cash += coinAmount;
   // update the UI
   UpdateTipCash ();
   TransactionComplete();
}
```

For the two game purchases, you will have to account for insufficient funds. You may also want to provide a sign when the transaction has gone though. Don't bother trying to save the script before you have added the transaction functions.

3. For the Wheelbarrow purchases, add the following:

```
public void BuyWheelbarrow () {
    // check for sufficient funds
    if(persistent.cash < wbPrice) {
        InsufficientFunds();
        return;
    }
    //add the coins
    persistent.wheelbarrows += 1;
    //take the money
    persistent.cash -= wbPrice;
    // update the UI
    UpdateBarrow ();
    UpdateTipCash ();
    TransactionComplete();
}
```

4. For the crusher purchase, add this:

```
public void BuyCrusher () {
    // check for sufficient funds
    if(persistent.cash < crusherPrice) {
    InsufficientFunds();
    return;
    }
    //add the coins
    persistent.candyCrushers += 1;
    //take the money
    persistent.cash -= crusherPrice;
    // update the UI
    UpdateCrusher ();
    UpdateTipCash ();
    TransactionComplete();
}
```

A sound effect or two would go well here. A bit of text will do the job for the message, but it will have to appear and then disappear. With the Credits panel, where there were several UI elements to be managed, you created another Canvas. The transaction messages are quite simple, an Image and Text, so you will be moving them up and down inside the Canvas to hide and show them. As a bonus, the images also will block the player from fast multiple picks. Let's see what they look like.

1. Drag the Transaction Complete object to the bottom of the Canvas.

    It appears (Figure 11-14), and you can see how it will block the store buttons.

Figure 11-14. The transaction message blocking picks for more purchases

2. Check your various screen presets to make sure the store buttons are always blocked.

3. Drag the Transaction Complete object back to the top and drag the Insufficient Funds object to the bottom to see what it looks like. Then drag it back up to the top.

4. In the Store Manager, create a variable for both Images:

    ```
    //transaction messages
    public Image insufficientFunds;
    public Image transactionComplete;
    ```

5. Save the script.

You can get away with using a single Audio Source component if you use PlayOneShot.

1. Add an Audio Source component to the Store Manager.

2. Add a variable to the StoreManager script so it can be quickly contacted:

    ```
    AudioSource theAudio;
    ```

3. Add a couple of sound effects:

    ```
    public AudioClip buzzer;
    public AudioClip dinger;
    ```

4. Assign the Audio Source in the Start function:

```
theAudio= GetComponent<AudioSource>();
```

To turn the images off and on after a short pause, you will use an IEnumerator and yield. The arguments sent to the co-routine tell it which image to bring forward and for how long.

5. Add the following just above the StoreManager's closing curly bracket:

```
IEnumerator TurnOffMessage (Image currentSibling,float pause) {
    yield return new WaitForSeconds(pause);
    currentSibling.transform.SetAsFirstSibling();
}
```

6. Add the following functions:

```
void InsufficientFunds() {
    insufficientFunds.transform.SetAsLastSibling();
    theAudio.PlayOneShot(buzzer);
    StartCoroutine(TurnOffMessage(insufficientFunds, 0.5f));
}

void TransactionComplete () {
    transactionComplete.transform.SetAsLastSibling();
    theAudio.PlayOneShot(dinger);
    StartCoroutine(TurnOffMessage(transactionComplete, 0.2f));
}
```

Feel free to adjust the times to your satisfaction.

7. Save the script.

8. Load the sound effects, BuzzerSoft and Ding, and the two transaction objects into the new parameters.

9. Hook up [add On Click events] the Buy Coins, Buy Wheelbarrows and Buy Candy Crushers buttons with their respective Store Manager functions, BuyCoins(),BuyWheelbarrow() and BuyCrusher().

10. Assign the corresponding UI elements to the Store Manager's Insufficient Funds and Transaction Complete parameters.

11. Set the Wheelbarrows and CandyCrushes to **0** in the Persistent script.

12. Play and test the store functionality.

The actual purchase of tipCoins is covered in Chapter 12, but your little game is now looking quite respectable.

Summary

In this chapter, you embellished your game's functionality to create a better environment for monetization. To support a "store" and its data, you made excellent use of the Persistent script so the various items and coinage would be retained and accessible throughout the various level or scene changes. Besides the in-game currency, tipCoins, you allowed your player to purchase the ability to rearrange the Banana Peels and, with the help of the character from Chapter 4, to eradicate peppermints. All the new functionality was tied together with enhanced GUI menus and elements.

For the Banana Peels, you introduced functionality that allowed the player to manually drag the Banana Peel objects around the board. In anticipation of the touch functionality prevalent on mobile platforms, the code was designed to work with both touch and mouse actions. When designing for both input schemes, you learned that the touch count from a mouse click will always return zero. To go for a full triple play, you added gamepad functionality by generating your own pointer object to give gamepad users a visual means to select and move the Banana Peels.

With the use of Time.timeScale, you learned that you can pause game play without affecting UI interaction. This provided you with a way to prevent the player from losing time during Marble resets, made rearranging the Banana Peels visually easier, and set your game up to be able to handle interruptions common on mobile devices.

Using the guard character to destroy the marauding peppermints gave you a chance to learn a little bit more about Mecanim and how you could also control the states through scripting. More important, the Guard's peppermint-crushing behavior provided a lot of eye candy to make your players feel like they was getting their money's worth for the purchases.

And finally, you learned a few new tricks for working with the Unity UI, including the use of multiple Canvases and controlling sibling order to make various UI elements visible and invisible on command as well as blocking unwanted interaction.

Chapter 12

Building for Windows Store

In this chapter, you will be getting firsthand experience with accelerometer code and functionality, provided, of course, you have access to a Windows 10 device that supports it. It is assumed you will be working with Windows 10. There are differences in procedure and requirements for Windows 8 and 8.1, but they are well documented on the Windows Dev Center in case you need them. The accelerometer functionality requires that you venture out from the (by now, comfortable) Unity environment, and discover the world of Windows Store, Windows Dev Center, and a host of new terms, procedures, and reference material.

This chapter also assumes that you have completed the section on porting in Chapter 1. It contains a very tiny project that will help you with the setup process. If you have not yet done so, please take the time now as there are several support files and Visual Studio tools that may not have been loaded when you installed Visual Studio. At the time of this writing, it appears that Visual Studio Service Pack 3 is not part of the Unity installation. Conspicuously missing are the Windows SDK and a suite of Visual Studio tools. Generally, when you are missing a Windows 10 or Visual Studio component or tool, you will be given a link to obtain it. The process of collecting all the necessary tools and installations could be time-consuming, so plan accordingly.

Once everything is in place, you will add the accelerometer functionality, address issues related to in-app purchases, and learn some testing procedures, both simulated and via Windows Store. Later, you will take a peek at additional monetization as well as additional UWP platforms and Visual Studio functionality.

> **Tip** A Unity forum dedicated to Windows Store apps and Windows Phone can be accessed at
> `http://forum.unity3d.com/forums/50-Windows-Development`

© Sue Blackman and Adam Tuliper 2016
S. Blackman and A. Tuliper, *Learn Unity for Windows 10 Game Development*,
DOI 10.1007/978-1-4302-6757-7_12

Reviewing Requirements

To properly support this chapter and build and test your game for Windows 10, you should be running Windows 10 (though you can package but not run Windows 10 apps on Windows 8) as well as have Visual Studio Community edition or greater installed. When you install the latest version of Unity, you'll have several options to choose (Figure 12-1).

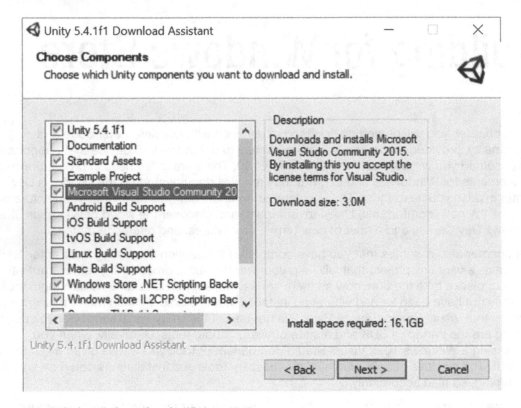

Figure 12-1. Unity installation options for Windows 10

The dialog box in Figure 12-1 may change slightly depending on the version of Unity that you install, so choose the options best fitting. Let's cover the options here:

> *Microsoft Visual Studio Community*: This option, which appears only if Visual Studio is not detected, installs Microsoft's completely free version of Visual Studio, called Visual Studio Community edition. *Select this option if you don't have Visual Studio installed.*
>
> *Microsoft Visual Studio Tools for Unity*: This option displays if Visual Studio is already installed. This option installs a Visual Studio add-in and configures Visual Studio to be able to talk to Unity to develop and debug your games, even while running in Unity. It also contains several great helpers covered below. *Select this option if you already have Visual Studio installed.*

Windows Store .NET Scripting Backend: This is the standard .NET compilation for Windows Store apps. In the future, this will be the "old way" of doing things, although it is currently the primary approach. As of this writing, if you want to use Unity's in-app purchase system (rather than write code to integrate directly with Microsoft's commerce system), you must install the .NET Scripting backend, as Unity's IAP libraries aren't yet supported with IL2CPP (though they may be supported by the time you read this). *Select this option.*

Windows Store IL2CPP Scripting Backend: This player takes all of your compiled C# code and converts it to C++, which means you'll need to also install (or have installed already) Visual C++ when you install Visual Studio. This has better API compatibility with Unity, but as of this writing is still in beta. Also if you want to debug code running on a device from Visual Studio, IL2CPP isn't supported yet (this may have changed by the time you read this). *This is optional as of this writing; consider trying this going forward. Be forewarned that it is possible that some Asset Store purchases may work only with IL2CPP. Be sure to test your purchases before incorporating them into your game, or contact the authors for compatibility with .NET.*

To complete this chapter, you need the following:

Visual Studio 2015 Community edition (or greater) with Update 3 or higher. Unity will install this for you by default on Windows if you don't already have it. (See Figure 12-1.)

Windows 10 SDK.

A computer with Windows 10 installed and running.

Optionally, a Windows 10 mobile device with an accelerometer.

A Microsoft account (free) to use Visual Studio. You can procure one at `http://account.live.com`.

If you wish to work through the entire chapter and publish your own applications to Windows Store, you will also need to obtain a developer account. They run about $19 USD and are a one-time nonrecurring charge. Get one at `http://dev.microsoft.com` or, if you are part of any of Microsoft's Startup programs such as BizSpark, they typically have free codes to register for Windows Store.

Developer mode enabled on your system

If you don't have these prerequisites but still want to try out building for Windows 10, you can create a Windows 10 Virtual Machine with Visual Studio already installed on it in Microsoft Azure, Microsoft's cloud service (Figure 12-2) in just a few clicks. You can then install Unity on it and be all set to build for Windows 10.

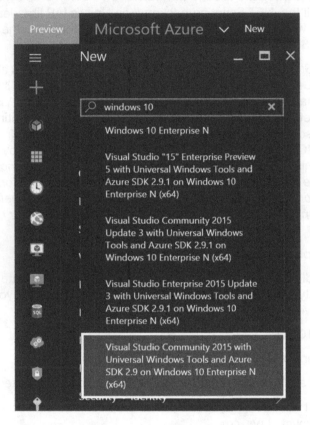

Figure 12-2. The option of running Visual Studio on a virtual machine in Microsoft Azure (Microsoft's cloud service)

Enabling Developer Mode

You need Developer mode enabled on your computer to be able to deploy (run) a Windows 10 application from Visual Studio to your computer. If Unity has installed Visual Studio for you, the first time you run it, you should be prompted to enable developer settings. If not, or if you already had Visual Studio installed, you can manually enable Developer mode:

1. Click the Start button from the Windows taskbar and click the Settings icon to load Windows settings.

2. Type in **developer** and select one of the resulting options. In Figure 12-3, both options do the same thing.

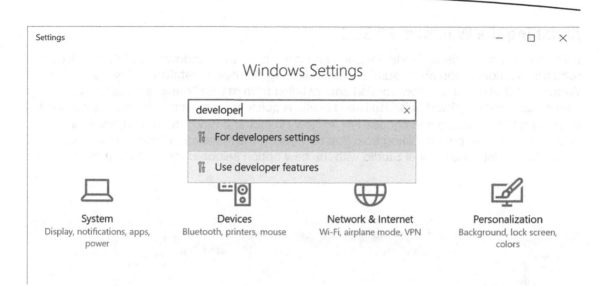

Figure 12-3. Searching for developer from Windows Settings

3. Select the Developer Mode radio button (Figure 12-4) and click Yes at the resulting prompt. You may then be shown a message to reboot; do so if prompted.

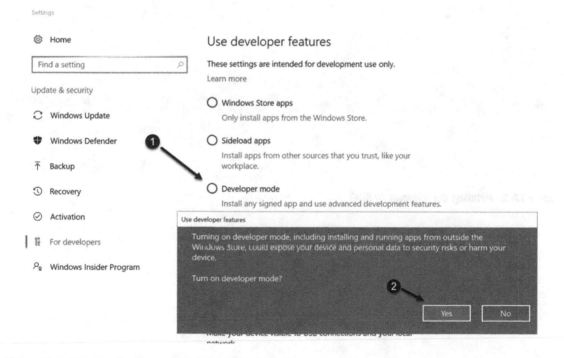

Figure 12-4. Activating Developer Mode in Developer Settings

Installing the Windows 10 SDK

If you already have Visual Studio installed and don't have the Windows 10 SDK installed, read this section. If you aren't sure, see the following "Verifying Installations" section. The Windows 10 SDK can be downloaded and installed from `https://developer.microsoft.com/en-us/windows/downloads/windows-10-sdk`. A quick way to check whether it's installed is to open Visual Studio and choose File ➤ New Project and navigate to the Universal section in the New project dialog box. You can launch the installation from here as well, which simply launches Visual Studio with the new option selected for the SDK (Figure 12-5).

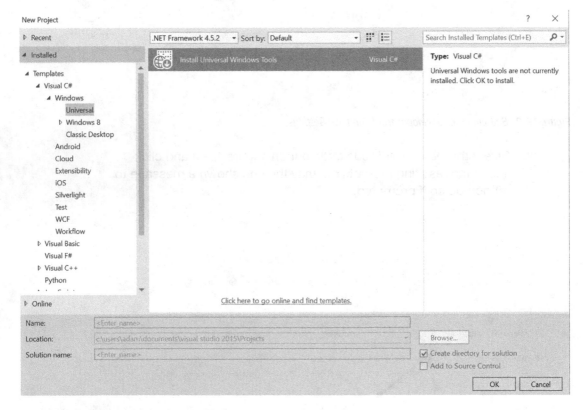

Figure 12-5. Installing the Windows 10 SDK

This launches the Visual Studio installer, where you can accept the defaults and click Next to install the Windows 10 SDK (Figure 12-6).

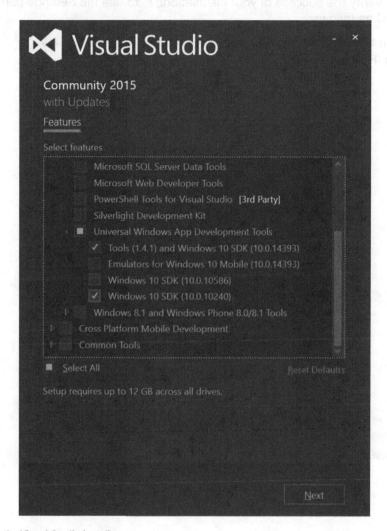

Figure 12-6. The the Visual Studio installer

Verifying Installations

A good way to verify the success of your installations is to use the Settings panel on your Windows 10 PC as follows:

1. From the Windows Start menu, type **settings** or click the Settings icon (Figure 12-7).

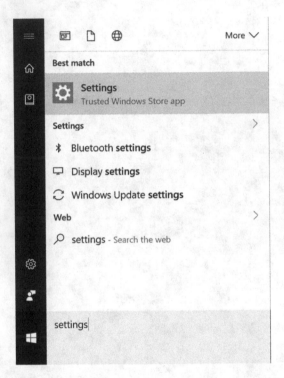

Figure 12-7. Accessing Setting in Windows 10

2. From Settings, choose System ➤ Apps and Features.

    If this isn't visible, just type in **Features**, and then select Apps and
    Features (Figure 12-8). You should now see the list of installed
    applications.

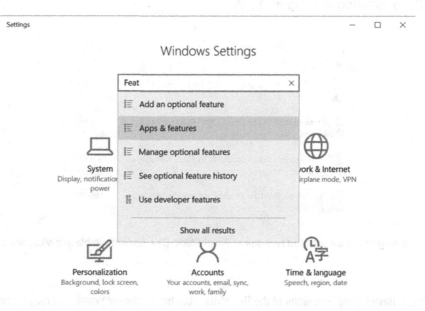

Figure 12-8. Locating Apps and Features

3. Scroll down to Microsoft Visual Studio C++ Redistributable.

   You should see a version for 2015 (x64) and (x86) as well as the build numbers.

4. Below those, you should see Microsoft Visual Studio Community 2015 with updates (Figure 12-9).

Microsoft Visual C++ 2015 Redistributable (x... Microsoft Corporation	23.5 MB 9/27/2016	
Microsoft Visual C++ 2015 Redistributable (x... Microsoft Corporation	19.5 MB 9/27/2016	
Microsoft Visual Studio 2015 Shell (Isolated) Microsoft Corporation	53.7 MB 9/30/2016	
Microsoft Visual Studio 2015 Tools for Unity Microsoft Corporation	55.9 MB 9/17/2016	
Microsoft Visual Studio Community 2015 with... Microsoft Corporation	1.99 GB 10/2/2016	

Figure 12-9. Checking to see the installed versions of Visual Studio C++ Redistributable and Microsoft Visual Studio

Tip   If you have multiple versions of the Redistributable from different years, you may be prompted to remove them.

5. Scrolling down farther, locate the Windows entries.

There you should have Windows SDK AddOn and Windows Software Development Kit (Figure 12-10).

Figure 12-10. Checking for installed versions of Windows SDK AddOn and Windows Software Development Kit

Obviously, this software undergoes regular updates, so you will want to use the most current versions.

If you do find that you are missing anything, you could modify the Visual Studio installation as shown next to select the new options. Again, ensure that you have at least Update 3 for Visual Studio. You can always check this via the Help ➤ About menu in Visual Studio.

To manually open the Visual Studio install to add the Windows 10 SDK when you don't yet have it, do the following:

1. In the Apps and Features opened previously, look for Visual Studio and click the Modify button (Figure 12-11).

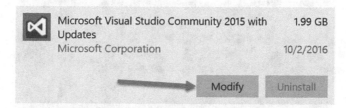

Figure 12-11. Modifying an installed version of Microsoft Visual Studio

2. When Visual Studio loads, click Modify again (Figure 12-12).

Figure 12-12. The Visual Studio updater

3. Choose the latest SDK version available to you.

If you have other items selected in the list beyond what is shown here, that is okay (Figure 12-13).

The Windows 10 SDK should now be installed.

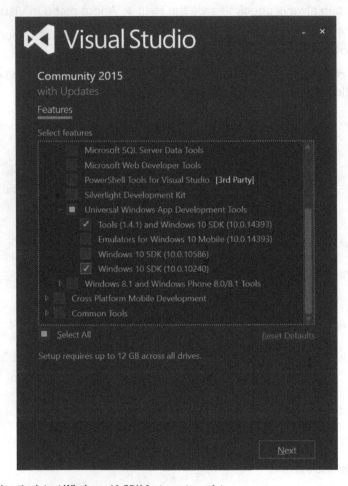

Figure 12-13. Selecting the latest Windows 10 SDK features to update

Setting Your Build Defaults

Now is a good time to set up the default build settings that Unity will use to package up your application for Windows Store. Each build is referred to as a *Player*. If you build for Windows Store, that's the Windows Store Player.

1. Bring up the Build settings in Unity with File ➤ Build Settings (Figure 12-14).

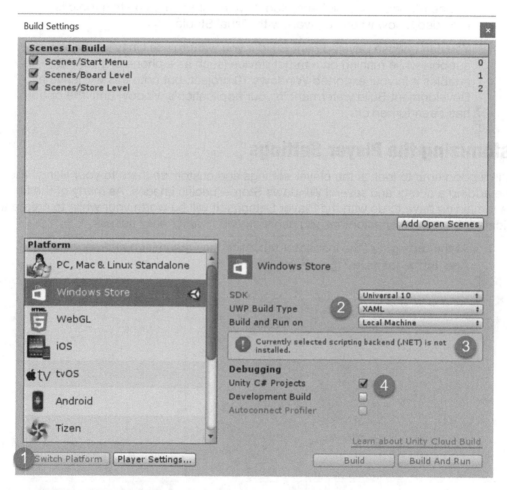

Figure 12-14. The Unity Build Settings

2. Select Windows Store in the list and click Switch Platform to set Windows Store as the default build platform (Figure 12-14, 1).

3. Select the SDK as Universal 10, UWP Build Type as XAML, and finally click Build (Figure 12-14, 2).

> **Tip**   If you notice an error that the currently selected scripting backend is not installed
> (Figure 12-14, 3), ensure that you have installed it in your Unity setup as mentioned earlier.

4.   Optional: Activate the Unity C# Projects check box (Figure 12-14, 4).

Activating the Unity C# Projects check box enables your build to contain
your Unity source code for debugging while running your app on your
device (Phone, PC, HoloLens, Xbox). More information on this topic is
provided below when you work with Visual Studio.

You can choose Development Build if you want to use Unity's profiler
support while running on a target device (such as a phone or your PC). This
enables it in your exported Windows 10 project, but note this will leave a
Development Build watermark in your application's window until the option
has been turned off.

Customizing the Player Settings

Now is a good time to look at the player settings and customize them to your liking. You
will be adding a cursor and several Windows Store–specific images. As many of the final
tasks remaining have to do with the Player Settings, it will be worth your while to create a
duplicate tab for the Inspector that you can lock and float for easy access.

1.   At the top right of the Inspector tab, click the Option icon and choose
Add Tab ➤ Inspector (Figure 12-15).

Figure 12-15. Adding another Inspector tab

2. Choose File ➤ Build Settings and then click the Player Settings button (Figure 12-16). Alternatively, choose Edit ➤ Project Settings ➤ Player.

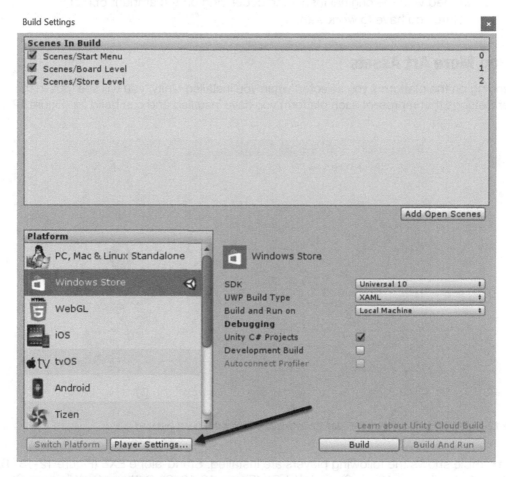

Figure 12-16. Accessing Player Settings through the Build Settings

3. As you have done in earlier chapters, turn on the lock icon to keep this tab from switching to your other objects or assets (Figure 12-17).

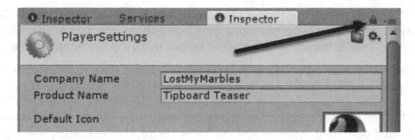

Figure 12-17. Locking the new Inspector tab

4. Optionally, drag the tab off to create a floating window (by dragging upward), a new column (by dragging downward), or just leave it tabbed with the original Inspector, depending on the amount of real estate you have to work with.

Adding More Art Assets

Depending on the platforms you selected when you installed Unity, you will see tabs in the Player Settings that represent each platform you have installed and can build for (Figure 12-18).

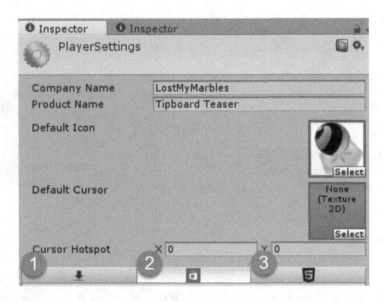

Figure 12-18. Player Settings showing a tab for each platform that has been installed

This example shows the following players are installed: Stand-alone EXE (Figure 12-18, 1), Windows Store (Figure 12-18, 2), and WebGL (Figure 12-18, 3). Settings for Windows Store are currently selected.

When you set the Build Settings to a particular platform, its corresponding tab will be active in the Player Settings. Before submitting your app to Windows Store, you should double-check each section to make sure everything has been covered.

In the top section, you added the Product Name, Tipboard Teaser, and a bogus Company Name, LostMyMarbles. When you have acquired a developer account, you will have created a publisher name. That is the name that should be put in as the Company Name.

You have already added an icon for desktop deployment, but have not yet added a custom cursor. With touch-enabled devices, a cursor is obviously not required and is in fact suppressed. In earlier versions of Unity, custom cursors required careful attention to layers to make sure they were drawn last, or on top of the rest of the scene. Now, however, Unity supports an actual operating system–type cursor (a.k.a. hardware cursor) making the use of simple custom cursors extremely easy.

A quick check of the Unity docs will *not* tell you that the hardware cursor size is going to be 32 × 32 pixels regardless of the image size or Windows pointer scheme. Oversized cursors would have to be made and handled through code as sprites. For this game, a simple hardware cursor will be fine.

Let's go ahead and create a cursor now:

1. Locate the Tipboard Cursor image in the Build Images folder.

2. Set its Texture Type to Cursor.

    In the Preview window, note that the image is 32 × 32 pixels.

3. Click Apply and drag the new cursor texture into the Default Cursor slot in the top section of the Player Settings.

4. Move the mouse so the cursor is over the Game view.

    The cursor changes.

    With the cursor less generic than that provided by the operating system, you will probably want to suppress it on mouse drags in the Board Level. The Cursor is handled from the Cursor class and can be accessed from any script. Because you will want to turn it off and on when the Board it tilting, you will be adding the code to the Tiltboard script.

5. Open the Tiltboard script.

6. At the top of the OnMouseDown function, add the following:

    ```
    Cursor.visible = false;
    ```

    To bring it back on, you will add the OnMouseDown function's counterpart, the OnMouseUp function.

7. Add the OnMouseUp function:

    ```
    void OnMouseUp()
    {
        Cursor.visible = true;
    }
    ```

8. Save the script and test the tilt functionality.

The cursor disappears during mouse drag as expected. The code, however, has nothing to do with the mouse-down so also works anywhere else onscreen. The UI elements may override the hide functionality, depending on focus and state of the element.

The last item in the top section of the Player Settings is the Cursor Hotspot. The location in pixels uses the upper-left corner of the image as 0, 0. The Tipboard Cursor image was also designed to use that location as the hotspot, so you are good to go.

Building for Windows

Now you are all set to create your first UWP build with the Tipboard project. As with your very first test build in Chapter 1, Unity will generate a UWP Visual Studio solution that you will open with Visual Studio and complete the build. You could have done this step right after the player settings were defaulted to the Windows Store previously, but any additional changes you made wouldn't have modified your generated Visual Studio solution.

Tip   Unity won't overwrite a generated Visual Studio solution. It will update its own files (such as your in-game assets), but it won't overwrite things like name or icons. Unity does, however, generate a file called UnityOverwrite.txt in your Build folder (or whatever you chose to name yours). This file can be customized to overwrite files upon build. For example, if you wanted Unity to overwrite the package.appxmanifest file, which contains your project name, icons (logos), and more, you could change the line in the UnityOverwrite.txt file as shown next. The next time you create a build from Unity, that file will be overwritten.

Old: `Tipboard Teaser\Package.appxmanifest: modified`

New: `Tipboard Teaser\Package.appxmanifest: overwrite`

---

1. Load up the Build Settings again via File ➤ Build Settings.

2. Ensure that Windows Store is selected as per the default you set up earlier in this chapter.

3. Click Build, and when the folder selection dialog box opens, choose a *new* folder to write your build to (unless this is a repeat step, and then you can write to the same folder). A good practice is to create a folder called Builds (outside your project folder).

   Unity will show you a status bar as your application, the Player, is being built. If successful, you should see either a folder open, or on your taskbar you'll see it highlighted.

4. Open the folder.

   If the folder doesn't appear, it is empty, or the build finished quickly, a problem likely occurred in building your application.

5. If there was a problem with the build, click the status line to open the Console window or open it from the Windows menu and inspect the message.

   Hopefully, you sorted out all of the installs in Chapter 1 with your test build. If not, read the error messages closely and double-check your installs as per the previous section.

6. If the build has failed and you are sure it should not have, restart
    Unity and attempt the build again.

Assuming now that you have had a successful build and that the folder you created was fill
and has opened, you are ready to move on to Visual Studio to continue the build process.

1. If you do not have Explorer showing file extensions, it is advisable
    that you set it to do so now.

2. To open the new build of your UWP application in Visual Studio,
    double-click the generated Visual Studio solution, which has the .sln
    extension (Figure 12-19).

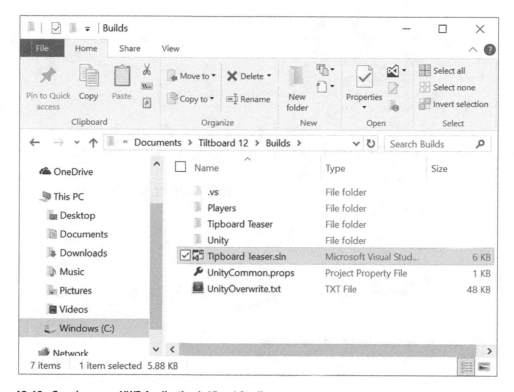

Figure 12-19. Opening your UWP Application in Visual Studio

When the solution opens in Visual Studio, typically you will have one to three projects
(Figure 12-20). If you selected Unity C# Projects in Unity's Build settings, you should see
three projects. Depending on where you have code in your project, Unity will generate
several additional C# projects. The first one you'll see, Assembly-CSharp, contains all of
your Unity C# game code contained within folders not called Plugins. If you opted for Unity
C# Project when you were setting up the Build Settings, you could go in there and make
minor modifications and recompile without Unity being open.

You could also set breakpoints in this code and debug your Unity code running on your device. *Breakpoints* halt the progress of evaluating code at that particular line in the code, allowing you to check on the status of variables and other information. From the breakpoint, you can step through the code one line at a time to see if it is going where you expected. When you have tracked down the problem or want to check in another place, you can tell Visual Studio to continue. For more information on breakpoints and stepping through code, see "Getting Started with Visual Studio" in the Dev Center.

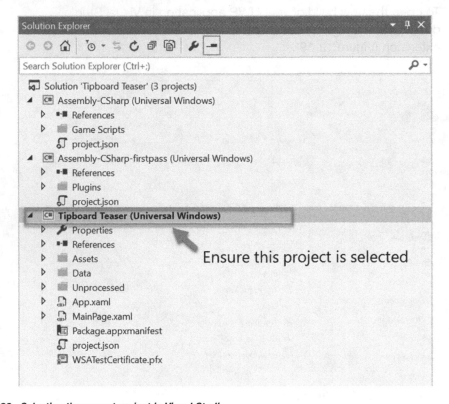

Figure 12-20. Selecting the correct project in Visual Studio

Next, you will select the processor type (Figure 12-21). The default build settings set your processor type to ARM—which is what you'll want *only* if you are building for or testing on a Windows Phone physical device. If you are testing for the Windows Phone by using the Windows Phone Emulator or for a Windows 10 PC (including HoloLens and Xbox), you'll want to choose x86. If you know you are on a 64-bit device (the majority of Windows 10 devices), you can alternatively choose x64. If you want to optimize your build and test it, you can choose Release or Master instead of Debug, called a Debug build, just to the left of the Processor drop-down).

Tip Release builds are optimized and still support Unity's profiler that you can run from within Unity, whereas Master is compiled with .NET Native and is fully optimized. Master builds take considerably longer to create (minutes) and are used for final testing and store submissions.

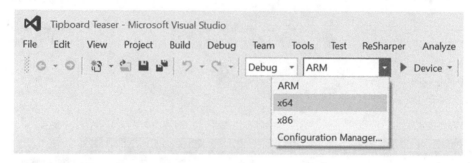

Figure 12-21. The processor type options

1. For testing on your local PC, set the processor to x64 and leave Debug selected (Figure 12-22).

Figure 12-22. Selecting the x64 processor type

2. Click the Local Machine play button to compile and *deploy* this UWP to your local machine.

You can view the build status in the lower-right corner of Visual Studio (Figure 12-23).

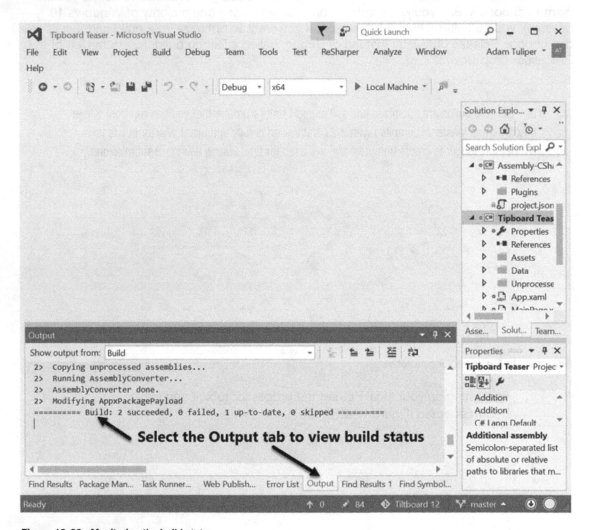

Figure 12-23. Monitoring the build status

When the application launches, you'll see Development Build in the lower-right corner (Figure 12-24, bottom right) because this is a Debug build (that is, you have Debug selected in the preceding step) or you still have Development Build selected in Unity's player settings for Windows Store Apps.

Also at the top of the screen is a debugging toolbar for XAML Windows applications. It isn't present in your Master builds—so this isn't something the end user sees. This debug toolbox is visible only because you are running your app from Visual Studio and you can collapse it by clicking its bar (Figure 12-24, top).

Figure 12-24. The launched Development Build

Having been deployed, the game is now running.

3. Give it a try to make sure things are working as expected.

4. To close the application, bring the mouse to the upper-right corner and click the window Close button, X (Figure 12-25, left).

Alternatively, you could click the Stop button in Visual Studio (Figure 12-25, right), but it's generally a safe practice to let an app safely close on its own if possible. While the Exit button would also stop the app, the convention for Windows Store apps or players is to use the window Close button. You will eventually swap out the Exit button for better game play instructions

Figure 12-25. Closing the Development Build

Exploring Screen Settings and Orientation

Let's look at options available for your Player. You can opt to attempt to have the application run in full-screen mode but you cannot force it to stay full-screen. This is up to the user, which was why GUI levels take more time and thought than 3D worlds. 3D space can be affected by a change in aspect ratio, giving your player a wider or narrower view of the environment. 2D screen space is affected by scale, in that it can become unreadable on small screens and overly large and clunky on large screens, hence the latest Unity UI system that allows you to compensate or even specify different configurations for different-sized screens.

Universal Windows applications have the ability to run on various rotations as well. They can support a single default orientation or autorotation, which automatically rotates your application when their device is turned, provided the device supports that. Choosing autorotation means you will want to select the supported rotations for your application. If the app is running on a device that supports rotation, it will not be redrawn for any of the deactivated rotations. In other words, if you rotate upside down but don't have Portrait Upside Down supported in the following dialog box, the application won't rotate. The little Tiltboard game requires a landscape orientation to give the player access to the HUD.

If the device doesn't support rotation, the application may get displayed in whatever default the orientation is for that device regardless of your specified settings. If I was on a device that didn't support rotation, and its default orientation was Portrait, if I specified only Landscape, it's possible the app would be launched in Portrait because that's all the device supports. These preferences apply to both the splash screen and the running game and should be kept in mind when you are setting the rotation options.

Let's set the default to be full-screen, and the default rotation (orientation) to be Landscape Right:

1. Open the Build Settings by choosing File ➤ Build Settings.

2. Click Player Settings and ensure that the Default Is Full Screen check box is activated (Figure 12-26).

3. For Default Orientation, choose Auto Rotation, and select Landscape Right and Landscape Left.

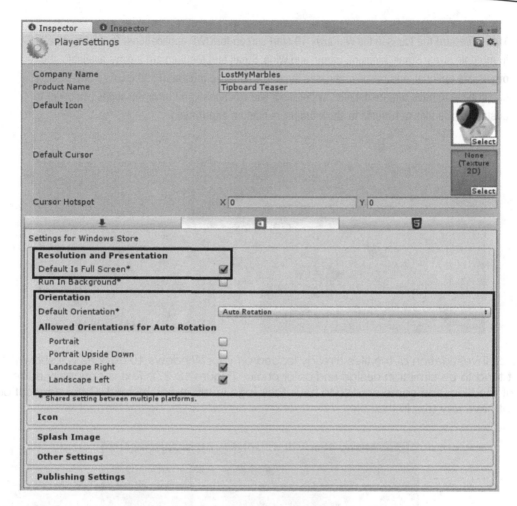

Figure 12-26. *Resolution, Presentation and Orientation in the Player Settings*

Providing Icons and Logos

If your curiosity has led you to investigate the Icon (called Logos in Windows Store applications) section of the Player Settings after you set the build to Windows Store, you may have been intimidated with the sheer number and sizes of images required. There are just a few required images (Unity generates these upon your first build). The rest are for an enhanced user experience to support users who could be running on a very wide array of screen resolutions and pixel densities. The images for Windows Store apps act as a logo (icon) in the Windows Store, the logo in your Start menu (which includes live tiles), and more. As such, they are an important tool for attracting players and supporting the most hardware possible.

Tip   *Tiles* are the icons in the Windows 10 start screen for UWP applications. They can come in multiple sizes: Small, Medium, Large, and Wide. Small and Medium are always available, the others are optional, and the user chooses them to customize their start screen. As a developer, you can choose to have a more detailed, wider tile if you so choose. You have the ability (via code) to customize the tiles at runtime to show the users custom information.

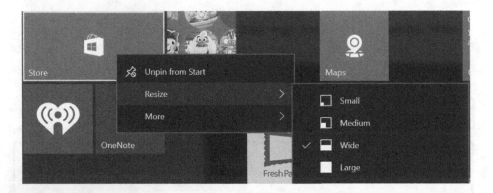

A quick investigation of the tiles already loaded on your Windows 10 devices will show that most tend to be similar in design and color choice (Figure 12-27). Text is optionally added on top of the tiles, and some choose to have their logo in the image instead. Other applications do not have any text in their tile.

Figure 12-27. Text added on top of tiles in Windows 10

By choosing a different wide logo, you can give a better layout when the user chooses to have a wide logo for your app on their start screen. Figure 12-28 shows an example of a medium and wide tile.

Figure 12-28. Regular and wide width tiles

By assigning these icons (a.k.a. logos and tiles) in the Player Settings, they will automatically get pushed down to Visual Studio. Note that Unity expects a Texture 2D type of image if you set these from within Unity. Since you are going to generate so many, it is recommended that you not set them at this time in Unity's Player Settings, but wait until you are working in Visual Studio.

Generating them one by one can be a tedious task, but several tools are at your disposal to generate the various icon sizes you need. The most important thing to understand is that you *should not use a single image and resize it to fit the various sizes*. For UWP, the scaling also includes various margin sizes that must be adhered to. This allows Windows 10 to automatically select the correct icon or tile sizes during the download for the target device as well as crop them depending on usage and device.

For the current guidelines, visit https://msdn.microsoft.com/windows/uwp/controls-and-patterns/tiles-and-notifications-app-assets or search the Windows Dev Center for "Guidelines for Tile and Icon Assets." It is highly recommended that you at least take a look through the article. The bare minimum tiles you must have are as follows:

> *Small*: 71 × 71, used on the Start screen
>
> *Medium*: 150 × 150, Start screen
>
> *Wide*: 310 × 150, Start screen
>
> *Large* (desktop only, not mobile): 310 × 310, Start screen
>
> *App List* (icon): 44 × 44, used in search results, shortcuts, Explorer

Microsoft recommends that for each tile size, you provide not only these sizes (referrred to as 100, or 100 percent) but in addition, 200- and 400-scale factors. So for the small logo, you should have at least 71 × 71, 142 × 142, and 284 × 284 sizes.

Unity will generate the placeholder images for the 100 percent scale. However, you will be happy to know that an extension is available in Visual Studio that will generate all the images for you. The UWP Tile Generator, available at `https://visualstudiogallery.msdn.microsoft.com/09611e90-f3e8-44b7-9c83-18dba8275bb2`, installs into Visual Studio (it is also open sourced at `https://github.com/shenchauhan/UWPTileGenerator`).

When you want a quick way to see these logos in action, check out a repository acquired from Paul Thomson (thanks Paul!) on GitHub at `https://github.com/adamtuliper/uwp-visual-assets` (Figure 12-29). This will allow you to run a sample project and see when the various logos/icons are used. Open this project's package.appxmanifest and click an icon to see its purpose if you ever forget it.

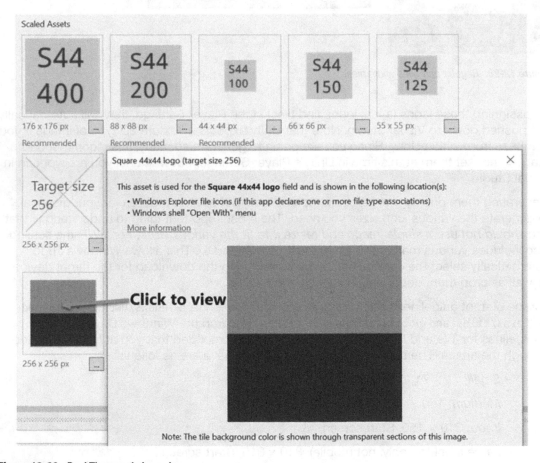

Figure 12-29. *Paul Thomson's icon viewer*

That sample project offers a nice way to view even the scaling sizes that Windows will choose because it lists the size on most of the icons. In Figure 12-30, you see a start screen using Square 44 × 44 at 150 percent scale (thus 66 × 66) and Square 150 at 150 percent scale (thus 225 × 225). Windows automatically chooses the scale factors based on display settings.

Figure 12-30. The test project's icon loaded in Windows

If you are familiar with and have access to a vector-based authoring program such as Adobe Illustrator, the simplest way to generate your icons is by creating a vector-based master (.svg extension) and letting the Visual Studio extension do the rest of the work for you. If you prefer a more complex raster-type image (.png is the recommended extension), you can also use the extension to generate the sizes and then touch up the images manually where required. For best results, it is recommended that you use an SVG image, and ensure that it has very little padding and scales the best across the various resolutions.

> **Tip** If you do not have Adobe Illustrator, a free alternative is the open source vector drawing program, Inkscape. While it may not be as full-featured as a fully commercial product, it has most of the functionality you will need and has a fairly shallow learning curve. Unfortunately, the UWP Tile Generator does not currently read Inkscape's version of the .svg format, but several users have devised a means of generating the various sizes required for your apps.

Let's give the UWP Tile Generator a try with a vector image and configure the icon options:

1. Follow the link provided to download the UWP Tile Generator.

2. Make sure Visual Studio is not running and then double-click the downloaded UWPTileGenerator.vsix file to install it.

3. Open Visual Studio and then open the Visual Studio *solution* for the
    Tipboard project.

    You will have to bring your SVG file into the Visual Studio solution manually,
    as it won't be automatically added by Unity. There are two ways to do this;
    both will be covered so you understand how files get added to your project.

    The icon loaded into Unity earlier in the project is more appropriate for a
    desktop solution. Locate the image, TileIcon.svg, in the Chapter 12 Assets
    folder.

4. Switch back to Visual Studio and bring the Explorer window into
    view.

5. Drag and drop TileIcon.svg from the Explorer window into the Assets
    folder in Visual Studio (Figure 12-31).

    The folder in Visual Studio named Assets isn't to be confused with the
    Assets folder in your Unity project. The two are unrelated.

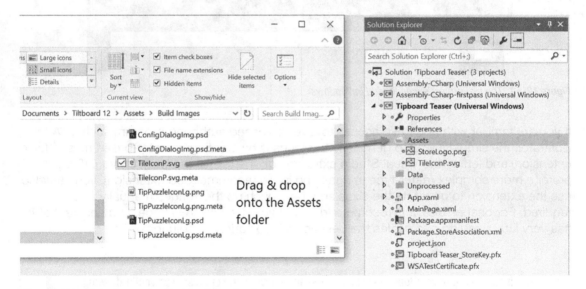

Figure 12-31. Bringing an svg file into Visual Studio

Alternatively, you can right-click the Assets folder in Visual Studio, choose Add/Existing Item, and navigate to the Chapter 12 Assets folder. Select TileIconP.svg to add it to the Assets folder in Visual Studio.

6. In Visual Studio, right-click Assets/TileIconP.svg and choose Generate UWP Tiles (Figure 12-32).

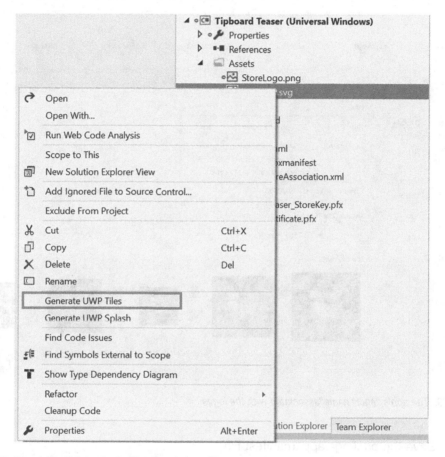

Figure 12-32. The right-click method of loading the svg file

7. Double-click the Package.appxmanifest file in Visual Studio's file list (the Solution Explorer window) and navigate to the Visual Assets tab to view all of the images that have been set up in the project.

8. Enable showing the application name printed on the logo in the Start screen by activating the deactivated check boxes under Show Name.

    The name displayed on the logo is what is entered in the Short Name field right above the check boxes, which is Tipboard Teaser (Figure 12-33).

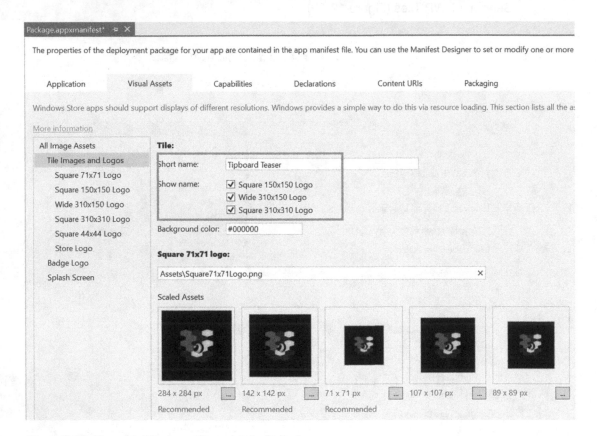

Figure 12-33. The app's "short name" associated with the logos

9. Save the package.appxmanifest file.

Anytime you go through the build process from Unity to generate the Visual Studio solution, these icon settings won't be overwritten. If for some reason you plan on deleting your generated project on occasion you'll either need to repeat the preceding image-generation process or bring the generated files into your Unity project and assign them in the Icon section of the Player Settings. (A use case for this is when you set up settings in Unity's Player Settings that you want to be pushed down to the Visual Studio solution.)

Once again, Windows Store doesn't require all of the images that were generated. You may have noticed that initially Unity generates five images for you. That is all you technically require. However, having all of the images will allow you to run on multiple display resolutions more effectively.

Having added the images to the built solution in Visual Studio, it is unnecessary to add them to the Unity project. If you want to do so anyway, just to keep all of the assets in the same place, follow these steps. Again, this is optional if you've successfully generated the tiles in Visual Studio.

1. Create a folder in Unity's Project view window under Assets and name it **Windows Images**.

2. Copy the new images from the Visual Studio solution's Assets folder and paste them into the new folder.

    If you have opted not to go through the image-generating process, alternatively you can import the Unity package, WindowsIcons. unitypackage, that contains all of the processed images. It can be found in the Chapter 12 Assets folder.

3. Open Unity, go to File ➤ Build Settings and click Player Settings.

4. Open the Icon section.

Figure 12-34 shows where you can assign names that will show up on the tiles as well as all of the individual tile sizes. Feel free to add names if you wish.

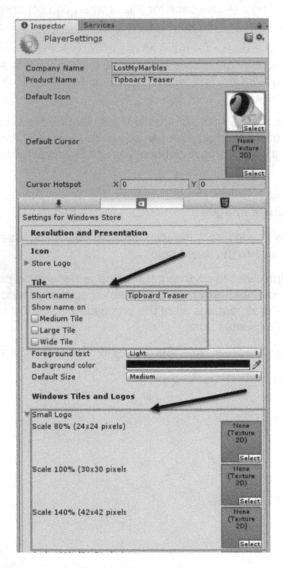

Figure 12-34. Unity Tiles and names assigned in Unity's Player Settings

5.   From the Build Images folder, locate and apply the corresponding texture to each tile or logo type by clicking the small Select button on each Texture 2D empty image preview or by dragging and dropping them directly from the Project view.

Adding the Splash Screen

If you have a Pro or a Plus Unity license, you have the option to customize or even remove the (Powered by) Unity splash screen that appears while your app loads. These settings are in the Player Settings (Figure 12-35). If you have only Unity Personal edition, this option is grayed out, but you can still customize your splash screen. If this option is enabled for you, you can assign your splash screen images here.

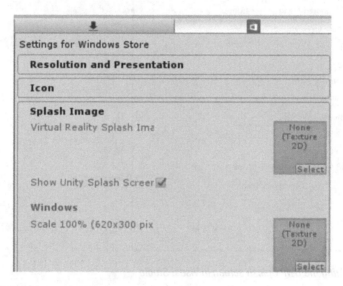

Figure 12-35. The Splash screen options in the Player Settings

If you do choose to use the Unity splash screen (and you have the Plus or Pro Unity license), you also have the option to use the light or dark color scheme. At the bottom of the Splash Screen section, you have the added option of setting the color of the Unity splash screen as well.

Let's customize the application's splash screen, independent of Unity's. If you have only an icon image to work with, the splash screen can be easily customized inside of the generated UWP solution in Visual Studio.

1. In Visual Studio, right-click the Assets/TileIconP.svg file and choose Generate UWP Splash (Figure 12-36).

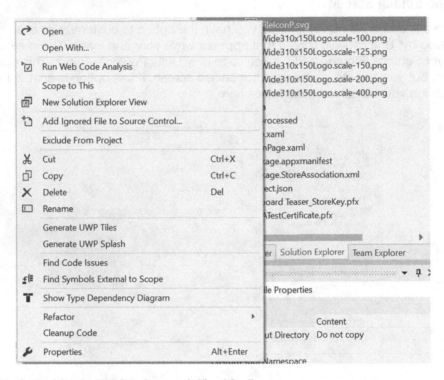

Figure 12-36. Customizing the UWP Splash screen in Visual Studio

2. Open Package.appxmanifest file and verify the various size splash screens that have been generated for you (Figure 12-37).

The next time you run the application, your custom splash screen will be displayed in addition to Unity's splash screen, unless you opted not to display Unity's.

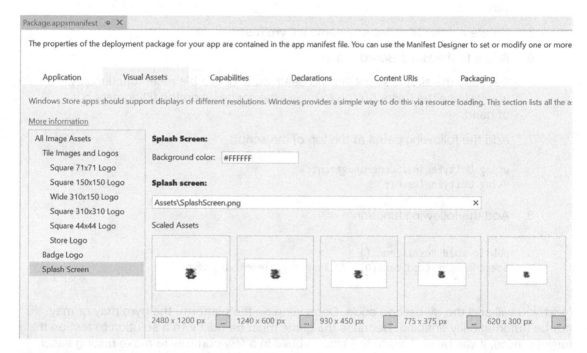

Figure 12-37. The generated Splash screens in Visual Studio

Enabling the Gyroscope Functionality

Most of the essentials have now been taken care of. With the confidence of knowing the app will successfully build for UWP and that you will be able to test on an Gyroscope-enabled device, you are now ready to tackle the gyroscope code. The Tiltboard project is far too complex at this point to be using to test new functionality, so you will reuse an early part of the Board Test scene to develop the basic gyroscope code. Aside from getting the gyroscope code to work, the most important goal is to make sure the camera has the correct orientation to match your finished scene. This will dictate which board axes get mapped to the gyro values returned by the gyroscope.

1. From the Chapter 12 Assets folder, load the BasicBoard. Unitypackage into your Porting Tests project.

2. Drag the Basic Board prefab into your Button Test scene's Hierarchy view.

3. Delete the original Main Camera from the scene and drag the imported camera and Directional Light out of the Basic Board group, agreeing to break the prefab instance.

4. In the Scene view, set to a Top view, move the Marble to the top of the board, and check that it appears in the same place in the camera view.

5. Create a new C# script and name it **GyroTest**.

6. Add it to the Basic Board group.

    Because the simple scene has no death zone or Marble reset functionality, you will use the Reset button to reload the scene when the tilting gets out of hand.

7. Add the following paths at the top of the script:

    ```
    using UnityEngine.SceneManagement;
    using UnityEngine.UI;
    ```

8. Add the following function:

    ```
    public void ResetScene () {
    SceneManager.LoadScene(0); // load the element 0 scene
    }
    ```

Next you will add the gyroscope code. Depending on the platform, the gyro may or may not be automatically enabled. Because the game must be built into a solution to test on the target device, it will be well worth the time to build in a few controls to make testing easer. You will eventually allow your player to switch between touch/mouse drag, gamepad, and gyroscope.

1. In the Start function, add the following:

    ```
    Input.gyro.enabled = true;
    ```

2. Add the following variables:

    ```
    float yRotation;
    float xRotation;
    float zRotation;
    float speed = 1f; // sensitivity adjustment

    public bool xOn;
    public bool yOn;
    public bool zOn;
    public Slider slider;

    public Text text;
    ```

As you have probably guessed, you will want a means of adjusting the sensitivity of the gyroscope. The speed variable will allow you to do so through a slider. The Boolean variables will allow you to isolate the axes while testing.

3.   Add the following code to the Update function:

```
if (xOn) xRotation += -Input.gyro.rotationRateUnbiased.x * speed;
else    xRotation = 0;

if (yOn) yRotation += -Input.gyro.rotationRateUnbiased.y * speed;
else    yRotation = 0;

if (zOn) zRotation += -Input.gyro.rotationRateUnbiased.z * speed;
else    zRotation = 0;

transform.eulerAngles = new Vector3(xRotation, yRotation, zRotation);
```

In this code, the gyro.rotationRateUnbiased value for each axis is added to the existing rotation and then multiplied or adjusted by the speed value. The last line sets the board's rotation by using the new values.

Next, you will add the function that will update the speed when the slider is accessed and report the number to the text object.

4.   Add the speed adjustment function:

```
public void SetSpeed (float value) {
    speed = value;
    text.text = value.ToString();
}
```

5.   And the functions for the on/off axes:

```
public void SetX (bool state) {
    xOn = state;
}
public void SetY (bool state) {
    yOn = state;
}
public void SetZ (bool state) {
    zOn = state;
}
```

6.   Save the script.

At this point, you are probably anxious to test the gyroscope code, so to save time, you can add the extra UI controls from a Unity package:

1. Delete the Button from the scene but leave the Event System.

2. Import the TestCanvas.unitypackage to your project.

3. Drag the Canvas into the Hierarchy view.

4. Select the Reset Button. In the existing On Click event, load Basic Board as the Object and GyroTest ➤ `ResetScene()` as the function.

5. Select Toggle X. In the existing On Value Changed event, load Basic Board as the Object and GyroTest ➤ SetX as the function.

   Note that there is also a SetX (bool) option. In the first, the check box state is passed directly into the SetX's argument, state. With the second, SetX (bool), you are provided with a check box just below the selected script/function, where you can dictate what value is sent to the function. While that may not make any sense with the simple true/false toggle state, if you were using the toggles as option or radio boxes, you could pass the appropriate value (of whatever type) directly to the function that would initiate the proper tasks.

6. Select Toggle Y, in the existing On Value Changed event, load Basic Board as the Object and GyroTest ➤ SetY as the function.

7. Select Toggle Z, in the existing On Value Changed event, load Basic Board as the Object and GyroTest ➤ SetZ as the function.

8. Select Slider, in the existing On Value Changed event, load Basic Board as the Object and GyroTest ➤ SetSpeed as the function.

9. Select the Basic Board and assign the Slider UI object as the Slider parameter and the Message UI object as the Text parameter.

10. Save the scene and save the project.

11. Click Play and test the check boxes, slider, and finally the Reset button.

With the test scene ready to go, it's time to build the solution and deploy it for testing:

1. Open up Build Settings and click Build.

2. Choose the same folder that you created for the first test project in Chapter 1.

3. Unity will overwrite its own data but won't overwrite any of the custom changes you've made. Power users can override Unity's overwriting behavior by editing the UnityOverwrite.txt file in the Build folder as mentioned earlier the chapter.

4. Open the solution again in Visual Studio. If it was already open, you will likely have been prompted to reload it; in that case, choose Reload All.

5. Because you are reusing the solution, the x86 setting has remained in place.

6. Click the Debug button on the top toolbar in Visual Studio and test the gyroscope by turning the axes on one at a time and adjusting the speed slider until the Marble has a reasonable amount of responsiveness.

    The first thing that you will have noticed is that the gyro axes are mapped wrong for the direction your camera is pointed. Experimentation will show that the last line in the Update function should be as follows:

    ```
    transform.eulerAngles = new Vector3(xRotation, zRotation, yRotation);
    ```

7. Feel free to make the changes if you wish, but you are now armed with the information required to add the acceleration code to the Tiltboard project.

Tip When running a Debug build, any output caused by using Debug.Log() will be written out to a UnityPlayer.log file. Note that output from print() statements will not be included. The player log is located under <user>\AppData\Local\Packages\<productname>\TempState. See also log files. These output values along with other helpful diagnostic information can also be viewed at runtime in Visual Studio's output window, accessible via Debug/Windows/Output.

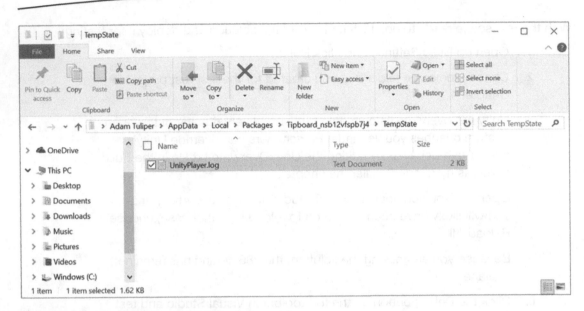

Figure 12-38. Visual Studio's Unity Player log

Finishing the Tiltboard Project

There are a few more things you will do to finish the functionality of the Tiltboard project and prepare it for deployment on Windows Store. The most obvious is, of course, adding the accelerometer code. Less obvious will be gracefully handling interruptions from other apps such as Skype, incoming phone calls, or text messages. A third consideration will be to test the in-app purchase of the tipCoins. A nice option with Windows Store is that you can allow players to "purchase" items for free.

Adding the Gyroscope Code

Let's begin by adding the gyroscope code to the project. When you test the game for the first time, you will probably notice that the gyroscope will suck up quite a bit of resources. That means that you should allow players to adjust the sensitivity of the tilting to better match their device. It also means that the speed value should be retained between levels so the player doesn't have to adjust it for each new game.

Another thing you will discover is that the mouse-drag functionality for tilting the board works with touch and drag. Although this is probably a pleasant surprise, you will want to restrict the player to one or the other input type at any one time.

Most of the code will be added to the TiltBoard script, so you will begin there:

1. Open the Tiltboard project.

2. Open the TiltBoard script.

3. Add the following variables:

```
// gyroscope ***
bool gyroEnabled = false;
internal float yRotation;
internal float xRotation;
internal float zRotation;

float speed = .065f; // sensitivity adjustment for gyroscope
public MarbleManager marbleManager; // to repress tilt when over tilted
public GameObject aCButton; //gyroscope/drag toggle
public GameObject aCSpeed; // gyroscope sensitivity slider
Slider slider; // the Slider component
Persistent persistent; // holder of data
```

The first variable controls whether gyroscope or dragging is in charge of tilting the board. The three floats manage the gyroscope changes. The speed is set to an amount that worked well on a Surface Pro. Feel free to adjust this number.

The MarbleManager is in charge of resetting the board when the Marble escapes, so it will need to tell the TiltBoard script to repress gyroscope functionality during a reset. The other variables are for the UI additions. Persistent is where you will store the player's speed preference.

4. In the Start function, identify and assign two of the variable's values:

```
slider = aCSpeed.GetComponent<Slider>();
persistent = GameObject.FindWithTag("Holder").GetComponent<Persistent>();
```

5. Also in the Start function, add the following:

```
if (SystemInfo.supportsGyroscope) {// check for acceleromter support
    Input.gyro.enabled = true; // enable hte acceleromter
    gyroEnabled = true;
    aCButton.SetActive(true); // show the toggle for acc/drag
    aCSpeed.SetActive(true); // show the speed slider
    GetACInfo(); // update the speed variable
}
else aCButton.SetActive(false);
```

In this code, you first check to see whether the device supports an gyroscope. If it does, you enable it. Next you set the variable that keeps track of which tilt functionality is active, and then you show the UI controls that are seen only if gyroscope functionality is present. Finally, you update the slider value to that stored in the Persistent script.

The code for setting the tilt is fairly straightforward. Note that the spin direction is always set to 0. The allowTilt flag is during board resets, while the gyroEnabled flag filters the tilt methods.

6. In the Update function, add the following:

```
if (!allowTilt || !gyroEnabled) return;

xRotation += -Input.gyro.rotationRateUnbiased.x * speed;
yRotation += -Input.gyro.rotationRateUnbiased.y * speed;

transform.eulerAngles = new Vector3(xRotation, 0, yRotation);
```

And now you will make the three functions that support the UI and manage the data. The first manages the tilt method.

7. Add the following function:

```
// gyroscope ***
public void ToggleGyroscope (bool state) {
    gyroEnabled = state;
    aCSpeed.SetActive(state); // if ac is on, show the slider
    persistent.gyroEnabled = gyroEnabled; // update enabled state
}
```

8. Add the function that manages the sensitivity:

```
// gyroscope ***
public void UpdateSpeed (float newSpeed) {
    speed = newSpeed;
    persistent.speed = speed; // update stored setting
}
```

9. Add the function that gets the data on startup:

```
// gyroscope ***
 void GetACInfo () {
    speed = persistent.speed; // get stored setting
    gyroEnabled = persistent.gyroEnabled;
    slider.value = speed; // update the slider
}
```

Note that you are also keeping track of the tilt functionality's current state.

The next section finishes up the functionality in the other scripts:

1. Open the Persistent script.

2. Add the following variables:

```
//gyroscope ***
internal float speed = .065f; // sensitivity adjustment
internal bool gyroEnabled ; // ac enabled state
```

3. Save the script.

4. Open the BoardManager script and add the following variable:

```
public TiltBoard tiltBoard; // gyroscope ***
```

5. In the `Update` function, below the `tiltBoard.UpdateBoard()` line, add this:

```
tiltBoard.allowTilt = true; // gyroscope ***
```

6. In the `StartBoardReset` function below the `resetBoard = true` line, add this:

```
tiltBoard.allowTilt = false; // gyroscope ***
```

7. Save the script.

8. Open the PathCellManagerscript.

9. In the `ProcessWinner` function, under the `marbleManager.repressInput = true` line, add the following:

```
Input.gyro.enabled = false; // gyroscope ***
```

10. Save the script.

Next you will add the new UI elements. To speed things up, you can bring these in from a Unity package and finish hooking them up to the code:

1. Open the Board Level scene.

2. Import the GyroscopeUI.unitypackage.

3. Locate the Gyroscope Group in the Prefabs folder and drag it into the Game Level GUI's Canvas.

4. Select the Toggle AC object in the Gyroscope Group and assign the Board Group as the Object in the On Value Changed event.

5. Set the function to TiltBoard ➤ ToggleGyroscope.

6. Select the AC Slider Speed object in the Gyroscope Group and assign the Board Group as the Object in the On Value Changed event.

7. Set the function to TiltBoard ➤ UpdateSpeed.

8. Save the scene and save the project.

Now you will build the updated project and test the new functionality on your Windows 10 device. For this test, a Surface Pro 4 was used, allowing the build to be deployed to Local Machine. If you are deploying to a device where installing Visual Studio is not practical, select Device instead and ensure that it is connected to your development machine by USB cable.

1. Create your build again from Unity.

2. Open the resulting Visual Studio solution and select Start Debugging from the Build menu.

3. Click Play, or press F5 on your keyboard.

    The Unity Load screen appears, and the newly updated game is loaded.

4. Test the game by toggling the gyroscope toggle button on and off.

    Note that when the gyroscope is off, you can tip the board with a finger touch and drag. Also note that there is no cursor.

5. Exit the debugging build.

Now that you know the mechanics of the game will work on devices with gyroscope functionality, it is time to think about managing the in-app and in-game purchases.

In-App Purchases

In this section, you will explore practical issues connected with in-app purchases. While you will want to test purchasing from an outside source, you will also want to consider what happens to the player's purchases should the game go down.

Saving Store and Game Data

In the scenario presented in the introduction to this section, you were made aware of a potential problem with both purchases made through Window Store, the tipCoins, and the in-game purchases of the Wheelbarrows (for moving the Banana Peels) and the Crushers (the guard character that destroys the peppermint candies).

In a networked game, especially those that are multiplayer, you would store player data on a server, where the player would be able to log in and run the game from different devices. Although many services offer cloud services, such as Microsoft Azure, server data storage is beyond the scope of this book.

Although it's not as flexible as a data store on a server, you can store data on the local device where the app has been deployed. Unity's PlayerPrefs allow you to store data in a format that is not easily hacked by typical casual players. Windows Store apps also have the ability to write roaming data that will get synchronized between your devices, though that is beyond the scope here, as it isn't integrated into Unity.

PlayerPrefs are easily updated, but it is important to know they are written back to disk only when you call `PlayerPrefs.Save()` or when the application exists gracefully (without a crash). It is best to explicitly save the values to prevent data loss (and angry players).

Before you begin coding the save and load functionality, you will be introduced to a slightly more advanced topic. Although most of the code involving the purchases resides in the StoreManager and Persistent scripts, the variables are accessed and updated from several scripts. The danger here is that you could theoretically change values before they were changed from an earlier call.

To safeguard against this happening, you will create copies of the main variables (currently fields) that will be *properties*. Properties provide you with a slightly different way to handle access to the variables. The first thing to do is to set the three main variables to `private`. Now the other scripts will have access to them only through their property counterparts' get and set accessors (methods). Note that the property names use the field names with the first letter changed to uppercase to keep things less confusing, though you'll find Unity uses nonstandard C# naming conventions for their property names.

1. Open the Persistent script.

2. Change the `cash`, `wheelbarrows`, and `candyCrushers` variables to private:

    ```
    private float cash;
    private int wheelbarrows = 0; // usable banana movers
    private int candyCrushers = 0; // usable peppermint crushers
    ```

3. Under the original variables, create the `Cash` property:

    ```
    public float Cash {
        get {
            return cash;
        }
        set {
            cash = value;
            PlayerPrefs.SetFloat("cash", Cash);
        }
    }
    ```

    With get, the value for the now `private` cash is immediately returned. To change it, the value sent through the set is immediately assigned to the private cash. Next, you will save the value to the device via the PlayerPrefs. For more information on PlayerPrefs, be sure to check out the Unity documentation. Something here on where exactly they are saved.

4. Create the Wheelbarrows property:

```
public int Wheelbarrows {
    get {
        return wheelbarrows;
    }
    set {
        wheelbarrows = value;
        PlayerPrefs.SetInt("wheelbarrows", Wheelbarrows);
    }
}
```

5. Create the CandyCrushers property:

```
public int CandyCrushers {
    get {
        return candyCrushers;
    }
    set {
        candyCrushers = value;
        PlayerPrefs.SetInt("candycrushers", CandyCrushers);
    }
}
```

In the CalculateWinCash function, you will save the three important values every time the player completes the game/level.

6. In the CalculateWinCash function, under the Cash = Cash + winCash line, add the following:

```
//user may have more points, but level
//has also ended save their current settings
SaveSettings();
```

The SaveSettings function is very simple. This forces the file containing your player preferences to be updated. Note that your preferences are not saved until this happens!

7. Save the player prefs to disk when SaveSettings is called:

```
//Saves player prefs to disk
public void SaveSettings() {
    //ensure the settings are saved when this is called (to disk)
    //Unity will save settings upon graceful exit, but let's ensure
    //user doesn't lose purchases now.
    PlayerPrefs.Save();
}
```

Now you will see about retrieving the properties from disk.

1. Create the following function to load the stored player prefs:

```
public void LoadSettings() {
    Cash = PlayerPrefs.GetFloat("cash", 0);
    Wheelbarrows = PlayerPrefs.GetInt("wheelbarrows", 0);
    CandyCrushers = PlayerPrefs.GetInt("candycrushers", 0);
}
```

These PlayerPrefs values are in what is called a *dictionary*. It's simply a key/value lookup. You ask for a key (for example, wheelbarrows) and you get the value back if one exists, or 0 for a default value.

You will want to load the saved data when the app is started.

2. At the bottom of the Awake function's if clause, add the following:

```
//Load the last saved values (if they exist)
LoadSettings();
```

3. Save the script.

The data is now saved when the level is completed, but it also should be saved after each purchase of tipCoins, Wheelbarrows, and candyCrushers. Because each transaction has a call to TransactionComplete, it will be a simple addition.

4. Open the StoreManager script.

5. At the top of the TransactionComplete function, add the following to ensure that we save our coin counts right after a successful purchase:

```
persistent.SaveSettings();
```

6. Save the script.

The data will be maintained nicely on the local device. Next you will investigate a practical means of testing the purchase of the tipCoins with "real" money.

Testing Purchases

At this point, you will want to test your purchases from outside sources. You have two choices for doing so. The first can be done using a simulator, which requires code changes to the Windows 10 simulator to fake a real purchase. The second is carried out through Windows Store and, as you may guess, requires an app developer license.

The Windows Store supports multiple types of in-app purchases (IAPs), covering consumables (for example, coins), subscriptions, and more. You are going to implement in-app purchases into Tiltboard to enable purchasing of coins—a consumable product.

Integrating in-app purchases is a problem that has several methods available for your implementation. Microsoft has this process documented in its developer documentation fairly extensively and has published source samples to do this from Unity at `https://github. com/Microsoft/unityplugins`. Even easier, though, is the fact that Unity has added in-app purchase support that can easily be extended to support additional platforms.

To use the built in in-app purchase support, you will have to do a couple of things. You will begin by enabling IAP services in your project. The IAP package will already be installed, but you may need a newer version.

> **Tip**   The Unity IAP, because it services many platforms, is constantly being updated. Unity recommends keeping up-to-date on this, and their dialog in services will help do this, but always back up your project before updating to ensure that your custom IAP code isn't overwritten.

1.   From the Window menu, select Services (Figure 12-39).

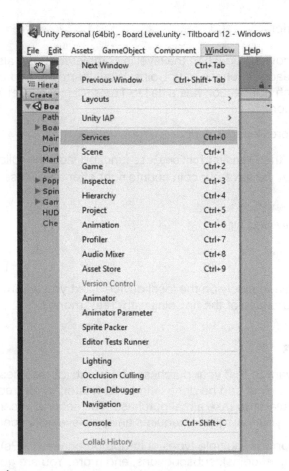

Figure 12-39. Selecting Services

2. In the resulting Services window, create a Unity Project ID—this is usually your Unity user ID (Figure 12-40).

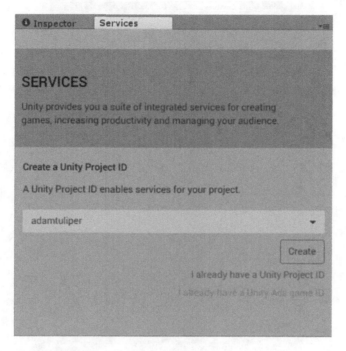

Figure 12-40. *Creating a Unity Project ID*

3.   Click to turn on IAP under In-App Purchasing (Figure 12-41).

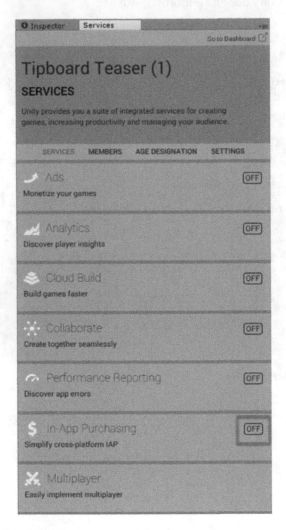

Figure 12-41. *Turning on In-App Purchasing*

4.   Confirm enabling IAP by clicking the Enable button (Figure 12-42).

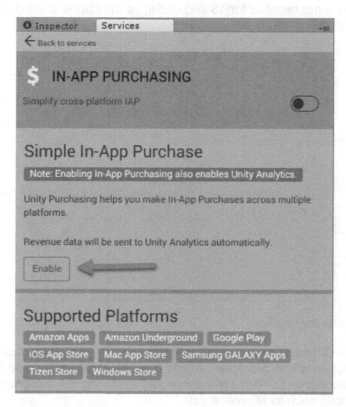

Figure 12-42. Confirming In-App Purchasing

5. Now choose the age range for your application.

    Tiltboard is not targeted for 13 and under, so the option is left deactivated (Figure 12-43).

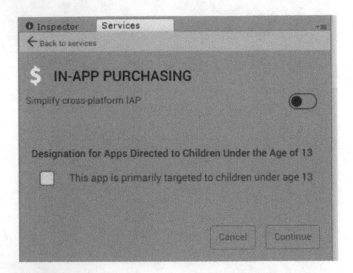

Figure 12-43. Selecting the age range

Note the Children's Online Privacy Protection Act (COPPA) compliance changes you will be prompted about. This affects ads that could be served up depending on COPPA compliance and assuming you integrate with an ad network, such as Microsoft Ads.

6. Click the Import or Reimport button if there are any updates to the in-app purchase libraries that Unity may prompt you about (Figure 12-44).

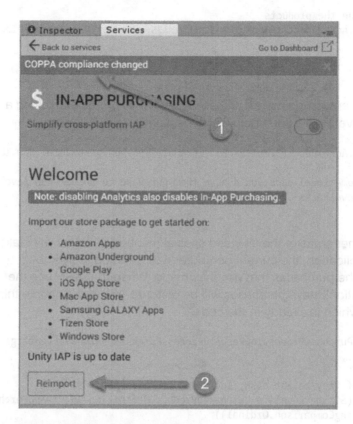

Figure 12-44. Checking for updates to in-app purchasing libraries

Configuring In-App Purchase Names

Follow the store submission process for the specific directions required to set up in-app purchases during the submission. The steps must be followed to ensure they match up with the names configured in the application.

In the Game Scripts ➤ WindowsStore/InAppPurchases file, you'll note there is a Coin75 in there with a specific string. This value is what needs to be set up in the Windows Store and defined in our in-app purchase API.

1. Examine the contents of the InAppPurchases script.

```
public class InAppPurchases
{
    //Note right side of the string is what needs to be registered in the store
    public const string Coins75 = "75.Coins";
}
```

2. Note that in the InAppPurchaseManager script in the `InitializeIAP` method, you let the system know about the IAPs you have:

```
// Define the products
builder.AddProduct(InAppPurchases.Coins75, ProductType.Consumable, new IDs
{
{InAppPurchases.Coins75, WindowsStore.Name}
});
```

3. If you were to add more purchase types (for example, unlocking a new Level Pack), you could do something like the following:

```
builder.AddProduct("LevelPack1", ProductType.NonConsumable, new IDs
{
    //Some level pack you'd have them purchase to unlock new levels
    {"LevelPack1", WindowsStore.Name}
});
```

4. Two other areas of the file need special mention. If a user reinstalls the application, the current computer won't immediately know about the purchases that user has made. When the user runs the application, these purchases will be restored. You must handle this case, which is already in the code.

```
public PurchaseProcessingResult ProcessPurchase(PurchaseEventArgs e){
    //......

    //If they bought cash, increment the amount and save it
    if (String.Equals(e.purchasedProduct.definition.id, InAppPurchases.Coins75,
    StringComparison.Ordinal))    {
        Persistent.instance.Cash += 75;
        //Ensure these are saved
        Persistent.instance.SaveSettings();
    }
}
```

Simulating Purchases

For localized testing of the purchasing process, you will require the built-in simulator. The simulator allows you to fake in-app purchases locally while developing rather than going to Windows Store. This gives you the ability to force different result codes for testing, such as success and failure.

1. Open the Game Scripts ➤ WindowsStore ➤ InAppPurchaseManager script and navigate to the `InitializeIAP` method.

2. In that method, change the following line of code to `true` to enable the simulation system for in-app purchases.

```
//***********************************
// You must remove this before building your release package
// for the store or you won't have real in-app purchases.
//***********************************
builder.Configure<IMicrosoftConfiguration>().useMockBillingSystem = true;
```

3. Save the script.

> **Important!**   Before you publish your application, you must set this value,
> useMockBillingSystem, to false or you will fail certification.

Running the simulator will give results as per Figure 12-45 when trying the in-app purchase while debugging.

Figure 12-45. Message from simulator while debugging

Making the Commitment

The second option for testing your in-app purchases is to upload a developer build to Windows Store. Before you can do so, you will be required to register as an app developer. A developer account lets you submit apps and add-ins to Microsoft marketplaces, including Windows Store, Office Store, and Azure Marketplace. A developer account is not required, however, to develop and test applications on your devices. That is a developer license, which is free. Note the difference in Visual Studio, which gives you the ability to register for either through the Project ➤ Store menu specifically when you are in a Universal Windows application project in Visual Studio (otherwise, the menu option for Project ➤ Store won't be visible, as it is context sensitive). See Figure 12-46.

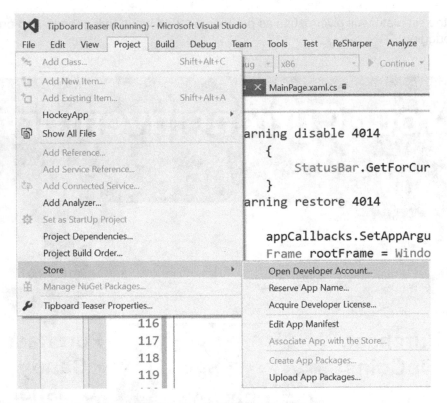

Figure 12-46. Registering for a developer account from within Visual Studio

Obtaining a Developer Account

Currently the cost is a one-time only fee of $19 USD for individuals and $99 USD for companies. To register as a developer and to learn more about the Universal Windows Platform in general, you can go to https://developer.microsoft.com and follow the Sign Up Now link. There you will be told what to expect and what you must provide during the sign-up process. You'll be asked to enter your contact information, choose a publisher display name, and provide a payment method.

To begin the sign-up process in earnest, you must be signed in with the Microsoft account that you want to associate with your developer account. If you don't already have a Microsoft account, you will be given a link to create one. If you downloaded Visual Studio components beyond the Unity install, you have probably already been asked to create a Microsoft account.

Following the next Sign Up prompt, you will be taken to the Microsoft Dev Center gateway, where you must either sign in or create a new account. If you create an account, you will have to return to the Microsoft Dev Center gateway to continue. The process is well documented, but is outlined here as well:

1. Go to `https://develop.microsoft.com` or choose Open Developer Account from Visual Studio, as shown in the prior section when a UWP application is open in Visual Studio.

2. Click Windows apps in the left column.

3. Click Get Started.

4. In Register as an App Developer, select Sign Up Now.

   You will be taken to the Window Dev Center and asked to sign in using the account you want to associate your app developer account with.

   Now you will be taken to the purchase page.

5. Select your account type: individual or company. Most small developers choose Individual, as company accounts require additional cost ($99) and business verification. Please research the account types via the link in the following Tip and choose what suits you best.

6. Provide a Publisher Display name.

> **Tip** It is a good idea at this point to click the Learn More link. It will take you to `https://msdn.microsoft.com/windows/uwp/publish/opening-a-developer-account#the-account-signup-process`, where you can get more in-depth information about the developer account.

In case you are not currently online, the paragraph on the Publisher Display Name is as follows:

Enter the publisher display name that you wish to use (50 characters or fewer). Note that if you enter a name that someone else has already selected, or if it appears that someone else has the rights to use that name, we will not allow you to select that name. For company accounts, the publisher display name must be your organization's registered business name or trade name. Select this carefully, as customers will see this name when browsing and will come to know your apps by this name.

7. Returning to the sign-up, fill in your contact information.

8. Pay a one-time registration fee (no prepaid credit cards are allowed). Students via a program at many schools called DreamSpark may have access to a Windows Store token to offset this fee. Those on Microsoft' BizSpark program also likely have this token available under their benefits.

9. On the next screen, read and accept the terms and conditions of the App Developer Agreement.

10. Select the check box to indicate you have read and accepted the terms.

11. Click Finish to confirm the purchase.

You will be taken to your account page, where the status will show that it is being processed. You will then receive an e-mail that you must respond to in order to confirm that the e-mail address is correct.

After responding to the e-mail, your dev account status should be active!

Packaging UWP Apps

To test or submit your app, you must first package it by choosing Create App Packages in Visual Studio. This process will create an appxupload file to send to Windows Store or an appxbundle that can be installed (side-loaded) onto another machine by double-clicking it. You will be creating the appxupload file to send to the store.

1. Ensure the Tipboard Teaser Universal Windows project is selected in Visual Studio (Figure 12-47).

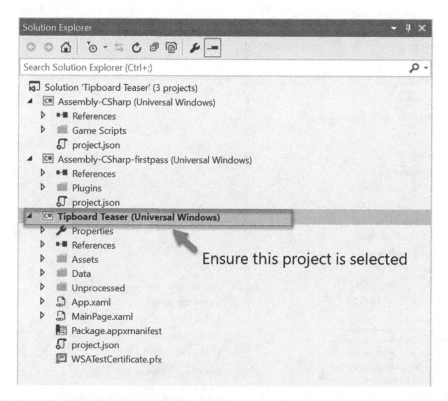

Figure 12-47. Selecting the project in Visual Studio

2. If you are building to run on the local machine, choose x64 (or if you know you are running on a 32-bit machine, choose x86).

3. Choose Project ➤ Store ➤ Create App Packages to tell Visual Studio to create a package that you can install onto devices (Figure 12-48).

You will eventually need to upload this package to Windows Store if you want to distribute it.

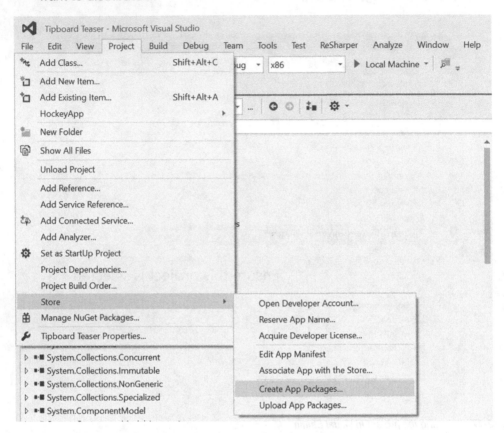

Figure 12-48. Creating a package that can be installed on devices

4. Confirm you want to build packages by choosing Yes on the next screen.

5. Enter a name for your application (Figure 12-49).

The name must be unique. Click Reserve, and it will process and reserve the application name for you. You have one year to publish your application before an unused name is returned back as available.

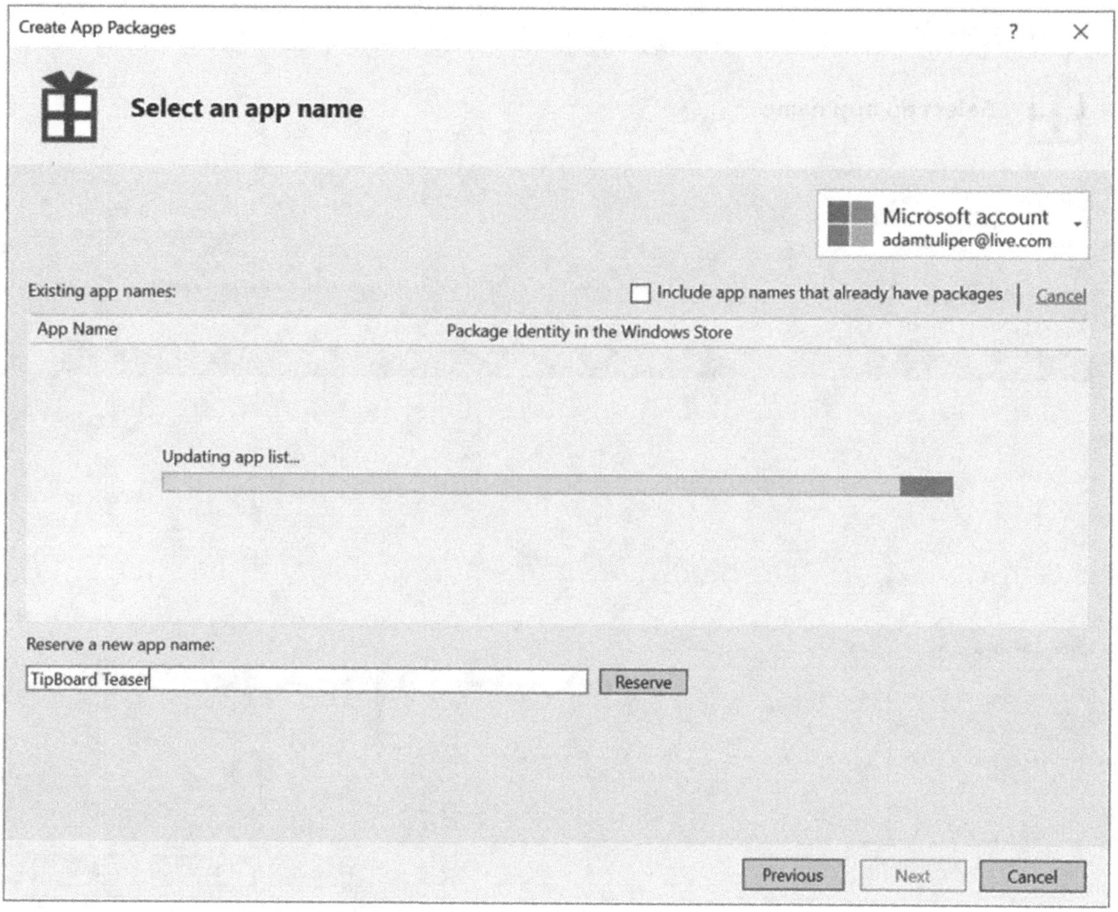

Figure 12-49. *Reserving an app name on Windows Store*

6. Choose your application from the Existing App Names list and click Next (Figure 12-50).

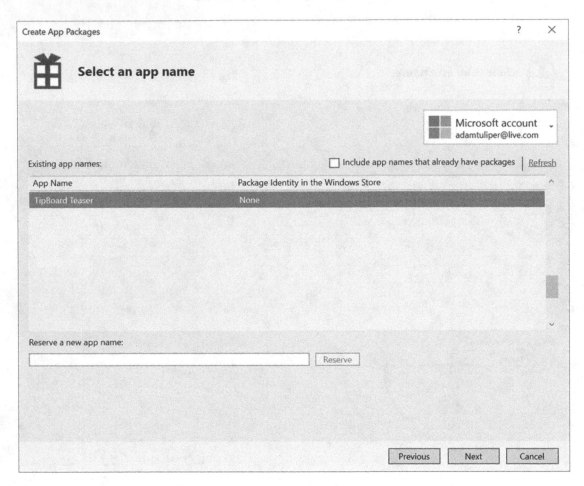

Figure 12-50. Selecting a name from your list of reserved names

7.   In the dialog box shown in Figure 12-51, select the following options to build for multiple platforms.

This will create multiple builds of your application that can run on 32-bit, 64-bit, and ARM processors. If you know you'll run on only, say, 32-bit machines at this time, then choose only 32-bit.

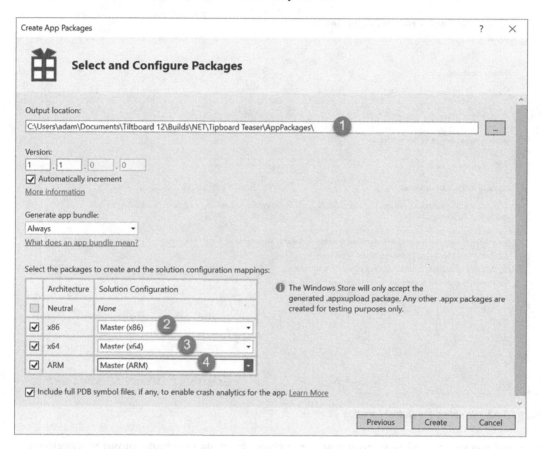

Figure 12-51. *Configuring the packages*

8.   Select or accept the location for the built package (Figure 12-51, 1).

9.   Choose Master x86 (Figure 12-51, 2).

10. Choose Master x64 (Figure 12-51, 3).

11. Choose Master ARM (Figure 12-51, 4).

Once completed, you'll either see an error to resolve (this should be rare) in Visual Studio or you'll see the completed dialog box.

12.   Click the link for the Output Location (Figure 12-52).

You will require it later on for submission to the store.

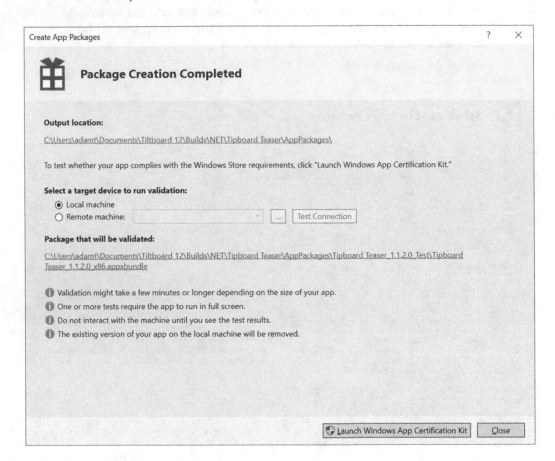

Figure 12-52. Selecting the Output Location

The resulting location should now have an .appxupload file you can upload to Windows Store (Figure 12-53).

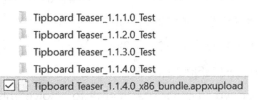

Figure 12-53. The generated appxupload file

You may have noticed in the preceding dialog box, the Launch Windows App Certification Kit. Microsoft recommends that you click it and read the next section at this time.

Windows App Certification Kit

Before submitting your app to the store for testing, purchase, free acquisition, or becoming Windows Certified, you should install and run the Windows App Certification Kit (WACK). This will help you validate and test it locally before you submit it for certification. Because you are using Visual Studio, you can run the Windows App Certification Kit when you create your app package.

The prerequisites are as follows:

- You must install and run Windows 10 with the Windows 10 SDK installed.

- You must have a valid developer license for your computer (if you've gone through the Create App Package procedure, you are all set up for this already).

Now, you will validate your Windows app by using the Windows App Certification Kit interactively.

1. You can run WACK from the completion of package creation in the prior step by clicking Launch Windows App Certification Kit; *if so, you can skip step 2.*

2. From the Start menu, search Apps, find Windows Kits, and click Windows App Cert Kit.

   a. From the Windows App Certification Kit, select the category of validation you would like to perform; in this case, select Validate a Windows App.

   b. Browse directly to the app you're testing, or choose the app from a list in the UI.

   c. When the Windows App Certification Kit is run for the first time, the UI lists all the Windows apps that you have installed on your computer. The next time you run the certification kit, the UI will display the most recent Windows apps that you have validated. If the app that you want to test is not listed, you can click My App Isn't Listed to get a full list of all apps installed on your system.

3. After you have input or selected the app that you want to test, click Next.

   From the next screen, you will see the test workflow that aligns to the app type you are testing. If a test is grayed out in the list, the test is not applicable to your environment. For example, if you are testing a Windows 10 app on Windows 7, only static tests will apply to the workflow. Note that Windows Store may apply all tests from this workflow.

4. Select the tests you want to run and click Next. If you are unsure, leave them all selected (Figure 12-54).

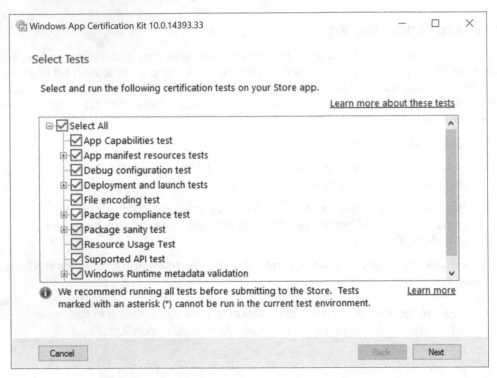

Figure 12-54. Selecting the tests to run

5. Once the test starts running, leave the machine alone until it finishes (Figure 12-55).

    This can take several minutes.

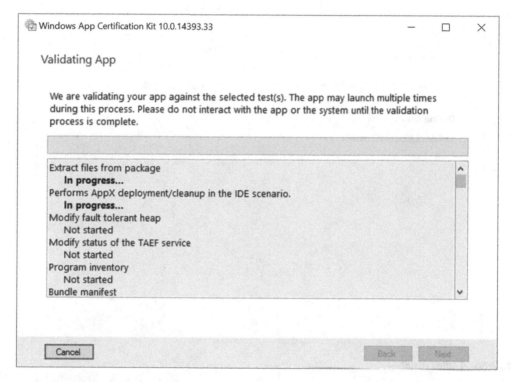

Figure 12-55. Progress reported for the tests

6. At the prompt after the test, enter the path to the folder where you want to save the test report.

    The Windows App Certification Kit begins validating the app.

    Be aware that paths containing ampersands may cause failure.

    The Windows App Certification Kit creates an HTML along with an XML report and saves it in the folder you specified.

If the report was successful, no further action is necessary. If it failed, as shown in Figure 12-56, further action will be required by clicking the link to view your results and determining what the error is. As simple as it sounds, search the Net for the same error you may receive. Also, double-check that you've created a Master build (not Release or Debug).

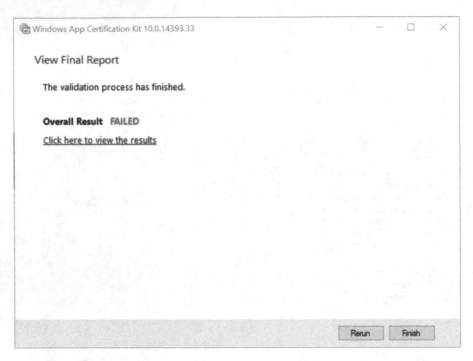

Figure 12-56. A failed result

Uploading to the Windows Store

Next you will want to send your application to Windows Store. This procedure assumes you have acquired a Developer Account that will enable you to publish to Windows Store.

The next step is context sensitive and requires this project to be selected.

1. Ensure that you have Visual Studio open and your Universal Windows project highlighted (Figure 12-57).

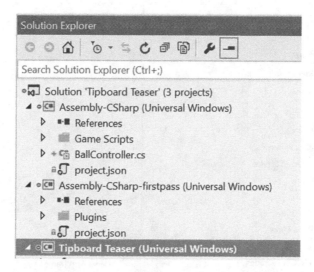

Figure 12-57. The project once again selected in Visual Studio's Solution Explorer

2.   In Visual Studio, choose Project ➤ Store ➤ Upload App Packages (Figure 12-58).

This launches your web browser, going to the Windows Dev Center specifically for the application name you've reserved.

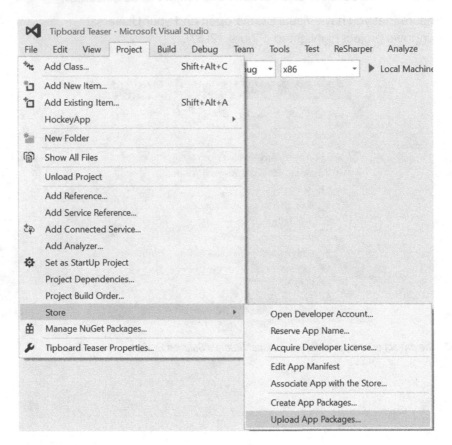

Figure 12-58. Uploading the App Packages

3. Click the Start Your Submission button (Figure 12-59).

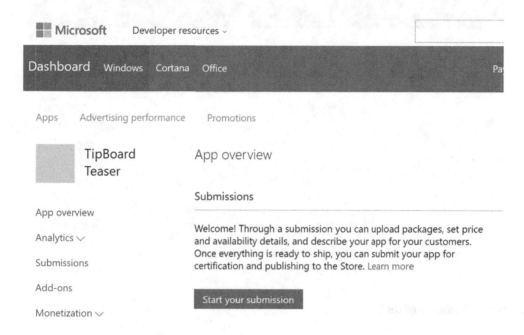

Figure 12-59. Starting your submission

4. Before you continue, take a moment to notice the notifications icon in the upper-right corner (Figure 12-60).

   When your application is published, it will contain information and helpful tips.

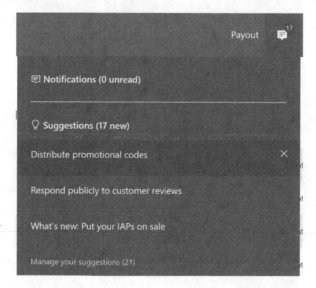

Figure 12-60. Inspecting the notifications icon

You will have numerous sections to fill out for your game (Figure 12-61).

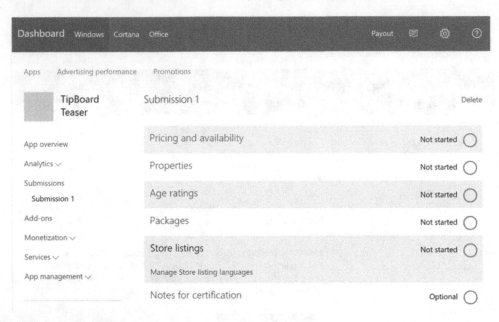

Figure 12-61. Sections to fill out

In Pricing and Availability (Figure 12-62), you will set the price for your applications and the countries where it will be available. Selecting many countries widens your market but may increase approval time for the store. Tipboard Teaser was marked as Free with No Free Trial, though if you wanted to make this a paid app, you could allow players to have a free trial period.

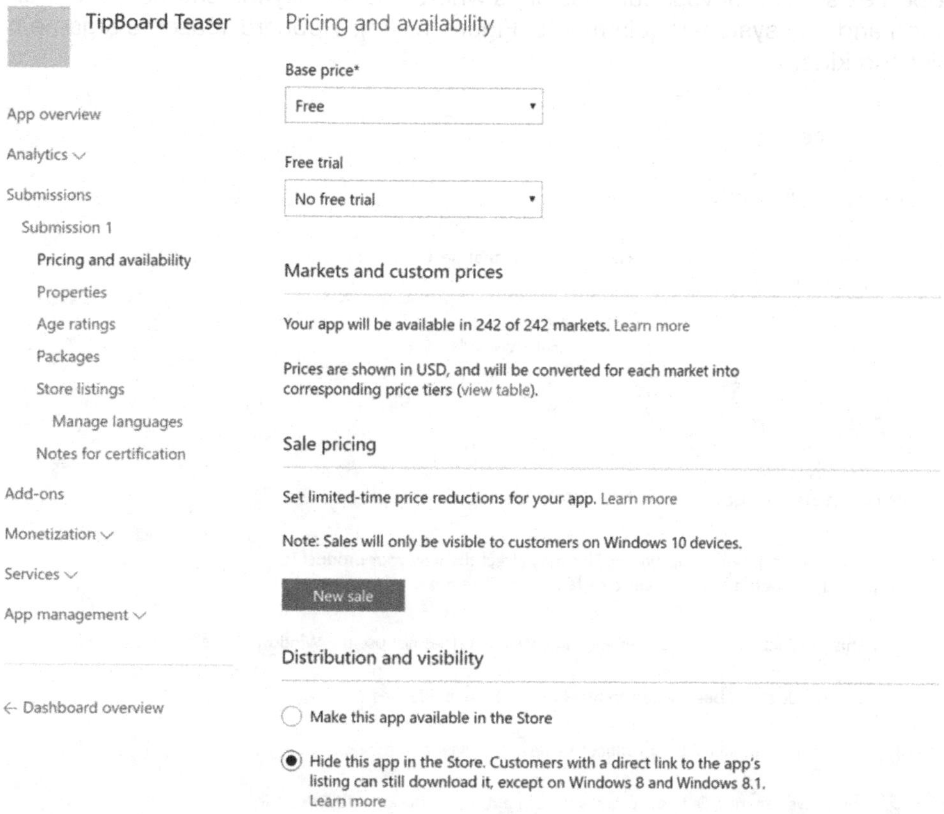

TipBoard Teaser

App overview

Analytics ∨

Submissions

  Submission 1

    Pricing and availability
    Properties
    Age ratings
    Packages
    Store listings
      Manage languages
    Notes for certification

Add-ons

Monetization ∨

Services ∨

App management ∨

← Dashboard overview

Pricing and availability

Base price*

| Free ▼ |

Free trial

| No free trial ▼ |

Markets and custom prices

Your app will be available in 242 of 242 markets. Learn more

Prices are shown in USD, and will be converted for each market into corresponding price tiers (view table).

Sale pricing

Set limited-time price reductions for your app. Learn more

Note: Sales will only be visible to customers on Windows 10 devices.

New sale

Distribution and visibility

○ Make this app available in the Store

◉ Hide this app in the Store. Customers with a direct link to the app's listing can still download it, except on Windows 8 and Windows 8.1. Learn more

Figure 12-62. Setting pricing and availability

Of notable mention here is the Distribution and Visibility section. You can make the app visible in the store once approved, or you can opt to not make it public. This way, you can send users the URL to your application, and they can install it and test it using real In-App Purchases before you do a larger launch. This is commonly called a *soft launch*.

The Properties section of your submission is where you specify the category for your application and any system requirements (Figure 12-63). Tipboard Teaser is a game meant for family and kids.

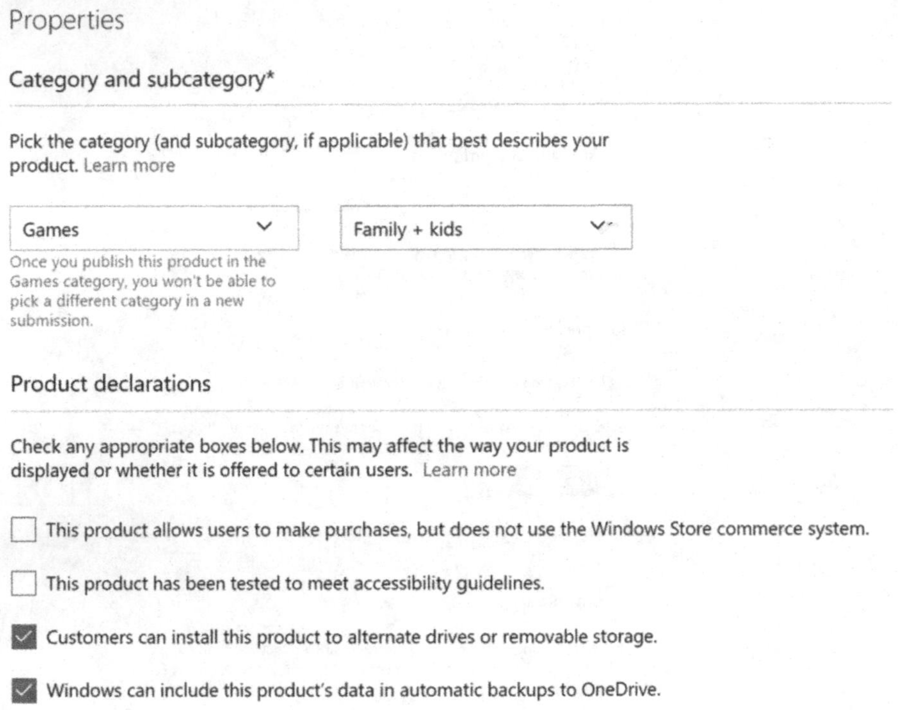

Properties

Category and subcategory*

Pick the category (and subcategory, if applicable) that best describes your product. Learn more

Games ∨		Family + kids ∨

Once you publish this product in the Games category, you won't be able to pick a different category in a new submission.

Product declarations

Check any appropriate boxes below. This may affect the way your product is displayed or whether it is offered to certain users. Learn more

☐ This product allows users to make purchases, but does not use the Windows Store commerce system.

☐ This product has been tested to meet accessibility guidelines.

☑ Customers can install this product to alternate drives or removable storage.

☑ Windows can include this product's data in automatic backups to OneDrive.

Figure 12-63. Setting category and system requirements

Tipboard Teaser can work with Touch, Keyboard, Joystick, and Mouse so you can add the entries for Recommended Hardware (Figure 12-64).

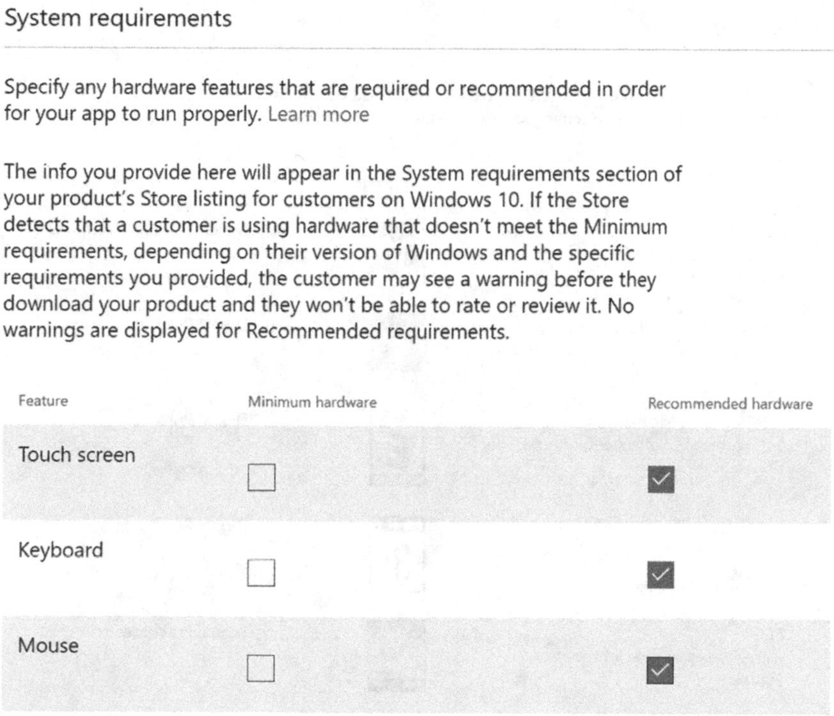

System requirements

Specify any hardware features that are required or recommended in order for your app to run properly. Learn more

The info you provide here will appear in the System requirements section of your product's Store listing for customers on Windows 10. If the Store detects that a customer is using hardware that doesn't meet the Minimum requirements, depending on their version of Windows and the specific requirements you provided, the customer may see a warning before they download your product and they won't be able to rate or review it. No warnings are displayed for Recommended requirements.

Feature	Minimum hardware	Recommended hardware
Touch screen	☐	☑
Keyboard	☐	☑
Mouse	☐	☑

Figure 12-64. Interactive hardware minimums and requirements

The next category, Age Ratings, will walk you through some questions to determine the rating for your game (Figure 12-65).

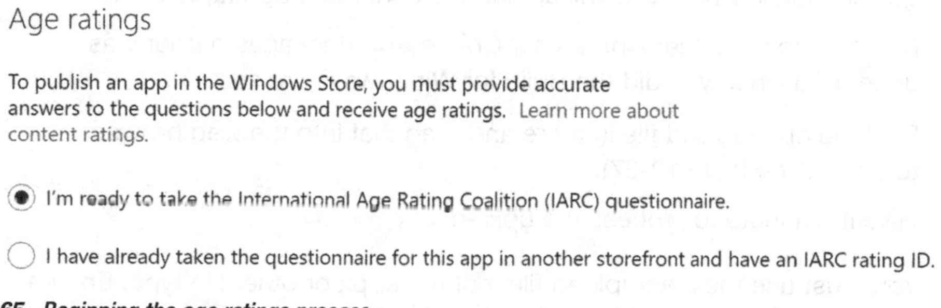

Age ratings

To publish an app in the Windows Store, you must provide accurate answers to the questions below and receive age ratings. Learn more about content ratings.

◉ I'm ready to take the International Age Rating Coalition (IARC) questionnaire.

◯ I have already taken the questionnaire for this app in another storefront and have an IARC rating ID.

Figure 12-65. Beginning the age ratings process

Once complete, you'll be assigned an Age Rating across various ratings organizations that are used in multiple countries to determine the appropriate audience for your application (Figure 12-66). You will want to review the results before moving on.

Figure 12-66. The generated ratings

The Packages section is where you will upload the generated appxupload file.

1. Navigate to the folder where your Create App Packages output was generated when you did the Build for Windows Store section.

2. Find the appxupload file in there and drag that into the web browser to upload it (Figure 12-67).

    Give it a minute to process the upload.

    You must use the appxupload file, not the appx or other file type. Ensure that you upload only a Master build, as the Release build would still have Unity profiler code within it.

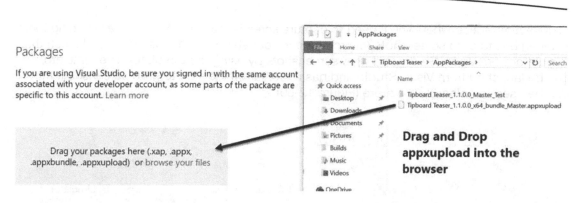

Packages

If you are using Visual Studio, be sure you signed in with the same account associated with your developer account, as some parts of the package are specific to this account. Learn more

Drag your packages here (.xap, .appx, .appxbundle, .appxupload) or browse your files

Drag and Drop appxupload into the browser

Figure 12-67. Dragging the packages into the browser

3.   Select the appropriate device families for your application.

Tipboard Teaser has been tested on the Desktop and Mobile device families (Figure 12-68). However, it could easily be tested on Xbox or HoloLens (there's a HoloLens emulator available for testing as well).

Figure 12-68. Selecting the device appropriate families

The Store Listings section is where you create a good description for your game. Creating a good description is an extremely important task. Feel free to examine other successful games for ideas on what they included in their descriptions. Coming up with a compelling description is an art form and should be given serious thought.

This section is also where you'll need to capture screenshots. Windows has a Snipping tool you can use to grab screenshots (search for it in your start screen). Also you can launch the Simulator from Visual Studio and grab screenshots by using the Simulator. The Simulator can be launched from Visual Studio and has a toolbar on the side to grab screenshots that can be used to upload to the store (Figure 12-69).

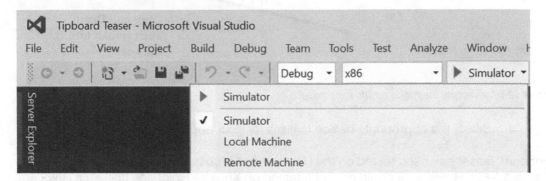

Figure 12-69. Using the Simulator to grab screenshots

In the left column in the web browser is a section for add-ons. This is where in-app purchases need to be configured (Figure 12-70).

Create a new add-on

Product type

Select the product type for this add-on. You can't change this once the add-on is created. Learn more

● **Developer-managed consumable:** After the add-on is acquired, it can be used up (consumed), then acquired again. Balance and fulfillment managed within your app. Supported on all OS versions.

○ **Store-managed consumable:** After the add-on is acquired, it can be used up (consumed), then acquired again. Balance tracked by Microsoft across the customer's devices running Windows 10, version 1607 or later (not supported on earlier OS versions). Note: the parent product must be compiled using Windows 10 SDK version 14393 or later.

○ **Durable:** After the add-on is acquired, it doesn't get used up. Once you create the add-on, you can optionally set the product lifetime so that it expires after a set period of time.

Product ID*

Type in the unique product ID that you'll use to refer to the offer in your code. Your customers won't see this product ID, just the description that you'll enter later.

You can't change or delete this product ID after you publish the add-on. Learn more

75.Coins

Figure 12-70. Selecting Developer-managed consumable

1. Click the Add-ons option and click to create a new add-on.

   Your in-app purchase is the 75 tipCoins, which is a consumable, meaning a player can use it up.

2. Select this as a Developer-managed consumable and ensure you specify the same name used in Game Scripts ➤ WindowsStore ➤ InAppPurchases, in this case 75.Coins.

   As of this writing Unity doesn't support Store-managed consumables so ensure you have selected Developer-managed.

3. After you are finished, review your certification and click Submit to the Store if everything is okay.

   A list of several of your settings appears (Figure 12-71).

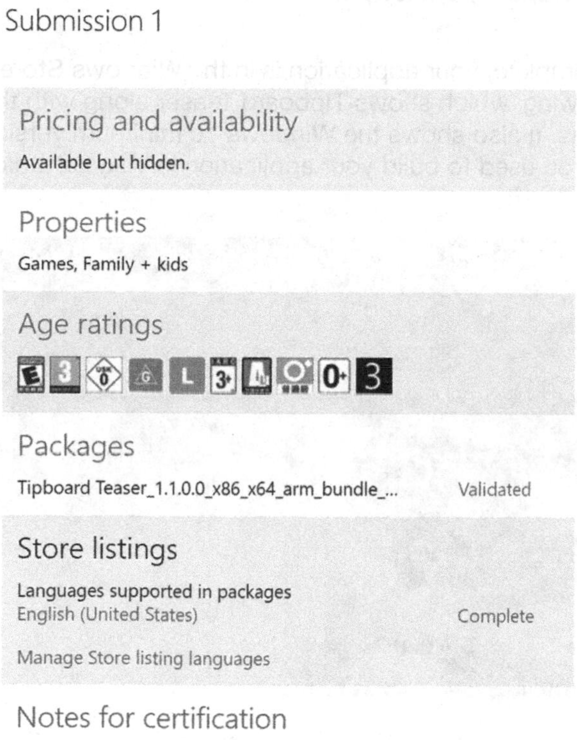

Submission 1

Pricing and availability
Available but hidden.

Properties
Games, Family + kids

Age ratings

Packages
Tipboard Teaser_1.1.0.0_x86_x64_arm_bundle_...   Validated

Store listings
Languages supported in packages
English (United States)   Complete

Manage Store listing languages

Notes for certification

Figure 12-71. A brief summary of your app's settings

You can review your progress then or wait for an e-mail that your submission has been approved (Figure 12-72).

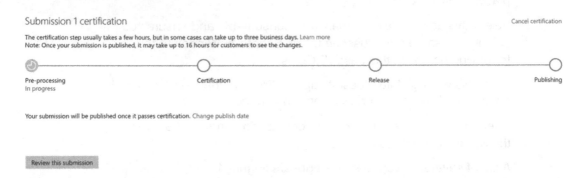

Figure 12-72. *The submission approval progress report*

Once certification is complete, your application is in the Windows Store (Figure 12-73). It will look similar to the following, which shows Tipboard Teaser along with the supported x86, x64, and ARM platforms. It also shows the Windows 10 minimum version—which is tied to the Windows 10 SDK you used to build your application in Visual Studio.

Figure 12-73. *The approved submission on Windows Store*

Monetization

In case you are wondering about monetization, you will find that there are currently four popular ways to earn money with your app. The first is to sell the app outright in Windows Store. Prices ranging from 99 cents to a few dollars tend to be the norm, but lately, a lot of developers opt to give the game away free and make money from in-app purchases or ads. You've had a test run with IAP, so now it's time to look at in-game advertisements. Basically, there are two types: banner ads and interstitial video ads. To utilize either type, you have to visit the Windows Dev Center, search for the Microsoft Store Services SDK, and install it on your developer machine. It contains the libraries and tools Visual Studio needs to let you add advertising to your Universal Windows Platform (UWP) apps.

1. Close Visual Studio if it is running.

2. Download and install the Microsoft Store Services SDK.

Once installed, it will be updated anytime you update Visual Studio. Always make sure that you have the latest version of both and that the versions match.

> **Tip**   For serious earning, you may want to make use of your Dev Center dashboard. It will allow you to easily run A/B testing, log, and evaluate results. That is beyond the scope of this book, but is well documented in the Dev Center and worth looking into when you are at that stage of your developer career.

Banner ads require you to design your app such that the ads will not interfere with your game or its UI. Because your little tip-puzzle game is already quite cluttered, you won't be giving this one a try. The coding for banner ads requires extensive use of XAML and layout coding and is beyond the scope of this book. If you are familiar and comfortable with XAML, feel free to give banner ads a try. As usual, they are well documented in the Dev Center docs.

Interstitial video ads are easier to manage than banner ads in that they use the entire screen and so require no placement coding. *Interstitial* means that they are run between scenes, levels, or other logical breakpoints, or at the player's choice. As the developer, it is up to you to decide where and how often they will appear, or how often a player may access them. Unity has an easy system for adding Unity-managed video ads, but unfortunately does not yet support Windows Store.

As you may have guessed, video ads are also well documented on the Dev Center. They come in two basic functionality types. Paywall ads are generally inserted between levels or scenes. The player must watch them before being rewarded with the next level. This is the more passive of the two types of video ads, but it could be set up to allow a player to spend a few tipCoins to cut the video short and get back to the game.

With rewards-based ads, you generally let the player access them on demand and for watching them, the player receives some type of reward. As the player can actively pursue rewards, you would want to set a limit as to how many and how often he could do so.

Due to time constraints, we were not able to provide a step by step procedure for testing Windows 10 ads. For more information on this topic, please visit the Windows Dev Center and search for interstitial ads in the Monetization section.

Exiting Apps

Windows Store apps leave the power to exit in the hands of the user. It is recommended that applications are not allowed to close themselves. All Windows Store apps are closed by the user closing the window. On the phone, when at the root page of your application, clicking back will close the application, and that is the expected behavior. On a desktop, users will click the X in the upper-right corner to close the application. If the app has been paused, the operating system determines that it wants to close to free up resources.

Having outlived its usefulness, you will want to remove the Exit button and replace it with something useful. The spot left would make a good place to access more in-depth instructions for the game now that it also has the flexibility to work for devices using a gamepad.

1. Open the Start menu in Unity and deactivate the Exit button (you may want to leave it in for stand-alone builds).

2. Import the NewInstructions.unitypackage from the Chapter 12 Assets folder.

3. Drag the More Button prefab into the Start Menu.

4. Save the scene, click Play, and test both the new instructions and exiting via mouse, touch, or virtual Enter button (for gamepad).

Suspended Apps

When the user switches away from your application, an event that can happen on any Windows 10 device, your application is paused. Unity provides you with the OnApplicationPause(bool paused) event. If it finds the code, it will call it. You will use this to pause the application during an interruption from outside the app. You have already implemented a pause in your game. This one will be very similar.

1. Import the PauseApp.Unitypackage from the Chapter 12 Assets folder.

    The package contains a new Canvas with a panel to block inadvertent input and a button to resume after the pause has been triggered.

2. Open the Game Level scene.

    The Start Menu and Store Levels are already waiting for user input so have no need of the pause functionality.

3. Drag the PauseScreen prefab into the scene.

4. From Game Scripts/WindowsStore, open ScreenManager and examine the code.

The only case that needs to be handled here is when OnApplicationPause(true) occurs. That is when the pause is triggered. When the user is ready to rejoin the game, he clicks or taps the Pause button that is on new screen overlay, or, he can press Escape or the back button (on phone or gamepad). Either alternative is mapped to the Escape key by the Input Manager.

The following is an outline of the actions taken for various pause scenarios. Resume is handled after being paused only by accepting user input to touch the onscreen Pause button or Escape/Back button input:

Game first loads ➤ Unity calls OnApplicationPause(false) ➤ Do nothing

Escape pressed and not paused ➤ Pause()

App loses focus ➤ Unity calls OnApplicationPause(true) ➤ Pause()

Focus returned to app ➤ Unity calls OnApplicationPause(false) ➤ Do nothing

Escape/Back Button/Pause button pressed and already paused ➤ Resume()

Typically, an application shows a pause screen, which is nothing more than an overlay Canvas (that blocks user input) with a button in the middle (to resume game play). Just as with the pause you created to stop the game while the player rearranges Banana Peels, you will stop time by setting the timescale to 0:

```
public void Pause(){
    // Set the game's timescale to 0 to pause
    originalTimeScale = Time.timeScale;
    Time.timeScale = 0;
    paused = true;
    Paused.SetActive(paused);
}
```

Note that before time is paused, you are saving the current timescale in originalTimeScale. This way, if your player was already in pause mode for the Banana Peel moving, the correct timescale will be restored.

The ScreenManager's pause code also must activate the imported Canvas object. Because the object is deactivated at startup, it *cannot* be identified by using GameObject.Find. So in this case, you must assign the Canvas manually in the Hierarchy view.

You have already set up several Button click events in both Chapters 10 and 11, so hooking up the Pause button to call Resume() will be easy:

1. Select the Pause button and add a new Button OnClick event.

2. Assign the ScreenManager (where the ScreenManager script resides) as the Object.

3. Select the ScreenManager's Resume() function.

Now, when the button is clicked, the Resume() method sets the Time.timeScale back to its original value and disables the Canvas.

In this instance, you were able to disable the Canvas and manually set a reference to it so it could be found later when it required activation. In some cases, that is not an option, making regular edit painful. A pro tip is that you can assign the canvas to a different layer and hide that layer in the Editor only via the Layers drop-down in the top-right corner of Unity. This method is used quite regularly for HUD GUI elements in general as they are automatically in the GUI layer.

Cleaning Up Unused Code

During the course of this book, you have created many new scripts. Because you have built upon some of them in multiple chapters, with a few exceptions, the default empty Start and Update functions were left intact for future use. Now, however, with the code finalized, you will want to go through and delete any empty functions, especially Update as it gets checked every frame. With this in mind, once you are creating your own scripts, best practice is to remove the default empty Start and Update functions from scripts that will never use them. Abandoned code is not as straightforward. You may want to archive it somewhere for use in other projects before you delete it.

While you are going through the scripts, feel free to delete old code that has been commented out. It doesn't cause a performance hit, but will keep your code cleaner and easier to read.

The list of scripts that have empty Start and/or Update functions is as follows:

> BaseCells.cs
>
> BoardManager.cs
>
> ColliderSwitch.cs
>
> Crusher.cs
>
> DeathZoneReset.cs
>
> GameManager.cs
>
> GridManager.cs
>
> HotSpotBooster.cs
>
> Neutralizer.cs
>
> PathCells.cs
>
> PathLister.cs
>
> PortalHopper.cs
>
> Rotator.cs
>
> SimplePool.cs
>
> StoreManager.cs
>
> WaypointManager.cs

Testing on Windows 10 Phone

If you want to test your game on a physical device such as a Windows 10 phone, there are a few different steps to go through. As with your development machine, the device must be set to Debug mode if you want to debug. Otherwise, you can choose Release or Master in Visual Studio for your build configuration, as we've done previously.

1. Locate the Developers Settings on your phone: Settings ➤ Update & Security, and then choose For Developers.

Tip   Enter **developer settings** into the Cortana search box in the taskbar.

---

2. Enable Developer mode.

3. Connect the device with a USB cable.

4. In Visual Studio, go to the debug target drop-down next to the Start Debugging button.

5. Choose Device to tell Visual Studio to deploy the app to your connected phone.

   Device will deploy the app to a USB connected device. The device must be developer unlocked (see step 1).

6. Next to the Debug, select ARM if it is not already showing.

7. Press F5 or from the Debugging menu, select Start Debugging.

Alternatively, you can test in the Windows Phone Emulator.

1. In the Device drop-down, select Download New Emulators (Figure 12-74).

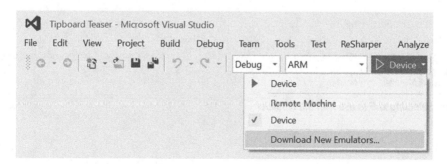

Figure 12-74. Selecting Download New Emulators from the Device drop-down

2. In the resulting web site, choose to install the emulator (Figure 12-75).

    The install may be about 4 GB.

Windows SDK and emulator archive

This archive contains SDK releases and updates for earlier Windows and Windows Phone platform versions, as well as emulator releases supporting development and UX testing for mobile device experiences.

For the latest editions of Visual Studio and the Windows 10 developer tools, see Downloads and tools for Windows.

Windows 10

Release

| Windows 10 SDK (14393) and Microsoft Emulator for Windows 10 mobile | Start building Universal Windows apps and desktop apps for Windows 10 with this SDK. Released August 2016. (Version 10.0.14393.0) | Install SDK | Released in-step with the SDK, the Microsoft Mobile Emulator for Windows 10 is a desktop application that emulates a mobile device running Windows 10. (Version 10.0.14393.0) | Install Emulator |

Figure 12-75. Installing the emulator

3. After installation is done, restart Visual Studio and open the Tipboard Teaser Universal Windows application project again.

4. This time, select one of the Mobile Emulators instead of Device.

    Because you are using an emulator on your local hardware, you'll also require x86 rather than ARM in the build configuration type (Figure 12-76).

Figure 12-76. Selecting x86 to use with the emulator

The emulator will load and eventually deploy your application to it and run (Figure 12-77).

Figure 12-77. A Windows Phone emulator

Extending the UWP

In this book, you have created a little game that was tailored for the conventional UWP devices that may contain accelerometers. This included phone, tablets, hybrid tablets/laptops, and, of course, conventional laptops and desktops, as an app rather than EXE. But you have also heard the occasional reference to Xbox One and HoloLens in that they also make use of UWP. In this short section, you will look a bit deeper into what it takes to author for the two devices. For both devices, you can build from your regular Windows 10 development machine. While there are emulators available for both, there are other factors that you will want to be aware of.

Xbox One

For Xbox One, the process is similar to what you have just finished working through, until you get to testing the app. The Xbox now allows you to experiment directly on the hardware without having to purchase a dev account. Unity even has an editor that can be run on the Xbox itself. To actually *develop* for Xbox, you will have to apply for an ID@Xbox. You will be asked about your company, school, or organization, whether you have a game ready to sell on Xbox, and various company and other information. Although there is a check box for home hobbyist, it is clearly geared toward people or teams that want to produce apps and/ or games for the Xbox.

Here is the interesting part. If you want to develop on a PC, there is an emulator available, but at present, for that, you must be an approved Xbox developer to gain access to it. So you can test your apps or games directly on an Xbox free of charge, but to use the emulator, you must go through the process of being an accepted Xbox developer. To jump into experimenting with Dev mode, all you have to do is download the Dev Mode Activation app on your Xbox One.

According to the Dev Center, "You don't need to be an ID@Xbox developer to experiment, create, and test games on your Xbox, but you do need to enroll with ID@Xbox if you want to publish and sell your game on Xbox One or take advantage of Xbox Live on Windows 10."

The other alternative is to build your game as a UWP, and then finish the build in Visual Studio and deploy it to the Xbox for testing. It will require a different SDK that can easily be downloaded and installed from the Dev Center.

As far as input, obviously, the gamepad is the primary device for games, but the handset is also important, especially with non-game apps. As you have already discovered, Unity's Input Manager makes authoring for the two input devices almost seamless.

For an excellent guide to creating apps with Xbox One, check out @schmosif's `http://forum.unity3d.com/threads/tips-and-tricks-for-building-for-uwp-and-deploying-to-xbox-one.395150/`.

HoloLens

For the HoloLens, the biggest barrier is the current price point, a whopping $3,000 USD. On the plus side, anyone in the United States can now purchase a developer version of the HoloLens if they can afford it (they cannot, however, sell it). In case the price is out of your budget, an emulator is available at no cost for the HoloLens. You already have most of the software HoloLens requires: Visual Studio 2015 Update 3 and the Windows 10 SDK (version 1511 or later). The Unity game engine is recommended as the game engine of choice to develop HoloLens apps. HoloLens support in Unity is available through a *custom version* of the Unity editor and runtime, which is available to download for free on the Unity web site. So you can install the HoloLens emulator to build holographic apps without a HoloLens.

The only restriction, is that the machine you plan to use it on must support Hyper-V for the emulator installation to succeed. The HoloLens emulator is based on Hyper-V and uses RemoteFX for hardware-accelerated graphics. 64-bit Windows 10 Pro, Enterprise, or Education Support Hyper-V, the Home edition does not support Hyper-V or the HoloLens emulator. To determine whether your system supports Hyper-V, go to Control Panel ➤ Programs ➤ Programs and Features. Turn Windows Features on or off and ensure that Hyper-V is present and selected.

Also be aware that HoloLens comes with a variety of less-than-conventional means of input referred to as *human understanding*. They include the following:

Spatial sound

Gaze tracking

Gesture input

Voice support

The emulator simulates these input types, but obviously there is no substitute for determining game flow and usability in the end than testing with the actual device.

A good starting place for researching the HoloLens is `https://developer.microsoft.com/en-us/windows/holographic/install_the_tools`.

Summary

In this final chapter, you began by reviewing the requirements for building a Visual Studio solution in preparation for deployment to Windows Store.

With the introduction of a Windows 10 device with accelerometer functionality, you made a simple test file to test the gyro code. In doing so, you found that mapping the gyro input to the correct axes required testing and adjustment.

The next step was to add the code to the Tiltboard project and allow the player to choose between touch-drag and accelerometer. Adding a toggle for the two methods used to tip the board, you made the game more flexible, especially as it became apparent that the accelerometer seemed to use a lot more power.

The next focus was on in-app purchases. To retain the player's purchases, both from Windows Store and in game, you added code to save the three key purchases to the local device at key times. This not only protected the player from losing purchases in case of a crash or power loss, but also retained them between sessions. While not as global as saving data to a server, it was a good solution on a small scale and gave you the opportunity to try more advanced coding with properties and to make use of Unity's PlayerPrefs for data storage.

With data saving under control, you moved on to testing the purchasing process. The first testing involved simulating the purchase on your local machine.

The next step required the commitment of obtaining an app developer account, where you also discovered a wealth of information in the docs found on the Windows Dev Center. Armed with a new publisher display name, you were ready to submit your game to be beta tested. This allowed you to invite others, as well as yourself, to test your game in a private setting to see how it behaved without fear of it garnering bad reviews in case there were bugs to be addressed.

With the tough bits taken care of, you turned your attention to filling in a few blanks in the Player Settings by adding icon and tile art, a cursor, and tweaking a few settings.

Finally, you took the plunge and submitted your app to Windows Store. While awaiting the results, you had a brief look at a few other platforms for which Visual Studio will be quite useful.

Index

© Sue Blackman and Adam Tuliper 2016
S. Blackman and A. Tuliper, *Learn Unity for Windows 10 Game Development*,
DOI 10.1007/978-1-4302-6757-7

Get the eBook for only $4.99!

Why limit yourself?

Now you can take the weightless companion with you wherever you go and access your content on your PC, phone, tablet, or reader.

Since you've purchased this print book, we are happy to offer you the eBook for just $4.99.

Convenient and fully searchable, the PDF version enables you to easily find and copy code—or perform examples by quickly toggling between instructions and applications.

To learn more, go to http://www.apress.com/us/shop/companion or contact support@apress.com.

All Apress eBooks are subject to copyright. All rights are reserved by the Publisher, whether the whole or part of the material is concerned, specifically the rights of translation, reprinting, reuse of illustrations, recitation, broadcasting, reproduction on microfilms or in any other physical way, and transmission or information storage and retrieval, electronic adaptation, computer software, or by similar or dissimilar methodology now known or hereafter developed. Exempted from this legal reservation are brief excerpts in connection with reviews or scholarly analysis or material supplied specifically for the purpose of being entered and executed on a computer system, for exclusive use by the purchaser of the work. Duplication of this publication or parts thereof is permitted only under the provisions of the Copyright Law of the Publisher's location, in its current version, and permission for use must always be obtained from Springer. Permissions for use may be obtained through RightsLink at the Copyright Clearance Center. Violations are liable to prosecution under the respective Copyright Law.